Palgrave Studies in Economic History

Series Editor
Kent Deng, London School of Economics, London, UK

Palgrave Studies in Economic History is designed to illuminate and enrich our understanding of economies and economic phenomena of the past. The series covers a vast range of topics including financial history, labour history, development economics, commercialisation, urbanisation, industrialisation, modernisation, globalisation, and changes in world economic orders.

Juan José Rivas Moreno

The Capital Market of Manila and the Pacific Trade, 1668–1838

Institutions and Trade during the First Globalization

palgrave
macmillan

Juan José Rivas Moreno
European University Institute
Florence, Italy

ISSN 2662-6497 ISSN 2662-6500 (electronic)
Palgrave Studies in Economic History
ISBN 978-3-031-71809-0 ISBN 978-3-031-71810-6 (eBook)
https://doi.org/10.1007/978-3-031-71810-6

Cover illustration: Lebrecht Music & Arts/Alamy Stock Photo

This Palgrave Macmillan imprint is published by the registered company Springer Nature Switzerland AG
The registered company address is: Gewerbestrasse 11, 6330 Cham, Switzerland

Acknowledgements

This book is the culmination of years of research in repositories across the world. As such, it was only made possible through the financial and academic support of countless institutions and individuals. Primarily, the ESRC financed the doctoral research that forms the basis of this work through an ESRC-LSE Doctoral Training Partnership. Similarly, research in the United States was financed by the Newberry Library through a short-term Newberry Library fellowship. The Economic History Society Power Fellowship also provided the necessary financial stability and academic mentorship to finalise this work. Smaller travel grants from the Radwan Travel Fund, the Francesca Carnevali Grant, the LSE-SEAC PhD Conference Support Fund, and financial support from the Economic History Society of Australia and New Zealand enabled me to present the first sketches of this book in a multiplicity of forums, whose feedback was instrumental in the final form of this research.

I am similarly indebted to Alejandra Irigoin, Guillermo Ruiz-Stovel, Francesca Trivellato, and Juan Mesquida, who read excerpts of this book and provided valuable insight, as well as Víctor Pérez-Sánchez and Safya Morshed, for their feedback on earlier chapter drafts. Ali Coşkun Tunçer helped immensely with advice throughout the process, as did Alejandra Irigoin. To both, I remain deeply obliged. Special thanks are due to Father Emiliano Pérez in the Archivo de la Provincia del Santísimo Rosario, and to the staff at the Newberry Library and the Institute of Historical Research in London.

This work benefitted from the helpful comments and advice of several scholars on the research that composes the bulk of this publication, including Kent Deng, Gerben Bakker, Tirthankar Roy, Patrick Wallis, and Karolina Hutkova, and especially Bartolomé Yun-Casalilla and Ron Harris. Francisco Cebreiro and Mario Cuenda offered comments and tips on the early stages of the research. Thanks are also owed to the staff at Palgrave, Ellie Duncan and Supraja Yagnaraman, for their work and guidance.

Finally, I am forever grateful to my wife and parents for their unwavering support. None of this research would have been possible without their patience and their love.

Contents

Abbreviations

ACCHS-CSIC	Archivo del Centro de Ciencias Humanas y Sociales
AESI-A	Archivo Histórico de la Provincia de Toledo de la Compañía de Jesús
AFIO	Archivo Franciscano Ibero-Oriental
AGI	Archivo General de Indias
AGN	Archivo General de la Nación
AMN	Archivo del Museo Naval
APSR	Archivo de la Provincia del Santísimo Rosario
AUST	Archive of the University of Santo Tomás
AYER	Newberry Library
BNE	Biblioteca Nacional de España
IOR	India Office Records

List of Figures

List of Graphs

List of Maps

List of Tables

CHAPTER 1

Introduction

1.1 Globalising Institutions

The Early Modern era witnessed the twin developments of the establishment of new direct trade between Europe and Asia and America, a spur of intercontinental trade of unprecedented dimensions that some have described as the "first wave" of globalisation,[1] together with a protracted period of economic growth and military innovation that culminated with the First Industrial Revolution at home and imperialism abroad, leading historians to question whether the development of long-distance trade and of industrialisation were related.[2] As a result, the Early Modern period has often been analysed from a teleological perspective, trying to

[1] On the debate around the Early Modern or "first wave" of Globalisation, see Flynn, Dennis, & Giráldez, Arturo, 'Cycles of Silver: Global Economic Unity through the Mid-Eighteenth Century', *Journal of World History* 13, n° 2 (2002): 391–427, O'Rourke, Kevin H., and Williamson, Jeffrey G., 'When did Globalisation begin?', *European Review of Economic History* 6, n° 1 (2002): 23–50, De Vries, Jan, 'The Limits of Globalization in the Early Modern World', *Economic History Review* 63, n° 3 (2010): 710–733.

[2] Berg, Maxine, 'Asian Luxuries and the Making of the European Consumer Revolution', in *Luxury in the Eighteenth Century: Debates, Desires and Delectable Goods*, ed. Maxine Berg and Elizabeth Eger (London: Palgrave, 2003): 228–244, De Vries, Jan, *The Industrious Revolution: Consumer Behavior and the Household Economy, 1650 to the Present* (Cambridge: Cambridge University Press, 2012), Broadberry, Stephen, & Gupta, Bishnupriya, 'Lancashire, India, and the Shifting Competitive Advantage in Cotton Textiles,

J. J. Rivas Moreno, *The Capital Market of Manila and the Pacific Trade, 1668–1838*, Palgrave Studies in Economic History,
https://doi.org/10.1007/978-3-031-71810-6_1

discern through backwards readings of historical processes the ultimate causes of Europe's predominance in the nineteenth century. The debate regarding Europe's supposed superiority has led to the revisionist stance of the Great Divergence question.[3] This criticism, exemplified in the work of Kenneth Pomeranz, brought evidence from Asia to qualify the extent to which Europe was on an inevitable track to predominance, and called into question the validity of a-historically searching for nineteenth-century hegemony in Eighteenth- and Seventeenth-century historical processes.

While the debate of the Great Divergence managed to change the focus into reciprocal comparisons between the experiences of Europe and Asia, the Spanish empire has remained in the fringes of this debate, referred to exclusively either as an example of institutional failure, or simply as a source of silver. No substantial efforts have been made to place the Hispanic Monarchy, one of the largest and most resilient polities of the Early Modern era, into a global context save for a few exceptions.[4] The closely related discussion on the importance of trade for economic growth in the Early Modern era, exemplified by the encyclopaedic work of Findlay and O'Rourke, has similarly approached the trade of the Hispanic world as an enabler, focusing exclusively on the silver transfers to Europe and elsewhere, but has failed to fully incorporate this important branch of global trade into the wider economic perspective of the world, ignoring for example the impact that American demand may have had on European

1700–1850: The Neglected Role of Factor Prices', *The Economic History Review* 62, nº 2 (2009): 279–305.

[3] Pomeranz, Kenneth, *The Great Divergence: China, Europe, and the Making of the Modern World Economy* (Princeton: Princeton University Press, 2000), Rosenthal, Jean-Laurent, and Bin Wong, Roy, *Before and Beyond the Divergence: The Politics of Economic Change in China and Europe*, (Cambridge (Mass.): Harvard University Press, 2011).

[4] See Irigoin, Alejandra, 'Rise and Demise of the Global Silver Standard', in *Handbook of the History of Money and Currency*, ed. Stefano Battilossi, Yousef Cassis and Kazuhiko Yago (Singapore: Springer, 2020): 383–410, Irigoin, Alejandra, 'The New World and the Global Silver Economy, 1500–1800', in *Global Economic History*, ed. Tirthankar Roy and Giorgio Riello (London: Bloomsbury Academic, 2019), Yun-Casalilla, Bartolomé, *Iberian World Empires and the Globalization of Europe, 1415–1668* (Singapore: Springer, 2019), more specifically on the Early Modern Iberian world and Global History, see Yun-Casalilla, Bartolomé, 'Early modern Iberian empires, global history, and the history of early globalization', *Journal of Global History* 17, nº 3 (2022): 539–561, Flynn, Dennis O., and Giráldez, Arturo, 'Spanish Profitability in the Pacific: The Philippines in the sixteenth and seventeenth centuries', in *Pacific Centuries: Pacific and Pacific Rim History since the sixteenth Century*, ed. Dennis Flynn, Lionel Frost, and A.J.H. Latham (London: Routledge, 1999), pp. 26–27.

industrial output, and the competition within Spanish America between European and Asian textiles.[5] The assessment of silver shipments exclusively as balance of trade settlements risks hindering the transformative effects that it had for the financial and monetary history of Europe.

Underscoring these debates is the question of how Europe managed to escape the trap of distance. The financing of long-distance trade has long been associated with the emergence of "modern" capital markets. The establishment of direct trade across continents presented challenges of unprecedented dimensions that required financial innovations to persist in time. Larger amounts of capital needed to be locked-in for unprecedentedly longer periods of time, while the vastness of the new mercantile landscape difficulted the monitoring and enforcement of contracts. Innovations were necessary to organise trade, structure investments, and for the emergence of impersonal capital markets capable of surpassing the constraints of personal networks or cultural coalitions. In this debate, the emergence in Early Modern Europe of the joint-stock corporations, the East India Companies, casts a long shadow.

For some historians, like Niels Steensgaard, the joint-stock corporation, whose alleged superiority was its capacity to interiorise protection costs, revolutionised the organisation of direct trade with Asia.[6] For others, like Emmer and Gaastra, the joint-stock company was the best way to channel resources from the home market to the trade, achieving an advantage in scale,[7] to the point that Emmer argued that incorporation was the *sine qua non* of sustained and meaningful trade between Europe and Asia.[8] More sophisticated still is the process presented by Gelderblom

[5] Findlay, Ronald, and O'Rourke, Kevin, *Power and Plenty: Trade, War, and the World Economy in the Second Millennium* (Princeton: Princeton University Press, 2007), see also de Zwart, Pim, and van Zanden, Jan Luiten, *The Origins of Globalization: World Trade in the Making of the Global Economy, 1500–1800* (Cambridge: Cambridge University Press, 2018).

[6] Steensgaard, Niels, *The Asian Trade Revolution of the 17th Century: The East India Companies and the decline of the Caravan Trade* (Chicago: Chicago University Press, 1973).

[7] Emmer, Pieter, & Gaastra, Femme, 'Introduction', in *The Organization of Interoceanic Trade in European Expansion, 1450–1800*, ed. Pieter Emmer & Femme Gaastra (Aldershot: Variorum, 1996), pp. xxiv–xxv.

[8] Emmer, Pieter, 'The Organisation of Global Trade: The Monopoly Companies, 1600–1800', *European Review* 22, n° 1 (2014), p. 109.

and Jonker on the one hand,[9] and Ron Harris on the other.[10] Both identify liquidity, the necessity to pool unprecedentedly large amounts of capital for equally long periods of time, as the core problem of Early Modern direct trade with Asia. Thus, they relate the birth of the corporation with the birth of globalisation. For both (although in different manners), the joint-stock corporation provided the tools to solve this problem and enable sustained long-distance trade between Europe and Asia. The corporation implied gains regarding the mobilisation of capital and the solution to the fundamental problem of how to sustain intercontinental trade in the context of the Early Modern era. Consequently, the joint-stock corporation has emerged as the normative model for how persistent trade with Asia would be organised.

This book analyses the business model of the European companies as one of scale. According to Harris, the complex organisational structure of the joint-stock corporation solved the problem of obtaining enough initial capital to launch intercontinental trading enterprises because it managed to create impersonal markets for the first time, thus being able to acquire an unprecedented scale of operations.[11] However, the East India Companies never truly solved the problem of how to acquire enough working capital to maintain operations, especially given that in the trade with Asia, this meant acquiring large amounts of silver which merchants in the content demanded to settle transactions. To palliate this problem, the East India Companies scaled operations, expanding continuously the volume of their trade, its composition, and its circuits. The English (EIC) and Dutch (VOC) East India Companies tried several strategies simultaneously to solve the problem of working capital, including dealing in intra-Asian trade, the issuance of bonds and corporate loans, and, importantly, the attempts to control markets through force, both abroad and at home. But this strategy also resulted in the expansion of costs. Navies, armies, forts, had to be maintained, rising extra-commercial costs and lowering the profitability of the trade. This explains the failure of the East India Companies at lowering transaction costs as identified by Jan

[9] Gelderblom, Oscar, Jonker, Joost, 'Completing a Financial Revolution: The Finance of the Dutch East India Trade and the Rise of the Amsterdam Capital Market, 1595–1612', *Journal of Economic History* 64, nº 3 (September 2004): 641–672.

[10] Harris, Ron, *Going the Distance: Eurasian Trade and the Rise of the Business Corporation, 1400–1700* (Oxford: Princeton University Press, 2020).

[11] Harris, *Going*, p. 5.

de Vries, and the failure of the first wave of globalisation in delivering price convergence.[12]

The present book argues that liquidity was determinant when it came to decisions on how to organise long-distance trade with Asia. Against the model of scaling and vertical integration of the East India Companies, the book proposes the alternative model of trade organisation represented by the Pacific exchange, the other instance of persistent long-distance trade with Asia during the period. From the conquest of Manila in 1571 by Miguel de Legazpi to the extinction of the direct trade with Mexico in 1821, America and Asia were directly linked through the intermediation of Manila. The Pacific trade, based on the exchange of Asian commodities and goods (primarily textiles) for Spanish American silver specie, was large, with an estimated annual amount of 2–4 million pesos (approximately 50–100 tons of silver) shipped across the Pacific Ocean,[13] and it was the most direct intermediation between Asian demand for silver and American supply. This trade rested on the financing originated in the city of Manila through retained earnings from its commercial activities. From 1668, capital pooling institutions emerged in the city in the form of legacy funds that mobilised working capital for investment in the trade, the so-called *obras pías* (lit. trans. "pious works").[14] Research has revealed 264 individual funds that operated in the city between 1668 and 1833, capable of pooling large amounts of capital without the need of incorporation, but more remain to be identified by future historians. The capital market of Manila, which adapted European institutions to satisfy of Asia's demand for silver specie, represented an alternative manner to organise and finance long-distance trade.

[12] De Vries, Jan, 'Understanding Eurasian Trade in the Era of the Trading Companies', in *Goods from the East 1600–1800: Trading Eurasia*, ed. Maxine Berg, Felicia Gottman, Hanna Hodacs, and Chris Nierstrasz (London: Palgrave Macmillan, 2015), pp. 32–33.

[13] Bonialian, Mariano, *El Pacífico Hispanoamericano: política y comercio asiático en el imperio español (1680–1784)*, (Mexico: El Colegio de México, 2012), pp. 45–48 & 233, & Flynn, Dennis, and Giráldez, Arturo, 'Arbitrage, China, and World Trade in the Early Modern period', *Journal of the Economic and Social History of the Orient* 38, n° 4 (1995), p. 429.

[14] By association, Manileños also used the term *obras pías* to refer to the organisations that managed the legacy funds too. In this dissertation, *obras pías* (unless specified otherwise in the text) will be used to refer to the institutions that administered funds, and the term "legacy funds" will be used to refer to the funds themselves.

The case of Manila poses several questions. First, how could Manila pool such large volumes of cash and transform it into working capital for the operation of the transpacific trade and the intra-Asian commerce that supplied the goods for the Galleon? Second, why was the capital market of Manila different? The Manila trade never adopted a joint-stock corporate form or used instruments such as bills of exchange that were important in European trade, even though Manileños were acquainted with them. Why did Manila opt for an alternative path? A third question that derives from this is whether the innovative elements of Europe's financial revolution were a *necessary* requisite for long-distance trade, or, as was the case of Manila, alternative institutional arrangements could work equally well to finance the Eurasian trade, and if so, what determined the appearance of one model or the other? This links to a further question, how could the model of Manila persist for so long and defeat all interloping attempts from "more efficient" businesses like the European companies; were they truly so efficient? or the *most* efficient? or was their organisational form just a response to problems that they alone faced or that were of a different magnitude in the context of Manila?

The aim here is to show that the city's capacity to intermediate Asia's demand for a silver means of payment and Spanish America's large production of a reliable coin dictated the process of institutional formation in Manila. The argument is that Manila enjoyed the most direct access with fewer costs to America's silver specie. To maintain its intermediary position between Spanish America and Asia, the city specialised in the provision of silver pesos, and in the process, it developed institutions and instruments that enhanced this advantage by pooling cash, offering working capital as pesos, and internalising the risks inherent in the exchange. Through specialisation, Manila managed to reach a degree of economies of scale in the provision of liquidity in Asian waters and organise its intermediation as efficiently as any of the existing alternatives. In other words, the nature of the trade was the determinant factor behind the process of institutional formation in Manila's capital markets.

The organisation of the Pacific trade differed from the companies' model of vertical integration and scaling. Instead, Manila followed a model of "Horizontal Specialisation", that is, a process through which transaction costs were unilaterally reduced because each participant in the commercial chain specialised in a specific aspect of the trade. Through specialisation, each link in the chain could achieve a degree of economies of scale, and thus reduce overall transaction costs. In the case of the

Pacific exchange, Manila specialised in mobilising cash as working capital, the American terminal specialised as silver and coin producer, and the Asian terminal specialised as a producer of textile manufactures. Through specialisation, Manila provided a comparatively efficient intermediation between American and Asian markets. This enabled the city to mitigate the Fundamental Problem of Exchange and capture the profits from this intermediary role. Furthermore, it will be argued that relative ease of access to liquidity—in the context of a similar trade environment of silver for goods—determined the differences between this model of horizontal specialisation and the European joint-stock companies' model of vertical integration and scaling: the East India Companies evolved to operate in a context of liquidity constraints, while the Manila trade evolved to maximise its advantages in a context of abundance of liquidity.

The case of Manila also qualifies the causal relationship between the economic context and the process of institutional formation as outlined by New Institutional Economics. North's assumptions that institutions are exogenous to the forces of supply and demand extracted institutions from the realm of the market mechanism,[15] leading to institutional analysis based purely on the capacity of institutional frameworks to lower transaction costs (however either might be defined).[16] This approach has tended obscure the process of how institutions came to being, since institutions are measured on their conduciveness for growth independent from the context in which they emerge, without considering how well they solved the problems that motivated the agents to create them in the first place, and leading to reductivism.[17] The case of Manila represents a counterfactual in which institutions equally capable of pooling large volumes of capital were created and adapted based on the imperatives of the trade they financed. Institutions cannot be considered exogenous and impervious to the economic context in which they operate, neither is their

[15] North, Douglass C., *Institutions, Institutional Change, and Economic Performance* (Cambridge: Cambridge University Press, 1990), pp. 27–28.

[16] Fundamental in North's conceptualisation is the influence of Polanyi's historicisation of market economies, North, Douglass C., 'Markets and Other Allocation Systems in History: The Challenge of Karl Polanyi', *Journal of European Economic History* 6, n° 3 (1977): 703–716.

[17] See for example Sokoloff, Kenneth L., and Engerman, Stanley L., 'Institutions, Factor Endowments, and Paths of Development in the New World', *Journal of Economic Perspectives* 14, n° 3 (2000): 217–232.

capacity to promote growth an act inherently derived from the quality of their design. Rather, the quality of their design has to be analysed within the historical and economic context in which they emerged. In the case of Manila, this was the global specie trade, the Asian demand for a silver means of payment, and the capacity of Manila to satisfy that demand and maintain its intermediation. The capital market of Manila demonstrates that many claims regarding uniqueness or superiority of the joint-stock corporation for trade with Asia are teleological, based on the outcome rather than the causes. A different process was possible. What needs to be understood is the underlying causes of the difference, and this was access to liquidity.

To understand how Manila solved the challenge of financing long-distance trade requires both a comparative analytical framework and connecting institutional processes with the real economy of the Pacific trade. The framework therefore explores the capital market of Manila in relation to the nature and evolution of the Manila trade (encompassing both its Pacific leg and its intra-Asian leg) and the comparative evolution of the European East India Companies, especially the English Company. Placing Manila in the mirror of the European companies through a reciprocal comparison—as described by Austin and Pomeranz[18]—allows us to better understand what was different in the city's alternative model of Horizontal Specialisation. Both the English East India Company and the Manileños faced the challenges of long-distance trade, and both were invested in a transcultural trade of large proportions with Asia. Yet both developed radically different business models and organisational forms. The comparison serves the purpose of questioning the conditions upon which an institutional regime or another is "successful" in obtaining its goals, as well as linking the theory on transaction costs with the economic fundamentals in which institutional frameworks developed. Much of the foundation of the historical literature on institutions and trade remains focused on theoretical analysis,[19] but it still remains to be more forcefully integrated with the economic reality of trade in the Early Modern

[18] Austin, Gareth, 'Reciprocal Comparison and African History: Tackling Conceptual Eurocentrism in the Study of Africa's Economic Past', *African Studies Review* 50, nº 3 (2007): 1–28, Pomeranz, *The Great*..., pp. 9–10.

[19] Harris, *Going*, Gelderblom, Oscar, *Cities of Commerce: The Institutional Foundations of International Trade in the Low Countries, 1250–1650* (Princeton: Princeton University Press, 2013).

era. This reciprocal comparison, especially its emphasis on how access to liquidity as a source of working capital impacted business strategies, bridges this gap and provides a novel explanation of the Pacific exchange.

There are three reasons for choosing the English East India Company. The first is a matter of space. Reconstructing the capital markets of Manila is in itself a daunting task, and a complete survey of the joint-stock companies is not possible, neither is it the purpose of this book. In the measure the European companies are reviewed here, it is to place the Manila trade in context to better understand its financial and organisational model. The second is that there is a wider literature that has developed a broad range of models for the EIC,[20] which provides a greater range for analysis. The third reason is that the EIC surpassed the VOC in trade and power during the eighteenth century. This makes the EIC a more relevant comparison for the period of this dissertation, but it is also important because there is a tendency to consider the EIC as superior organisationally to the VOC, an example of "finer" vertical integration or trade organisation.[21]

1.2 Institutions and Trade

The literature regarding institutions and trade has placed the emphasis on the study of transaction costs and how institutions mitigated them. This has been established as the link through which institutional and organisational innovation impacted trade. This section reviews the relationship between institutions and the way they mitigated transaction costs. North defined institutions as "the rules of the game in a society", the set of

[20] For example, Chaudhuri, K.N., *The Trading World of Asia and the English East India Company* (Cambridge: Cambridge University Press, 1978), Anderson, Gary M., McCormick, Robert E., and Tollison, Robert D., 'The Economic Organization of the English East India Company', *Journal of Economic Behavior and Organization* 4, nº 4 (1983): 221–238, Erikson, Emily, *Between Monopoly and Free Trade: The English East India Company, 1600–1757* (Princeton: Princeton University Press, 2014), Carlos, Ann, and Nicholas, Stephen, '"Giants of an Earlier Capitalism": The Chartered Trading Companies as Modern Multinationals', *The Business History Review* 62, nº 3 (1988): 398–419.

[21] Neal, Larry, 'The Dutch and English East India companies compared: evidence from the stock and foreign exchange markets', in *The Rise of Merchant Empires: Long-Distance Trade in the Early Modern World, 1350–1750*, ed. James Tracy (Cambridge: Cambridge University Press, 1990), Harris argues that the EIC represents the completion of the organisational revolution of Eurasian trade, in which the VOC was a fundamental—yet not final—step, Harris, *Going*, p. 290.

constraints devised by human beings that direct social and economic interaction.[22] According to his model, the economy is embedded in the institutional framework, and growth stems from this institutional framework and spills to the economy at large. North relies on the idea of transaction costs, as explained by Coase and Williamson.[23] He argued that institutions emerge to lower the costs of transacting, which are essentially information and enforcement costs. Transaction costs permeate all economic activity.[24] In this model, economic growth is ultimately reliant on the success of the institutional framework to create the right incentives. North argued that changes in relative prices in themselves were not enough to lead Europe beyond Malthusian constraints.[25] Secure property rights, however, provided the right incentives for investment and invention. The entwined nature of property rights and the government led to a deeper study of the structure of the state. Economic growth is impossible without institutions that protect private property rights, and such institutions are impossible without "credible commitment" of the ruler, a term that denotes a constitutional arrangement of checks and balances and limited government capable of preventing the state from succumbing to its predatory instincts.[26]

The importance of both transaction costs and the state are obvious when it comes to trade.[27] According to North, the high transaction costs

[22] North, *Institutions*..., p. 3.

[23] See Coase, Ronald H., 'The Nature of the Firm', *Economica* 4, n° 16 (1937): pp. 386–405, Williamson, Oliver E., 'The Theory of the Firm as a Governance Structure: From Choice to Contract', *The Journal of Economic Perspectives* 16, n° 3 (2002): pp. 171–195, Williamson, Oliver E., *The Economic Institutions of Capitalism: firms, markets, relational contracting* (London: Collier Macmillan, 1987), and North, *Institutions*, p. 27.

[24] North, *Institutions*, p. 28.

[25] North, Douglass C., and Thomas, Robert P., *The Rise of the Western World: A New Economic History* (New York: Cambridge University Press, 1973), pp. 69–70.

[26] North, Douglass C., and Weingast, Barry, 'Constitutions and Commitment: The Evolution of Institutional Governing Public Choice in Seventeenth-Century England', *The Journal of Economic History* 49, n° 4 (1989): 824–828.

[27] North, Douglass C., 'Institutions, Transaction Costs, and the Rise of Merchant Empires', in *The Political Economy of Merchant Empires*, ed. James D. Tracy (Cambridge: Cambridge University Press, 1991), pp. 22–23.

of Early Modern trade led to institutional and organisational innovation in a push to partially integrate faraway markets.[28] High transaction costs forced merchants to cooperate and pool resources together, and the chartered joint-stock company emerged. Capital pooling could not be achieved without the reassurance of credible commitment against the expropriation of property.[29] North's model of transaction costs and political ordering of the state has been the basis for some empirical tests on Early Modern trade and growth, including the work of Acemoglu, Johnson, and Robinson.[30] The application of Northian constitutionalism implied a dualistic understanding of institutions divided into inclusive (or good) institutions and extractive (or bad) institutions. This eschatological reduction is not only an oversimplification of the institutional landscape of the Early Modern world, but the method employed by Acemoglu et al. represents a logical contradiction: countries with extractive institutions could have long-distance trade but did not manage to capture the profits derived from it, even though North's model clearly states that *good* institutions are a *pre*-condition for the emergence of trade.

The problem with North's constitutionalism is double when it comes to Manila. First is the empirical issue that Manila had the capacity to pool large amounts of cash and supply capital at low rates in the absence of a similar constitutional ordering to that described by North. A large literature has discredited the idea that composite monarchies like the Hispanic Monarchy had the drive and the capacity to extract the large amounts of resources as claimed by NIE, instead of focusing attention to the bargained and negotiated nature of sovereignty.[31] Manila, and the

[28] North, 'Institutions', pp. 27–29, this argument links with North's previous works on institutions and freighting costs, North, Douglass C., 'Ocean Freight Rates and Economic Development, 1750–1913', *The Journal of Economic History* 18, n° 4 (December 1958): 537–555.

[29] North, 'Institutions', pp. 25–26.

[30] Acemoglu, Daron, Johnson, Simon, and Robinson, James, 'The Rise of Europe: Atlantic Trade, Institutional Change, and Economic Growth', *The American Economic Review* 95, n° 3 (2005): pp. 546–579, Acemoglu, Daron, and Robinson, James, A., *Why Nations Fail? The Origins of Power, Prosperity and Poverty* (London: Profile Books, 2012).

[31] Irigoin, Alejandra, and Grafe, Regina, 'Bounded Leviathan: Fiscal constraints and financial development in the Early Modern Hispanic world', in *Questioning Credible Commitment: Perspectives on the Rise of Financial Capitalism*, ed. D'Maris Coffman, Adrian Leonard, and Larry Neal (Cambridge University Press, Cambridge, 2013), Yun-Casalilla, Bartolomé, 'Las instituciones y la economía política de la Monarquía Hispánica

Hispanic Monarchy at large, had legal ways to protect private property. Neither is the adjective "extractive" much of a predictive variable when ascertaining the volume and growth of trade. When the fiscal burden of England and Spain in the eighteenth century is compared quantitatively as Grafe and Irigoin did,[32] it turns out that England was the more extractive of the two. Similarly, Yun-Casalilla and Comín Comín question extractiveness as the root of the problem.[33] Lack of fiscal capacity constrained the action of the state, and instead ended solidifying highly inegalitarian modes of production and redistribution of wealth.[34] The relationship between constitutional ordering and increased volume of trade is not as simple as envisioned by NIE.

The second problem is that it suffers from an empirical contradiction. Long-distance trade without the right institutions should not be possible since there are no guarantees to protect investment. Yet there was trade, and there was long-distance direct trade with Asia long before the 1688 Glorious Revolution. Thus, the available evidence from England, collected by Gregory Clark, contradicts North's assumptions that institutional reform and credible commitment allowed the pooling of capital, and thus worked to lower interest rates, permeating to private credit.[35] The reality is that private rates were already low before the Glorious Revolution, and it was the government's interest rates that were exceptionally

(1492–1714). Una perspectiva trans- "nacional"', in *Economía Política desde Estambul a Potosí: Ciudades estado, imperios y mercados en el Mediterráneo y en el Atlántico ibérico, c. 1200–1800*, ed. Fernando Ramos Palencia and Bartolomé Yun-Casalilla (Valencia: Publicacions de la Universitat de València, 2012), Cardim, Pedro, Feros, Antonio, and Sabatini, Gaetano, 'The political constitution of the Iberian monarchies', in *The Iberian World 1450–1820*, ed. Fernando Bouza, Pedro Cardim, and Antonio Feros (London: Routledge, 2020): 34–61, Cardim, Pedro, Herzog, Tamar, José Javier Ruíz Ibáñez, and Sabatini, Gaetano, 'Polycentric Monarchies: How did Early Modern Spain and Portugal Achieve and Maintain a Global Hegemony?', in *Polycentric Monarchies: How did Early Modern Spain and Portugal Achieve and Maintain a Global Hegemony?*, ed. Pedro Cardim (Eastbourne: Sussex Academic Press, 2012).

32 Irigoin, and Grafe, 'Bounded', p. 206.

33 Yun-Casalilla, Bartolomé, and Comín Comín, Francisco, 'Spain: From Composite Monarchy to Nation State, 1492–1914. An Exceptional Case?', in *The Rise of Fiscal States: A Global History, 1500–1914*, ed. Bartolomé Yun-Casalilla and Patrick K. O'Brien (Cambridge: Cambridge University Press, 2012): 233–266.

34 Yun-Casalilla, 'Las instituciones', pp. 150 & 160.

35 Clark, Gregory, 'The Political Foundations of Modern Economic Growth: England, 1540–1800', *Journal of Interdisciplinary History* 26, nº 4 (1996): pp. 563–588.

high for European standards, supporting Epstein's suggestion that the English Financial Revolution reflect a process of catching up rather than breaking ahead,[36] and the anomality to explain was not the low interest rates following 1688, but the high public rates that preceded it. Similarly, since NIE's evidence of credible commitment at work is based on the low interest rates, it is important to highlight that the Hispanic world, operating on a completely different constitutional order, had low interest rates by the eighteenth century.[37] If the price of money was not substantially different, neither is the causation attributed to the constitutional ordering by NIE a plausible explanation.

Vertical integration through the firm was another way to solve high transaction costs.[38] The history of the Early Modern joint-stock companies, especially the EIC and VOC, have advanced this interpretation. Niels Steensgaard, argued that when a comparatively more efficient institution enters the game, less efficient ones will disappear following the Smithian logic of competition: either they will adapt and mimic the more successful counterpart, or they will be expelled from the game, a theory used to explain Portugal's quick decline in Asia when challenged by the Dutch.[39] Others, like Erikson, ascribe to the companies informational advantages and outsourcing efficiency that others lacked.[40] These theories present problems in terms of deficient predictive power and lack of economic context. While Steensgaard's model of internalising protection costs may explain the advantage of the Dutch over the Portuguese, it cannot explain why other joint-stock companies with the exact same model fared worse,

[36] Epstein, S.R., *Freedom and Growth: The Rise of States and Markets in Europe, 1300–1750* (Routledge, London, 2000), p. 25.

[37] Irigoin and Grafe, 'Bounded', pp. 210–212, Grafe, Regina, 'An Empire of Debts? Spain and Its Colonial Realm', in *A World of Public Debts*, ed. N. Barreyre, and N. Delalande (Singapore: Springer, 2020), p. 8.

[38] Coase, 'The Nature', & Williamson, 'The Theory'.

[39] Steensgaard, *The Asian*, this process was characterised by Subrahmanyam and Thomaz as "institutional Darwinism", Subrahmanyan, Sanjay, and Thomaz, Filipe F.R., 'Evolution of Empire: The Portuguese in the Indian Ocean during the Sixteenth Century', in *The Political Economy of Merchant Empires*, ed. James Tracy (Cambridge: Cambridge University Press, 1991): 298–331. In fact, the Portuguese attempted to emulate the Dutch East India Company and briefly organised their own joint-stock enterprise to integrate their Asian trade, but its performance was lacklustre, Disney, A.R., 'The First Portuguese India Company, 1628–33', *The Economic History Review* 30, n°2 (1977): 242–258.

[40] Erikson, *Between Monopoly*.

or why the joint-stock corporation worked in Asia but was a failure in America, where eventually the Portuguese defeated the Dutch West India Company.[41] It also fails to explain why the joint-stock companies were eventually expelled from trading activities in Asia by private merchants organised around partnerships. Efficiency in these writings is rarely associated with company fundamentals such as profit margins or debt ratios. The role of the government and violence is sometimes minimised, and in some cases, Asian trade is paradoxically a fixture of the background rather than the backbone of the enterprise.

While Steensgaard did not explicitly address transaction costs in his book, some historians like Ann Carlos and Stephen Nicholas clearly state that the vertical integration of the chartered companies served as a *more efficient* alternative to the open market.[42] The data to reach this conclusion is missing, not only because of the problems associated with the accounts of the East India Companies, but because of the impossibility to define—let alone measure—the "market" across such a vast expanse as Asia and across such a long period of time. However, focusing the analysis of efficiency on transaction costs risks forgetting about fundamentals. Transaction costs are not a substitute for fundamentals. This thesis argues that the joint-stock companies problems arose when mounting expenses put stress on the economic fundamentals of their trade.

When it comes to Manila, the question of Company efficiency, whether it was through better internalising of protection costs or better informational flows, is paradoxical. Manila, like the Portuguese *Estado da India*,

[41] Brandon, Pepijn, 'Between Company and State: The Dutch East and West India Companies as Brokers between War and Profit', in *The Corporation: A Critical, Multi-Disciplinary Handbook*, ed. Grietje Baars and Andre Spicer (Cambridge: Cambridge University Press, 2017), pp. 219–220.

[42] Carlos and Stephen developed this argument in reference to the Hudson Bay Company and the Royal African Company, however they considered it applicable across the chartered companies. Carlos, Ann M., and Nicholas, Stephen, 'Agency Problems in Early Chartered Companies: The Case of Hudson's Bay Company', *Journal of Economic History* 50, n° 4 (1990): 853–875, and the debate with Jones and Ville. Jones, S.R.H., and Ville, Simon P., 'Efficient Transactors or Rent-Seeking Monopolists? The Rationale for Early Chartered Trading Companies', *The Journal of Economic History* 56, n° 4 (1996): 898–915, Carlos, Ann M., and Nicholas, Stephen M., 'Theory and History: Seventeenth-Century Joint-Stock Chartered Trading Companies', *The Journal of Economic History* 56, n° 4 (1996): 916–924, Jones, S.R.H., and Ville, Simon P., 'Theory and Evidence: Understanding Chartered Trading Companies', *The Journal of Economic History* 56, n° 4 (1996): 925–926.

always resisted integration. A fundamental aspect of it was because Manila was an intermediary in a trade predicated on arbitraging the price of pesos and Asian goods between Asia and America. As an intermediary, Manila partially caused such transaction costs. If integration was to occur, it would likely be by bypassing Manila. And yet, Manila successfully defeated the interloping attempts of the EIC, the VOC, and the Real Compañía de Filipinas (RCF), a joint-stock company chartered by Spain. This, as will be discussed in Chapters 5 and 6, is an indication that Manila was at least as efficient as the existing alternatives of the time, the East India Companies. Absent from much of this literature was the inefficiency in commercial terms of the Companies, forced to maintain armies, forts, and navies to internalise those protection costs and which lowered their profit margins and thus, their capacity to compete in prices with private merchants.

Dealing with liquidity constraints that arose from long-distance trade and its unprecedented capital demands was a fundamental factor behind the decision to form joint-stock corporations. Gelderblom & Jonker explain how the shares of the VOC, supported by their dividend, were able to perform as money substitutes, channelling liquidity in the form of cash into the VOC and solving the issue.[43] The work of Ron Harris develops a holistic explanation of the institutional formation process. Harris deconstructed every institutional structure into individual "building-blocks", arguing that their capacity to be exported to different cultural settings, and to be mixed with others to produce a resulting overall *institution*, depends on their history and setting.[44] The main strength of the joint-stock corporation, however, resides it is legal components, which were capable of offering security and guarantees to investors as well as informational advantages.[45] What the combination of the joint-stock and the legal personhood of the corporation achieved was the creation for the first time of impersonal markets, capable of bringing

[43] Gelderblom and Jonker, 'Completing', pp. 659–660.

[44] Harris, *Going*, p. 65, Harris, Ron, 'The institutional dynamics of early modern Eurasian trade: The commenda and the corporation', *Journal of Economic Behavior & Organization*, 71 (2009): 606–622.

[45] Harris, *Going*, p. 308.

"impersonal cooperation", and thus to obtain resources beyond the limitations that family firms and state enterprises had managed to achieve before them.[46]

The enhanced capacity to pool resources and mobilise capital is what unites the transaction costs literature with the more historical approaches of historians like Steensgaard, Harris, and Gelderblom and Jonker. This book wholly agrees with placing liquidity at the centre of the analysis, a result of the increased demands posed by a new way of long-distance trading. What the case of Manila's capital market shows is that there was an alternative path to achieving impersonal cooperation that went beyond the networks of mercantile dynasties and cultural groups, and yet did not need incorporation or constitutionalism as defined by North. Neither did it have recourse to chartered proto-national banks or to the spillover effect of public debt to form.[47] Instead, in Manila, religious institutions of an urban nature evolved to provide the intermediary link between the broader population and trade finance. These were the brotherhoods and religious orders that played such a fundamental role in structuring the capital markets elsewhere in the Iberian world, but whose analysis until now has been confined to local and public debt markets.[48] Manila shows that, given the right economic context, these institutions could also mobilise the necessary resources to finance long-distance trade.

[46] Harris, *Going*, p. 330.

[47] Adrianova, Svetlana, Panicos, Demetriades, and Xu, Chenggang, 'Political Economy Origins of Financial Markets in Europe and Asia', *World Development* 39, nº 5 (2011): 686–699, Fratianni, Michele, and Spinelli, Franco, 'Italian city-states and financial evolution', *European Review of Economic History* 10, nº 3 (2006): 257–278, Pezzolo, Luciano, 'Sovereign debts, political structure, and institutional commitments in Italy, 1350–1700', in *Questioning Credible Commitment: Perspectives on the Rise of Financial Capitalism*, ed. D'Maris Coffman, Adrian Leonard, and Larry Neal (Cambridge: Cambridge University Press, 2013): 169–198.

[48] Lavrín, 'El Capital Eclesiástico y las Élites Sociales en Nueva España a Fines del siglo XVIII', *Mexican Studies* 1, nº 1 (1985): 1–28, von Wobeser, Gisela, 'Las fundaciones piadosas como fuentes de crédito en la época colonial', *Historia Mexicana* 38, nº 4 (1989): 779–792, Rodrigues, Lisbeth, 'Institutional investors in the Portuguese credit market (1550–1800): The case of the *Misercórdias*', *Revista de Historia Económica/Journal of Iberian and Latin American Economic History* 41, nº 1 (2024): 1–29.

1.3 Market Structure and Horizontal Integration

An alternative approach to vertical integration through the firm was to integrate markets horizontally. Epstein developed such a model, arguing that the deciding factor for growth was not so much the inherent capacity of institutions to credibly commit, but rather their capacity to integrate markets.[49] According to Epstein, jurisdictional fragmentation across and within territories gave rise to coordination failures: markets do not integrate because those that control the unintegrated market would stand to lose their controlling position if they open up without any *ex-ante* guarantee that their actions would be reciprocated. Thus, those agents that can make the decision face a prisoner's dilemma. Without any overarching authority that can offer guarantees, markets remain unintegrated. Epstein's model not only places agent motivation at the core of the analysis but does not treat trade endogenously: trade exists prior to market integration, but in the absence of political will or capacity, fragmentation would remain, hampering the emergence of economies of scale. While Epstein still agreed that causation emanates from institutions, he wrote about a stronger feedback mechanism, in which larger, integrated markets make fragmentary, rent-seeking institutions non-existent.[50]

The problem of coordinating disparate territories and markets resonates much more with the political economy of the Spanish empire than NIE's idea of a despotic government.[51] The template of Epstein institutionalist model has been explicitly applied by Regina Grafe and Alejandra Irigoin to the Hispanic Monarchy.[52] As they rightfully stress, and as was the case of Manila, capital pooling took place in Spain and

[49] Epstein, S.R., *Freedom and Growth: The Rise of States and Markets in Europe, 1300–1750* (London: Routledge, 2000), p. 167.

[50] Epstein, *Freedom*, p. 173.

[51] Yun-Casalilla and Comín Comín, 'Spain', Yun-Casalilla, *Iberian World*, Cardim, Feros, and Sabatini, 'The Political'.

[52] Irigoin and Grafe, 'Bounded', Grafe, Regina, and Irigoin, Alejandra, 'A Stakeholder Empire: the political economy of Spanish Imperial rule in America', *Economic History Review* 65, n° 2 (2012), Grafe, Regina, *Distant Tyranny: Markets, Power, and Backwardness in Spain, 1650–1800* (Princeton: Princeton University Press, 2012), Grafe, Regina, and Irigoin, Alejandra, 'The Spanish Empire and its legacy: fiscal redistribution and political conflict in colonial and post-colonial Spanish America', *Journal of Global History*, vol. 1 (2006): 241–267, & Irigoin, Alejandra, and Grafe, Regina, 'Bargaining for Absolutism:

the Hispanic world, and interest rates were low.[53] There is no indication that North's "absolute tyrant" affected investment in the Spanish empire. Instead, following Epstein, the problem was one of coordination failure among the myriad jurisdictions that composed the empire. The very strength of the Hispanic polity was the capacity of the king to arbitrate the relationship between all the political units of this body, but this came at the expense of guaranteeing each one's jurisdictional domain to the detriment of integration.[54] This fragmentation is what raised transaction costs and led to inefficiencies in trade. Efficiency, not investment, was the problem. In this model, trade and institutions are endogenous to each other. Trade can exist and persist, and it is the level of jurisdictional fragmentation and the resulting absence or reduction of market integration that affects trade through higher transaction costs. This approach developed by Epstein, Grafe, and Irigoin suits best the situation of the Pacific exchange. The limitations faced by the Manileños in the Acapulco negotiation resulted in their adoption of the one-Galleon system (Chapter 4), which limited trade, making market risk nil but at the expense of reducing market integration. In the case of the Pacific exchange, however, the origin of the coordination failure was economic, embedded in the monopsonic market for silver pesos, rather than institutional. Manila's specialisation as a provider of liquidity was a strategy to mitigate this coordination failure to the extent it was possible in the absence of perfect market integration or vertical integration.

The work of Avner Greif, Yadira González de Lara, and Sumitra Jha, developed game theoretical tools to explore how commitment issues, ex-ante guarantees, and formal and informal institutions affected international trade in the Early Modern world. This framework, the Fundamental Problem of Exchange (FPOE),[55] has proven crucial to understand the

A Spanish Path to Nation-State and Empire Building', *Hispanic American Historical Review* 88, nº 2 (2007): 173–209.

[53] Irigoin and Grafe, 'Bounded', p. 220.

[54] Irigoin and Grafe, 'Bounded', p. 218.

[55] Greif, Avner, 'The fundamental problem of exchange: A research agenda in Historical Institutional Analysis', *European Review of Economic History*, vol. 4 (2000): 251–284, Greif, Avner, *Institutions and the Path to the Modern Economy: Lessons from Medieval Trade* (New York: Cambridge University Press, 2006), González de Lara, Yadira, 'The Secret of Venetian Success: A Public-Order, Reputation-Based Institution', *European Review of Economic History*, vol. 12 (2008): 247–285, González de Lara, Yadira, Greif, Avner, and

cost–benefit analysis that merchants in the Early Modern period faced, and thus to understand institutional formation. This model incorporates the motivation of those involved in institution-building as the foundational part of the process, but it still failed in placing these institutions in their economic context. In other words, what factors may have motivated the agents other than to keep transacting among themselves was lost. Therefore, Greif's model derived into a dichotomy between personal and impersonal institutions, according to which personal institutions were cheaper to enforce but limited in their scope, while impersonal institutions were more expensive but could handle a larger volume of trade.[56] While the Fundamental Problem of Exchange as developed by Greif and others applies on a micro scale to issues of trust and guarantees between merchants, it has obvious synergies with the Northian model of constitutional commitment, and can be translated into a broader political scale. The work of Epstein and the concept of coordination failures mentioned above, similarly has recourse to game theoretical settings to explain the absence of market integration. This book adopts a wider perspective on the Fundamental Problem of Exchange, seeking to understand how contracts could be monitored and enforced both on a transactional level and on a broader political and institutional level.

This model faces two problems. Firstly, the role of trade is endogenous to it. Trade is not only the outcome of personal and impersonal institutions, but also the cause for switching from one to the other. This leads to its second problem. Lacking a contextualisation of the motivation of the agents in the macroeconomic landscape, and with trade being both cause and consequence, Greif resorts to ontological explanations, arguing that impersonal institutions emerge in "individualist" cultures like Genoa, and personal institutions emerge in "collectivist" cultures like the Maghrebi traders. And that cultural variable is unexplainable and

Jha, Sumitra, 'The Administrative Foundation of Self-Enforcing Constitutions', *American Economic Review* 98, n° 2 (2008): 105–109.

[56] Greif, 'The fundamental', p. 278, González de Lara, 'The secret', pp. 278–279, an interesting take is presented by Grafe, Regina, and Gelderblom, Oscar, 'The Rise and Fall of the Merchant Guilds: Re-thinking the Comparative Studies of Commercial Institutions in Pre-Modern Europe', *The Journal of Interdisciplinary History* 4, n° 10 (2010): 477–511.

immutable.[57] Finally, personal and impersonal institutions can coexist. Francesca Trivellato revealed how personal networks could overcome the barrier of cultural homogeneity that guarantees monitoring and enforcement in Greif's model.[58] Similarly, impersonal financial institutions like banks have never surrendered their personal networks, even today. Formal and informal institutions coexist and enhance each other.

This complementarity of private order and public order institutions can be seen in operation in Manila, in the way in which notarial archives and contracts enabled fund managers and its beneficiaries to monitor each other and to punish transgressions while circulating the news widely, fast, and cheaply across the city's financial networks. It will be argued through Chapters 5 and 6 that networks enhanced the function of formal institutions, and that formal institutions were often used to the benefit of networks. This last part is especially the role of Chapter 6, which examines the coordination failure of the Acapulco negotiation as it was crystallised by law into fragmented jurisdictions across the Pacific, and how Manila used the legal tools at its disposal to mitigate the issue by doubling down on specialisation.

Yet another strand of economic history gives primacy instead to relative factor price differentials to explain different paths to growth. In a seminal book co-edited by Gareth Austin and Kaoru Sugihara, *Labour-Intensive Industrialization in Global History*,[59] several historians demonstrate how differences in prices of the factors of production led to different approaches to economic growth and industrialisation, including the emergence of different institutional frameworks. Since these alternative paths are characterised by the difference in price of capital, labour,

[57] Greif, Avner, 'Cultural Beliefs and the Organization of Society: A Historical and Theoretical Reflection on Collectivist and Individualist Societies', *Journal of Political Economy* 102, nº 5 (1994): 912–950.

[58] Trivellato, Francesca, *The Familiarity of Strangers: the Sephardic diaspora, Livorno, and cross-cultural trade in the Early Modern period* (London: Yale University Press, 2012). There is similarly great debate on the importance of associative organisations in contract enforcement and their impact on the market. An example is the case of guilds in Europe. See Ogilvie, Sheilagh, *Institutions and European Trade: Merchant Guilds, 1000–1800* (Cambridge: Cambridge University Press, 2011), Ogilvie, Sheilagh, 'Thinking carefully about inclusiveness: evidence from European guilds', *Journal of Institutional Economics* (2020): 1–16, also Grafe and Gelderblom, 'The Rise'.

[59] Austin, Gareth, and Sugihara, Kaoru (editors), *Labour-Intensive Industrialization in Global History* (Abingdon: Routledge, 2013).

and land across the world, it is ultimately the given abundance of labour, land fertility and usage, and resource endowments relative to other factors that define the path to growth taken by different societies. This is a useful framework for the present work, although the emphasis is taken away from factors of production and focused instead on the trade, especially the arbitrage to be made between Asian demand for specie and Spanish American production.

This is related to the importance of silver in the Early Modern global trade. As Irigoin has argued, the role of silver has often been mischaracterised.[60] For Pomeranz, silver was simply a way to settle negative balance of accounts for Europeans trading with Asia.[61] Flynn and Giráldez offer a different theory, in which silver bullion is treated as a commodity for trade.[62] Irigoin has explained that Asia's—and especially China's—demand for silver differentiated between bullion and coins, and between specific coins. Irigoin argued that the development of the peso coin in Spanish America after 1680 shifted Chinese demand for silver into a demand for a certifiable means of payment.[63] China demanded pesos because China lacked a reliable silver coin for its monetary system. This, in turn, drove global demand due to China's size in the world economy during the period. The peso became a currency of trade, and this minimised transaction costs because it provided a standard to settle transactions with Asia.[64] The core of the argument regarding the Manila trade is that, when faced with a coordination failure that raised transaction costs due to the skewedness between demand and provision of pesos, the city developed institutions that allowed it to mitigate the coordination failure. Manila devised a different strategy towards partial integration

[60] Irigoin, 'Rise', pp. 386–387. Nothing evidences better this discrepancy regarding the role of silver than the debate between Flynn and Giráldez and O'Rourke and Williamson, Flynn and Giráldez, 'Cycles of silver', O'Rourke, Kevin H., and Williamson, Jeffrey G., 'When did Globalisation begin?', *European Review of Economic History* 6, n° 1 (2002): 23–50, Flynn, Dennis O., and Giráldez, Arturo, 'Path dependence, time lags, and the birth of globalisation: A critique of O'Rourke and Williamson', *European Review of Economic History*, vol. 8, n° 1 (2004): 81–108, O'Rourke, Kevin H., and Williamson, Jeffrey G., 'Once more: when did globalisation begin?', *European Review of Economic History* 8 (2004): 109–117.

[61] Pomeranz, *The Great*, p. 270.

[62] Flynn, and Giráldez, 'Path dependence', pp. 85–86.

[63] Irigoin, 'Rise', p. 396.

[64] Irigoin, 'Rise', p. 403.

horizontally, through specialisation. This horizontal approach allowed Manila to maintain its intermediary status at the expense of verticalisation, while enabling enough specialisation to mitigate the foregone gains of integration through economies of scale in the origination of working capital. The primary cause is nevertheless to be found on the economics of the Pacific exchange rather than the institutional framework. The specific set of institutions that Manila devised were the response.

1.4 The Spanish Philippines and the Manila Trade

Incorporating the reconstructed capital market of Manila has the potential to change our understanding of the processes taking place in the islands during the long eighteenth century. The historical literature on the Spanish Philippines has suffered from problems of legacy. This is most notable in the case of the English-speaking literature, which has often relied on the work of William Schurz and has therefore carried on several of the problems associated with it.[65] The most important one is that Schurz's work on the Manila Galleons lacks a chronological dimension, following instead a straightforward thematic composition that gives the impression that the Manila trade was unchanging. Schurz does not seek to historicise the evolution of the Manila trade. Without a historical dimension, it is impossible to discern changes or processes, which in turns hides the interests and motivations of Manileños. Another problematic issue of Schurz's work is that he often fortuitously considers practices and usages of the Manila trade as plain corruption, crafting a picture of negligence and venality which has been carried on by the literature all the way to the most recent publications by Arturo Giráldez.[66] This approach hides the complex process of bargaining that reveals to historians the true motivation of Manileños behind an inscrutable barrier termed simply as "corruption". This is a mischaracterisation and oversimplification of the political economy of the Hispanic Monarchy, and crucially, it compounds

[65] Schurz, William, *The Manila Galleon* (New York: E. P. Dutton & Co, 1939). See for example Giráldez, Arturo, *The Age of Trade: The Manila Galleons and the Dawn of the Global Economy* (London: Rowman & Littlefield, 2015), Flynn, Dennis O., 'Comparing the Tokugawa Shogunate with Hapsburg Spain: Two silver-based empires in a global setting', in *The Political Economy of Merchant Empires*, ed. James D. Tracy (Cambridge University Press, Cambridge, 1990) or Pearson, M.N., 'Spain and Spanish trade in Southeast Asia', *Journal of Asian History*, 2 (1968): 109–129.

[66] Giráldez, *The Age*.

the problems derived from Schurz's thematic approach because it similarly prevents any analysis of change by simply writing off everything that did not stick to the legislation as "corruption". The motivation of Manileños was to remain intermediaries in the direct silver trade between America and Asia. From this foundation, it is possible to understand how Manileños used the political tools available to them to protect their intermediation.

A second problem of the literature on the Spanish Philippines is the dispersal of the sources. This dispersion is not entirely fortuitous. The lack of coordination of the Hispanic Monarchy meant that sources were produced by different entities and kept in different repositories depending on the nature of the document. The causes and challenges of this dispersal are developed later, what matters is that no one repository presents a complete picture of what was taking place in Manila. As a result, the literature has focused on one specific aspect of Manila and the Pacific exchange while remaining oblivious to the rest of the evidence. This is compounded by the fact that private documents produced for the trade and by the trade have remained dispersed in the archives of the institutions that created them and have therefore been the least utilised to date. Historians are missing the private market of the city, the commercial enterprises of merchants, religious orders, investors, and financiers. Without this crucial piece of the puzzle, the literature has reverted to explanations that are weighted towards the kind of sources that they are using.

For example, some historians have focused on the fiscal side of the Spanish domination of the archipelago. The work of Luís Alonso Álvarez refuted the long-held assumption, inherited from the work of Leslie E. Bauzon, that the Philippines were a deficitary province sustained by transfers from Mexico.[67] Alonso Álvarez proved that it was in fact the transfer of the local *tributo indígena* to the religious orders that provoked this situation of fiscal deficit.[68] But fiscal historians have only interpreted the trade in its relation with the accounts of the local government, which

[67] Alonso Álvarez, Luis, *El costo del imperio asiático: La formación colonial de las islas Filipinas bajo dominio español, 1565–1800* (Mexico: Instituto Mora, 2009), Bauzon, Leslie E., *Deficit Government: Mexico and the Philippine Situado, 1606–1804* (Tokyo: Centre for East Asian Cultural Studies, 1981).

[68] Alonso Álvarez, Luis, 'Financing the Empire: The Nature of the Tax System in the Philippines, 1565–1804', *Philippine Studies* 51, nº 1 (2003): 63–95.

has tended to both give the authorities a disproportionate weight in the commerce than was really the case. Fiscal historians fail to place the evidence they see in the broader context of the political economy of the Hispanic Monarchy. The devolution of authority meant that fiscality was often subservient to local imperatives,[69] and in the case of Manila, this meant the silver trade. Not only do Alonso Álvarez and Bauzón lack the information regarding the private capital market, without it they cannot understand the privatisation of public resources that was underway as they cannot know the true motivation of Manileños. For example, Chapter 6 shows that the deficit of the Philippines served a bigger purpose: to monetise the taxes on the trade and return them to the Philippines to repay debts that the local treasury had been forced to incur to prop up private market rates. This cannot be ascertained by only looking at the fiscality in the islands without contrasting it to the broader economic imperatives of the Pacific trade, and fundamentally, the capital market of Manila.

Recent scholarship from Latin America exemplifies the problems that can arise from a territorially oriented interpretation of the sources of the Manila trade. The works of Carmen Yuste López and Mariano Bonialian interpret the Manila trade from the perspective of Spanish America. Yuste argued that Manila was a Mexican outpost in the Far East, where relatives and agents of the powerful wholesalers of Mexico City (the *almaceneros*) controlled the trade.[70] According to Yuste, Mexican merchants were capable of switching from the Pacific negotiation to the Atlantic and vice versa whenever it was more profitable for them, an argument also followed by Bonialian.[71] This was allegedly done to the detriment of Spanish official policy, as the silk trade of Manila competed against that of the Andalusian cities, and because the king hardly received any rents in the form of taxes from the Pacific exchange.

Yuste's and Bonialian's interpretation of the Pacific as an alternative commercial space for local merchants outside of the control of the

[69] Grafe, *Distant*, Ch. 6, Grafe and Irigoin, 'A stakeholder', pp. 637–638.

[70] Yuste López, Carmen, *Emporios Transpacíficos: Comerciantes Mexicanos en Manila (1710–1815)*, (Mexico: Universidad Nacional Autónoma de México, 2007), a more nuanced view for the earlier seventeenth century is presented in Gasch-Tomás, José Luís, 'Mecanismos de funcionamiento institucional en el imperio Hispánico. El comercio de los Galeones de Manila y el Consulado de comerciantes de México en la década de 1630'. *Revista de Historia Jerónimo Zurita*, 90 (2015): 55–74.

[71] Bonialian, *El Pacífico*.

metropolis has relegated Manila to the role of simple waystation of the Mexican merchants. This interpretation however suffers from several inconsistencies. Foremost is the issue that it projects identities that belong to the nineteenth century back in time in an effort to interpret the history of the Pacific as one of "*indianos*".[72] Had Yuste or Bonialian expanded their family connections beyond Mexico, they would have found that the merchants operating in Manila were not Mexicans, but belonged to a series of families that hailed originally from specific regions of Spain, and that operated across the entire empire.[73] Yuste is correct in noting that the Manileños had family and business relations with their counterparts in Mexico, but they were far from mere agents. Many of them remained in Manila, where they married, raised their children, and died. Their profits were often spent in Manila and their prosperity was tied to the city. Relying exclusively on American sources even conceals Manileños as historical agents, transforming them into a sub-category of American merchants.

Finally, there has been a resurgence of interest for the history of the Philippines in later years. The Spanish experience in Asia has received renewed attention among Spanish scholars,[74] while recent research in America—especially the work of Guillermo Ruiz-Stovel and Joshua Kueh[75]—has shed new light in the relationship of the Spanish and the

[72] The term *indiano* is commonly used to denote the peninsular Spaniard who earns a fortune in the Indies and returns to Spain. *Criollo* refers to creole, descendants of Spaniards born in the Americas. Bonialian however uses the term *indiano* in contrast to Schurz's and Spate's description of the Pacific as a "Spanish Lake", giving the term *indiano* a meaning as antonym of Spanish.

[73] Cebreiro Ares, Francisco, 'Redes comerciales y traslado de herencias entre el Imperio Hispánico y Galicia: Andrés de Losada Sotomayor y los retornos monetarios a Compostela (1744–1790)', *e-Spania*, 34 (October 2019): 1–26.

[74] Gasch-Tomás, José Luís, 'Transport Costs and Prices of Chinese Silk in the Spanish Empire. The Case of New Spain, c. 1571–1650', *Revista de Historia Industrial*, nº 60 (2015): 15–47, Pérez-García, Manuel, *Global History with Chinese Characteristics: Autocratic States along the Silk Road in the Decline of the Spanish and Qing Empires, 1680–1796* (Singapore: Palgrave, 2021), Pérez-García, Manuel, 'Beyond the Silk Road: Manila Galleons, trade networks, global goods, and the integration of Atlantic and Pacific markets (1680–1840)', *Atlantic Studies* 19, nº 3 (2022): 373–383.

[75] Ruiz-Stovel, Guillermo, 'Chinese Shipping and Merchant Networks at the Edge of the Spanish Pacific: The Minnan-Manila Trade, 1680–1840' (PhD diss., University of California Los Angeles, 2019), Kueh, Joshua Eng Sin, 'The Manila Chinese: Community,

Chinese in Manila, and on Manila's Chinese trade. The work of Ruiz-Stovel on the trade of the Philippines has been especially important. For the first time since 1960, historians have a more accurate picture of the commerce between Manila and Asia thanks to Ruíz-Stovel's Manila Intra-Asian Trade (MIAT) database.[76]

However, regardless of how promising this recent wave of interest in the Spanish Philippines is, the capital market of Manila is still missing. Without it, it is not possible to fully comprehend the role that the city played in Asia, and its importance for intra-Asian trade. Neither is it possible to truly understand the motivation of Manileños. This links to the problems presented by the literature. Whether Manila is analysed from a fiscal point of view like Alonso Álvarez and Bauzón did, or from the perspective of Spanish America, Manila itself and its role in the trade remains hidden. Without this, it is not possible to analyse how the Fundamental Problem of Exchange was solved in the Pacific. This is the main contribution of this book, the missing piece of the puzzle that can help scholars make sense of the Iberian Pacific: the capital markets of Manila. Once they are brought into the equation, it can be seen that *obras pías* guaranteed Manileños' intermediation in the Pacific silver trade, and therefore, they aligned the motivation of everyone in Manila towards protecting the *obras pías* and the rents they obtained from financing the trade.

1.5 Sources

Many of the shortcomings of the literature are explained by the challenges presented by the primary documentation. There are three main problems with sources of the Spanish empire. The first problem is hermeneutical and relates to the authority of the sources and the context in which they were produced. Most of the sources that have survived were produced in the context of the complex bargaining for legislation that characterised the political framework of the Hispanic Monarchy.[77] As a result, the accuracy of the information contained is not free from bias, as groups

Trade, and Empire, c. 1570–1770', (PhD diss., Georgetown University, Washington D.C., 2014).

76 Ruiz-Stovel, Guillermo. (2021). Manila Intra-Asian Trade Database (MIAT) (1.0) [Data set]. Zenodo. https://doi.org/10.5281/zenodo.4836052, accessed 25/07/2022.

77 Irigoin and Grafe, 'Bargaining', pp. 204–205.

of interest lobbied for their respective causes. The compilations on the Manila trade done by Juan Grau y Monfalcón in 1637[78] and Antonio Álvarez Abreu in 1734,[79] provide an example. Both works were recordings of judicial processes ordered by the king in which the authors were interested parties, as both were representatives of the city of Manila in the court of Madrid. Importantly, they essentially contain the cases of the litigants, presenting the points of view of both Manileños and Sevillians. The information they contain is valuable to the historian if critically used and interpreted within the context of bargaining. The problem is that this layer of hermeneutical analysis is missing in the literature, which takes assertions made by litigants at face value. These types of sources are useful, but their richness is to be found on what they reveal regarding the process of bargaining and the red lines of the different parties involved. They need to be interpreted in their broader context.

A second problem is related to the previous one and pertains to the fragmentary and dislocated nature of the sources that remain. Because of the nature of the trade and the fragmented jurisdictions of the Hispanic world, there is a general lack of serialised hard data. The state never truly had the aim or the authority to record information in a centralised way, and the dichotomy between Civil and Canonical jurisdiction meant that the sources of the religious (whether clerical or lay) institutions that financed the trade remained separate. While *almojarifazgo* (import and export tax)[80] records for the whole of the Spanish period exist, this data is suspicious of underreporting the real conditions of Manila, although the recent work of Ruiz-Stovel has done much to correct previous inaccuracies.

[78] BNE, Ms/899, *Juan Grau y Monfalcón, Memorial Informatorio al Rey en su Real Consejo de Indias*, 1637.

[79] Álvarez de Abreu, Antonio, *Extracto Historial del expediente que pende en el Consejo Real, y Supremo de las Indias, a instancia de la Ciudad de Manila, sobre la forma en que se ha de hacer y continuar el Comercio, y Contratación de los Texidos de China en Nueva España*, Madrid, 1736.

[80] The *almojarifazgo* was to all effects a tax on maritime trade, and the series is an important source of information for the Manila trade because it recorded its provenance of the ships that arrived in Manila, their captains, and—through the tax receipt and tax rates—the value of the goods transported in each vessel. However, it did not include a detailed breakdown of the items and goods that were brought into Manila. Chapter I discusses further the issues with the *almojarifazgo* series.

The final problem is the geographical dispersion of the sources. This is partly the result of historical accidents, with some collections being moved to places like the Newberry Library in Chicago, while large amounts of documents remain in Manila or are scattered across Spain. But mostly it reflects the multiple jurisdictions of the Hispanic Monarchy. Thus, the administrative papers of religious orders are still largely kept in the orders' archives, notarial protocols remain in Manila, while documents regarding the administration of justice such as the proceedings of the freighting of the Manila Galleons are kept in the AGI, in Seville. Adding to this dispersion is an issue of survival and loss through the history of the repositories. Many books of the notarial protocols of Manila have been lost due to the vicissitudes of war, while entire repositories such as the archive of the Misericordia of Manila were destroyed during the American invasion of the Philippines. This poses a problem of survival bias that is impossible to solve with any degree of certainty.

To overcome these problems of bias and lack of serialised data, it is important to use independent sources, sources produced by the trade for its management and financing. This is one of the strengths of this book, which relies on private sources from the notarial protocols of Manila and the religious orders that managed legacy funds. These include the contracts of transactions incurred in financing the trade and the account books of the funds that provided the capital. These sources are not only novel, but they represent the commercial and financial life of the city, overcoming problems of bias and placing Manila at the centre of the analysis. Two main corpora of sources are used in reconstructing the capital markets of Manila. The first are private financial documents related to operation of the market. This includes the sea loan contracts (known in Manila as *correspondencias*)[81] that were used to finance the trade, the account books of the legacy funds that issued the *correspondencias*, as well as the management books of the institutions that administered the funds. These documents provide a picture of the operation of the financial market and of the agents involved. *Correspondencia* contracts were

[81] *Correspondencias* belonged to the category of respondentias, that is sea loans imposed on the cargoes of merchant vessels as opposed to those sea loans imposed on the ship itself, which are termed "bottomry" loans following the English nomenclature. The different categories of sea loans are analysed in depth in Chapter 3 Section Correspondencias a riesgo de mar. From here on, *correspondencias* will be used when referring to the contracts issued in Manila. *Respondentia* will be used whenever the text refers to the broader category of sea loans imposed on the cargo of a vessel.

collected from the notarial protocols of Manila, since the parties involved in the contract always had them notarised. The information on legacy funds had to be collected from the archives of the brotherhoods and Third Orders that administered the funds, and whose archives remain private. This is the case specifically of the funds managed by the Franciscan (kept in the Archivo Franciscano-Ibero Oriental in Madrid, AFIO) and Dominican orders (kept in the Archivo de la Provincia del Santísimo Rosario in Ávila, APSR). The papers of the Jesuit funds were collected from the Newberry Library in Chicago. The information on the funds managed by the archbishopric of Manila was collected from the archive of the University of Santo Tomás in Manila (AUST).

The second body of sources is composed of documents related to the governance of the financial markets of Manila. These include documents pertaining to many hierarchical and jurisdictional levels, that is, from litigation in the Council of the Indies and reports of royal officials in Manila, to the legal opinions of the University of Santo Tomás on cases involving legacy funds, as well as documents with legal authority such as powers of attorney, testaments, and bills of lading in the Galleons. These sources reveal valuable information regarding the motivation of Manileños and are crucial in understanding how contracts were enforced and monitored, and how the law was bargained and implemented. In short, how institutions worked in the Pacific. These sources were collected from many repositories. The documents regarding litigation and bargaining in the Council of the Indies is archived in the Archivo General de Indias in Seville. These include reports from officials and audits of fund managers involved in judicial proceedings. The private papers of many of the early nineteenth-century governors of the Philippines have been kept in the Archivo del Museo Naval in Madrid, and these included several reports and statistics from earlier periods that were undoubtedly part of the information gathered by the officials during their careers. Similarly, because the Manila Galleon was the privilege of the citizens of Manila, the freighting proceedings were notarised and sent to the Council of the Indies, where some of the manifest books of the Galleons have survived.

The value of the first body of sources is that they are private in nature and are not affected by the bias of sources produced for litigation and bargaining before the king and the authorities. This is precisely the kind of sources that can afford researchers a glimpse of the activities and motivations of Manileños. The analysis of private sources like sea loan contracts, legacy funds' account books, last wills, and freighting bills allows for a reconstruction of how the capital market of Manila worked, which in turn is fundamental to better contextualise the second body of sources, obtaining even more information from the latter than has been possible until now. Fundamentally, they allow for a new perspective, one in which Manila is an active agent of the Pacific exchange. These are sources produced by the trade and for the trade, intended to be used for commercial and financial operations.

1.6 Structure

The book is divided into seven chapters. Chapter 2 describes the nature of the Manila trade, focusing on the global specie trade of the Early Modern period. It highlights Manila's unique role as a provider of liquidity in maritime Asia, and analyses the consequences of this, namely the Dutch Disease that the archipelago experienced. In short, it illustrates that Manila's best option given the broader macroeconomic context was to specialise. Chapter 3 reconstructs the capital markets of Manila from 1668 to 1833. It expands the lessons of Chapter 2 to argue that Manila developed a capital market oriented towards maximising its advantageous access to silver specie. It shows that the capital market of Manila could solve the problems associated with long-distance trade and foster impersonal cooperation just like the joint-stock companies did, but following an alternative model based on optimising the abundance of cash in the city.

Chapter 4 examines the business model of the transpacific trade and the one-Galleon system given the economic and institutional context developed in the previous chapters. Asian demand for silver and their preference for Mexican peso coins skewed the bargaining power in the retail chain in favour of New Spanish merchants. The chapter shows that Manileños palliated this by limiting the volume of the trade through the one-Galleon system so as to maintain their negotiating position in the Acapulco fair. Limiting the scale of the exchange in turn led Manileños to prioritise profitability over volume.

Chapter 5 addresses the Fundamental Problem of Exchange in the context of the capital markets of Manila. It explains the city's position within the Pacific retail chain. It is divided in two parts. The first part studies how the institutional framework of Manila's capital markets mitigated the risks of the Pacific exchange, while the second part analyses in depth the concept of Horizontal Specialisation. Essentially, it argues that

Manila's capability to pool large amounts of cash and mobilise capital while internalising the risk meant it could perform as an intermediary, while the economies of scale in the provision of liquidity that stemmed from its specialisation meant that the city remained competitive compared to the alternatives of the time, being able to issue capital at relatively low rates.

Chapter 6 examines how the Pacific trade fitted within the broader political economy of the Hispanic Monarchy, and how the system of territorial bargaining offered enough guarantees to mitigate the Fundamental Problem of Exchange on a political level. It shows how trade was institutionally organised within the Spanish empire, and how Manila managed to use its position within the body politic to protect its intermediary role and sustain the trade. Chapter 7 concludes by more explicitly contrasting the financial and business model of Manila's specialisation with the strategy of scaling of the EIC and the VOC, demonstrating that it was different access to liquidity which determined the different institutional outcomes even when both models were faced with the similar challenges that direct long-distance trade with Asia entailed.

CHAPTER 2

The Manila Trade

2.1 The Global Silver Trade and the Pacific

One of the most salient features of Early Modern European trade with Asia was its reliance on silver. Throughout the period, Europe paid for Asian commodities and manufactures by shipping treasure. According to Chaudhuri, in the years 1660–1720, the EIC exported a total worth of £12,588,296 from England to Asia (approximately 1,500 tons of silver or 25 annual tons).[1] Bowen calculates £18,342,417 for 1760–1820 (approximately 2,200 tons or 36.7 tons annually).[2] The VOC also exported great quantities of silver to Asia from Europe despite the exclusive access they enjoyed to Japanese silver. The Dutch transported a total of 573,926,000 guilders to Asia between 1602 and 1795 (approximately 5,545 tons of

[1] Chaudhuri, K.N., 'Treasure and Trade Balances: The East India Company's Export Trade, 1660–1720', *The Economic History Review* 21, nº 3 (1968), pp. 497–500.

[2] Bowen, Huw V., 'Bullion for Trade, War, and Debt Relief: British movements of silver to, around, and from Asia, 1760–1833', *Modern Asian Studies* 44, nº 3 (2010), pp. 454–455. Bowen's data only captures silver exports from London to Asia, so it excludes the large shipments from within Asia, which became a feature after the capture of Bengal, the increase importance of the Canton trade, and the clandestine trade of Manila.

J. J. Rivas Moreno, *The Capital Market of Manila and the Pacific Trade, 1668–1838*, Palgrave Studies in Economic History,
https://doi.org/10.1007/978-3-031-71810-6_2

silver, 28.7 annually),[3] while between 1788 and 1809, British and private traders exported an annual average of 70 tons of silver to Asia (the peak of British exports eastwards).[4] De Vries estimated that from 1725 to 1800, an annual average of 160 tons of silver were shipped from all of Europe to Asia.[5] The magnitude and continuity of the silver flow to the East resulted in seasonal scarcities of currency in London whenever the EIC fleets were readied for the crossing to Asia.[6]

Europeans' trade in Asia was framed within a larger commercial phenomenon. The discovery of large deposits of the white metal in America led to the first global trade in which Europeans intermediated between Spanish America's supply of silver specie and Asia's demand for it.[7] Stemming from America, there were two official routes that carried the outflows of silver used to pay for Spanish American consumption, the Atlantic Run represented by the *flotas* of New Spain and the *galeones* of Perú, and the Pacific Run or Manila Galleon. Both were officially sanctioned routes since the sixteenth century and were broadly based on the same terms: importing consumer goods, mostly textiles, into Spanish America in exchange of silver specie. From Seville and Cádiz, silver specie permeated into the European monetary circuits as payments for exports. Other unofficial routes, such as the trade between Buenos Aires and the Plate estuary to Brazil and onwards on to Europe and Africa, or the contraband trade through the British Caribbean, mobilised large quantities of silver specie, although their volumes are less documented[8] (Map 2.1).

[3] Gaastra, F.S., 'The exports of precious metal from Europe to Asia by the Dutch East India Company, 1602–1795', in *Precious Metals in the Later Medieval and Early Modern Worlds*, ed. J.F. Richards (Durham: Carolina Academic Press, 1983), pp. 451.

[4] Irigoin, 'Rise', pp. 396–397.

[5] De Vries, 'The limits', p. 718.

[6] Chaudhuri, 'Treasure', pp. 480–481.

[7] Irigoin, 'The New', pp. 272–273, for a study on the nature of China's demand for silver, see Von Glahn, Richard, *Fountain of Fortune: Money and Monetary Policy in China, 1000–1700* (Berkeley: University of California Press, 1996).

[8] Pearce, Adrian J., *British Trade with Spanish America, 1763–1808* (Liverpool: Liverpool University Press, 2007), Bohorquez, Jesus, 'Linking the Atlantic and Indian Oceans: Asian textiles, Spanish silver, global capital, and the financing of the Portuguese-Brazilian slave trade (c. 1760–1808)', *Journal of Global History* 15, n° 1 (2020): 19–38.

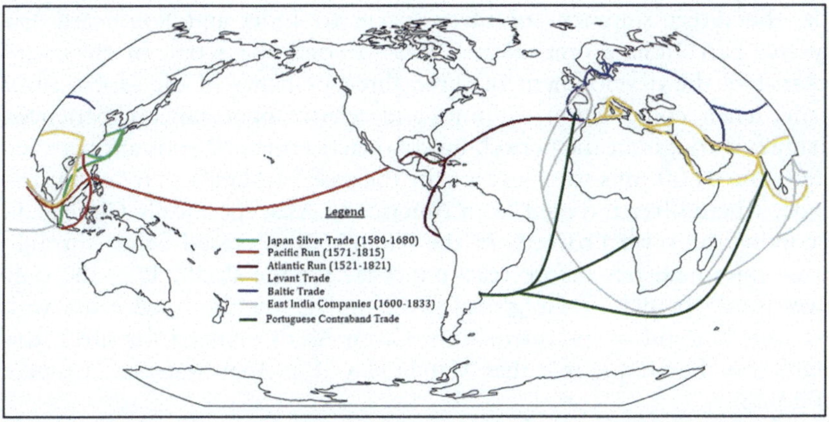

Map 2.1 Global silver trade routes 1500–1800 (*Source* Frank, André Gunder, *Re-Orient: Global economy in the Asian Age*, Berkeley: University of California Press [1998], Barrett, Ward, 'World Bullion Flows, 1450–1800', in *The Rise of Merchant Empires: Long-Distance Trade in the Early Modern World, 1350–1750*, ed. James D. Tracy, Cambridge: Cambridge University Press [1990], Flynn, Dennis O., & Giráldez, Arturo, 'Cycles of Silver: Global Economic Unity Through the Mid-Eighteenth Century', *Journal of World History* 13, n° 2 [2002], Irigoin, Alejandra, 'Rise and Demise of the Global Silver Standard', in *Handbook of the History of Money and Currency*, ed. Stefano Battilossi, Yousef Cassis and Kazuhiko Yago, Singapore: Springer [2020], Bohorquez, J., 'Linking the Atlantic and Indian Oceans: Asian Textiles, Spanish Silver, Global Capital, and the Financing of the Portuguese-Brazilian Slave Trade [c. 1760–1808]', *Journal of Global History* 15, n° 1 [2020])

From Europe, three large routes channelled the silver eastwards: the Italian states used it to settle payments in the Levant, where silver specie entered the Ottoman empire and circulated eastwards into Persia and India[9]; Dutch and other European merchants sent it through the Baltic as payment for bulk goods like wood, tar, wheat, and furs, from where it went to modern-day Russia and eventually China[10]; the third channel

[9] Barrett, Ward, 'World Bullion Flows, 1450–1800', in *The Rise of Merchant Empires: Long-Distance Trade in the Early Modern World, 1350–1750*, ed. James D. Tracy (Cambridge: Cambridge University Press, 1990), p. 252.

[10] Barrett, 'World Bullion', pp. 250–252.

was the direct shipment of silver specie to India and Southeast Asia by the East India Companies.[11] It is beyond the scope of this work to analyse the development of these three branches of the global silver trade. Their composition, volume, and relative importance experienced changes throughout the period, but two facts remained constant between 1500 and 1800: this was—except for the case of Manila—an "eastward" trade, where silver travelled from America to Asia, specifically China; and secondly, the silver proceeds of the Atlantic Run passed hands through many intermediaries before reaching Asia. Yet the Pacific leg—the only "westward" branch of the global silver trade—was the trade route with the least amount of intermediation. Given Asia's demand for silver, this highlights the unique role that Manila played in Asian waters as a source of liquidity.

An explanation of this fixture of Eurasian trade needs to consider the distribution of silver production worldwide during the period. Silver was plentiful in Spanish America. According to TePaske and Brown, from the conquest of Mexico in 1521 to the revolt of Hidalgo in 1810, Spanish American mines produced an average of almost 300 tons of silver annually, for a grand total of approximately 86,000 tons.[12] Therefore, Spanish America was the largest provider of silver throughout the entire Early Modern era. In comparison, Asia lacked any significant sources of silver by the start of the eighteenth century. Apart from a small silver boom during the Ming dynasty, silver mines in China only produced an average of 6 tons annually, with the highest peaks only representing 20 tons.[13] The VOC shipped silver from Persia during the seventeenth century, but many of these exports were coins brought in from the Levant trade, and this line ended in 1722.[14] Japan did produce great quantities of silver, and during the late sixteenth century and the first half of the seventeenth century, it was the most important supplier of silver to China, a role shared—and later dominated—by direct imports of silver from Manila to Fujian.[15]

[11] Prakash, Om, *European Commercial Enterprise in Pre-Colonial India* (Cambridge: Cambridge University Press, 1998), pp. 84–85, Irigoin, 'Rise', pp. 396–397.

[12] TePaske, John J., *A New World of Gold and Silver*, ed. Kendall W. Brown (Boston: Brill, 2010), p. 113.

[13] Von Glahn, Richard, 'Myth and Reality of China's Seventeenth Century Monetary Crisis', *The Journal of Economic History* 56, n° 2 (1996), p. 432.

[14] Gaastra, 'The Export', pp. 467 & 474.

[15] Flynn and Giráldez, 'Born', p. 260.

Japanese mines were said to produce 150–200 tons of silver a year in the early seventeenth century, but production later dropped to 60 tons annually by the 1640s and the export of silver was restricted.[16] In 1695 the Japanese silver *keicho* standard was debased from 80% silver content to 64%, and according to Glamann, variations in the value of the *keicho*, forced upon Dutch merchants, seriously undermined the profitability of exporting silver from Japan.[17]

Production in America skyrocketed in the second half of the eighteenth century. After the defeat of the Seven Years' War, the government of Carlos III of Spain adopted a reformist programme, sending José de Gálvez as superintendent of the Indies to New Spain.[18] This was followed by policies that aimed to help the mining industry. Prior to Gálvez's appointment, the king subsidised the inputs used by the mines offering gunpowder and mercury at lower rates than the market,[19] but in the 1760s, a further reduction of gunpowder prices, selective tax exemptions for risky enterprises, and the creation of the Mexico mining guild in 1770 with its own bank led to a second expansion of silver output.[20] Spanish American silver production entered two distinct phases of acceleration, as noted in Graph 2.1. The first bar refers to the 1695 debasement of the Japanese *keicho*, while the second points the end of the Seven Years' War in 1763. The Graph shows that production reached previously unknown levels by 1741–1750 with Mexico leading the boom. With a total of 4,878 tons mined between 1801 and 1810, production was over three times above the 1,274 tons mined in 1691–1700, the decade of the Japanese debasement. Spanish American silver production experienced a boom as Japanese silver deposits dried up.

There may not have been a causal relationship between both events, but this coincidence was important for the Manila trade because Japan was the most direct alternative source of silver for much of East Asia. With the drying-off of a competing source of silver, so did competing

[16] Irigoin, 'Rise', p. 385.

[17] Irigoin, 'Rise', pp. 395–396, Glamann, Kristoff, *Dutch-Asiatic Trade, 1620–1740* (Copenhagen: Danish Science Press, 1958), p. 68.

[18] Brading, D.A., *Miners and Merchants in Bourbon Mexico 1763–1810* (Cambridge: Cambridge University Press, 1971), p. 28.

[19] Irigoin, 'Rise', p. 387.

[20] Brading, *Miners*, pp. 157–159.

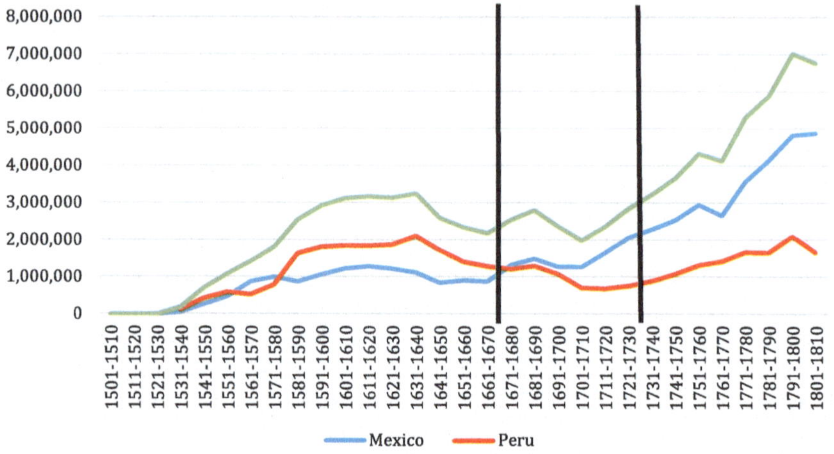

Graph 2.1 Total Spanish American silver production (kgs) 1501–1810 (*Sources* TePaske & Brown, A New World of Gold and Silver, Leiden: Brill [2010])

trade lines come to an end, enhancing the importance of Manila as a silver provider regionally. This was the case of the silver-for-silk exchange that had operated between Macao and Nagasaki first,[21] and then between Canton-Batavia-Nagasaki inherited by the Dutch after the Portuguese were expulsed from Japan in 1639. The end of Japanese silver exports was felt in Asia. Blussé documented the rise of a sugar plantation economy in Java between 1690 and 1740,[22] but he failed to notice that this coincided with the debasement of the *keicho* and the lower supply of silver from Japan in the 1680s and 1690s. This may indicate that the Dutch partially retreated from the intra-Asian silver trade by encouraging product substitution and the cultivation of crops locally.

The search for alternatives is illustrated by Dutch shipments of silver to Asia from Europe between 1602 and 1795 as shown by Gaastra

[21] Boxer, C. R., *Fidalgos in the Far East, 1550–1770: Fact and Fancy in the History of Macao* (The Hague: M. Nijhoff, 1948), Boxer, C.R., *The Portuguese Seaborne Empire 1415–1825* (London: Hutchinson, 1969), pp. 63–64, Flynn, Dennis O., and Giráldez, Arturo, 'Silk for Silver: Manila-Macao Trade in the 17th Century', *Philippine Studies* 44, n° 1 (1996): 52–68.

[22] Blussé, Leonard, 'Batavia, 1690–1740: The Rise and Fall of a Chinese Colonial Town', *Journal of Southeast Asian Studies* 12, n° 1 (March 1981): 159–178.

(Graph 2.2). The era of greatest splendour for the VOC in Asia between 1630 and 1680 witnessed relatively small shipments of silver from Europe on average despite the expansion of trade, but at the time the VOC had access to silver from Japan. The decline of Japanese silver exports in the second half of the seventeenth century and the beginning of the eighteenth century meant an increasing use of American silver shipped from Europe.[23] The debasement of the Japanese silver standard similarly coincided with a period of borrowing from the Amsterdam Wisselbank in search for silver to export to Asia.[24] This does not necessarily mean that the VOC's business was growing, but it implies that the terms of trade were such in Asia that liquidity was needed. In fact, the Dutch company sent 61% of all the treasure it ever sent to Asia between 1720 and 1790, when the VOC was in open decline.[25] As Glamann noted, shipments from Europe escalated because the VOC had drained Asian sources of silver.[26] The case illustrates two points that were fundamental for Europeans' trade in Asia: payments had to be settled in cash, mostly silver, and due to the wide arrange of goods, routes, and wind patterns involved in intra-Asian trade it was imperative for European factors to have ready liquidity available in Asia.[27]

On the other hand, the number of ship arrivals in Manila harbour confirm that the city's importance as a silver provided grew by the end of the century: Manila received 544 ships from China in the three decades between 1685 and 1715 as opposed to 157 between 1654 and 1684, an annual average of 18 ships compared to 5.[28] Arrivals from China reached a peak of 62 ships in 1686, an unprecedented number of ships

[23] Gaastra, Femme, 'The Dutch East India Company and its Intra-Asiatic Trade in Precious Metals', in in *European Commercial Expansion in Early Modern Asia*, ed. Om Prakash (London: Routledge, 1997), p. 106.

[24] Van Dillen, J. G., 'The bank of Amsterdam', in *History of the Principal Public Banks* (London: Frank Cass & Co. Ltd, 1934), pp. 110–112 & 117–123, according to Gaastra, the amount of money paid in Amsterdam on bills of exchange from Asia also tripled between 1660 and 1680, in Gaastra. 'The exports', p. 462.

[25] Gaastra, 'The exports', p. 451.

[26] Glamann, *Dutch-Asiatic*, p. 69.

[27] Chaudhuri, K.N., 'The East India Company and the Export of Treasure in the Early Seventeenth Century', *The Economic History Review* 16, nº 1 (1963): 23–38. p. 29.

[28] Ruiz-Stovel, MIAT, 2021, Chaunu, Pierre, *Les Philippines et le Pacifique des Ibériques (XVI, XVII, XVIII siècles)*, (Paris: S.E.V.P.E.N., 1960), pp. 148–198.

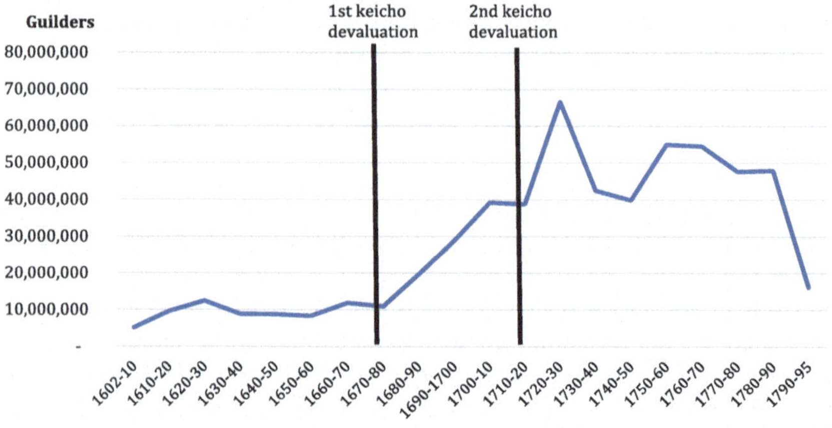

Graph 2.2 VOC Exports of precious metals from Europe to Asia 1602–1795 (guilders) (*Sources* F.S. Gaastra, 'The Export of Precious Metal from Europe to Asia by the Dutch East India Company, 1602–1795' in *Precious Metals in the Later Medieval and Early Modern Worlds*, ed. J.F. Richards, Durham: Carolina Academic Press, 1983, p. 451)

that surpassed the peak of 54 arrivals in 1637.[29] Manila's position as a source of silver within Asia's maritime world was unique after the 1680s, and the expansion of Spanish American silver output in the eighteenth century enhanced this role.

The exact volume of the Manila trade is not known. However, different authors have attempted to estimate its value using a variety of sources. According to TePaske, an average of 9 tons of silver crossed the Pacific between 1600 and 1660 based on Hamilton's data, but—according to his own admission—this is a very low estimate, especially given that on average 5 million pesos were said to have crossed the Pacific annually between 1610 and 1630.[30] Ward Barrett calculated that approximately 800,000 pesos, around 34 tons of silver, crossed the Pacific from Mexico to Manila, but this may be an underestimation based on a too-literal reading of production figures from local mints and money sent via the

[29] Ruiz-Stovel, MIAT, 2021, Chaunu, *Les Philippines*, pp. 157 & 177.

[30] TePaske, John, 'New World Silver, Castile and the Philippines 1590–1800', in *Precious Metals in the Later Medieval and Early Modern Worlds*, ed. J.F. Richards (Durham: Carolina Academic Press, 1983), pp. 436 & 445.

Atlantic.[31] Chuan Hang Sheng estimated a volume for the eighteenth-century trade that varied between 2 and 4 million pesos annually, with an increasing trend.[32] Giráldez and Flynn used Chuan's estimates and extended them to argue that between 50 and 71 metric tons of silver may have crossed the Pacific during the Early Modern period annually.[33] Flynn and Giráldez' lower figures comprise the maximum value of silver volume ascribed to the Pacific by Jan De Vries, whose figures have become standard. However, De Vries did not provide an explanation for this choice, and he used Barrett's and TePaske's figures as his low estimates.[34] Finally, Mariano Bonialian created his own series which was largely in accordance with Chuan's, although revised for higher volumes during the first half of the eighteenth century.[35] This largely agrees with reports from contemporaries like Bernardo Iriarte, who in 1781 estimated the annual amount of pesos shipped to Manila at 3 million annually.[36] It is important to notice too that Chuan's estimation is in accordance with Ng's suggestion that between 2 and 4 million pesos reached Fujian annually,[37] but still leaves behind the annual 300,000–350,000 pesos from "outright sales" in Manila that made it back to Madras between 1690 and 1762 according

[31] Barrett, 'World bullion', pp. 248–250, Von Glahn also offered estimates of the volume of silver crossing from Manila to China based on the *almojarifazgo* receipts for the period between 1580 and 1700, but the *almojarifazgo* series is not reliable, Von Glahn, *Fountain*, pp. 134–139.

[32] Hang-Sheng, Chuan, 'Trade Between China, the Philippines and the Americas During the Sixteenth and Seventeenth Centuries', in *Metals and Monies in an Emerging Global Economy*, ed. Dennis O. Flynn and Arturo Giráldez (Aldershot: Variorum, 1997), p. 283.

[33] Flynn and Giráldez, 'Arbitrage', p. 437.

[34] De Vries, Jan, 'Connecting Europe and Asia: A Quantitative Analysis of the Cape-route Trade, 1497–1795', in *Global Connections and Monetary History, 1470–1800*, ed. Dennis Flynn, Arturo Giráldez, and Richard von Glahn (Aldershot: Ashgate Publishing, 2003), pp. 80–81. Besides, the upper estimate of Flynn and Giráldez of 71 tons of silver for four million pesos seems to be a clerical mistake. At slightly higher than 24.81 grams of silver per peso, four million pesos would translate into almost 99 tons of silver.

[35] Bonialian, *El Pacífico*, pp. 45–48.

[36] AGI Filipinas 941 N. 1, *Expediente sobre los desórdenes del comercio de Filipinas*, Manila, 1769.

[37] Ng, Chin-Keong, *Trade and Society: The Amoy Network on the China Coast, 1683–1735* (Singapore: Singapore University Press, 1983), p. 85.

to Quiason.[38] It is important to notice that those authors who used direct observations on the cargoes of the Galleons such as Chuan and Bonialian agree on a higher volume of between 2 and 4 million pesos, while cargo loads of shipwrecks far surpassed this average. The shipwreck of the *San* José, which sunk in 1698, carried an estimated 7,694,742 pesos (approximately 185 tons of silver).[39] It is likely, therefore, that the Galleons moved between 50 and 100 annual tons of coined silver, as argued by Chuan and Bonialian.

The fragmentary nature of the observations prevents a definitive appraisal of the evolution of specie imports through the Pacific. Manila used between one or two annual galleons to trade across the Pacific for reasons that will be analysed in Chapter 4. While the regularity of the number of vessels may create the impression that the volume of specie imports was equally regular, there was room for variance. Graph 2.3. plots the volume of Pacific cargoes of pesos from the Galleons collected from Chuan and Bonialian against the number of ships calling at Manila harbour from the MIAT database crafted by Ruiz-Stovel. The observations are fragmentary and only represent return cargoes that are known. The lack of data also conceals the number of shipwrecks and failed trips to Acapulco, and the series ends in 1784, not capturing the late century increase in arrivals to Manila. The result, however, broadly matches the activity of Manila's harbour. The long eighteenth century represented a recovery from the crisis of the mid-seventeenth century,[40] and had fluctuations between 1680–1740, 1740–1780, and 1780–1800, which are largely in accordance with the fluctuations observed by Ruiz-Stovel for the Manila-Minnan trade that composed the bulk of Manila's Asian trade.[41]

Between 2 and 4 million pesos, accounting for 50–100 tons of silver, arrived to Manila each year during the century. In comparative terms, this was more than the annual average of any of the other participants in the direct trade with Asia during the period. Its two largest competitors, the EIC and VOC, only achieved a similar volume during the late eighteenth

[38] Quiason, Serafin, *English "country trade" with the Philippines, 1644–1765* (Quezon City: University of the Philippines, 1966), pp. 74–76.

[39] Arteaga, Fernando, Desierto, Desiree, & Koyama, Mark, 'Shipwrecked by Rents', MPRA Paper N° 102974 (2020), p. 1.

[40] The cycles of the trade are explained later in Section The Asian Leg.

[41] Ruiz-Stovel, 'Chinese Shipping', pp. 29–37.

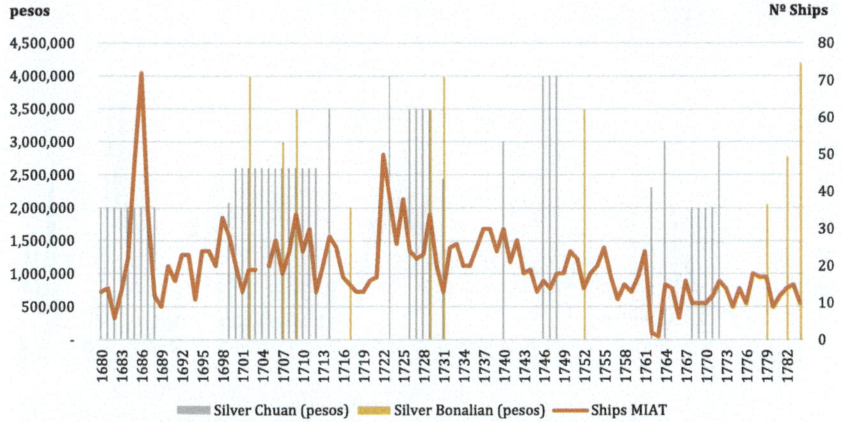

Graph 2.3 Galleons' returns in pesos compared to N° of ship arrivals in Manila harbour 1680–1784 (*Sources* Hang Sheng, Chuan, 'Trade Between China, the Philippines, and the Americas during the Sixteenth and Seventeenth centuries', in *Metals and Monies in an Emerging Global Economy*, ed. Dennis O. Flynn & Arturo Giráldez, Aldershot: Variorum, 1997, Bonalian, Mariano Ardash, *El Pacífico Hispanoamericano: política y comercio asiático en el imperio español [1680–1784]*, México: El Colegio de México, 2012, & Ruíz-Stovel, Guillermo [2021] Manila Intra-Asian Trade database [MIAT] [1.0] [Data set]. Zenodo)

century and the early nineteenth century (see Graph 2.4). The VOC shipments of precious metals from Europe to Asia have already been discussed above. According to Gaastra's figures, at its peak the VOC sent an annual average of 52.5 tons to Asia during the decade of 1750–1760.[42] For the period between 1660 and 1820, the EIC sent an annual average of 40 tons of silver from Europe to Asia, mostly in specie.[43] However, the EIC shipments were more volatile, combining years in which no treasure was sent eastwards with years of high shipments like 1802 with 205 tons and 1804 with 234 tons, as seen from Graph 2.5.[44] This highlights Manila's role as a source of liquidity in Asia.

[42] Gaastra, 'The exports', p. 451.

[43] Calculated from Chaudhuri, 'Treasure', Chaudhuri, *The Trading*, & Bowen, 'Bullion'.

[44] Bowen, 'Bullion', pp. 454–455.

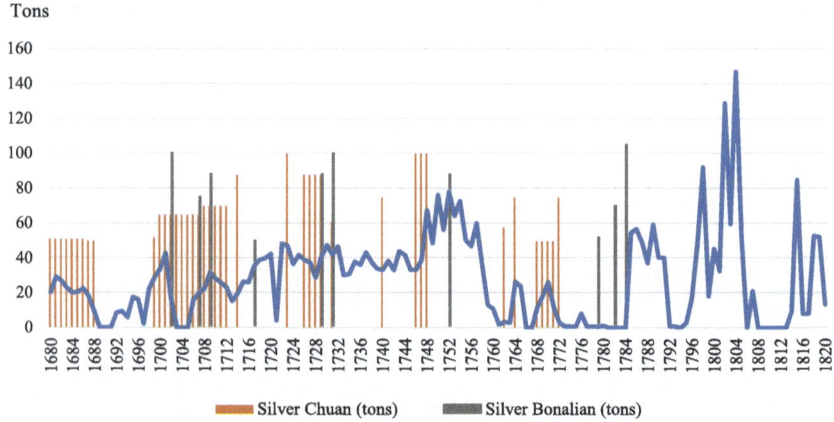

Graph 2.4 Estimated silver shipments to Asia: Manila Galleon and EIC compared 1680–1820 (*Note of sources* 1968 Chaudhuri provides a breakdown of kind of treasure sent to Asia. Here, only silver has been included. This distinction is not included in Chaudhuri 1978, which includes gold. However, the amounts of gold flowing out of England after Newton's recoinage were low. Bowen does not differentiate, and his figures may have also included some gold. *Sources* Manila: Hang Sheng, Chuan, 'Trade Between China, the Philippines, and the Americas during the Sixteenth and Seventeenth centuries', in *Metals and Monies in an Emerging Global Economy*, ed. Dennis O. Flynn & Arturo Giráldez, Aldershot, 1997, Bonialian, Mariano, *El Pacífico Hispanoamericano: política y comercio asiático en el imperio español [1680–1784]*, México, 2012. EIC: K.N. Chaudhuri, 'Treasure and Trade Balances: The East India Company's Export Trade, 1660–1720' [1968], K.N. Chaudhuri, *The Trading World of Asia and the English East India Company 1660–1760*, Cambridge 1978, & Huw Bowen, 'Bullion for Trade, War, and Debt-Relief: British Movements of Silver to, around, and from Asia, 1760–1833', *Modern Asian Studies* 44, nº 3 [2010]: 445–475)

The engine of the global silver trade was the large profits that could be realised by arbitraging the price of silver across the world. Historians like Giráldez, Flynn, and Gasch-Tomás have used the difference in bimetallic ratios of gold and silver between America, Europe, and Asia to measure the profitability of the Pacific silver trade.[45] The differences

[45] Flynn and Giráldez, 'Arbitrage', Gasch-Tomás, 'Transport costs', also mentioned in Bonialian, *El Pacífico*, and Fradera, Josep M., *Filipinas, la Colonia más peculiar. La*

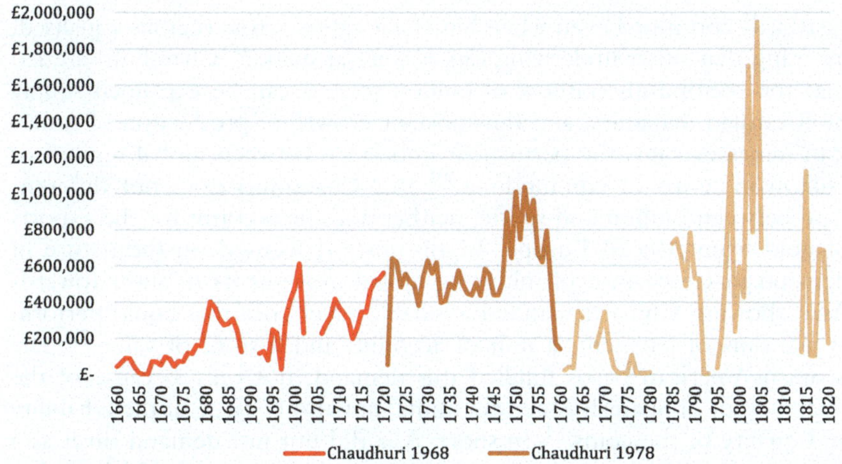

Graph 2.5 EIC shipments of precious metals from Europe to Asia 1660–1820 (in £) (*Note of sources* 1968 Chaudhuri provides a breakdown of kind of treasure sent to Asia. Here, only silver has been included. This distinction is not included in Chaudhuri 1978, which includes gold. However, the amounts of gold flowing out of England after Newton's recoinage were low. Bowen does not differentiate, and his figures may have also included some gold. *Sources* K.N. Chaudhuri, 'Treasure and Trade Balances: The East India Company's Export Trade, 1660–1720' [1968], K.N. Chaudhuri, *The Trading World of Asia and the English East India Company 1660–1760* (1978), & Huw Bowen, 'Bullion for Trade, War, and Debt-Relief: British Movements of Silver to, around, and from Asia, 1760–1833' [2010])

in bimetallic ratios of gold to silver between Europe and Asia stood at 1:5.5 to 1:7 at Canton, 1:9 in Moghul India, 1:10 in Japan, and 1:12.5 to 1:14 in Spain during the late sixteenth century and the early seventeenth century.[46] During the second half of the century they equalised, and diverged again during the early eighteenth century, when they stood at 1:10 in China and 1:15 in Europe,[47] only to equalise again by the half of the century. However, as Irigoin has noted, the shipments of silver

Hacienda Pública en la definición de la política colonial, 1762–1868, Madrid: Consejo Superior de Investigaciones Científicas (1999).

[46] Flynn, Giráldez, 'Arbitrage', p. 432.

[47] Giráldez, *The Age*, p. 171.

eastwards continued even when bimetallic ratios across regions equalised, meaning that other underlying causes were at work.[48] Chaudhuri argued that the continuous outflow of bullion to Asia can be explained simply by Ricardian dynamics, and the constant growth of production of American mines explains the permanent imbalance between global regions of bullion in terms of commodities.[49] But Chaudhuri does not differentiate between bullion and specie, neither does he account for the exports of gold from Asia to Europe. Irigoin instead focused on the nature of demand in China in explaining the global movements of silver towards Asia, showing China demanded a reliable silver coin that could perform as a means of payment, a unit of account, and a store of value.[50] The Spanish American pesos fulfilled this demand, not only because of the large output of Spanish American mints, but also because of the reliability and quality of the coins.[51] In short, Asia did not just demand silver as a precious metal, it demanded Spanish American silver pesos, which further increased the importance of Manila within the commercial networks of maritime Asia as the most direct source of the coveted coins.

The demand for pesos increased the profits of arbitraging this specific currency across the world. Contemporary merchants were quick to understand the importance of the peso for trade with Asia. Holden Furber reports different prices at which the *peso* traded against the silver sterling in various ports in 1789 (Table 2.1).[52] It is noticeable that when measured against the sterling, a peso, whose metallic equivalent was 4s 2d, traded at 14% above its inherent silver content in Batavia, 26% in Bombay, and 60% in Basra. For the period covered in this study, the peso performed as a currency for trade. As Charles Boxer noted regarding the European trade with and within Asia:

[48] Irigoin, 'The New', p. 272.

[49] See Chaudhuri, K.N., 'The Economic and Monetary Problem of European Trade with Asia in the Seventeenth and Eighteenth Centuries'. *Journal of European Economic History* 4, n° 2 (1977): 323–358.

[50] Irigoin, 'Rise', p. 396 & Von Glahn, 'Foreign', p. 71.

[51] Irigoin, Alejandra, 'A Trojan Horse in Daoguang China? Explaining the Flows of Silver in and Out of China', Working Paper n° 173/13 (Department of Economic History, LSE, London, 2013), p. 7.

[52] Furber, Holden, *John Company at Work, A Study of European Expansion in India in the Late Eighteenth Century* (New York: Octagon Books, 1970), pp. 349–350.

Table 2.1 Price of the Peso in regional comparison, 1789

City	*Exchange value*	*% Above par*
Basra	6s 8d	60
Bombay	5s 3d	26
Batavia	4s 9d	14
Par	4s 2d	

Sources Holden Furber, *John Company at Work*, Cambridge: Harvard University Press (1951): Appendix C, pp. 349–350

From a purely financial point of view, therefore, it was profitable to carry silver to Asia and import commodities for which there was a ready demand in Europe. Since silver was at a premium in Asia, the European traders, whether Portuguese at Goa and Macao, Spaniards at Manila, or English and Dutch at Surat, Batavia and Bantam, could buy cheap and sell dear when they were well-supplied with the coveted pesos de a ocho reales.[53]

Given Manila's access to Spanish American market and its privileged position in the global silver trade with Asia, the large demand for the peso had important implications for its trade. Because the need for cash to settle payments in Asia and the demand for pesos made this currency difficult to substitute, Manila performed a unique role within maritime Asia as a source of liquidity that had direct access to the origin of the pesos via trade. Through Manila's commerce with the rest of Asia, goods from across the continent arrived in the city for transhipment across the Pacific in exchange for silver pesos. Thus, Manila's specie trade permeated across the maritime networks, integrating intra-Asian trades and the Pacific exchange through the city, buttressing transactions elsewhere.

Manila's role within Asia is especially evident when the flow of pesos through the Pacific were interrupted. Thus, in 1715, East India Company agents in Madras wrote to the Directors in London saying:

We cannot wait for the usual shipments [of specie] from Manila, as trade between that city and New Spain has come to a standstill [...] the scarcity

[53] Boxer, C.R., 'La Plata es sangre: Sidelights on the Drain of Spanish-American Silver in the Far East, 1500–1700', *Philippine Studies* 18, nº 3, (1970), p. 463.

and high cost of silver is very discouraging for trade with Bengal and China.[54]

The relationship between Manila and the EIC is illustrative of the role the first played in enabling Asian trade. The importance of Spanish American specie cannot be understated and is evidenced by the eagerness with which the EIC sought a reliable supply. In 1630, the English obtained an agreement with Spain to market pesos through London instead of Genoa, although this deal was short-lived.[55] The EIC specifically created a Committee for Rials in the early decades of the seventeenth century (rials being the term for Spanish *reales*, the lower denomination of the *pesos de a ocho reales*) with instructions to buy all pesos from Seville and Mexico they could find.[56] Already in 1644 the Enlgish tried to open negotiations with Manila, but in 1668, when the EIC could not acquire enough silver from open market purchases in Europe to finance all its Asian operations, the head of the Surat factory suggested sending an embassy to Spain to negotiate direct trade with Manila.[57] The proposed deal came to nothing, but in 1669 a ship from Surat arrived in Manila.[58] In 1683 there was a financial crisis in London, during which many goldsmiths, which had provided specie to the company, were forced out of business and the EIC was forced to announce that it would stop all exports of treasure until its debts were repaid.[59] This coincided with the signing of a treaty between the Company and the Armenian nation in 1688 which made Armenian

[54] Chaudhuri, K.N., 'Circuits monétaires internationaux, prix comparés et spécialisation économique, 1500–1750', in *Études d'Histoire Monétaire*, ed. John Day (Lille: Presses Universitaires de Lille, 1984), p. 53.

[55] Chaudhuri, 'The East India', p. 37.

[56] Chaudhuri, 'The East India', p. 23.

[57] Chaudhuri, 'Treasure', p. 492.

[58] Chaunu, *Les Philippines*, p. 165.

[59] Chaudhuri, *Trading*, p. 170.

trade in Asia a subsidiary of EIC trade.[60] Through Armenians and Luso-Indians, the EIC established an important direct trade with Manila that provided a large volume of cash to the Madras Presidency.[61]

In time, as Chaudhuri says, a triangular relationship between India, Manila, and Canton developed with the increasing importance of the China trade.[62] Goods from India were sold in Manila for pesos and brought to Canton, thus financing operations in China.[63] This triangular relationship is illustrated by the dearth of silver that followed the English occupation of Manila in 1762–1764, during which the Pacific trade was interrupted. Pesos became scarce in Canton and the EIC's Canton Committee was close to bankruptcy. During these years, the EIC factors in Canton entered a series of currency exchange deals with Manila-based private merchants, who provided Spanish pesos on exchange of Indian gold pagodas.[64] Between 7th November and 8th December 1764 alone, the Canton factors realised seven such exchange transactions with 6 different individuals (mostly residents of Manila) for a total of 32,980 pesos.[65] Already in 1763, the EIC government in Manila had to divert silver shipments from England that had been earmarked for Canton, forcing the factors in China to incur a debt of 60,000 *taels*.[66]

[60] The treaty reflected years of increasing rapprochement between the EIC and the Armenian merchants, Aslanian, Sebouh, 'Trade Diaspora vs Colonial State: Armenian Merchants, the English East India Company, and the High Court of Admiralty in London', *Diaspora: A Journal of Transnational Studies* 13, n° 1 (2004), p. 50.

[61] Quiason, *English*, pp. 74–76, see Bhattacharya, Bhaswati, 'Making Money at the Blessed Place of Manila: Armenians in the Madras-Manila Trade in the Eighteenth Century', *Journal of Global History*, vol. 3 (2008): 1–20, & Baena Zapatero, Alberto, and Lamikiz, Xavier, 'Presencia de una diáspora global: comerciantes armenios y comercio intercultural en Manila, c. 1660–1800', *Revista de Indias* LXXIV, n° 262 (2014): 693–722.

[62] Chaudhuri, *Trading*, p. 173.

[63] Cheong asserts that the silver peso was a fundamental part of the Canton system as a recognised medium of exchange by the East India Companies, the Hong merchants, and the private traders, Cheong, W.E., 'Trade and Finance in China 1784–1834: A Reappraisal', *Business History* 7, (1965), p. 36. See also Cheong, W.E., 'The Beginnings of Credit Finance on the China Coast', *Business History* 12, n° 2 (1971): 87–103.

[64] *Letters to Fort St. George*, 1763; Letter 46, p. 39.

[65] *Letters to Fort St. George*, 1764; Letters 13, 15, 16, pp. 10–16.

[66] *Letters to Fort St. George*, 1763; Letter 13, p. 10.

The drought was made more intolerable because the Chinese merchants specifically demanded pesos. In the same letter, the Canton factors requested the Madras authorities that they send them specifically Spanish silver pesos "as our Payments are made in Dollars or money of the same fineness, and therefore all Silver that comes here, must be reduced to that Standard".[67] Some of the exchange deals that the factors had to enter into priced the peso above its metallic content, giving an idea of the premium the Chinese were willing to pay.[68] The EIC learnt from its reliance on the procurement of pesos in Canton, and in the 1770s launched a system through which the Bengal Presidency sold bills of exchange payable in London to independent country traders, specifying purchases exclusively in Canton and in silver pesos.[69] Manila's peso trade was fundamental in buttressing maritime exchange across Asia.

In short, the engine that motivated the Manila trade was the profit that could be derived from arbitraging the purchasing power differentials of the peso from America to Asia. When it came to the Manila trade, which enjoyed the least costly, most direct access to the *pesos* of Spanish America, profits were large. There is not much information on profits due to the private and unregulated nature of the Pacific commerce. Schurz conservatively estimated returns of 100–300% without concreting the period, although he mentioned that detractors of the trade elevated this to 1,000%.[70] Bernal estimated that mark-ups in the sixteenth century were on the range of 1,100–1,300%,[71] but did not estimate net profits, although the implication is clear that these must have been high. For the late-seventeenth century and the eighteenth century, Bonialian estimated mark-ups of 1,400–1,600%, and rates of return of 400–600%.[72] However, it is unclear how Bonialian estimated the costs to such a reduction between mark-ups and profits since, as will be seen later in this work, Manila incurred few costs in its Pacific intermediation.

[67] *Letters to Fort St. George*, 1763; Letter 46, p. 38.

[68] *Letters to Fort St. George*, 1763; Letter 13, p. 10.

[69] IOR HMS 795, *Extract of such paragraphs of the Letters from the Court of Directors to the Bengal Government as regard China Remittances*, 11th November 1768, ff. 92–96.

[70] Schurz, *The Manila*, p. 190.

[71] Bernal, Antonio Miguel, 'La "Carrera del Pacífico": Filipinas en el sistema colonial de la Carrera de Indias', in *España y el Pacífico. Tomo I: Legazpi*, ed. Leoncio Cabrero (Madrid: Sociedad Estatal de Conmemoraciones Culturales, 2004), p. 517.

[72] Bonialian, *El Pacífico*, p. 177.

Estimates for the latter half of the eighteenth century show smaller price differentials of goods between Manila and Acapulco than those estimated by Bonialian, but still very large in absolute terms. Cheong provided estimates for 1796 of price differentials in goods traded by the RCF between Manila and a series of American ports. Most items earned between 100% and 233%, with a few returning over 300% and 400%, showing the resilience of price differentials between Asia and America.[73] An appraisal of confiscated goods in Acapulco for public auction in 1767 reveals price differentials between Manila and Mexico ranging from 120 to 300% depending on the item.[74] Yet it is important to notice that the prices of such goods in the market could have been higher, since the criteria for the appraisal—whether based on market or fiscal valuation—is not specified and the auction took place after the rightful sale of the legal part of the Galleon's cargo at the Acapulco fair, meaning that at least a sizeable part of the demand for Asian goods had already been satisfied. Over a decade later, in 1778, a list of prices for 83 items sold in the Acapulco fair can be contrasted with a 1777 valuation list of 324 goods in Manila.[75] The gross price differentials of comparable items (since weight and quantity were not recorded consistently in Acapulco) ranged between 112 and 280%, with the possibility that some of the more specific and value-added goods listed in Manila but not in Acapulco may have reached higher prices. These price differentials do not account for the cost of transporting the goods from Manila to Acapulco, but most of the operational costs were deflected to the royal treasury of Manila, or were mitigated through subsidies, including wages to the merchants enrolled in the Galleon as officials or crew, payable in Acapulco.[76] Such profits were not exceptional for Europeans' direct trade with Asia. Steensgaard calculated that the Dutch monopoly in spices rendered the VOC

[73] Cheong, 'The Decline', p. 152.

[74] AGI Filipinas 941 N.1., 1769.

[75] AGN, GD 48 Filipinas (1778) vol 13.exp.11, *Relación de precios de la Feria que se celebró el 9 de marzo de 1778 en este puerto de Acapulco*, ff. 261–263.

[76] On the cost of the Galleon, AGI Filipinas 941 N. 1, includes the expenses on building the Galleon *San Carlos*, on the salaries of the Galleons' crew, Cosano Moyano, José, *Filipinas y su Real Hacienda (1750–1800)*, (Córdoba: Publicaciones del Monte de Piedad y Caja de Ahorros de Córdoba, 1986), pp. 355–377.

returns of 300%-460% between the mid-seventeenth century and the mid-eighteenth century.[77]

In sum, from the start of direct trade between Asia and Europe, silver played a fundamental role. This was the case for all participants, chartered joint-stock companies, the Portuguese *Carreira*, and independent merchants alike. Organisational and business models played no fundamental difference. Even the later independent US trade with Asia, carried on mostly by private entrepreneurs, relied heavily on the export of large quantities of silver specie.[78] Having cash in hand in Asia improved the terms of trade, and the demand for Spanish American pesos increased this advantage. Pesos traded above their metallic content, and for all Europeans wishing to trade with Asia, the challenge was to obtain a timely and regular supply of pesos to operate their business. An important distinction must be made regarding the role of liquidity in long-distance trade during the Early Modern period: its role in providing initial capital, and its role in providing working capital. Incorporation and the issuance of tradable shares helped with the first challenge, yet East India Companies had a permanent problem acquiring enough cash to operate the direct trade with Asia.[79] The situation was different for Manila, which enjoyed the most direct access to Spanish American silver of all Asian trading ports. This meant that the city performed a unique role as a provider of liquidity that permeated other trades through intra-Asian networks. The Pacific silver trade and the intra-Asian trade in goods were integrated. This unique role of Manila is fundamental in understanding the financial model that developed in the city.

[77] Steensgaard, Niels, 'The Growth and Composition of the Long-Distance Trade of England and the Dutch Republic Before 1750', in *The Rise of Merchant Empires: Long Distance Trade in the Early Modern World, 1350–1750*, ed. James D. Tracy (Cambridge: Cambridge University Press, 1990), pp. 122–123.

[78] Irigoin, Alejandra, 'The End of a Silver Era: The Consequences of the Breakdown of the Spanish Peso Standard in China and the United States, 1780s–1850s', *Journal of World History* 20, n°2 (2009), pp. 212–213, Fichter, James, *So Great a Proffit: How the East Indies Trade Transformed Anglo-American Capitalism* (Cambridge (Mass.): Harvard University Press, 2010), pp. 119–123.

[79] Chaudhuri, 'The East India', p. 24.

2.2 The Organisation of the Manila Trade

Ever since Legazpi's arrival to Cebú in 1565, life in the Spanish Philippines up to the end of the American empire was defined by trade. The demand for specie was such that Manila soon became a cosmopolitan city, attracting Chinese, French, English, Armenian, Portuguese, and many other merchants.[80] By the mid-seventeenth century there are reported to have been 42,000 people inhabiting the city, most of them permanent sojourners from China that formed their own neighbourhoods outside the walled Spanish city, known as *Intramuros*.[81] William Draper, the English conqueror of Manila in 1762, claimed that the city and its suburbs had approximately 100,000 inhabitants.[82] Although this was an exaggeration, the city was undoubtedly large. A census of *Intramuros* from 1778, a time when the commercial activity had moved to the neighbourhood of Binondo, reveals that only in the reduced inner city, crowded with religious and official buildings, lived 6,345 people.[83] Manila attracted merchants from all over because it connected Asian demand for silver specie with American supply. Thus, it is important to take a bird's-eye view of the commercial universe of the city.

The Manila trade consisted of two legs. The Asian leg revolved around the importation of goods and manufactures from all over Asia to Manila. This was an open trade in which merchants from all across the Indo-Pacific sailed to Manila to sell their wares in exchange of specie. These goods were for local consumption and, most importantly, for re-export to Spanish America. The American leg was conducted by the annual Galleons that sailed from Manila loaded with Asian goods bound to Acapulco, where they were sold for pesos. This trade was limited in scale to the annual Galleon, and it was the privilege of the city of Manila. It was an intra-imperial trade that connected two imperial regions, the Philippines

[80] Reed, Robert R., 'The Colonial Origins of Manila and Batavia: Desultory Notes on Nascent Metropolitan Primacy and Urban Systems in Southeast Asia', *Asian Studies* 5, n°3 (1967), p. 560.

[81] This figure was approximately the same population as Barcelona or Marseilles, Flynn, and Giráldez, 'Born', p. 263.

[82] Letter of William Draper to the Secretary of War, Manila 2nd November 1761, in *Documents Illustrating the British Conquest of Manila, 1762–1763*, ed. Nicholas P. Cushner, Doc. 70, pp. 145–149.

[83] AMN *Padrón General de todos los habitantes dentro de los muros de esta ciudad de Manila*, 1778.

and New Spain, and was circumscribed to the control of its respective authorities, the Mexico *Consulado* and the city of Manila. Despite the differences in their formal organisation and legal standing, both the intra-Asian and trans-Pacific trades were horizontally integrated. Asian goods composed the outgoing cargoes of Galleons and were paid for by the pesos that returned as proceeds from sales in Acapulco. Manila acted as the intermediary between both, redistributing pesos across Asia through purchases of goods for export.

In its Asian leg, Manila was part of an ever-changing pattern of intra-Asian trade. Manila's capacity to provide the silver that settled commercial transactions in Asia made it a fixture of this intra-Asian exchange. Participants changed with time according to circumstances in Asia, but three broad lines of trade converged in Manila throughout the Early Modern period bringing goods from China, India, and Indonesia. In its American leg, Manila's Pacific trade was part of a broader empire-wide system of trade networks designed to import textiles and other consumption goods to Spanish America in exchange for silver.[84] From the sixteenth century, this intra-imperial trade system was organised around chartered towns with licences to conduct trade, the merchant associations of these towns (*Consulados*), the convoy systems that shipped goods and silver (*flotas*), and the trade fairs in which transcontinental transactions took place. This system functioned until changes in the eighteenth century led to its demise.

Trade in this system of kingdoms and fairs was organised around convoys which agglutinated all the goods to be exported to America since 1561.[85] The original system of fleets obeyed the need for security, but it was quickly coaxed into the territorial fragmentation represented by the fairs. The arrival of the fleets to their destination started a hectic period of negotiations and transactions that would end with the timed departure

[84] On the organisation of the Atlantic trade, see García Fuentes, Lutgardo, *El Comercio Español con América, 1650–1700* (Sevilla: Escuela de Estudios Hispanoamericanos, 1980), García-Baquero, Antonio, *Cádiz y el Atlántico, 1717–1778* (Sevilla: Escuela de Estudios Hispanoamericanos, 1976), Fisher, John, *The Economic Aspects of Spanish Imperialism in America, 1492–1810* (Liverpool: Liverpool University Press, 1997). The *consulados* as organisations of licensed merchants had precedents going back to the wool trade with the Low Countries. See González Arce, José Damián, 'La universidad de mercaderes de Burgos y el consulado castellano en Brujas durante el siglo XV', *En la España medieval* 33 (2010): 161–202.

[85] García Fuentes, *El Comercio*, p. 159.

of the squadron back to Spain. Up to the changes of the Bourbon period, and intermittently halted during the late seventeenth century, Spanish American fleets would depart from Seville and sail across the Atlantic towards Havana in Cuba, where the squadrons would divide into two: the *Galeones de Tierra Firme* continued to Portobello in the Panama isthmus, where they met fleets of Peruvian merchants that came to sell their silver in the Portobello fair; a second squadron sailed to Veracruz in modern-day Mexico, where the fair (later moved to Jalapa) would take place. The return voyage paralleled these trips, with the whole Treasure fleet congregating in Havana before setting sail for Seville and later Cádiz.[86] The Manila transpacific trade was organised as one such fleet system, relying on the sailing of one or two Galleons instead of a whole convoy of vessels. The carefully timed sailing patterns favoured control from importers, who, as will be seen in Chapter 4, could use these limitations to strengthen their bargaining position. After all, silver specie had no immediate substitutes[87] (Map 2.2).

Local merchants that controlled international trade were organised in corporate bodies known as the *Consulados*. Merchants in Mexico and Lima founded *Consulados* with royal assent in 1592 (Mexico) and in 1613 (Lima), however Manila lacked a *Consulado* until 1769.[88] Instead, the city of Manila enjoyed exclusive jurisdiction over the Manila-Acapulco line as a privilege granted in 1593 by King Felipe II. This privilege—which will be explored in detail in Chapter 6—implied that Manila enjoyed a unique regulatory regime embodied in the *reglamentos*, the pieces of legislation that regulated the Manila-Acapulco trade. The first *reglamento* was issued in 1593 with the recognition of the privilege of exclusive freighting across the Pacific. Additions or changes could be negotiated in further legislation. A major overhaul of the 1593 *reglamento* was issued in 1734 as a conclusion to the litigation between Manila and Seville that raged from 1702 until 1734.[89] This new *reglamento* was in force until the dissolution

[86] Rahn Phillips, Carla, 'The Growth and Composition of Trade in the Iberian Empires, 1450–1750', in *The Rise of Merchant Empires: Long-Distance Trade in the Early Modern World, 1350–1750*, ed. James D. Tracy (Cambridge: Cambridge University Press, 1990), p. 77.

[87] Irigoin, 'Rise', p. 389.

[88] Yuste, *Emporios*, pp. 150–151.

[89] A complete reproduction of this *reglamento* can be found in AGI Filipinas 268 N.1, *Expediente sobre alteraciones del comercio. Primera parte*, 1754–1756.

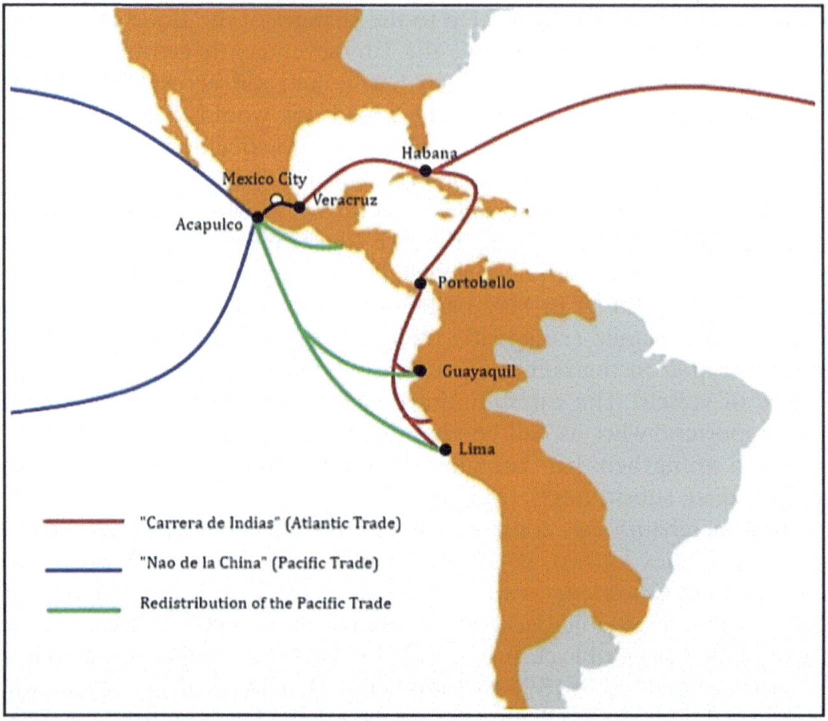

Map 2.2 Main trade routes in the Spanish Empire ca. 1700 (*Sources* Own creation from Rahn Phillips, Carla, 'The Growth and Composition of Trade in the Iberian Empires, 1450–1750', in *The Rise of Merchant Empires: Long-Distance Trade in the Early Modern World, 1350–1750*, ed. James D. Tracy, Cambridge: Cambridge University Press [1990], Baskes, Jeremy, *Staying Afloat: Risk and Uncertainty in Spain's Atlantic World Trade, 1760–1820*, Stanford: Stanford University Press [2013], & Bonialian, Mariano, *El Pacífico Hispanoamericano: política y comercio asiático en el imperio español [1680–1784]*, Mexico: El Colegio de México 2012])

of the Galleon privilege in 1815, together with the addendum of 1769 which created the Manila *Consulado*.[90] Under this regime, freighting in the Galleon belonged to the citizens of Manila, which in turn had unique

[90] AGI Filipinas 941 N.1, 1769.

institutions that enforced the privilege, such as the *junta de repartimiento*, a body composed by the governor, the archbishop, the *fiscal* (attorney) of the *Audiencia* (local court of justice), as well as representatives from the city and the trade, and which was in charge of allotting the cargo space of the annual Galleon among the citizens.[91]

Both legs were related to different trading systems, one with Asia's local trade networks, and the other with the Hispanic transcontinental silver trade. However, this separation was more apparent than real: both the Asian and the American legs were integrated by Asian demand for silver, which meant that goods flowed to America and pesos crossed the Pacific in the opposite direction. The role of this demand in structuring and organising the trade has not been analysed so far. Chapter 4 is devoted to bringing Asian—and especially Chinese—demand for silver into the equation. This present section will review the formal characteristics of the Asian and American legs of Manila's trade for later analysis.

The Asian Leg

Manila was considered the "mart of the East", and goods from all over Asia could be found in its markets.[92] The lion's share of the Manila trade was reserved to the cotton and silk textiles that were brought over from India and China and made the main cargo of the Galleons that sailed to Acapulco. These various goods were all brought to Manila to sell for pesos, a dynamic that remained stable throughout the 250 years that this exchange lasted. The attraction that Manila exerted over Asian trade with its offer of liquidity highlights one of the main aspects of Manila's peso trade: similar to an extent to Batavia, but unlike most European intra-Asian trade, where European vessels visited Asian harbours, it was the Asian merchants themselves—Gujaratis, Chinese, Armenian, Malabaris, etc.—that flocked to Manila. Manila was indispensable due to the liquidity it offered. The persistence of Manila's position in intra-Asian trade and of the specie flow was remarkable, lasting throughout the entire Early Modern period (Map 2.3).

[91] Schurz, *The Manila*, p. 156.

[92] Díaz-Trechuelo, Lourdes, 'El comercio de Filipinas durante la segunda mitad del siglo XVIII', *Revista de Indias*, vol. 23 (1963), pp. 465–466.

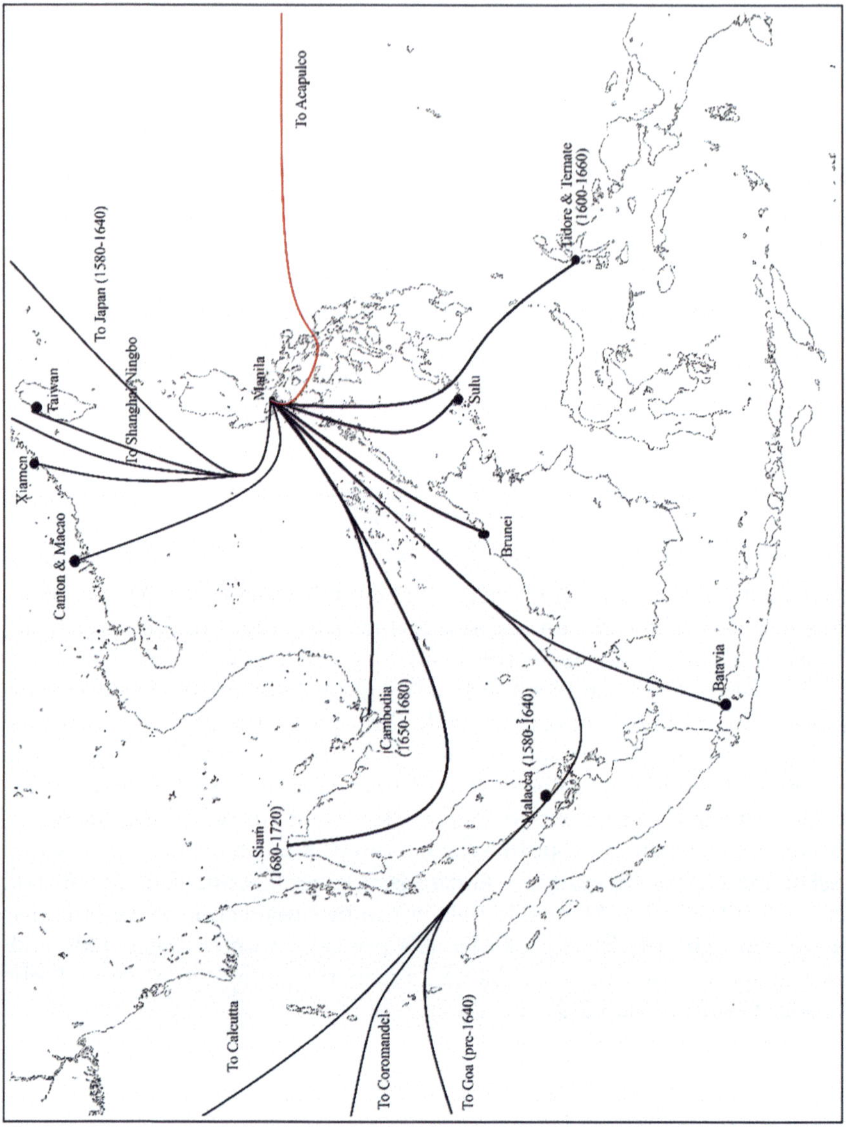

Map 2.3 The Manila trade 1571–1815

Manila's main trading partners were China, India, and Southeast Asia. Virtually since the conquest of the city in 1571 until the early nine teenthcentury, Manila received the visit of a fleet of between 15 and 40 junks annually from Amoy.[93] Chinese merchants from Fujian were the most consistent and numerous exporters of goods to Manila for the whole period under research. Ng has estimated that an average of 2–4 million silver pesos annually reached Fujian during the centuries that this trade lasted.[94] This is not surprising given that China was the region with the highest demand for pesos. The Chinese junk fleets moved with the monsoon winds, arriving in Manila between March and April, and sailing back to China between August and October.[95] Initially, Manileños attempted to subject Chinese merchants to a buyers' cartel called the *pancada*. Representatives from the Manileño buyers would set the prices for Chinese goods each season in negotiation with Chinese representatives.[96] The *pancada* was a term used by the Portuguese to describe the buyers' cartel they faced in the Nagasaki market.[97] It is also interesting that this system of cartel negotiation was also the transaction method of the Acapulco fair.[98] The *pancada* in the Philippines, however, did not last long, and by the second half of the seventeenth century it had been abandoned.[99] Instead, a large community of Chinese sojourners and settlers, known in Manila as *Sangleyes*, migrated to the city as tradesmen, manual labourers, and merchants, opening shops and dominating the local retail trade.

The peak of the commercial season of Manila took place between June and August. Returning Galleons, laden with pesos from Acapulco, usually arrived in June and July, while the outgoing Galleon departed in July or August. During these months, Manila was bristling with Asian goods and silver pesos. Contracts were signed, payments were settled,

[93] Díaz-Trechuelo, 'El comercio', p. 157, Ruiz-Stovel, MIAT, 2021.

[94] Ng, *Trade*, p. 85.

[95] Ruiz-Stovel, MIAT, 2021.

[96] Schurz, *The Manila*, pp. 77–78.

[97] Souza, George Bryan, *The Survival of Empire: Portuguese Trade and Society in China and the South China Sea 1630–1754* (Cambridge: Cambridge University Press, 1986), p. 59, also Cooper, Michael, 'The Mechanics of the Macao-Nagasaki Silk Trade', *Monumenta Nipponica* 27, nº 4 (1972): 423–433.

[98] The Acapulco fair is examined in Chapter 4, Sect. 4.2.

[99] Schurz, *The Manila*, p. 78.

and cargoes were purchased. The *correspondencias* used to finance the procurement of Asian goods for export to America were often signed in a short period of time: of the 89 surviving *correspondencia* contracts for the year 1789, 59 were signed in the two months between 11th of June and 11th of August.[100] Of the 50 surviving contracts for the 1766 season, 29 contracts were signed only in the month of July but represented all the extant *correspondencias* to Acapulco for that year (25 contracts).[101] *Correspondencias* originated by legacy funds contractually specified that repayment had to take place no longer than 15 days after the return of the Galleon loaded with the proceeds of the Acapulco fair. This means that between the return of the previous year's Galleon and the departure of the next Galleon for Acapulco, *correspondencias* were repaid, legacy funds were recapitalised and issued the *correspondencias* for the next season, using the pesos to buy goods brought from China, India, and Southeast Asia. Manila was thus a clearinghouse through which contracts were settled and pesos were exchanged for the consumption goods that were then re-exported to America.

The dynamics of the three main trade lines that stretched from Manila (to China, India, and Java), can be seen in Graph 2.6. This table has been created by multiplying Chaunu's recorded *almojarifazgo* tax payments by the established tax rate to obtain the actual total value of the cargo of the vessels involved. The first thing to notice is that the amounts recorded are significantly smaller than what sources at the destination of the ships testify (2–4 million pesos just for Amoy according to Ng, and approx. 300,000 pesos only for Madras according to Quiason). This disparity is most likely due to underreporting, which is known to have been endemic in Manila at the time.[102] This information can be contrasted with the number of ships arriving to the harbour of Manila. Graph 2.7 presents the number of ships entering Manila from three main destinations, China, India, and Java, as well as plotting the total arrivals recorded in the

[100] Escribano José Flores, 1789 [Legajo #21A] Colección de Microfilmes de la Sección de Documentos Españoles del Archivo Nacional de Filipinas. Archivo del Centro de Ciencias Humanas y Sociales (CSIC), Madrid, Spain.

[101] Escribano Martín Dominguez Zamudio, 1766 [Legajo #8], ACCHS-CSIC.

[102] Von Glahn, 'Myth', p. 438, Manila prosecutor Viana argued that this was due to collusion between the authorities of the Manila harbour and the merchants, AMN 533 MS1576 Doc. 1, *Informe de Viana sobre los perjuicios causados a la Real Hacienda en la percepción de los impuestos, especialmente el de almojarifazgo*, 1760.

city. Together, these three locations represented almost the entirety of all recorded arrivals except for the decades after 1780, as seen in the gap between the "total" line and the piled bars. The graph has been crafted using the more recent research of Ruiz-Stovel on the *almojarifazgo*, which extends back to 1680. Chaunu's data is still used for the period between 1620 and 1680.[103] Using the number of ships, however, also has some limitations. Something not recorded by Graph 2.7 but that is evident in Graph 2.6 is that the importance of India as a trade partner of Manila rose in the last decades of the century.[104] This is most likely related to the growing carry capacity of English vessels in Asia.[105] Thus, the data presents important limitations, but using both graphs together and with enough caution there are some overall conclusions that can be drawn regarding the evolution of the Manila trade between the seventeenth and eighteenth centuries.

The data shows a period of overall decline in trade in Manila during the second half of the seventeenth century that only starts to improve by the 1670s. Many explanations for this have been advanced. The fall of the Ming dynasty and the temporary emergence of the kingdom of Koxinga in Taiwan, which led to the Kangxi maritime ban of 1661 (only lifted in 1680s) could have affected demand.[106] On the other hand, the stagnation of silver production in Spanish America could have affected supply.[107]

[103] Ruiz-Stovel' MIAT databases record a larger number of arrivals than in Chaunu's work and correct some inaccuracies regarding the origin of vessels. However, the overall trends of ship arrivals in MIAT and Chaunu's book are comparable.

[104] Fradera quotes evidence from an 1842 report according to which, in 1810, imports from India were valued at 1,150,000 pesos, the same as imports from China, while exports were worth 1,190,000 and 1,675,000, respectively. Quoted in Fradera, *Filipinas*, p. 94.

[105] According to Bowen (Bowen, Huw V., *The Business of Empire. The East India Company and Imperial Britain, 1765–1833* (Cambridge: Cambridge University Press, 2009), p. 269), the carry capacity of East Indiamen more than doubled between 1760 and 1780–1790. This only refers to the vessels used by the EIC, and not to those used by country traders, which were Manila's main trade partners. However, the types of vessels recorded in MIAT also show a progressive change towards larger vessel types like "frigates" or "brigs" instead of the lighter "packet-boats" and "pataches" of previous periods (Ruiz-Stovel, MIAT, 2021).

[106] Giráldez, *The Age*, p. 90.

[107] Chaunu, Pierre, 'Le galion de manille: Grandeur et décadence d'une route de la soie', *Annales, Histoire, Sciences Sociales*, 6e Année, n° 4 (1951): 447–462. On the debate, see TePaske, John J., and Klein, Herbert, 'The Seventeenth-Century Crisis in New Spain: Myth or Reality?', *Past & Present*, n° 90 (1981): 116–135, Kamen, Henry, and Israel,

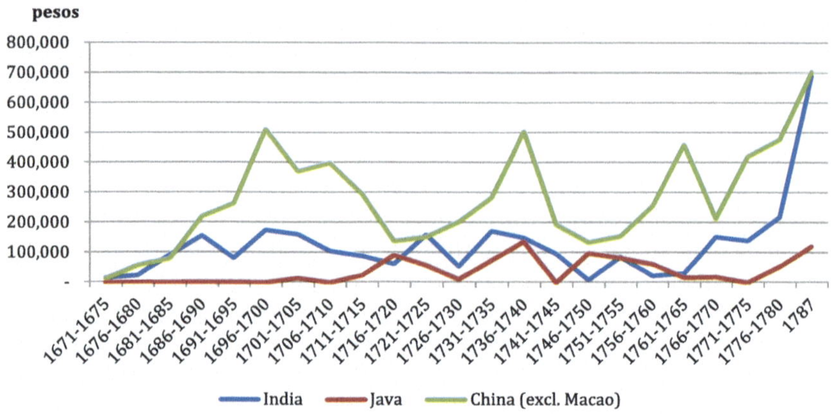

Graph 2.6 Volume of trade by origin of vessels, 1671–1787 (*Sources* Own calculation from data from almojarifazgo tax receipts in Manila harbour collected by Pierre Chaunu, quinquennial estimates. Pierre Chaunu, *Les Philippines et le Pacifique des Ibériques,* Paris: SEVPEN [1960]. India refers to three destinations marked in Spanish records [Bengal, Coromandel, Surat])

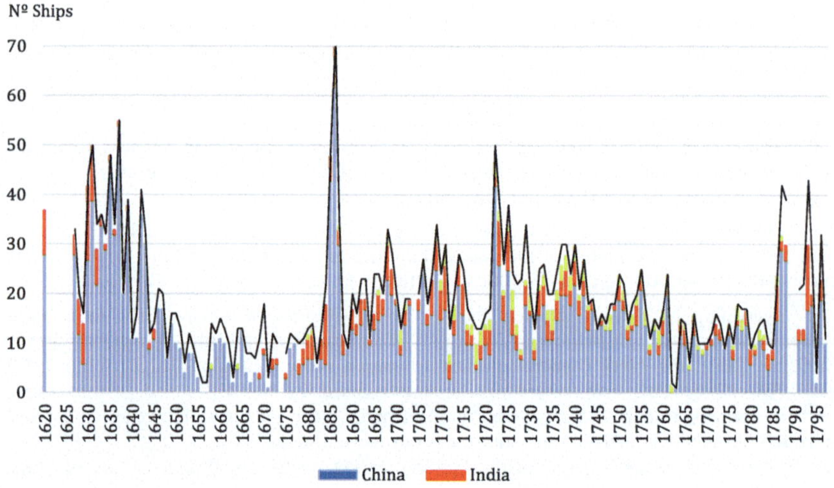

Graph 2.7 Number of ships in Manila harbour by origin, 1620–1797 (*Sources* Pre-1680, Chaunu, Pierre, *Les Philippines et le Pacifique des Ibériques (XVIe, XVIIe, XVIIIe siècles)*, Paris: SEVPEN, 1960, post-1680 Ruíz-Stovel, Guillermo [2021] Manila Intra-Asian Trade database [MIAT] [1.0] [Data set]. Zenodo)

Other factors affected the Manila trade negatively. The breakup of the Union between Spain and Portugal in 1640 led to a meltdown of the Iberian trading circuits that impacted Manila,[108] while changing climatic conditions during the second half of the seventeenth century prolonged the navigation up to 40% of its normal duration.[109] Finally, there may have been a change in the nature of trade that the sources do not capture properly.[110]

Regardless of the exact cause of the decline in the *almojarifazgo* series, deep changes in the Manila trade took place during the 1660s and 1680s that were of crucial importance for the later development of commerce. While from 1570 to 1650 most of the intra-Asian trade of Manila (other than China) was directed to Portuguese and Spanish possessions in Goa, Malacca, Macassar, Ternate, and Tidore, from the 1670s onwards a new pattern emerged that remained constant for most of the eighteenth century until the end of the Galleon trade in the 1820s.[111] The new main partners of the Manileños were the English in Surat and Madras (and after the 1760s, Bengal), and the Dutch in Batavia. The English attempted to open a direct line with Manila as early as 1644,[112] and by the 1670s this

J.I., 'The Seventeenth-Century Crisis in New Spain: Myth or Reality?', *Past & Present*, nº 97 (1982): 144–156, TePaske, John J., and Klein, Herber, 'The Seventeenth-Century Crisis in New Spain: Myth or Reality? A Rejoinder', *Past & Present*, nº 97 (1982): 156–161.

[108] Boxer, Charles R., 'Portuguese and Spanish Rivalry in the Far East in the Seventeenth Century', *Journal of the Royal Asiatic Society* 78, nº 3 (1946), pp. 162–164, Souza, *The Survival*, pp. 101–102. See also AGI Filipinas 31 N. 22, *Carta del gobernador Fajardo sobre prisión de portugueses*, 1650.

[109] Parker ascribes this to changing El Niño patterns, which were periodic and could lengthen the trip up to a third of its normal duration. Parker, Geoffrey, *Global Crisis: War, Climate Change, and Catastrophe in the Seventeenth Century* (London: Yale University Press, 2013), pp. 15 -16, also see Calvo, Thomas, *Espacios, climas y aventuras: El Galeón de Filipinas y la fragata de las Marianas en el Pacífico occidental (1680–1700)*, (San Luís Potosí: El Colegio de San Luís, 2016). According to Giráldez, this was rather the effect of changes in sunspot activity during the period, Giráldez, *The Age*, p. 128.

[110] For a broader view of this period in Southeast Asian history, see Reid, Anthony, *A History of Southeast Asia: Critical Crossroads* (Oxford: Wiley-Blackwell, 2015), Reid, Anthony, *Southeast Asia in the Age of Commerce 1450–1680: vol. 1. The Lands below the Winds* (New Haven: Yale University Press, 1988), and Reid, Anthony, 'An 'Age of Commerce' in Southeast Asian History', *Modern Asian Studies* 24, nº 1 (February 1990): 1–30.

[111] Chaunu, *Les Philippines*, pp. 148–198.

[112] Quiason, *English*, p. 5.

link with English India had been established.[113] This trade was usually carried on by ex-company agents that disguised themselves as pilots of Asian ships, or by intermediaries such as Armenians or Luso-Indians.[114] From 1743, the Batavia branch of the trade was directed from Manila by Swiss national César Faillet, who sent an annual ship to Batavia.[115] While it is difficult to know with any accuracy the volume of these lines of trade, Serafin Quiason has estimated that between 1690 and 1762, between 25 to 30% of all the silver that arrived to the Presidency of Madras came directly from Manila, representing around 300,000–350,0000 silver pesos a year.[116]

The 1680s were a period of recovery for Manila's trade, which boomed to dimensions not seen since the 1630s. A series of events coincided in this decade. In 1681, the maritime ban in China was repealed, and Chinese merchants flocked to the city searching for the Galleons' silver. Similarly, the EIC signed a treaty of alliance with the Armenian nation in 1688, which indirectly opened the trade of Manila to the EIC, as Armenians were permitted to sail to Manila and settle there. Armenians traded goods in the Philippines with the capital of EIC agents, channelling flows of specie back to India.[117] During the 1670s and 1680s, Japanese silver exports came to end. As mentioned previously, this increased Manila's importance as a source of silver within Asia. An even more important event for the silver trade, as argued by Irigoin, was the introduction of a new peso coin in America, the famous "pillar" dollar (whose name derived from the use of the Pillars of Hercules in the coin's stamp). This new coin supplanted previous designs and included a rimmed edge that made it

[113] Quiason, *English*, pp. 42–45.

[114] Quiason, *English*, pp. 64–65.

[115] Manilha Consultations, vol. 4, 1763, p. 2, see also the case of Thomé Gaspar de León, Flannery, Kirstie, and Ruiz-Stovel, Guillermo, 'The Loyal Foreign Merchant Captain: Thomé Gaspar de León and the Making of Manila's Intra-Asian Connections', *Vegueta*, 20 (2020), p. 196.

[116] Quiason, *English*, pp. 74 & 76.

[117] This relationship is detailed in the work of Quiason and Bhattacharya. According to Souza, the VOC also attempted to establish a similar relationship with Portuguese and Armenian country traders since the later seventeenth century, Souza, *The Survival*, pp. 154–155, as did the French East India Company, Manning, Catherine, 'French Country Trade on Coromandel (1720–50)', in *European Commercial Expansion in Early Modern Asia*, ed. Om Prakash (Aldershot: Variorum, 1997), p. 287.

more difficult to clip.[118] The impact of these changes is further examined in Chapter 4. For now, what matters is that the period between 1680 and 1740 was one of expanded trade in Manila.

A second cycle of stagnation started in 1740 and lasted until 1780. During this period, the number of vessels sailing to Manila was reduced, and Manila suffered a series of setbacks. In 1743, the British captured the Galleon *Covadonga*.[119] This was followed by a series of failures to celebrate the Acapulco fair: between 1743 and 1751, only three Galleons managed to return from Acapulco.[120] The Seven Years' War and the English capture of Manila in 1762 further impacted the trade. The English captured the Galleon *Santísima Trinidad* and looted the *obras pías*, causing a stoppage of trade financing in the city,[121] the restoration of Spanish control, on the other hand, resulted in a general expulsion of *sangleyes*, who were said to have sided with the British.[122] During the 1780s, an expansionary cycle set in. Trade expanded and became more direct across the Spanish empire, which slowly supplanted the previous system of fairs and fleets. The Manila-Acapulco trade remained the exclusive privilege of Manileños, but in the 1760s direct trade between Spain and the Philippines started,[123] and in 1785, the Real Compañía de Filipinas was chartered with the right to intermediate between Asia and America across the Atlantic, and between Perú and the Philippines in the Pacific.[124] The causes and the effect of this transformation are analysed in Chapter 6, but it is certain that this period witnessed a generalised increase of competition and the expansion in the volume of trade across the empire.

Altogether, three distinct cycles can be observed between 1640 and the early nineteenth century. These cycles obeyed causes originating from

[118] Irigoin, 'Rise', p. 391.

[119] Schurz, *The Manila*, pp. 330–337.

[120] Yuste, *Emporios*, Cuadro I.

[121] Mesquida, Juan, 'Pious funds across the Pacific (1668–1823): Charitable Bequests or Credit Source?', *The Americas* 75, n° 4 (2018), p. 687, Schurz, *The Manila*, pp. 340–341.

[122] Escoto, Salvador, 'Expulsion of the Chinese and Readmission to the Philippines: 1764–1779', *Philippine Studies* 47, n° 1 (1999): 48–76.

[123] Díaz-Trechuelo, 'El comercio', pp. 478–480.

[124] Díaz-Trechuelo, María Lourdes, *La Real Compañía de Filipinas* (Escuela de Estudios Hispanoamericanos, Sevilla, 1965), p. 34.

Asia, America, and Manila itself, where the capital market reacted to maritime disasters and commercial failures. This highlights the global and entangled nature of Manila as a hub connecting the Pacific branch of the global silver trade, but it also shows that, with the emergence of its own financial markets, local circumstances and conditions increasingly participated in the evolution of this trade. Manila needs to be traced back into the story as an active participant rather than a passive observer, and its local history needs to be woven into the intricate intercontinental web that connected the Early Modern world.

The American Leg

For most of the Early Modern period, Manileños were the only ones to consistently cross the Pacific. During the late sixteenth century, small flotillas of up to four ships crossed the Ocean. However, during the seventeenth century the number was reduced to two Galleons annually, and by the eighteenth century only one ship made the crossing. The *reglamento* of 1593 limited the trade to two annual ships of 300 tons each. It is however doubtful that the decree of 1593 was the real reason for the limitation. The decree's stipulations regarding the tonnage of the vessels were widely ignored, and thousand-ton vessels were often in use since 1614.[125] Even more puzzling was the Manileños' insistence on the use of one single Galleon. The royal instructions of 1718, 1720, and 1730 clearly insisted on diversifying the risk of the Pacific crossing among two ships. The Manileños refused and counter-offered to concentrate all the shipping in one single vessel representing less than the combined allowed tonnage of the two ships stipulated in the orders.[126] Despite the insistence of the authorities, the Manileños only sent one single Galleon annually across the Pacific.

On paper, the cargo of the Galleon was also regulated to specific sums known as *permiso* (lit. trans. allowance). The *reglamento* of 1593 established that cargo could only be shipped from Manila to Acapulco for the value of 250,000 pesos, and only 500,000 pesos could be brought back in the concept of payments for those goods.[127] This amount was increased

[125] Schurz, *The Manila*, p. 194.

[126] Álvarez Abreu, *Extracto*, ff: 50–56.

[127] Schurz, *The Manila*, p. 155.

to 300,000 and 600,000 respectively in 1702, 500,000 and 1 million in 1734, and 750,000 to 1.5 million in 1769.[128] The *permiso*, however, was equally ignored. There was no effective way to monitor the real value of the shipments as port authorities never had the power to open trunks, and they had to accept the declaration and valuation that the owners made of their own cargoes by law.[129] The *permiso* was also complemented with the *situado*. The *situado* was a cash transfer from the Treasury of Mexico to that of the Philippines to cover the deficit in Manila. *Situados* were a common feature of the Spanish empire, and their function in the political economy of the empire has been analysed by Grafe and Irigoin.[130] The *situado* of the Philippines averaged 200,000 pesos a year,[131] and was essentially composed of the *almojarifazgo* tax collected from the Galleon in Acapulco, which was then sent back to the islands.[132] It was, as will be argued in Chapter 6, a strategy to monetise the fiscal burden of the Galleon and return it to Asia in the form of the coveted pesos.

As seen in the previous section, estimates suggest that the transpacific trade moved far more than the allowed sum, showing that the *permiso* was hardly adhered to. The law specifically ordered custom officials to accept the sworn declarations presented by the owners of the trunks at face value.[133] The attorney Leandro de Viana in 1760 complained to the king that this system allowed freighters to consistently under-value their shipments.[134] The traditional interpretation of the secrecy regarding the Galleon's cargo is one of corruption and fiscal evasion. However, protests from the Galleon freighters involved in the investigation of the *San Carlos Borromeo* in 1767 indicate that the right to the secrecy of their bills of lading was protected by a sentence from the Council of Castile,

[128] Fradera, *Filipinas*, p. 56.

[129] Schurz, *The Manila*, p. 179.

[130] Grafe and Irigoin, 'A stakeholder'.

[131] TePaske, 'New World silver', p. 434. *Situados* were transfers between different territorial districts, Grafe and Irigoin, 'A stakeholder', p. 612.

[132] Alonso Álvarez, *El costo*, pp. 283–287, see Flynn and Giráldez, 'Spanish profitability', pp. 29–30.

[133] AMN 533 MS1576, Doc. 2, *Informe de Viana sobre engaños con que se hace el comercio de los galeones*, 1760, ff. 9–10.

[134] AMN 533 MS1576, Doc. 2, ff. 1–2.

meaning that it enjoyed institutional and royal protection.[135] This same process highlights that for freighters in the Pacific—like the freighters in the Atlantic *flotas*, who enjoyed the same privilege of handing only their sworn declaration[136]—secrecy was not a strategy to protect themselves from the fiscal burden of the exchange, which was, in any case, monetised and sent back to Manila as the *situado*, but to reduce the flow of information on the goods carried by the Galleons to the Mexican purchasers in the Acapulco fair,[137] something that is analysed in depth in Chapter 4.

The volume and value of goods, in any case, must have been high. Manila Galleons were among the largest vessels of their times. The *Santísima Trinidad* had a cargo capacity of 2,000 tons, while the *Nuestra Señora del Rosario* carried 1,710 tons.[138] Together, these two Galleons performed 15 crossings between 1743 and 1762 out of a total of 18.[139] Even comparatively smaller vessels were large for any standard. Vessels of 1,600, and 1,500 tons were common, and the *Magallanes*, a modern war frigate of the closing days of the line, had a capacity of 933 tons.[140] By comparison, standard East Indiamen employed by the EIC during the 1760s could carry 500 tons, and the largest Indiamen used in the last decades of the eighteenth century were 1,200 tonners.[141] According to Parthesius, VOC ships plying the direct Europe-Asia route up to the 1660s reached 625 tons of cargo capacity.[142] Packing was done by Chinese workers in Manila and was highly efficient.[143] The goods

[135] AGI Filipinas 941 N. 1, 1769.

[136] Del Valle Pavón, Guillermina, 'La lucha por el control de los precios entre los consulados de México y Andalucía', *Revista Complutense de Historia de América*, vol. 32 (2006), p. 44.

[137] AGI Filipinas 941 N.1, 1769, this is explored further in Chapter 4.

[138] Schurz, *The Manila*, pp. 194–195.

[139] Yuste, *Emporios*, Cuadro I, pp. 384–391.

[140] Blanco Núñez, José María, 'La fragata de S.M. *San Fernando* a. *El Magallanes* en el servicio del Galeón de Manila-Acapulco', in *El Galeón de Manila: la ruta española que unió tres continentes* (Madrid: Ministerio de Defensa, 2016), p. 205.

[141] Bowen, *The Business*, p. 269.

[142] Parthesius, Robert, *Dutch Ships in Tropical Waters. The Development of the Dutch East India Company (VOC) Shipping Network in Asia* (Amsterdam: Amsterdam University Press, 2010), p. 68.

[143] Schurz, *The Manila*, p. 182.

that were transported in the Galleons were also value-added manufactures, mostly silk cloths and later Indian cotton goods. As the century progressed, it became more common to ship finished and semi-finished goods from India, and raw materials like silk from China, although finished goods like stockings from Nanjing and Zhangzhou were also included.[144]

Other smaller luxury goods were also transported to Mexico. These included from religious imagery commissioned and manufactured in China, lacquered boxes and furniture,[145] to spices, and even mercury to feed the silver industry of Spanish America. The *Magallanes* itself carried no less than 1,588 Castilian *quintales* (73 tons) of mercury from Manila to Acapulco in 1794.[146] The shipment of mercury from China was encouraged during the late seventeenth century, when the production of the mines of Almadén in Spain went into decline. Governor Fausto Cruzat y Góngora sponsored the trade, but it was finally banned by Felipe V in 1709 to avoid competition with a resurgent Almadén.[147]

While the Asian leg of the trade was open to anyone that came to sell to Manila, the American leg was the consuetudinary right of the registered citizens (*vecinos*), encompassed in the formula of the "City and Commerce" by the *reglamento* of 1593.[148] Local Manileños of Spanish descent were the only ones with the right to freight in the Galleon. Up to

[144] AGI Filipinas, 936, N. 3, *Testimonio sobre la fragata San José y el paquebot San Carlos, El Filipino*, 1781. This is the freighting proceeding of the Galleons *San José* and *El Filipino*. The document includes an evaluation in Manila of the list of items for export to America.

[145] Gasch-Tomás, José Luis, 'Asian Silk, Porcelain and Material Culture in the Definition of Mexican and Andalusian Elites, c. 1565–1630', in *Global Goods and the Spanish Empire, 1492–1824: Circulation, Resistance and Diversity*, ed. Bethany Aram and Bartolomé Yun-Casalilla (London: Palgrave Macmillan, 2014).

[146] Blanco Núñez, 'La fragata', p. 200, in the meantime, the administration of Almadén had been placed under the control of the Consulado of Seville, and its distribution within New Spain was monopolised by the merchants of the Consulado of Mexico that financed the silver mines of New Spain and contracted at the fairs, del Valle Pavón, Guillermina, 'Bases del poder de los mercaderes de plata de la ciudad de México. Redes, control del Consulado y de la Casa de la Moneda a finales del siglo XVII', *Anuario de Estudios Americanos* 68, nº 2 (2011), pp. 584–585, Lang, M.F., 'Las minas de Almadén bajo la superintendencia de Miguel de Unda y Garivay', *Hispania*, 32 (1972): 261–276.

[147] AGI Filipinas, 129, N. 150, *Carta del conde de Lizárraga sobre azogue de China*, 1712.

[148] Schurz, *The Manila*, p. 154.

the creation of the *Consulado* of Manila in 1769, the hold of the Galleons had been divided into 4,000 equal shares, and citizens had been given a *boleta* (ticket) representing their share in the vessel's lading space,[149] although the 1734 *reglamento* allocated half of all *boletas* (2,000) to the *obras pías* of Manila until the practice was discontinued in 1769.[150] *Boletas* were assigned annually by the *junta de repartimiento*.[151] Since the freighting of the Galleon belonged to the city, the allotment process was regulated by a hierarchy of institutions. The first allotment was done by the *junta*, but any aggrieved individual could challenge the *junta*'s decision regarding their share through appeals to the *Audiencia*, which had a reserve of *boletas* allocated to improve the share of any citizen.[152] Similarly, citizens that could not ship were to return their *boletas* before a specified date, after which a second allotment was made, concentrating *boletas* in the hands of those that could freight.[153] The sale of *boletas* was forbidden except for widows and the ambiguous "poor", which may have included the *obras pías*, although there is no solid evidence of how the *obras pías* dealt with their allotted 2,000 *boletas* from 1734 until 1769. Finally, the governor also had a reserved number of *boletas* that he could allocate to those that merited them or among his protégés.[154]

Boletas were also allotted to corporate bodies like the chapter of the cathedral of Manila and to officials, meaning that the same person could receive several of them (i.e. as a citizen, as an official, and as the member of a corporation).[155] This could lead to large concentrations of *boletas* in the hands of a few holders. In a letter to the king in 1750, Archbishop Pedro Martínez de Arizala complained that widows and poor received too few *boletas*. Arizala reproduced the allotment list of the year 1750, which shows that in the first allotment, 56 individuals had received 875 *boletas*

[149] Schurz, *The Manila*, p. 158.

[150] AGI Filipinas 941 N.1, 1769.

[151] Schurz, *The Manila*, p. 156.

[152] AGI Filipinas 229 N.1, *Carta del Tribunal de Cuentas de México con el Libro de Sobordo del Santo Cristo de Burgos*, 1724, & AGI Filipinas 268 N.1, 1752. Both documents include the proceedings of the *repartimento* of *boletas* for their respective years.

[153] AGI Filipinas 229 N.1, 1724, & AGI Filipinas 268 N.1, 1752.

[154] AGI Filipinas 229 N. 1., 1724.

[155] AGI Filipinas 229 N. 1., 1724.

out of 2,000, representing 43.75% of all available *boletas* out of a list of 1,041 eligible citizens.[156]

Citizenship could be granted to those willing to reside in the city for at least eight years. Manileños had often complained of merchants coming from New Spain with abundant capital, capable of outbidding their Manileño competitors in the purchase of Asian goods.[157] Foreigners from kingdoms outside of the Hispanic Monarchy could also become citizens. Among the freighters of the Galleon in the eighteenth century there were Antonio Piñón, an Armenian, as well as Irishmen like the O'Kennery brothers, or Germans like Ignacio Herman.[158] Other foreigners also received *boletas* even if they did not necessarily freight or received capital to do so even if they were not eligible for *boletas*. Stanislaus Termeyer belonged to the first group,[159] while Doña Manuela Rosa Paasines, a Filipino headwoman of the suburb of La Hermita, received 400 pesos from Tomás de Endaya in a *correspondencia* to Acapulco.[160] Surnames such as Diculesit[161] or Bagge,[162] reveal that foreigners participated in the American leg.

Most *boleteros* (ticketholders) did not freight in the Galleon themselves. During the eighteenth century, only a small group of between 30 and 50 wealthy citizens did freight on the Galleon frequently.[163] This small group was the only one that was truly in contact with the merchants on both ends of the exchange, and their commercial activity was therefore circumscribed to the two fairs that delimited the Manila trade: the Manila fair and the Acapulco fair. They had contact with many Mexican merchants, who were often of the same family, and established family connections that extended over the empire and stretched back to

156 AGI Filipinas 292 N. 32, Doc. 2, *Carta de Pedro Martínez de Arizala sobre reparto de boletas*, 1750.

157 Yuste, *Emporios*, pp. 135–137, & Schurz, *The Manila*, p. 364.

158 Yuste, *Emporios*, p. 107.

159 APSR Tomo 282, *Obra pía del Capitán Juan Bautista de Uriarte*, f. 21.

160 Escribano Baltasar Xavier Sanchez, 1740–1741 [Legajo #2], ACCHS-CSIC, ff. 174a-175a.

161 Escribano Domingo Cortes de Arquiza, 1755 [Legajo #5], ACCHS-CSIC, ff. 40b-41b.

162 Escribano Baltasar Xavier Sanchez, 1740–1741 [Legajo #2], ACCHS-CSIC, ff. 170b-171b.

163 Schurz, *The Manila*, p. 160.

Spain.[164] This reduced number of freighters also held public offices in the Philippines, serving as mayors, military officials, and presiding over the powerful Third Orders and confraternities that controlled the legacy funds. And often too, they did not sail themselves in the Galleon across the Pacific but gave their powers of legal representation to agents.[165] These agents, called consignees, were often family relations or protégés, and it was common for several freighters to give their powers to the same person. When the *Consulado* of Manila was established in 1769, two requirements were set for membership: first, a capital of 8,000 pesos, and second, either to have been born in Manila or Spain, or to have resided in the island for at least ten years.[166] The freighters and their agents soon coped all important positions in the *Consulado*.[167]

The organisation of the American leg of the Manila trade, like the Asian leg, experienced changes throughout its 250-years-long history. Most important was the enactment of the 1593 *reglamento* that established the basics of the transpacific trade, including a limited number of Galleons that sailed exclusively to Acapulco, a *permiso* of 250,000–500,000 pesos, and the recognition of the Galleon trade as the consuetudinary right of the citizens of Manila that was allocated through *boletas*. The long-standing animosity between Seville and Manila also left their mark on the legislation of Manila's trade. The litigation between both in 1702–1734 ended with Manila's final victory. The significance of this is not so much revealed on changes to the organisation of the line, but on the fact that the king recognised the privileges enjoyed by Manila and augmented the *permiso* to 500,000–1,000,000 pesos. A third change came in 1769 with the creation of the *Consulado* of Manila and the deposition in the institution of the right to receive and allocate the *boletas*. This virtually disembedded the merchant community from the broader citizenry, although the reform was not complete, with widows, religious bodies, and other important institutions of the city still participating in the trade and receiving *boletas*, while the *permiso* was also augmented to 750,000–1,500,000 pesos.

164 Yuste, *Emporios*, p. 126.

165 An exemplary list of consignors and their agents for the 1767 Galleon *San Carlos Borromeo* can be found in AGI Filipinas 941 N.1, 1769.

166 Yuste, *Emporios*, p. 154.

167 Yuste, *Emporios*, pp. 239–240.

Ever since Schurz's work, this evolution has been interpreted as the result of a fiscal struggle between the Spanish government and the city of Manila, with the consequent emphasis on the persistence of corruption and devious practices that were oriented to defrauding the central government from the rents of the trade.[168] But this approach hides some of the most important motivations for regulation that existed from the late seventeenth century onwards. The purpose of these changes very often also arose from motives that were endogenous to trade itself, from the management of risk to the menace of interlopers that threatened to reduce the profits of Manileños, to the economic link that tied the prosperity of the trade with the supply of public goods in Manila. Understanding the challenges and dilemmas that Manileños faced is fundamental for studying the trade, as this evolutionary process forced them to change and adapt the institutions they knew to an ever-evolving environment.

2.3 Transactions Map of the Manila Trade

The purpose of mapping the retail chain of the transpacific trade is to highlight two aspects of the exchange that are important for future analysis. The first is that Manila was an intermediary, and as such, it derived large profits from matching Asian demand for pesos to Spanish American supply. But Manila's intermediation could be bypassed. The second, is that the Pacific exchange was not vertically integrated, which meant that Manileños were vulnerable to hold-ups. Vertical integration in the trade could have solved the problems of hold-ups and made the trade more efficient, but this would have been at the expense of the intermediary: Manila. Vertical integration was not in Manila's interest. Instead, Manila managed to maintain its position as an intermediary by specialising as the financier of the Pacific exchange.

Thus, understanding the complicated financing process that took place at Manila requires first mapping the transactions of the Pacific silver trade all the way from Asia to America. In such a map (Fig. 2.1), two extremes appear at the end of each terminal of the trade with the major transactions entered by the participants. One was the Manila fair, during

[168] Schurz, *The Manila*, Yuste, *Emporios*, Bonialian, *El Pacífico*, Bjork, Katharine, 'The Link that Kept the Philippines Spanish: Mexican Merchants Interests and the Manila Trade 1571–1815', *Journal of World History* 9, nº 1 (1998): 25–50, Flynn and Giráldez, 'Spanish profitability', pp. 28–29.

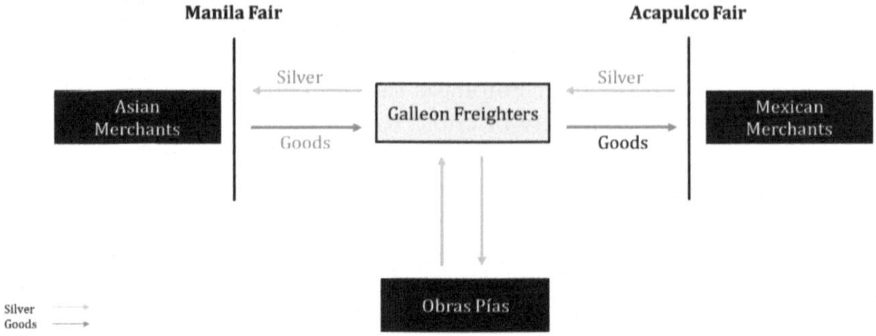

Fig. 2.1 Transactions map of the Manila trade, 1700–1800

which merchants from all over Asia sold their wares to the Manileños in exchange of silver pesos.[169] The other was the Acapulco fair in New Spain, where the Galleon freighters or their agents sold these Asian goods to a wide array of purchasers from Spanish America, but principally New Spain.[170] These two fairs were the major commercial events of the Pacific run, and both strictly revolved around the annual sailing of the Galleon.

This created the first barrier to trade, which was of a seasonal nature: the departure dates of the Galleon both from Manila and Acapulco were carefully timed with the prevailing monsoon winds and the typhoon season. The outgoing voyage to America usually started with the Galleon's departure from Cavite between July and August and took on average six months to complete. The inbound trip to Manila started in February/March and took on average three months. That way, the Galleons could clear Filipino waters before the typhoon season started in September. Fairs were usually short, lasting around one or two months. The Acapulco fair lasted from January to late February or early March, while the Manila fair took place in June–August.[171] This deadline was the more important because Manileños, as *peninsulares* in the Atlantic, did not have the right to stay in New Spain or to penetrate the interior. Manileños were only allowed to travel inside New Spain once the

[169] Schurz, *The Manila*, pp. 74–75.

[170] Schurz, *The Manila*, p. 363.

[171] Schurz, *The Manila*, pp. 71–72, 279.

fair had ended, and upon receiving a special permit.[172] Stocking goods, staying over in New Spain, or travelling to the interior were expensive enterprises, thus Manileños only had the one/two months of the fair to satisfy Mexican demand for Asian goods, and most importantly, Asia's demand for silver. This helped Mexican buyers in Acapulco to make a unified front against the Manileños in order to delay the transactions and push down prices, as they were aware that the Manileños had to clear before a certain date.[173] This strategy was also followed in the mirror fair of Jalapa, where the Atlantic Run ended.[174] However, the timing of the fairs and the sailing of the Galleons was not the cause of Mexicans' position of power in the transpacific exchange.

The Mexican wholesalers' capability to present a unified front resembling a cartel was based on the structure of the Mexican commercial circuits. A small cliqué of wholesalers from Mexico City, grouped in the local *Consulado*, virtually controlled the exchanges of the Jalapa and Acapulco fairs.[175] These merchants mobilised most of the silver pesos available in New Spain, which allowed them to be the main buyers in both fairs, pushing prices down. Once the fairs were concluded, these wholesalers redistributed the goods internally, sending them to the faraway mining camps and to the smaller retailers in the interior.[176]

Mexican wholesalers derived their power from their deep connections with the silver mining industry within New Spain. The Mexican silver industry was not integrated. Mining required high sunk costs for the development of shafts, the payment of salaries, and the creation of mills and other engineering works,[177] yet mining itself was highly unpredictable, since the deeper the mines went, the more vulnerable they became to flooding, which drove many miners out of business.[178] The Mexican wholesalers positioned themselves in an intermediary role. Some of them became bankers and financiers of the mines (*aviadores*), which allowed them to have preferential access to silver bullion without the risk

[172] Yuste, *Emporios*, p. 292.

[173] Yuste, *Emporios*, p. 382.

[174] Bonialian, *El Pacífico*, p. 177.

[175] Brading, *Miners*, p. 97, Yuste, *Emporios*, pp. 15–16.

[176] Brading, *Miners*, p.98.

[177] Brading, *Miners*, Ch. 4.

[178] Brading, *Miners*, pp. 132–135.

of bankruptcy.[179] Some others made fortunes by providing the isolated silver camps with goods and resources necessary for mining and refining silver, partaking in the profits.[180] Their intermediary role also benefitted them, as the wholesalers were the agents collecting silver bullion, both as proceeds from their sales to the miners and as the royal agents charged with collecting the payments for taxes and mercury, and bringing it to the mint of Mexico City—the only mint in New Spain for most of the period—to be coined into pesos.[181] Finally, wholesalers controlled the supply of mercury, a necessary input for the amalgamation of silver ore that had to be imported from Spain. Mercury was provided by the king from the mine of Almadén and shipped to America in the Atlantic *flotas*, but its distribution within New Spain had to be outsourced and the wholesalers' managed to monopolise the supply mercury from royal agents and its distribution to the mining towns.[182] Thus, they controlled the inputs and outputs of silver mines without bearing the risk of ownership, which allowed them to control the flows of silver bullion into the Mexico City mint, and—consequently—the flow of pesos to either the Pacific and Atlantic fairs, which brought consumption goods to New Spain.

As both the Pacific and Atlantic Runs were mostly defined by the trading of goods for silver pesos, the position of the Mexican merchants as purveyors of the silver towns enabled them to accumulate large amounts of cash that would be mobilised at once for the fairs. This meant that Manileños faced a de facto peso cartel in the Acapulco fair, a situation that could only be alleviated by the timely arrival of Peruvian merchants willing to compete against their Mexican counterparts.[183] However, by the eighteenth century Peruvians rarely intervened directly in the Acapulco fair, and instead contracted via the Mexican wholesalers, who then re-exported the goods from Jalapa and Acapulco to Perú.[184] Thus, the wholesalers' control of the distribution of pesos within New Spain and the careful

[179] Brading, *Miners*, pp. 149–150 & Del Valle Pavón, 'Bases', pp. 565–598.

[180] Brading, *Miners*, p. 150.

[181] De Elhuyar, Fausto, *Indagaciones sobre la amonedación en Nueva España*, México: Tipografía Literaria de Filomeno Mata, 1880 (1814), p. 7.

[182] Del Valle, 'Bases', pp. 570 & 594.

[183] Schurz, *The Manila*, p. 382, Bonialian, *El Pacífico*, p. 279.

[184] Bonialian, *El Pacífico*, p. 290.

timing of the navigation put the Manileños at a disadvantage and allowed the Mexicans to become price-setters.[185]

At the Asian end of the trade, Galleon freighters faced two different kinds of transactions, the acquisition of goods for trade, and the financing of trading operations, that is, the acquisition of working capital. The procurement of goods took place in the Manila fair. As seen previously, Chinese merchants settled in Manila becoming a group of their own, the *Sangleyes*. *Sangleyes* lived in the Parián, but soon extended into other neighbourhoods like Binondo or Santa Cruz, where they kept shops opened all year long, renting locales from religious orders or the city's commons.[186] The result was the emergence of the Manila fair, a fair for Asian products that started around June, as the Chinese junks would arrive from April to May, and lasted until the southern monsoon forced them to depart for China in August–September. Most of the junks that arrived at Manila did so from Fujian, where also most of the *Sangleyes* hailed from.[187] The fair gave the potential Galleon freighters the freedom to buy merchandise in the market, although attempts to corner or limit the *Sangley* community always remained. Ships from other destinations also arrived in Manila around June, including from the Portuguese possessions, from English-controlled India, and from Batavia.[188] Very little is known about the Manila fair itself. The term "fair" referred to the hectic period of contracting between the arrival of the returning Galleon loaded with pesos and of the Chinese junks, and the departure of the outgoing Galleon, which all coincided in the space of a few months between May/June and July/August. The only fair-like aspect of the Manila transaction was that the commercial activity was concentrated between the arrival of the ships from Asia and the departure of the Galleon. This left a very short period for re-stocking the *Sangley* shops year on year and realise the purchases for the Galleon and the financing of the commerce.

[185] Bonialian, *El Pacífico*, pp. 182–183, and Yuste, *Emporios*, p. 285.

[186] Alva Rodríguez, Inmaculada, *Vida Municipal en Manila (Siglos XVI-XVII)*, (Córdoba: Universidad de Córdoba, 1997), pp. 60–61.

[187] Chia, Lucille, 'The Butcher, the Baker, and the Carpenter: Chinese Sojourners in the Spanish Philippines and Their Impact on Southern Fujian (Sixteenth-Eighteenth Centuries)', *Journal of the Economic and Social History of the Orient* 49, n° 4, 2006, p. 510.

[188] Chaunu, *Les Philippines*, pp. 199–219.

The second transaction that Galleon freighters faced in Manila was the purchase of *boletas*. Since 1593, freighting in the Manila Galleons had been the right of the Spanish citizenry of Manila. As seen in previous sections, *boletas* were legally allocated among the neighbours of Manila, although their distribution was unequal, and only a small number of freighters sent goods across the Pacific. The sale or transfer of *boletas* may never had reached the high proportions and prices that many royal officials claimed.[189] For one thing, *boletas* were a consuetudinary right that could not be transferred. If any transactions took place, these must have been the purchase of the usufruct of *boletas* for one trading season. While widows and the ambiguous "poor" were always allowed to sell their usufruct in the open market, they never had enough volume to critically swing the market in one way or another.

Similarly, it is complex to pin down in time when—if ever—this kind of transaction really dictated the freighting market in Manila. There is the possibility that the 2,000 *boletas* granted to *obras pías* from 1734 to 1769 were sold, and at least the addendum of 1769 implies that,[190] but not much is known about how they were used. Yet, the Galleon proceedings of the mid-eighteenth century reveal that, apart from the 2,000 *boletas* allotted to the *obras pías*, the great majority of the annual shares granted to the citizenry were eventually concentrated in the hands of a few freighters through the legally established process of the *junta de repartimiento* and the *Audiencia*,[191] which questions the extent to which these freighters were in desperate need for additional cargo space, and therefore the inflated prices they were willing to pay according to royal officials.

Even more important is the fact that by the eighteenth century, *boletas* were divorced from the actual cargo loaded in the Galleons. *Boletas* were each meant to represent one *pieza* (bundle) in the Galleon's hold. While every Galleon was divided into 4,000 *boletas*, the number of *piezas* (bundles) loaded into the Galleon varied, sometimes not reaching 1,000 *piezas*, sometimes surpassing 6,000. Similarly, the number of freighters in the Galleons' roster does not identify all citizens that sent goods to

[189] Schurz, *The Manila*, pp. 158–159.

[190] AGI Filipinas 941 N.1, 1769.

[191] The notarised proceedings of the freighting of the 1723 and 1753 Galleons included the process of *repartimiento* of *boletas*, AGI Filipinas 229 N.1, 1724, & AGI Filipinas 268, N.1.,1752.

Acapulco. The secret instructions of the *San Carlos Borromeo* in 1766,[192] as well as the signature in the trunks of the *Santo Cristo de Burgos* in 1723,[193] reveal that many freighters gathered goods from individuals and loaded them as their own, making the receipt of *boletas* for freighting less crucial than imagined from officials' reports. What seems to have been the convention for freighting in the Galleon in the eighteenth century was for individuals to purchase goods and trust them to the care of freighters, who then inscribed them in the Galleon roster as their own, while detailing to their consignors which bundles belonged to their associates. *Boletas* were not as important as Schurz assumed them to be.[194] If *boletas*—or more accurately, their seasonal usufruct—were purchased, this probably reflected freighters adjusting their hold share based on orders, and likely buying them from one another or the *obras pías*, rather than a full-blown secondary market on financial instruments or an annual rent. Importantly, by the eighteenth century *boletas* do not feature prominently in contemporary documents or chronicles other than in some prosecutors' reports to the king and are absent in the notarial protocols of the city, meaning that their relevance was secondary for the freighting of the Galleon.

Far more important was the financing of the trade by the *obras pías*. The nature, volume, and operation of this financial market is explored in depth in the following chapter, but from the late seventeenth century onwards, the investment of the *obras pías* financed the purchasing of Asian goods. Obtaining capital from the *obras pías* remained one of the largest and most important transactions that were to be incurred to enable the negotiation at Acapulco. Through the legacy funds, *obras pías* pooled liquidity and transformed it into the working capital needed to finance the purchase of Asian goods for re-export to America, smoothing the operation of the trade.[195] The Manila fair relied on the timely arrival of the returning Galleons and the Asian trading fleets. A delay in this schedule had the potential to complicate contracting in Manila. *Obras pías* solved this problem. Through their deposits of pooled pesos, they

192 AGI Filipinas 941 N. 1., 1769.

193 AGI Filipinas 229 N. 1., 1724.

194 Schurz, *The Manila*, pp. 157–164.

195 The role of legacy funds is further explained in Chapter 3.

could provide financing to purchase Asian goods and wait for the return of the Galleons or absorb the loss of a vessel, obviating waiting times.

The structure of the Pacific exchange reveals that the whole chain was subject to many potential hold-ups and disruptions. In Manila, the late arrival of a returning Galleon loaded with silver could negatively affect the negotiations with Asian merchants, which took place between June and August. In Acapulco, Mexican wholesalers could force a waiting strategy upon Manileños, shielded by their control of a fragmented internal market in which they were positioned as providers to everyone, but kept a distance from the risks and heavy investments of mining. At any point, a myriad variables could impact the flow of trade. Manila as an intermediary was vulnerable to many of them, but also worked to smooth them, ensuring that Asian goods and silver pesos could reach their respective markets.

2.4 The Consequences of the Pacific Silver Trade

The unique role of Manila as a hub for liquidity and distribution of silver cash not only enhanced its commercial role and enabled—to an extent—the trade of its partners, but it also had unintended consequences that affected the economic choices available to the local merchants. The city was in a unique position to become a specialised provider of capital in Asia due to its intermediary role in the Pacific peso trade and its high rates of returns, but Asian demand for Mexico-minted pesos and the profits that accrued from this trade similarly made other products grown in the islands uncompetitive in the international market. Wealthy Spanish citizens with accumulated capital preferred as a result to invest in trade rather than in the development of a local plantation economy that could not compete with the deluge of Chinese and Indian goods that were sold in the archipelago to obtain pesos. The absence of market-oriented agriculture and the difficulties of Spanish merchants to develop cash crops in turn increased the reliance of the city on trade and oriented financing towards commerce given the lack of productive enterprises in which capital could be invested.

With the accession of the Bourbon dynasty in the eighteenth century, the promotion of a vigorous plantation system became a priority for reformists that compared the relative poverty of the archipelago with the seeming prosperity of the English and the Dutch possessions in Asia.[196] The reality was more complex. The Pacific intermediation between Asia and Spanish America resulted in an abundance of liquidity in Manila that affected the relative prices of tradable goods. Relative to India or China, Manila's main trading partners—and the largest economies of the era—Manila channelled a large flow of silver specie. This was compounded by Asian demand for specie. As a result, Indian and Chinese goods were therefore comparatively cheap. Thus, it was more expensive to invest in local production in the Philippines than it was to import all kinds of goods, including foodstuffs. It is difficult to directly observe relative prices given the lack of price series for the Philippines and for Asia, and the difficulty in making the goods comparable due to the differences in weights and measures. But Manila's reliance on imports for its day-to-day existence, combined with the annual flows of between 50 and 100 tons of silver, paint a picture in which prices in Manila for tradable goods were high, making it worthwhile to import everything. And that is what Manileños did.[197]

In short, Manila suffered a Dutch Disease. The abundance of liquidity and Asia's demand for silver made it more profitable for Manileños to trade than to produce. Some contemporaries understood the link between the trade and the lack of a plantation economy. An anonymous report written in the last quarter of the eighteenth century by an agricultural administrator that had lived in Manila for 23 years and had managed three different estates noted that:

> Among the many causes that prevent the flourishing of Agriculture in these islands, the principal is undoubtedly that the Spaniards prefer the Commerce, attracted by the easiness and quickness with which they enrich

[196] Francisco Leandro de Viana, 'Viana's Memorial of 1765', in Emma H. Blair & James A. Robertson, *The Philippine Islands*, Cleveland, Ohio, 1903–1909, vol. 47, p. 226, this process has been documented by Dolores Elizalde, although the Dutch Disease is not mentioned as one of the causes holding back the development of a plantation economy, Elizalde, Dolores, 'El viraje de Filipinas hacia Asia en el filo de los siglos XVIII y XIX', *Vegueta. Anuario de la Facultad de Geografía e Historia*, 20 (2020): 163–187.

[197] According to Ruiz-Stovel, Manileños even imported plaster from China, 'Chinese Shipping', p. 425.

> themselves, especially with that of New Spain, which promises much wealth.[198]

The same author noticed the problem associated with the seasonal flooding of the Philippines with low-cost Chinese textiles and suggested protectionist measures:

> Being Chinese textiles [...] the most consumed in the islands by the natives, who dress with them, the Chinese extract great quantities of money to the detriment of the islands. Their introduction must therefore be absolutely prohibited, not only to the Chinese but also to the Spaniards, so that the natives will be forced to produce their own textiles.[199]

Filipino products were too expensive compared to Indian and Chinese products, and this affected even local trade. In his 1810 report, Comyn informed that while the locals were skilled in producing cotton and *abacá*—a textile produced from the *nipa* tree—cloths, these goods rarely were exchanged even within the islands, and only did so when Chinese and Indian goods were scarce.[200] This shows the extent to which the Dutch Disease made Filipino products uncompetitive and hindered the development of a local plantation economy. The effects can be seen in the attempts to grow two commercial crops for export: cinnamon and cotton.

The best documented project to grow cinnamon in the Philippines was undertaken by English-born Manila resident Nicholas Norton Nicols in the 1760s. In a letter to king Carlos III in 1760, Nicols presented a project to start the cultivation of cinnamon and indigo in his estate of Mindanao.[201] Nicols reported that some indigo samples that he had cultivated in his estate at the cost of 500 reales had reached a price of 2,600 reales in London, a mark-up of 420%.[202] Nicols intended to supply Spain

[198] AMN 553 MS1576, *Disertación sobre la agricultura de Philipinas*, undated, ca. 1790, fol. 66.

[199] AMN 553 MS1576, ca. 1790, ff. 74–75.

[200] Comyn however failed to link this to the relative prices of silver coins, arguing instead that it was the result of inefficient production methods, De Comyn, *Estado*, pp. 40–41.

[201] Norton Nicols, Nicolás, 'Commerce of the Philippine Islands', in Emma H. Blair & James A. Robertson, *The Philippine Islands*, Cleveland, Ohio, 1903–1909, vol.47, p. 253.

[202] Norton Nicols, 'Commerce', p. 271.

with cinnamon from the Philippines at the expense of Dutch cinnamon. Spain imported most of its cinnamon from the Dutch East Indies, representing an annual drain of four million pesos according to Nicols.[203] He estimated instead that cinnamon of good quality could be grown in Mindanao in enough quantities to satisfy Spanish demand at half the price. Nicols conducted quality experimentation comparing the cinnamon grown in the Philippines to that grown in Ceylon, arguing that samples of the former had been better received in Manila.[204] Nothing came out of Nicols' efforts despite the king's support, and he was said to have died defending Manila from the English in 1762. In a 1765 report, attorney-general Leandro de Viana suggested that Nicols' failure was partly to blame on the indifference from the Manileños themselves.[205] This indifference is understandable. Manila profited from the premium that the peso enjoyed abroad, which added to the opportunity cost of import substitution through investment in the local economy.

Other individuals also made attempts to develop the local economy, such as Francisco Javier Salgado in his estate of Calanvang during the last quarter of the century,[206] or Augustinian friar Matías Octavio, who tried to process indigo in the town of Tambobo.[207] However no attempt can be compared, either in magnitude or consistency, to that carried out by the Real Compañía de Filipinas from 1785 to 1804. The Real Compañía de Filipinas (RCF) was established in 1785 out of the Real Compañía Guipuzcoana de Caracas. It was a joint-stock corporation that enjoyed the support of the king and the powerful director of the Bank of San Carlos, Francisco Cabarrús.[208] The main objective of the company was to wrestle the trade monopoly away from the Galleon freighters by opening a direct route from Manila to Spain through the Cape of Good Hope. This project had been floated several times since the early eighteenth century, and although the king had supported private companies by granting them access to the Philippines, including the wealthy *Cinco*

203 Norton Nicols, 'Commerce', p. 272.

204 Norton Nicols, 'Commerce', p. 275.

205 Quoted in Quiason, *English*, p. 91.

206 Díaz-Trechuelo, *La Real Compañía*, pp. 252–253.

207 Díaz-Trechuelo, *La Real Compañía*, p. 265.

208 Schurz, *The Manila*, p. 412.

Gremios de Madrid,[209] or the Cádiz-based house of Ustáriz, San Ginés, y Cia,[210] none of the previous attempts had persisted.

The RCF had an initial capitalisation of 8 million pesos divided in 32,000 shares of 250 pesos each.[211] A proportion of these shares were to be offered in America and the Philippines, although the company was deeply resented in the archipelago and considered a threat.[212] The creation of the company was welcomed by the English East India Company, which hoped to sign a treaty whereby it could regularly supply the RCF with Indian products in exchange for silver pesos, something that would ease its chronic shortage of cash. A letter from 1790 written by EIC employees in India clearly stated that an agreement with the RCF would mean that "the necessity of sending bullion from England to China would be materially obviated".[213] One such deal was signed with the EIC during Cornwallis' tenure as Governor-General of India for the supply of "manufactures of Bengal and Madras [...] to the amount of six hundred thousand hard or new Mexico dollars" in 1790, negotiated by Fermín de Tastet, factor of the RCF in Calcutta.[214] The deal, however, never came to fruition, and instead the RCF decided to negotiate with private agencies, but the eagerness of the EIC demonstrates the RCF's potential to mitigate its liquidity constraints.[215]

The RCF had jurisdiction to trade in all continents, and had offices in Madrid, Cádiz, Calcutta, Manila, Canton, Lima, and half a dozen other

[209] Cosano Moyano, José, 'Un nuevo intento de comercio directo con las Filipinas: la compañía de Aguirre, del Arco, y Alburquerque', *Anuario de Estudios Americanos*, n° 35 (1978): pp. 261–281.

[210] Ruiz Rivera, Julián B., 'Intento Gaditano de romper el monopolio comercial novohispano-filipino', *Actas de la IV Jornadas de Andalucía y America*, Tomo I (1985): pp. 147–179.

[211] Schurz, *The Manila*, p. 412.

[212] AMN 533 MS1576, *Disertación sobre la agricultura de las Filipinas,* undated, ca. 1790, ff. 174–188.

[213] IOR/HMS/606, *Notes Relatives to the Affairs of Native and Foreign European States*, fol. 435.

[214] IOR/D/150, *Report of the Secret Committee of Correspondence of 23 Jul 1788 on the proposed trade agreement with the Royal Spanish Philippine Company*, 1783–1788, fol. 193.

[215] Cheong, 'Changing the Rules', p. 4. See also Furber, Holden, 'An Abortive Attempt at Anglo-Spanish Commercial Cooperation in the Far East in 1793'. *The Hispanic American Historical Review* 15, n° 4 (November 1935): 448–463.

places. The only trade route that was closed to them was the Manila-Acapulco line, which remained the exclusive domain of the city of Manila as per the privilege of 1593. However, they could access New Spain via Veracruz and Central America, from 1785 to 1789.[216] Shipments to Peru were also common, and ships from the company tended to use El Callao as a stopover in their return trip to Cádiz via Cape Horn. In the first years between 1785 and 1795, five ships of the company stopped at Callao or Lima out of a total of 8 ships that crossed the Pacific.[217] The geographic extension of the company's operations and the connections it established with other players meant that the first years of the RCF were relatively profitable, and the volume of its sales in Europe between 1785 and 1806 totalled 384,778,000 reales.[218]

The authorities had conceived the RCF as a vehicle to develop the economy of the islands. The RCF's foundational charter forced the company to plunge 4% of its profits back into the economy of the Philippines.[219] The company focused its efforts on the development of five main cash crops: cotton, pepper, silk, indigo, and sugar.[220] The original plan was for the RCF to use the profits from its trading activities to develop the cultivation of these cash crops.[221] The company would then use its established distribution channels to sell the products of the archipelago, and when possible, to incentivise the emergence of a local industry by reserving some of its cargo capacity for the manufactures of

[216] Díaz-Trechuelo, *La Real Compañía*, p. 216.

[217] Díaz-Trechuelo, *La Real Compañía*, pp. 183–196.

[218] Schurz, *The Manila*, p. 416.

[219] Legarda, Benito J., *After the Galleons: Foreign Trade, Economic Change, & Entrepreneurship in the Nineteenth-Century Philippines* (Quezon City: Ateneo de Manila University Press, 1999), p. 78.

[220] AMN 552 MS1662, Doc. 97, *Ynforme del Comisionado D. Juan Francisco de Urroz sobre el estado de la Agricultura e Industria de las Yslas, 1802*, ff. 262–300.

[221] Concepción de la Isla seems to hint that the previous, short-lived *Compañía de Manila* established by governor Arandía in 1755 also attempted to invest in the landed economy of the Philippines. The constitutions of the company did include provisions to reinvest profits into the development of cotton agriculture in the islands. The company, however, did not last beyond a year in operation, being wound-up in 1757. Concepción de las Isla, Fr. Juan, *Historia General de Philipinas*, vol. 14., Sampaloc (1792), p. 170, *Ordenanzas de la Compañía de Comercio que se ha formado en esta ciudad de Manila*, Imprenta del Colegio y Universidad de Santo Tomás, Manila (1755), rules 8–12, see also AGI Filipinas 98, N. 8, *Consulta sobre Compañía de Comercio de Filipinas*, 1756.

the country.[222] A report from 1802 written by the factor of Manila Juan Francisco de Urroz informed the directors that, since its creation in 1785, the company had invested 2.3 million reales (280,000 pesos) into a wide array of activities, including iron mines, the nascent textile industry, and botanical experimentation.[223] The figures were broken down by sector and province (Table 2.2). The largest investment was given to the cultivation of cotton, with 846,622 reales, followed by pepper (420,605 reales), silk (294,903 reales), and the textile industry (187,471 reales). The cultivation of cinnamon, which had so prominently featured in the projects of early reformists, only received 3,772 reales during the period.[224]

The production of native cotton highlights the problems that the RCF faced in international markets. Díaz-Trechuelo has documented the lengths to which the RCF went to produce this good. Cotton was the most appreciated cash crop of the Philippines. Early samples sent to China demonstrated that Philippine-grown cotton was of exceptional quality and competed favourably against Indian cotton. In 1796, Filipino cotton sales in Canton commanded a premium over Indian cotton of 23%. Yet, not even with these prices was the cultivation of cotton profitable relative to its importation. Much of it was earmarked for manufacture in the nascent textile industry, and the Spanish tried to imitate the Coromandel cotton cloth in the Philippines,[225] but such industry did not develop until the end of the Pacific trade.

Urroz's report shows the scope of the Company's investment in the development of the local economy. The RCF's project was a broad one that invested in several areas, from cash crops to manufactures and botanical exploration, across many provinces. The company subsidised the purchase of plants, offered to pay entire harvests year on year with advanced sales contracts, offered prizes, and freely provided roots or trees for their cultivation.[226] When it came to pepper, the company shipped copses and trees at its own expense to several provinces, including

222 Díaz-Trechuelo, *La Real Companía*, p. 27.

223 AMN 552 MS1662, Doc. 97, 1802, f. 300.

224 See Díaz-Trechuelo, María Lourdes, 'The Economic Development of the Philippines in the Second Half of the Eighteenth Century', *Philippine Studies* 11, n° 2 (1963): pp. 195–231.

225 Díaz-Trechuelo, *La Real Compañía*, p. 273.

226 Díaz-Trechuelo, *La Real Compañía*, p. 267.

Table 2.2 Report on the investments of the RCF on the Philippines, 1785–1802

Cotton		*Pepper*		*Silk*		*Other sectors*		*Total*	
Cebu	14,393.32	Tayabas	213,231.14	Camarines	149,756.7	Estate of Calavang		Cotton	846,622.26
Isla de Negros	59,716.4	Ilocos	2,140.0	Tondo	145,147.8	Manufactures	76,775.14	Pepper	420,605.7
Bataan	127,259.23	Pampanga	392.17	Total	294,903.15	Ilocos & Manila	187,471.25	Silk	294,903.15
Bulacan	69,410.0	Bataan	81,828.4			Iron		Cinnamon	3,722.16
Tayabas	52,406	Camarines	110,950.33	*Cinnamon*		Angal	8,130.0	Others	3,536.29
Ilocos	507,915.30	Batangas	5,642.30	Calavang	3,102.16	Botany			
Batangas	2,286.8	La Laguna	6,288.25	Tiaong	670	Manila	458,655.29		
La Laguna	150	Huerta de los Angeles	130			Others			
Others	13,084.31								
Total	846,622.26	Total	420,605.7	Total	3,722.16	Total	3,536.29	**Total**	**2,300,473.25**

Sources AMN 552 MS1662, Doc. 97, *Ynforme del Comisionado D. Juan Francisco de Urroz sobre el estado de la Agricultura e Industria de las Yslas*, 1802, ff. 262–300

Tayabas, Camarines, Batangas, Laguna, Pampanga, and Albay, and replenished lost ones. It also employed experts occasionally, such as botanist Juan de Cuéllar,[227] and imported machinery from Catalonia to help peel cotton.[228]

The results, however, were not promising despite the great efforts of the company. Urroz's report recommended the abandonment of all economic activities within the islands and blamed the incapacity of the company to force the natives to work the fields and the workshops as the ultimate cause of the lack of competitiveness.[229] The inefficiency of labour was a common complaint, but the reality was that production was expensive in the Philippines and the RCF could not compete in the long run with the cheaper products from India and China. In 1804 the RCF stopped investing in the local economy of the archipelago and turned exclusively to its trading operations. The several failures to develop the economy of the islands were the result of the lack of competitiveness that Filipino products faced in the international and local market. This, in turn, was the counterpart to the demand for pesos in Asia, which increased their value abroad and, consequently, the opportunity costs for Spaniards to invest in the development of a local economy.

Silver specie was the key to trading with Asia, and the Manileños had the most direct access route to the source in New Spain. An example of the choice between investing in the trade and in the economy is presented in the early failure of the *encomienda* in the Philippines. While *encomiendas* were adapted to the archipelago during its conquest in the late sixteenth century, by the late seventeenth century they had almost disappeared.[230] *Encomiendas* persisted as a concept more related to pensions granted by the state, than as actual grants of lands and population.[231] The failure of the *encomienda* was precisely the profits that could be realised in the Pacific trade, which meant that the Spanish lay

[227] Legarda, *After*, p. 82.

[228] Díaz-Trechuelo, *La Real Compañía*, p. 275.

[229] AMN 552 MS1662, Doc. 97, 1802, ff. 297–298.

[230] Phelan, John L., *The Hispanization of the Philippines: Spanish Aims and Filipino Responses, 1565–1700* (Madison: The University of Wisconsin Press, 1959), p. 97.

[231] Alonso Álvarez, *El costo*, p. 50, & BNE MSS/11014(H.435R.-442R.), *Informe sobre las encomiendas de la Corona y de particulares en Filipinas*, undated, ca. 1700.

population soon crowded in and around Manila, abandoning the countryside.[232] The provinces were soon devoid of Spaniards except for garrisons in strategic forts (*presidios*) and *alcaldes mayores*. In 1781, French visitor Le Gentil observed that the Spanish did not move further than 15 leagues away from Manila.[233] Spaniards had a bigger incentive to reside in Manila and finance the trade than they did in administering *encomiendas* whose products could not compete with those from the larger Asian nations.

All these failed attempts at developing the local economy of the Philippines point to two important conclusions. First, the consistent failure to develop a plantation economy was due to the Dutch Disease that made Filipino products uncompetitive even in the local market. The Manileños owned the most direct access route to silver specie, and they understood that the Pacific silver trade was the most profitable activity to which they could apply their savings. Second, the lack of a local productive economy of the Philippines was not the symptom of a failure, but of the success of the trade. Manileños simply had better options. All the attempts to develop a local plantation economy came from participants that were outside the Manila-Acapulco trade and did not have access to its great profits, from Nicholas Norton Nicols to Matías Octavio, to the RCF. The relationship between the trade in pesos and the production of goods in the islands is illustrated by the fact that, according to Rafael Díaz Arenas, already by 1838 the Philippines enjoyed a positive balance of trade of half a million pesos, becoming a net recipient of cash.[234] The sudden reversal of the balance of trade went hand in hand with the development of a local export-oriented economy and the end of the Manila Galleons.

Within intra-Asian trade circuits, Manila performed a unique role as a source of liquidity, and it was the abundance of silver pesos in the city, not the fertility of its soil, that attracted the annual fleets from India, China, and Southeast Asia. Asia's demand for silver specie was as well a function of how developed their economies were, and the productive capacity of their manufacturing industries. The Philippines sat at the door of India, China, and America, as much as the peso trade was a match made in

[232] Alonso Álvarez, *El costo*, pp. 65–68.

[233] Guillaume Le Gentil, 'Voyages dans les mers de l'Inde' (1781), in Emma H. Blair & James A. Robertson *The Philippine Islands*, Cleveland, Ohio, 1903–1909, vol.28, pp. 170–191.

[234] Díaz Arenas, Rafael, *Memoria sobre el Comercio y Navegación de las Islas Filipinas* (Imprenta de Domingo Ferós: Cádiz, 1838), p. 81.

heaven, it also meant that alternatives to the specie trade were difficult to develop.

CHAPTER 3

The Capital Markets of the Manila Trade

The strategic position of Manila as an intermediary between Spanish America and Asia made it lucrative for the Manileños to gear their activities towards financing the trade with New Spain. This intermediation also led to the city playing a unique role as a source of liquidity in Asia through the pesos that arrived in Manila as returns to the Galleon trade, integrating the Asian commercial circuits with the Pacific. Yet such an enterprise, which implied crossing the largest body of water on Earth, had to be financed. In this regard, Manileños faced challenges similar to those encountered by the English and the Dutch in their direct trade with Asia: long waiting times, need to lock-in investments, and—most importantly—the challenge of mobilising large volumes of capital. This chapter explores how capital was raised in Manila. It reconstructs the financial market of the city from their emergence and operation to the institutional framework that regulated them.

3.1 The Emergence and Development of the Capital Markets of Manila

There has never been a complete study of the *obras pías* of Manila and the legacy funds that mobilised a large part of the capital used to finance the city's trade. Those studies that exist have focused more on the urban

J. J. Rivas Moreno, *The Capital Market of Manila and the Pacific Trade, 1668–1838*, Palgrave Studies in Economic History,
https://doi.org/10.1007/978-3-031-71810-6_3

and social function that the legacy funds played in financing welfare and providing social cohesion through religious activities, as is the case of the work of Díaz-Trechuelo,[1] or the relationship with the trading establishment in New Spain, as is the case of Yuste.[2] This, compounded by the secrecy regarding the actual cargoes of the galleons and the profits of the Manila trade, has led to an overreliance on regulation as the engine of change in the history of the Spanish Pacific.

An alternative chronological approach needs to focus on the institutions that managed legacy funds, of which the most important was the *Santa Casa de la Misericordia* or House of Mercy. The Misericordia of Manila is the most appropriate choice as a proxy to understand the development of the financial market. As the largest manager of legacy funds, the history of the Misericordia parallels the capital market of Manila, which has been largely absent from the periodisation of the transpacific commerce. Similarly, the charitable nature of legacy funds meant that the profits of the trade were linked to the livelihood of many Manileños through welfare it provided.[3] The history of the Misericordia, thus, offers us a glance to the financial history of Manila.

Misericordias were lay brotherhoods that developed in the urban centres of medieval Mediterranean towns. The first Misericordia was the Brotherhood of Our Lady of Mercy of Florence, established in 1244.[4] Misericordias soon spread to other towns, including Naples and Seville, and they were tasked with multiple civic duties, including burials for the executed, visiting prisoners in jail, ransoming captives, and executing the wills of the deceased. However, it was in the Portuguese empire that Misericordias became more closely entangled with the dynamics of European expansion. Misericordias in the Portuguese world also had a decentralised, medieval origin, but in 1498 the Misericordia of Lisbon was

[1] Díaz-Trechuelo, Lourdes, 'Religiosidad Popular en Filipinas: Hermandades y Cofradías (Siglos XVI–XVIII)', *Hispania Sacra*, 53 (2001): 345–366.

[2] Yuste, *Emporios*, p. 95–96.

[3] Mesquida, Juan, 'Negotiating Charity, Politics and Religion in the Colonial Philippines: The Brotherhood of the Misericordia of Manila (1594–1780s)', in *Faith's Boundaries: Laity and Clergy in Early Modern Confraternities*, ed. Nicholas Terpstra, Adriano Prosperi, and Stefania Pastore (Turhnhout: Brepols, 2012), pp. 188–189, Díaz-Trechuelo, 'Religiosidad Popular', p. 365.

[4] Russell-Wood, A.J.R., *Fidalgos and Philanthropists: The Santa Casa da Misericórdia of Bahia, 1550–1755* (London: Macmillan, 1968), p. 3.

founded with complete hierarchical control over the rest of the Misericordias of the kingdom, which spread on the wake of empire to places such as Goa (1519), Salvador de Bahía (1552), and Macao (1569),[5] becoming a fundamental part of an imperial fabric that was based on an intercontinental network of cities.[6] Following the precepts of the works of mercy, Portuguese Misericordias soon performed fundamental charitable activities wherever they were founded,[7] and became an essential foundation of the urban network that composed the Portuguese empire and were critical in maintaining the foundations of the Portuguese polity through their provision of welfare and their capacity to pool capital in times of need.[8]

The Portuguese Misericordias obtained most of their money from donations and legacies.[9] The Misericordia of Macao functioned very similarly to the way the Misericordia of Manila did, and it is probable that part of this similarity was based on the importance of Macao in the silk-for-silver trade of East Asia and its early connections with the Spanish settlement in the Philippines.[10] Like in Manila, Macao's Japanese trade was organised through a chartered annual Galleon, the "Great Ship of Amaçon" as it was known,[11] a model that perhaps inspired the later Manila Galleon.[12] From the late seventeenth century on, the Macao

[5] Russell-Wood, *Fidalgos*, pp. 17–18.

[6] Bethencourt, Francisco, 'Political Configurations and Local Power', in *Portuguese Oceanic Expansion, 1400–1800*, ed. F. Bethencourt and D. Ramada Curto (Cambridge: Cambridge University Press, 2007), p. 199.

[7] Boxer, *The Portuguese Seaborne*, pp. 288–289 & 293.

[8] Rodrigues, 'Institutional', pp. 4–5, see also dos Guimarães Sá, Isabel, *Quando o rico se faz pobre: Misericórdias, caridade e poder no imperio portugués 1500–1800* (Lisbon: CNCDP, 1997).

[9] Boxer, *The Portuguese Seaborne*, pp. 290–291, Souza, *The Survival*, p. 28.

[10] On this relationship, see Boxer, 'Portuguese and Spanish Rivalry', Martínez Torres, José Antonio, 'Integrate the empire: proposals for commercial and defensive cooperation in South-East Asia during the incorporation of Portugal into the Monarchy of the Spanish Habsburgs', in *A Global Trading Network: The Spanish empire in the world economy (1580–1820)*, ed. José Ignacio Martínez Ruiz (Sevilla: Editorial Universidad de Sevilla, 2018): 221–237.

[11] Boxer, Charles R., *The Great Ship from Amacon* (Macau: Instituto Cultural de Macau, 1985), and Souza, *The Survival*, pp. 58–59.

[12] Regarding the possible Portuguese influence in the foundational years of Manila and the Pacific trade, see Villamar, Cuauhtémoc, *Portuguese Merchants in the Manila Galleon System, 1565–1600* (London: Routledge, 2021).

Misericordia—like the legacy funds of the Misericordia of Manila—invested in both the maritime and interior trades through *respondentias*, called in Macao *riscos de mar*.[13]

The Misericordia of Manila was founded in 1594—during the Union of the Crowns of Spain and Portugal—with the same statutes as the Misericordia of Lisbon.[14] Just like its Portuguese counterparts, the Misericordia played an important role in providing public services to the population of Manila, including the maintenance of hospitals, orphanages, and schools, and distributed alms and dowries.[15] This charity soon became an integral part of the livelihood of the city. According to Uriarte, by 1728 the Misericordia had given 508,916 pesos in the dowries of orphan girls since the beginning of the dowry fund in 1634, as well as housing, educating, and providing dowries for a total of 13,270 women.[16]

Similarly, given its central role as a pillar of urban life, the Misericordia also extended loans to the Governor in times of urgency. For example, during the Dutch onslaught of 1646, the Misericordia lent 10,000 pesos to outfit a naval squadron.[17] Other loans took the form of government appropriations in times of extreme urgency. This was the case of the retention of the legacy funds left by Bartolomé Thenorio, who had died in 1643 leaving 45,000 pesos in his will at a time when the war against the Dutch in Indonesia was at is most intense phase.[18] Appropriations however differed from confiscations: the government eventually repaid these amounts. In 1728 Juan Bautista de Uriarte estimated that, since 1619, the Misericordia had lent a total of 454,119 pesos to the government.[19]

[13] Dos Guimarães Sá, Isabel, 'Ganhos da Terra e Ganhos do mar: caridade e comércio na Misericórdia de Macau', *Lér Historia*, 44 (2003): 45–57, Guedes Cosme, Marco Antonio, 'Elites e Poder Local em Macau (1750–1848): Os Proveedores da Santa Casa da Misericórdia' (Dissertação de Mestrado em História, Universidade de Coimbra, 2020).

[14] Díaz-Trechuelo, 'Religiosidad Popular', p. 347, de Uriarte, Juan Bautista, *Manifiesto y Resumen Histórico de la fundación de la Venerable Hermandad de la Santa Misericordia*, Manila, 1728, fol. 55.

[15] Díaz-Trechuelo, 'Religiosidad popular', pp. 355–356.

[16] De Uriarte, *Manifiesto*, f. 46.

[17] De Uriarte, *Manifiesto*, f. 28.

[18] De Uriarte, *Manifiesto*, f. 25.

[19] De Uriarte, *Manifiesto*, ff. 43–44.

While Misericordias were a fundamental element of municipal governance, they were also an integral part of the Catholic order. Any institution that administered legacies—such as lay confraternities or Third Orders—were under the jurisdiction of Canon Law and subject to the local diocesan authorities, but the Council of Trent (1545–1563) granted an exception to the Portuguese Misericordias, placing them under the tutelage of the king instead.[20] This exception provided the Misericordia of Manila with the arguments to resist the visitations of the Archbishop of the city, since its foundation was based on the Lisbon statutes.[21] The ambiguity of the legal status of the Misericordia gave ample independence to the institution but provoked long-drawn legal battles between the Archbishops and the House, until the Misericordia petitioned to be placed under royal patronage, which the king accepted in 1733.[22] The now *Real Casa de la Misericordia* (Royal House of Mercy) remained the largest manager of legacy funds throughout the period.

Most of the money of the Misericordia were legacies held in the form of investment funds whose proceeds were destined to charitable ends. These legacy funds were opened by an individual through a testament.[23] There was no impediment in principle for any person to open a legacy fund with either money or property. In fact, the identity of founders was varied, including men and women of different means and social status, as will be seen in later sections. The founder would usually set some money apart to be invested in different ways, on condition that the returns of the investments be used to recapitalise the original foundation and the profits be destined to charitable ends.[24] "Ends" could be incredibly diverse. For example, Italian missionary Juan Bautista Sidoti created a legacy fund to promote the conversion of Asia and the establishment of new religious

[20] Mesquida, 'Negotiating Charity', p. 191, Álvarez-Dardet Espejo, Concha, López Manjón, Jesús D., and Baños Sánchez-Matamoros, Juan, 'Accounting at the Boundaries of the Sacred: The Regulation of the Spanish Brotherhoods in the Eighteenth Century', *Accounting History* 11, n° 2 (2006), p. 134.

[21] De Uriarte, *Manifiesto*, ff. 47–48.

[22] Mesquida, 'Negotiating charity', p. 197.

[23] The dispositions specified in the testaments were included at the start of the account books held by the Third Order of Saint Dominic. See for example APSR, Tomo 232, *Obra pía de Dª Paula González, doncella difunta*, 1778.

[24] AMN 552 MS1662, Doc. 6, *Extracto General de la fundación de las Obras Pías de la Misericordia*, undated, ca. 1790, ff. 25–66. This is a summarised report of the legacy funds under the management of the Misericordia.

orders in the Philippines—something that infringed upon the authority vested in the king of Spain as patron of the missionary church in his domains.[25] In the late eighteenth century, legacy funds, by then established beyond the Misericordia across dozens of different corporations, supported a whole welfare system that included two universities, two orphan houses for girls, three hospitals, several schools, the dowries of orphaned women, alms, masses, the maintenance of priests (so-called *capellanías*), and the salaries of professionals like doctors or professors among many other expenditures.[26]

Most legacy funds in the Hispanic Monarchy invested in *censos*, a Spanish instrument similar to English leases.[27] The *censos* were imposed on a property, usually land, and were widely used by the Church as the main landholder and credit provider.[28] The interest payment of the *censos* were regulated across Spain by royal *pragmáticas* (orders), and for most of the eighteenth century, nominal interest remained at 5% in Manila.[29] The Misericordia lent on *censos* at least since 1637, according to Uriarte—a secretary of the Misericordia in the early eighteenth century—from which date and up to 1728 the Misericordia had distributed 301,028 pesos to the community in the form of charity.[30] The *censo* funds of the Misericordia, however, suffered severe shocks during the seventeenth century. A Chinese revolt in 1639 seriously affected the countryside around Manila, and was almost immediately followed by the great earthquake of 1645, and another seism in 1654. To help the community cope

[25] Manchado López, Marta, '"Desamparo en que con la vida se pierde el alma" Las controversias en torno a la obra pía del abad Sidoti para la recogida de niños chinos abandonados (Filipinas, 1705–1740)', *Revista de Indias* LXXI, nº 252 (2011): 415–448.

[26] AMN 552 MS1662, Doc. 6, ca. 1790, ff. 25–66, see also APSR section in Bibliography.

[27] Von Wobeser, 'Las fundaciones piadosas', p. 782, von Wobeser, Gisela, *El crédito eclesiástico en la Nueva España, siglo XVIII* (Mexico: UNAM, 1994), pp. 54–59, on the censo, Ena Sanjuan, Íñigo, 'The imperceptible financial (r)evolution of the censo', *Investigaciones de Historia Económica-Economic History Research*, 17 (2021): 1–12.

[28] Von Wobeser, 'Las fundaciones piadosas', pp. 788–789. An example is seen in the endowments of the University of Santo Tomás, which both imposed *censos* and owed them to different individuals and corporations. AUST, Becerros 13, *Manual para los M.M.R.R.P.P. rectores del Colegio de Santo Tomás año de 1775*, 1775–1783.

[29] APSR Tomo 218, *Extracto de aquellas obras pías de la VOT cuya noticia puede ser interesante al Padre Prior del Convento*, 1820.

[30] De Uriarte, *Manifiesto*, f. 44.

with these events, the Misericordia released 77,142 pesos of a total investment it held in real estate of 89,855 pesos, which severely diminished the principal invested in *censos* by 86%.[31] This came together with the serious damage of property and the loss of labour that followed, which devalued the underlying assets of the *censos*. As a result, by 1655, the Spanish population of Manila scarcely amounted to 200 souls, although this number is disputed.[32]

According to Juan Mesquida, these adverse shocks could have motivated citizens to create legacy funds that invested directly in the trade by originating sea loans—or *correspondencias*, as they were known in Manila.[33] This was unique to Manila, although shared to an extent with neighbouring Macao. Uriarte, made a clear distinction between the funds that "invested in estates" and the legacy funds that invested directly in the trade.[34] The first such legacy fund that invested in *correspondencias* was opened by a merchant named Captain Diego Martínez Castellanos in 1668.[35] Soon enough others followed, with merchant Tomás García de Cárdenas establishing his in 1675, Governor Manuel de León creating one in 1677, and another 5 belonging to individuals and the "common of this republic" opening before the turn of the century.[36] By 1728 there were 26 legacy funds that issued *correspondencias*, and by 1750 they had expanded to 48.[37] By 1816 this number had increased to 58.[38] The *correspondencia* funds soon became the largest providers of public goods in the city. Just in the period of 1677–1728, the Misericordia's *correspondencia* funds distributed proceeds of 657,383 pesos, compared to 301,028 pesos from *censos* funds for 1637–1728, an average annual expenditure of 12,900 annual pesos from *correspondencia* funds as opposed to 3,300

[31] De Uriarte, *Manifiesto*, ff. 28–32.

[32] Mesquida, 'Negotiating Charity', p. 194, Alva Rodríguez, *Vida Municipal*, pp. 31–32.

[33] Mesquida, 'Pious', p. 669.

[34] De Uriarte, *Manifiesto*, ff. 40–41.

[35] Mesquida, 'Negotiating Charity', p. 195.

[36] AMN 552 MS1662, Doc. 6, ca. 1790, ff. 25–66.

[37] AGI Filipinas 303 N. 6., *Expediente sobre interferencia de privilegios de las obras pías*, 1750–1752.

[38] AFIO 52/9, *Balance del caudal de las obras pías de la Misericordia*, 1817.

pesos from *censo* funds.[39] This would scale up during the eighteenth century as more *correspondencia* funds were opened in the Misericordia.

The quick propagation of *correspondencia* funds illustrates the returns they offered. While in 1700 there were 8 such funds, all under the management of the Misericordia,[40] by 1833 this had increased to at least 264 identifiable funds under the management of seven different institutions.[41] The Third Order of Saint Francis (*Venerable Orden Tercera de San Francisco*, usually abbreviated as VOT) became one of the most important managers of the city with 83 funds established between 1708 and 1833.[42] The Jesuits managed 45 funds by the time of their expulsion from the isles in 1769,[43] and the VOT and Dominican Province of the Santísimo Rosario managed a combined total of 46 funds by the late 1820s.[44] By the second half of the eighteenth century, the number of institutions managing *correspondencia* funds becomes too diverse to count accurately, although the surviving notarial protocols from Manila show 38 brotherhoods, Third Orders, and other corporations that originated *correspondencias*. These formed a network extending from the Manila suburbs of Dilao, Binondo, Sampaloc, and La Ermita, to the towns of Cavite, Cebú, and Nueva Cáceres.[45] The expansion of funds and of fund managers point to an increase of liquidity in the city as more institutions entered the game and increased the supply of capital for trade.

[39] De Uriarte, *Manifiesto*, ff. 44–45.

[40] AMN 553 MS 1662, Doc. 6, ca. 1790, ff. 25–66.

[41] Gathered from AMN 552 MS1662, Doc. 6, AMN 552 MS1662, Doc. 5, *Extracto que manifiesta todas las obras pías que administra la junta de la VOT de Penitencia de nuestro Padre Santo Domingo*, 1829, AGI Filipinas 1034, *Libros de obras pías administradas por la junta de la Orden Tercera de San Francisco de la ciudad de Manila*, 1805–1806, Archive of the University of Santo Tomas (AUST), Manila, Libros Tomo 20, *Consultas y sus Respuestas*, undated, Eighteenth Century, ff. 157–166, & Newberry Library Vault Ayer MS1349, 1797.

[42] AGI Filipinas 1034, 1805–1806.

[43] Newberry Library, Vault Ayers MS 1448, *Documents pertaining to the Administration and Liquidation of the obras pías of the Jesuits following their expulsion from the Philippines, 1743–1804*, see also Escoto, Salvador P., 'Governor Anda and the Liquidation of Jesuit Temporalities in the Philippines, 1770–1776', *Philippine Studies* 23, n° 3 (1975): 293–319.

[44] AMN 552 MS1662, Doc. 5, 1829, fol. 23.

[45] 1783, 1796, 1799, 1800, 1789, 1792, 1795 [Legajos 14, 15, 15a, 18, 19, 21a, 24, 26] ACCHS-CSIC.

Correspondencia funds attracted plenty of savings, and the size of the market seems to have expanded throughout the century. Misericordia secretary García del Villar estimated that between 1734 and 1766 the Misericordia had invested 3,319,787 pesos only on the Galleon trade, while Schurz estimates that another unspecified "eight" managers may have given around 5 million pesos during the same period, an average of 260,000 pesos annually.[46] Tomás de Comyn estimated the total assets of the *obras pías* in 1809—at a time during which the Pacific trade was in decline after no Galleons had managed to return from Spanish America to Manila since 1804—to be 3 million pesos,[47] while he estimated the assets held by private merchants to be 2.5 million pesos, for a combined total of 5.5 million pesos (or approximately 137.5 tons of silver).[48] The paucity of sources impedes any statistical reconstruction of the total capital pooled through legacy funds, but fragmentary evidence from the Misericordia presented in Table 3.1. reveals the overall growth of capital under management and the resilience of the funds. In 1752, the Misericordia held less than 200,000 pesos in its legacy funds,[49] the result of a series of catastrophes that prevented 7 of the 10 Galleons scheduled between 1742 and 1752 to complete the round voyage across the Pacific. By 1755, this had expanded to 577,738.[50] Similarly, in 1765, after the capture of the outgoing and incoming Galleons and the looting of the *obras pías* by the English in 1762, the Misericordia had 350,273 pesos in its legacy funds.[51] Three years later they reached 455,200 pesos,[52] an annual growth rate of 10%. By 1783, the capital of the legacy funds stood at 1,037,449 pesos.[53] According to the wills of the fund owners, two-thirds of this capital was to be invested annually between Asia and America. If this clause was rigidly followed, that would imply that in 1783 the Misericordia alone issued

[46] Schurz, *The Manila*, p. 169.

[47] De Comyn, *Estado*, p. 56.

[48] De Comyn, *Estado*, p. 54.

[49] AGI Filipinas 303 N.6, *Expediente sobre interferencia de los privilegios de obras pías en la visita eclesiástica*, 1752, f. 37.

[50] AGI Contaduría 1282, *Caja de Filipinas. Cuentas de la Misericordia*, 1755.

[51] AGI Filipinas 595 N. 1, *Cuentas Casa de la Misericordia y Colegio de Santa Potenciana*, cuaderno 1, cuentas 1765–1768.

[52] AGI Filipinas 595 N. 1, cuaderno 1, cuentas 1765–1768.

[53] AGI Filipinas 595 N. 1, cuaderno 4, cuentas 1784–1788, f. 8.

around 691,632 pesos in *correspondencias* for the Pacific trade. Similarly, by 1806, the legacy funds of the Third Order of Saint Francis held 502,411 pesos under management.[54] In short, the legacy funds absorbed the shocks of the transpacific trade, rebounding from the problems of 1752 and 1764, and expanded their accumulated capital over the course of the century.

This in turn increased the supply of working capital for trade. While their emergence can be attributed to innovation in the context of profound changes taking place between the 1640s and the 1670s, their expansion coincided with periods of booming trade activity as presented in Chapter 2. Two distinct phases emerged, with the foundation of legacy funds accelerating between the late 1680s and up to 1740, peaking in the 1730s.[55] This was the same boom in arrivals recorded in the

Table 3.1 Holdings of Obras Pías under the management of the Misericordia

Year	*Pesos*
1707	81,587
1708	94,247
1741	217,763
1752	194,577
1755	577,738
1764	250,093
1765	350,273
1766	363,066
1767	408,603
1768	455,200
1778	790,463
1783	1,037,449
1788	911,859
1793	947,372
1816	962,375

Sources AGI Filipinas 193, AGI Filipinas 303, AGI Filipinas 595, AGI Contaduría 1282, Mesquida, Juan, 'Pious Funds across the Pacific (1668–1823): Charitable Bequests or Credit Source?', *The Americas* 75, nº 4 (2018)

[54] AGI Filipinas 1034, 1806.

[55] Based on data gathered from APSR, AMN 553 MS 1662, Doc. 6 ff. 25–66, AUST Libros Tomo 20, *Consultas y sus Respuestas*, undated, Eighteenth Century, ff. 157–166, AGI Filipinas 1034, & Newberry Library Vault Ayer MS1349, *Report concerning the liquidation of obras pías formerly owned by the Jesuits in the Philippines,* 1797.

harbour, with an increasing number of ships arriving from India under the command of Indian and Armenian merchants, and the largest fleets of Chinese junks since the 1640s.[56] A period of relative stability followed between the 1740s and the 1760s, before a second sustained boom set up from the 1770s until 1800.[57] These two distinct phases (1690–1720 and 1770–1800) coincided with greater amounts of pesos being brought through the Pacific. The first period overlapped not only with the expansion of mining in Mexico, but also with the partial closure and rerouting of the Atlantic *flotas* due to the War of Spanish Succession and the brief invasion of Spain.[58] The second expansion followed the steps of the reform plans promoted by José de Gálvez in New Spain after the defeat of the Seven Years' War, which managed to more than double silver production in Spanish America between 1770 and 1808.[59] For Manila, the increased arrival of Spanish American pesos from the Pacific meant higher liquidity, and thus an increased capacity to pool capital through legacy funds. Given the importance of silver pesos for Asian trade, higher liquidity in Manila also implied an expansion of commercial activity in maritime Asia, and more liquidity to establish funds. A symbiotic cycle encompassing Manila, Asia, and America was at work, with expanded trade with America resulting in more capital pooled in Manila, and this in turn leading to more investment from Manila into the Asian and American trades and more specie circulating across maritime Asia.

The exact date of the end of the Manila trade system is unknown. The privilege of the Galleon trade itself was revoked by king Fernando VII in 1815,[60] although some vessels continued sailing to New Spain up to 1821, the year of Mexican independence.[61] Nevertheless, the investment model of *obras pías* must have died at some point before 1838, in which year the Misericordia petitioned the Governor of the Philippines become a premium insurance company.[62] The deathblow to this

[56] See Quiason, *English*, pp. 42–45, & Ruiz-Stovel, MIAT, 2021.

[57] Ruiz-Stovel, MIAT, 2021.

[58] Bonalian, *El Pacífico*, p. 229.

[59] TePaske, *A New World*, p. 113.

[60] Schurz, *The Manila*, p. 60.

[61] Cheong, 'The Decline of Manila', p. 153, Elizalde, 'El viraje', p. 172.

[62] AMN 700 Ms 2287, Doc. 47, *Informe de Pascual Enrile a consecuencia del expediente instruido por la petición de la Casa de la Misericordia de Manila de permiso para destinar*

model of trade finance was exogenous. Legacy funds never closed, but in 1808, the monetary standard of the peso broke down. This process, documented by Irigoin, resulted in several different coins of varying quality and content being minted in Spanish America, which in turn were rejected in China.[63] The peso was no longer a reliable coin, and subsequently the terms of trade changed. The trade disappeared gradually, as stocks of the pre-1808 pesos were transported out of Spanish America into Asia. The disappearance of the peso as an item of exchange resulted in structural changes to the trade, including the unstoppable rise of opium as an alternative good to penetrate Chinese markets, in which Manileños played a role and whose rise has already been linked to the progressive end of the peso trade.[64] Thus, the transpacific trade ended as the pillar in which the exchange rested, the Spanish American silver peso, disappeared, and the financial markets of Manila had to reorient their operations.

The financial history of the Misericordia offers a narrative of the evolution of the investment markets in Manila. A relative period of prosperity based on individual financing of the trade through *correspondencias* and the development of a welfare system that rested on *censos* ended abruptly by the seventeenth century. The response was a reorientation of investment towards trade that was achieved through the adaptation of legacy funds to invest directly in the Pacific exchange through *correspondencias*. This led to a new system of trade financing throughout the eighteenth century that marked the financial life of the city of Manila for as long as the peso trade remained in existence, from the 1680s to the late 1820s. Shifting the perspective to Manila provides a chronology that identifies the crises and changes that defined the Manila trade. This is the first step

de los fondos que tiene una cantidad para establecer una casa de seguros marítimos, 1838, ff. 254–260, according to Leoncio Cabrero, the obras pías also contributed capital to the establishment of the Banco Español Filipino de Isabel II in 1851, Cabrero, Leoncio, 'Las entidades económicas y financieras filipinas en el siglo XIX', *Revista Complutense de Historia de América*, 17 (1991), p. 197.

63 Irigoin, 'A Trojan', & Irigoin, 'The End', see also Irigoin, Alejandra, 'Gresham on Horseback: The Monetary Roots of Spanish American Political Fragmentation in the Nineteenth Century', *The Economic History Review* 62, n° 3 (August 2009): 551–575.

64 Irigoin, 'The End', pp. 237–238, Cheong, 'Trade and Finance', p. 38, see also Permanyer-Ugartemendia, Ander, 'Opium after the Manila Galleon: The Spanish involvment in the opium economy in East Asia (1815–1830)', *Investigaciones de Historia Económica - Economic History Research*, n° 10 (2014): 155–164.

to analyse how the financial model that emerged in Manila responded to challenges the city faced.

3.2 Organisations and Agents

Legacy Funds

Asian demand for specie represented a challenge for those willing to trade in the continent, for it meant that large amounts of liquidity needed to be pooled and shipped across the oceans. Joint-stock companies found a way to mitigate the problem of liquidity when it came to raising initial capital but did not manage to solve the issue of acquiring enough working capital consistently, especially since in the context of trade with Asia this involved a regular flow of silver specie. In Manila, legacy funds were the primary vehicle used to pool liquidity and supply working capital through *correspondencias*, solving liquidity constraints and providing regular access to cash to settle transactions.

Legacy funds were investment funds created through a deposition of money given by a founder. The deposit originated the fund, which had the purpose of financing whatever charitable deeds the founder considered pertinent for the salvation of their soul and was placed under the professionalised management of elected boards in confraternities, Third Orders, or other lay or clerical institutions.[65] Such legacy funds were common across the entire Hispanic world and were divided into many different types. A common one were *capellanías*, which could be founded with a cession of productive land which could be rented out and whose proceeds went to finance the ecclesiastical careers of a relative of the original founder.[66] Legacy funds usually invested in land through *censos* as the safest possible investments. Only in Manila did funds invest directly in long-distance trade by originating *correspondencias*, as documented in the previous section. These are the funds that are analysed in this section.

[65] APSR, Tomo 232, 1778, includes the process of opening a fund.

[66] Mesquida, Juan, 'La población de Manila y las capellanías de misas para españoles: Libro de registros, 1642–1672', *Revista de Indias* LXX, nº 249 (2010): 496–500, in Mexico: del Valle Pavón, Guillermina, 'Estrategias de inversión de los mercaderes de México: la fundación de capellanías a finales del siglo XVIII', *Investigaciones de Historia Económica*, 16 (2020): 30–43. A complete foundational document for a capellanía in Manila has survived in Escribano Miguel José Flores, 1792 [Legajo #24], ACCHS-CSIC, ff. 36A-37A.

Legacy funds appeared in Roman times, when paternalistic foundations created by rich members of the Roman elite provided subsidised credit as part of their patron-client networks.[67] The legal basis of Manila's legacy funds can be found in two Roman legal principles. The first was the *depositum*, essentially the deposition of something, including money, under the stewardship of another person who becomes contractually obliged to keep the thing and surrender it when requested by the owner.[68] The second was the *fideicomissum*. A simplified way of explaining the *fideicomissum* is to view it as a specific kind of deposit. The *fideicomissum* functioned similarly to English trusts: the founder would leave a deposit of money, property, or goods under the management of a *fideicommisarius*, a third party, for the benefit of a person named by the founder, called the *heres* (heir). The *fideicommisarius* had the obligation to manage this deposit until the beneficiary met certain requirements (often related to reaching adulthood), upon whose completion the property of the deposit was turned over to the beneficiary.[69]

Thus, legacy funds involved three parties, a beneficiary (*heres*), a founder, and a manager (*fideicommisarius*). The next section will analyse the managing agents in Manila. This section will explore the founders and beneficiaries of Manila's legacy funds. Legacy funds that originated *correspondencias* were opened with a cash endowment, always in pesos, that was transferred from the founder himself or their testamentary executor to the managing institution in which they wished to open their funds. Funds did not have a minimum cash requirement to be opened. Endowments varied from maximums of 50,000 pesos in the funds of Governor Manuel de León and Archbishop Fray Andrés González in the Misericordia,[70] to minimums of 300 pesos as those of the funds of priest Lucas de Souza and damsel Paula González in the VOT of Saint Dominic.[71]

[67] Andreau, Jean, *Banking and Business in the Roman World* (Cambridge: Cambridge University Press, 1999), p. 120.

[68] For the depositum, see Martínez Gijón, José, 'La comenda en el Derecho español. I. La comenda-depósito', *Anuario de Historia del Derecho Español* XXXVI (1966), pp. 38–42.

[69] D'Ors, Álvaro, *Derecho Privado Romano* (Pamplona: ENUSA, 1997), pp. 406–411.

[70] AMN 552 MS1662 Doc. 6, ca. 1790, ff. 26 & 29.

[71] APSR, Tomo 281, *Obra pía del bachiller Don Lucas de Souza*, & Tomo 232, *Obra pía de Paula González, doncella difunta*.

The identity of those that opened legacy funds varied widely. Among the first and most important founders were governors of the islands like the aforementioned Manuel de León or Fernando Valdez Tamón, who governed the Philippines between 1729 and 1739.[72] There were nobles like the Marquess of Salinas and the Marquess of Montecastro,[73] as well as noblewomen like the Countess of Lizárraga.[74] Clergymen and academics also opened funds: bishop Santiago Fernández, Aspostolic Vicar to Tunkin, left 5,000 pesos to the Dominican Third Order in 1775,[75] and Andrés González, bishop of Nueva Cáceres, left 50,000 pesos to the Misericordia in 1706,[76] while Doctor Luis de Beltrán Medrano opened a legacy fund in Manila in 1780.[77] Women also opened legacy funds. Of the 264 identified legacy funds, 43 belonged to women, as were the cases of damsel, Paula González,[78] and the two funds opened by María Balansao on behalf of her daughter, a nun named Clara de la Cruz.[79] Founders included foreigners. Prior to their expulsion, the Jesuits managed the funds of Joanes Zena and Juan de Santa Cruz Cachic, two Armenians residing in Manila.[80] Yet most of the funds belonged to lay citizens, including wealthy freighters like Francisco David,[81] Tomás de Endaya,[82] Domingo Antonio de Otero Bermúdez,[83] or Juan de Infante y Sotomayor.[84] Finally, there were some funds opened by unspecified associations of individuals and corporate funds, opened by an institution like the Archbishopric of Manila with profits earmarked for a specific purpose, as was the case of the *obra pía de los niños seises*, whose proceeds went to

[72] AMN 552 MS1662 Doc. 6, f. ca. 1790, 26 & APSR, Tomo 229, *Obra pía del Sr. Fernando Valdez Tamón*.

[73] AMN 552 MS1662 Doc. 6, ca. 1790, ff. 51–52.

[74] APSR Tomo 289.

[75] APSR Tomo 284.

[76] AMN 552 MS1662 Doc. 6, ca. 1790, ff. 29–30.

[77] APSR Tomo 226.

[78] APSR Tomo 232.

[79] APSR Tomo 274 & 275.

[80] Newberry Library, Vault Ayers MS 1349, 1797.

[81] APSR, Tomo 276.

[82] AMN 552 MS1662 Doc. 6, fol. 28.

[83] AMN 552 MS1662 Doc. 6, ff. 43–44.

[84] APSR, Tomo 228.

pay for the choirboys of the cathedral.[85] Essentially anyone could open a fund in Manila.

The Pacific exchange presented a good investment opportunity, and this attracted founders of legacy funds from outside the Hispanic Monarchy. Yuste has recorded that many Mexican merchants, like Francisco Echeveste and Francisco Carriedo y Peredo, opened legacy funds in Manila.[86] However, it is unlikely that *obras pías* were a strategy of Mexican wholesalers to provide their Manila agents with funds to finance their purchases as Yuste argues.[87] In fact, the Manila trade attracted individuals from regions further away than Mexico. In 1708 Sabino Mariani an Italian missionary of the entourage of cardinal Tournon, opened a legacy fund under the management of the Misericordia that was meant to pay dividends to Rome.[88] However, Spanish law prevented proceeds to be paid outside of the Monarchy, leading to a dispute that had to be intermediated by cardinal Acquaviva, the Spanish representative in Rome, and ended with the eventual closure of the fund.[89] But this was not the only case. In the closing decades of the seventeenth century, the Duchess of Aveiro gave the Jesuits a large endowment of money to finance the evangelisation of the Mariana islands.[90] This endowment was most likely made into *correspondencia* funds for investment in the trade, and corresponds to the *Obras pías de las Marianas* that appear in the notarial protocols as an issuer of *correspondencias* in the late eighteenth century.[91] In another example, the French Jesuit mission of Madura in India attempted to place 20,000 pesos of their funds under the management of the Misericordia to invest in *censos* in 1735. The Misericordia declined the proposal alleging that it could not place such investment.[92]

[85] Escribano Baltasar Javier Sánchez, 1741 [Legajo #2], ACCHS-CSIC, ff. 106a-106b.

[86] Yuste, *Emporios*, pp. 95–96.

[87] The criticism of Yuste's characterisation of Manileños as agents of Mexican merchants is developed in detail in Chapter 4.

[88] AGI Filipinas 149 N. 2, *Carta de Valdés Tamón sobre depósitos de Sabino Mariani*, 1737.

[89] AGI Filipinas 149 N. 2.

[90] Newberry Library, Vault Ayers 1398, *Letters Manila, to the Duquesa de Aveyro Arcos y Maqueda*, 3 July, 16 August, 12 December 1698.

[91] Escribano Miguel José Flores, 1795 [Legajo #26], ACCHS-CSIC, ff. 25a-26a.

[92] AGI Filipinas 96, N. 7, *Consulta sobre censo para jesuitas franceses de la India Oriental*, 1735.

The fact that the Misericordia should refuse this scheme points to the affluence of liquidity in the city and confirms the notion that the problem of Manila was to find enough investment options given the Dutch Disease that afflicted the islands. More importantly, it reveals that actors outside of the Manila market, from Rome to Mexico and Madura, were aware of the financial institutions of the city, and considered it to be a viable investment option.

The varied cast of individuals that opened funds demonstrate the easy availability of savings in cash that existed in Manila, as well as the need to find an appropriate investment opportunity given the lack of options in the land. It also shows the extent to which participation was open to anyone, including outsiders to the transpacific trade, which signals that this was an impersonal market capable of fostering impersonal cooperation like the joint-stock East India companies did.[93] The question then becomes what motivated citizens of Manila, beyond pious regards for their souls, to open *correspondencia* funds. Legacy funds not only had a charitable and religious aspect, but they were also vehicles for making profit. There is little evidence that legacy funds paid dividends directly to their owners, but establishing a fund in a brotherhood must have offered access to the pooled capital of lay confraternities.

In fact, that there was a significant overlap between managers of legacy funds, members of brotherhoods, and those that received *correspondencias* in the capital market. This overlap was not only across roles (i.e. someone may open a fund, sit in the board of the *obras pías*, and request *correspondencias* from the same brotherhood), but also across organisations. Thus, the Marquess of Montecastro in the eighteenth century, owned funds in the Misericordia and the Third Order of Saint Francis, was a member of the board of the Misericordia, freighted in the Galleon, and issued *correspondencias* as much as he requested them,[94] which could lead to conflicts of interest. This conflict is addressed in Chapters 4 and 5, but it is important to notice here that legacy funds were not a direct source of wealth for their founders and did not pay dividends directly to their pockets. Instead, they buttressed someone's social position in the economic and social fabric of Manila, offered access to the capital pooled

[93] Harris, *Going*, p. 4 & pp. 312–313.

[94] AMN 552 MS1662 Doc. 6, ff. 51 & 54, AFIO 530/9, Escribano Domingo Cortés de Arquiza, 1755 [Legajo #5], ACCHS-CSIC, ff. 145a-145b,

by the legacy funds, and through the boards of managers, granted influence in the taking of decisions that were fundamental for the trade, such as the annual premium rates for each trading destination, as will be seen later.

Regarding the beneficiaries, legacy funds differed from trusts in that the latter tended to be dissolved once the requisites that the beneficiary needed to accomplish were met. In Manila however, *correspondencia* legacy funds usually had no specific beneficiary but a long list of charitable activities that needed financing. Rarely did funds specify that the proceeds of their investment were to be granted to relatives or specific individuals. Most commonly they went to finance hospitals, monasteries, festivals, masses, scholarships for students as well as missionary efforts in China, Vietnam, Cambodia, and Siam. The beneficiary was therefore an abstract, non-physical entity that could never meet the requirement for the fund to be redeemed. This can be seen in a judicial sentence issued by Fr. José Torrubia in 1753 regarding the embezzlement of money from some funds destined to the dowries of women in Manila.[95] Fr. Torrubia recognised the impossibility to both identify those that had been wronged during the period, as well as to calculate how much money would have accrued to them, and therefore the total extent of the damage they had incurred.[96] The result of all of this was that unlike trusts but similarly to *waqf s*, legacy funds had no end date.

Legacy funds were not donations, they remained the property of the immortal soul of their founders, which meant that the foundational wills were legally binding.[97] Nevertheless, the management of legacy funds was professionalised, and the wills of the founders could be legally overruled in specific instances, giving legacy funds a greater flexibility than the *waqf*.[98] The casuistic approach of Canon Law meant that the wills

[95] Torrubia was also the author of a monograph on the Philippine islands that described the Misericordia as a communal "montepío" of the city of Manila, Torrubia, Fr. Joseph, *Disertación Histórico-Política, y en mucha parte Geográfica, de las Islas Philipinas*, Madrid, 1753.

[96] BNE, MSS/11014 (H.449R.-452V.), *Informe de la Mesa de la Misericordia*, undated (early 1700).

[97] See, for example, AGI Filipinas 291, N. 33, *Expediente sobre dar a riesgo los principales redimidos de capellanías*, 1739, in which the authorities discuss the capacity of overruling the wills of the founders to turn *censos* funds into *correspondencia* funds.

[98] On the *waqf*, see Kuran, Timur, 'The absence of the Corporation in Islamic Law: Origins and Persistence', *The American Journal of Comparative Law* 53, n° 4 (2005):

of the donors were judged against the real circumstances of the time. Canon Law jurists had recourse to the principle of *epikeia* to help them take managerial decisions. *Epikeia* is an Aristotelian principle according to which a law could be broken or bypassed if enacting it would have been damaging, or if a greater good that respected the spirit of the law could be achieved through alternative means.[99] *Epikeia* and casuistry allowed for legal flexibility and enabled the administrators of funds to adapt to changing conditions.

Legacy funds were well suited to channel liquidity to the trade by providing an institutional vehicle that transformed savings into working capital through *correspondencias*. They offered investment opportunities given their lack in the local landed economy along with professional management. The legacy funds allowed individuals to participate in the profits of the trade and solved the problem of long waiting times before the gains of trade could be realised and locked-in capital that joint-stocks' tradable shares came to mitigate.[100] Because legacy funds effectively pooled capital perennially, long-waiting time until the realisation of profits became unimportant for individual traders. Legacy funds and the institutions that managed them provided access to working capital upfront whenever it was needed.

Fund Managers: Brotherhoods, Third Orders, and the Misericordia

Whoever had money saved and wished to finance charity in Manila had the option to open a legacy fund and place it under the management of any institution or organisation they deemed appropriate. The bulk of the legacy funds were managed by brotherhoods and Third Orders, but they

785–834, Kuran, Timur, 'Why the Middle East is Economically Underdeveloped: Historical Mechanisms of Institutional Stagnation', *Journal of Economic Perspectives* 18, nº 3 (2004): 71–90, Kuran, Timur, 'The Islamic Commercial Crisis: Institutional Roots of Economic Underdevelopment in the Middle East', *The Journal of Economic History* 63, 2 (2003): 414–446. For a later survey of the Ottoman cash *waqf*, see Karagedikli, Gürer, & Tunçer, Ali Coşkun, 'Microcredit in the Ottoman Empire: A Review of Cash Waqfs in Transition to Modern Banking', in *Financing in Europe*, ed. M. Lorenzini., C. Lorandini, and D. Coffman (London: Palgrave Macmillan, 2018): 239–268.

99 St. Thomas Aquinas, *Summa Theologica*, Part 2, Treatise on the Cardinal Virtues, Q 120, translated by the Fathers of the English Dominican Province, New York: Bezinger Bros. (1947), pp. 2267–2268.

100 Gelderblom and Jonker, 'Completing', pp. 648 & 653.

were not the only trustees charged with administering the legacies. The *Colegio de Santa Potenciana*, a school for orphaned girls owned by the Misericordia, managed two funds directly.[101] The Hospital of San Juan, the archbishopric, and even the town hall of Manila (*cabildo*) managed their own legacy funds.[102] The largest managers were the Brotherhood of the Misericordia, the Jesuit Order, and the Third Orders of Saint Francis and Saint Dominic. Yet there was a profusion of smaller brotherhoods and confraternities that appear as investors in the trade, such as the *Cofradía del Santo Sepulcro*, from the Manila suburb of Binondo, or the *Cofradía de Jesús Nazareno*.[103] In time, other capital pooling institutions that did not necessarily manage legacy funds but that had corporate identity and originated *correspondencias* in the capital market of the city emerged, as the *Montepío Político y de Hacienda* and the mutual fund of the *Príncipe* regiment both appearing in the last quarter of the eighteenth century.[104] There was ample freedom to establish both *correspondencia* legacy funds and fund-managing organisations.

Most of these fund managers were lay organisations who in turn managed a portfolio of legacy funds. The Brotherhood of the Misericordia, from its Italian and Portuguese medieval origins, was an association for lay members, and so were all confraternities and brotherhoods. Tertiary or Third Orders were composed of the laymen and laywomen of a Religious Order, as opposed to the First Order (monks) and the Second Order (nuns). Membership into a Third Order or Brotherhood was regulated by the constitution of each organisation, and thus varied across them, although it seems to have been both relatively open and to have composed a large segment of the population of Manila. The list of brothers that joined the Order of Saint Dominic between 1697 and 1818 has survived. This list is composed of a total of 1,070 members, 422 men

[101] AFIO 530/9, *Estado de los fondos de las dos únicas obras pías de Sta. Potenciana*, 1834.

[102] Carriedo left two legacy funds to the *cabildo* for the purpose of providing sewage to Manila, de Mas y Oztet, Francisco, *Carriedo y sus obras* (Manila: Ramírez & Giraudier, 1882), gathered from notarial protocols, see ACCHS-CSIC section in Bibliography.

[103] Escribano Miguel José Flores, 1789 [Legajo #21A], ACCHS-CSIC, ff. 117b-118b, & Escribano Baltasar Javier Sánchez de Cuenta, 1758 [Legajo #4], ACCHS-CSIC, ff. 97–98.

[104] Escribano Miguel José Flores, 1792 [Legajo #24], ACCHS-CSIC, ff. 34b-35b, & Escribano Miguel José Flores, 1795 [Legajo #26], ACCHS-CSIC, ff. 178b-179b.

and 648 women.[105] Third Orders do not seem to have enforced exclusion based on race or nationality, as evidenced by surnames such as Wilson or Qiambao among its members. In fact, race was sometimes recorded among female members from 1780 onwards showing that, of the 139 women whose race is recorded, 80 (57%) were Spanish, while 59 (43%) of them were either native (26 individuals), mestizas (29, including mixed-Portuguese parentage), Chinese (1), and even African (1).[106] Among the men, race was never recorded. Most importantly, members of the Third Order received indirect benefits from the legacy funds, including the payment of funerals or almsgiving, which explains the large membership.[107] Brotherhoods and Third Orders were religious in that they were recognised as the lay part of the Catholic Church—as opposed to the clergy—their social purpose was ostensibly charitable and devotional, and they were usually attached to a broader order and a chapel or convent where the membership met, prayed, marked religious festivities, and kept their records and money.

The governance of brotherhoods and Third Orders was complex. Brotherhoods had their own statutes that regulated conflicts within the organisation, but as religious institutions, they were under the jurisdiction of the local bishop. The only exception to this rule, as mentioned previously, was the Misericordia, which managed to obtain royal patronage in 1733. The relationship between the lay Third Order and the regular First Order differed. Among the Franciscans, Third Orders existed in Manila, Dilao, Sampaloc, and Binondo, and managed their own funds independently, with little connection to the first order.[108] The Dominican Third Orders of Manila and Cavite were clearly distinct from each other as well as from the funds managed by the Regular Province, but they were more integrated amongst themselves and all the funds were unified in 1799 under the management of the Third Order of Manila.[109] Regardless of their level of coordination, all Third Orders were ultimately supervised

[105] APSR, Tomo 194, *Orden Tercera. Lista de terciarios*, 1697–1818.

[106] APSR, Tomo 194.

[107] These were the dispositions of the 1735 legacy fund of Francisco Echeveste, founded with the VOT of Saint Dominic, APSR, Tomo 304a, *Obra Antigua del General Francisco de Echeveste*, 1735.

[108] The different confraternities invested separately as per 1789, 1792, 1795 [Legajos #21A, #24, #26] ACCHS-CSIC.

[109] APSR. Tomo 282, 284.

and regulated by the head of the Province in the Philippines, called the *prior provincial*, who inspected and approved the accounts of the Third Orders. In the ecclesiastical division of territory, all regions in which a religious order was present represented a province (*provincia*) with defined borders that encompassed First, Second, and Third Orders.

The day-to-day activities of brotherhoods and Third Orders, including the management of the legacy funds, were done by an elected board of members called *mesa* (lit. trans. "table", meaning board). The election process of *mesas* was stipulated in the statutes of each organisation, but most of them were elected among the members annually through a vote.[110] *Mesas* had discretionary powers to administer the funds of the brotherhood or Third Order they managed but had to follow the statutes and important decisions had to be put down to a vote amongst members. Regarding the management of funds, the *mesas* had to obey the foundational wills, which often stated the initial capital of the fund, the amount of capital the fund had to reach before paying out its charity,[111] how the money was to be invested in each leg of the Manila trade, and how to spend the proceeds.[112] However, the *mesas* still had ample room for management. Even though they were required to follow these foundational instructions as closely as possible, *epikeia* allowed them to divert from the instructions in justified circumstances. Instructions also did not specify details regarding who to give *correspondencias* to or how much money to invest. *Mesas* administered the whole process of originating *correspondencias* and decided which requests to accept. In Manila, the process to issue a *correspondencia* is represented in Fig. 3.1: a *principal* (the applicant) with his joint-guarantors would approach a *mesa* (as giver or *otorgante*) and ask for money in *correspondencia* for a specific destination. The *mesas* would then review the request and accept it or reject it. If the request was accepted, the *mesas* decided how much to invest and from which funds the money should come. Usually, the cash for a *correspondencia* was gathered from several funds.[113] Upon the expiration of the *correspondencia*, the *principal* or his guarantors would repay the

110 Díaz-Trechuelo, 'Religiosidad popular', pp. 349–351 describes the election process of the Misericordia.

111 This practice can be seen in the account books (APSR) and is mentioned in some foundational documents (AMN 533 MS1662 Doc. 6).

112 AMN 553 Ms 1226, Doc. 6., ca. 1790., ff. 25–66.

113 AGI Filipinas 303 N. 6., 1752.

money. If the *principal* failed to repay, his guarantors could pay the *correspondencia* and its premium, in which case they could ask the *mesa* to expedite them a *carta de lasto*, a notarised document that verified that the guarantors had repaid the amounts owed, and thus entitled them to seek judicial satisfaction from the *principal* if necessary.[114] This whole process, except the granting of *correspondencias* and the expeditions of *cartas de lasto*, was private and was not notarised, instead, *mesas* recorded the process in the institutions' *Libro de Acuerdos* (Minutes Book).[115]

Mesas were also responsible for keeping the accounts of legacy funds. Each fund had an accountant tasked with crafting the books in which all the annual transactions were recorded, while the *mesa* had its own separate accounts for the whole Third Order.[116] Accounts were submitted

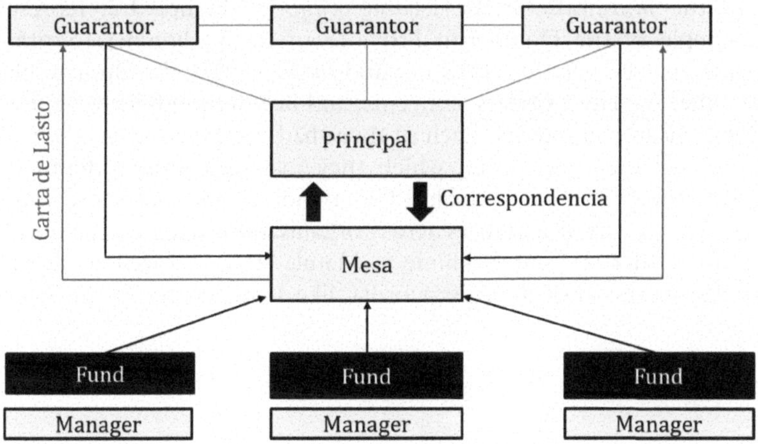

Fig. 3.1 The contractual process of correspondencias (*Source* Own creation from information gathered from the notarial protocols [see Bibliography ACCHS-CSIC section] and references in the account books of the legacy funds [APSR section])

114 An example can be found in Escribano Baltasar Javier Sánchez de Cuenca, 1752 [Legajo #3] ACCHS-CSIC, ff. 13b-15a.

115 Cross-references to the *Libro de Acuerdos* can be found in many account books. See APSR section in Bibliography.

116 APSR Tomo 213, *Libro de Cuentas de los Apoderados de la VOT de Santo Domingo*, 1784–1804.

to the *prior provincial* for supervision. Third Orders also had to accept the visit of the archbishop of Manila, and like the Misericordia, they all resented it.[117] It was not until the 1780s that the archbishops managed to establish their authority over the brotherhoods and religious orders, following changes that were taking place across the empire.[118] The Misericordia, however, successfully resisted episcopal control and placed itself under royal patronage, as seen previously. *Mesas*, in any case, remained as the main governing bodies and interlocutors with the overall hierarchies. In exchange for all of this, many legacy funds dictated that the *mesas* would receive a remuneration from the net profits of the funds each season, often standing at 5.25%.[119]

Thus, the overall governance structure of brotherhoods was hierarchical, and resembled more a corporate structure than the personalist role of the *mutawalli* in the Islamic *waqf*.[120] Figure 3.2. represents the example of the Dominican Province of the Philippines (*Santísimo Rosario*). As seen here, the Province and its *prior* were the ultimate heads of the different Third Orders, convents, and brotherhoods associated with the Dominican community. Each of them had their own *mesa*, their own statutes, and their own fund, which they managed independently, and each had their own membership. This is not to say that there was no substantial overlap of members across organisations. In fact, members of the Third Order of Saint Dominic in Manila appear as well as members of the Brotherhood of the Misericordia, like Juan Infante de Sotomayor,

[117] They argued that this would let the archbishop confiscate their property, but there was not much evidence that any archbishop of Manila confiscated property from the Third Orders and the Brotherhoods. Newberry Library, Vault Ayers MS1331, *Deffensa canónica por las Sagradas Religiones sobre la vista que intentó y en parte executó el Ilmo. Sor. D. Diego Camacho, arzobispo de Manila*, ca. 1698, AFIO 101/14, *Copia de un Informe del Arzobispo de Manila, Juan, elevado al Rey, acerca de las Obras Pías que administra la VOT de Manila*, 1806. A good summary of the controversy up to the start of the eighteenth century is presented in Coello de la Rosa, Alexandre, 'Los conflictos jurisdiccionales entre los arzobispos de Manila y los jesuitas por las doctrinas de indios (siglos XVI-XVIII)', *Boletín Americanista* LXIII, nº 67 (2013): 105–124.

[118] Álvarez-Dardet Espejo, López Manjón, and Baños Sánchez-Matamoros, 'Accounting', pp. 135–142.

[119] AMN 553 MS 1662 Doc. 6. Ca. 1790, ff. 25–66.

[120] Kuran, 'Why the Middle East', p. 75.

who was a member of the Third Order of Saint Dominic, acted as accountant for some of their funds, opened one himself in 1760,[121] and was a member of the *mesa* of the Misericordia in 1755,[122] or the case of the Marquess of Montecastro mentioned previously. What seems to have been the norm was for brotherhoods and Third Orders to elect the wealthiest amongst their members to the board, which often tended to be seasoned merchants.[123] This may have been the result of unobservable clientelism at work, but to all effects it guaranteed that the savings pooled by a multitude of individuals in the form of legacy funds were administered and invested by those members that had the most expertise on the trade. Most importantly, professionalisation was instrumental in overcoming information asymmetries for potential investors that were outsiders to the Manila trade.

A fundamental aspect of these organisations was their social dimension, both as a network of *vecinos* (citizens of Manila) and as a source of public welfare. Brotherhood and Third Orders are best described as

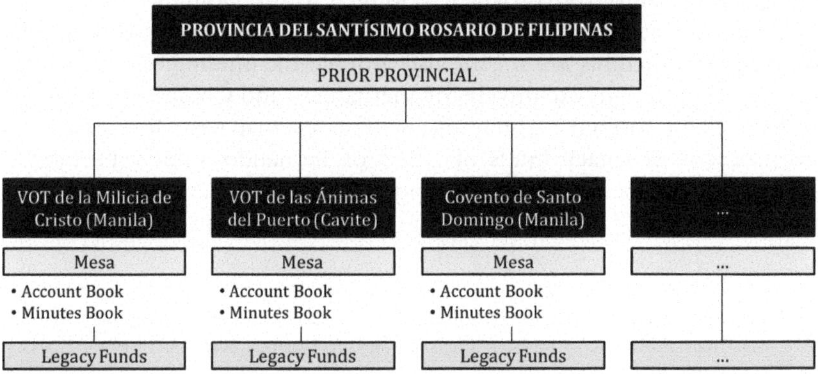

Fig. 3.2 Governance structure of the Dominican Province of the Philippines (*Source* Own creation from APSR (see Bibliography) and issuance of correspondencias from the notarial protocols [ACCHS-CSIC])

121 APSR Tomo 228, *Obra pía fundada por el Gral. Don Juan Infante de Sotomayor*.

122 AGI Filipinas 199 N. 3, *Expediente sobre préstamos de la casa de la Misericordia*, 1756, f. 4.

123 There was a clear parallel in this regard with the Misericórdia of Macao, Guedes Cosme, 'Elites', p. 174.

urban organisations that essentially created networks of social care and help among its members.[124] The literature has noted the role of brotherhoods and religious orders in structuring the financial markets in the Hispanic world,[125] but only in Manila did these institutions develop such a direct link with the financing of intercontinental trade. The legacy funds of Manila pooled money, provided access to capital, and financed the welfare of the city through their proceeds. At the same time, they provided expert and transparent management through the *mesas*.

The social network of brotherhoods and Third Orders is visible in how the profits of legacy funds were redistributed. While there is no distinctive connection among the 23 founders of legacy funds in the Third Order of Saint Dominic by gender, profession, or geographical origin, the proceeds of their funds were destined to fund the different needs of the Order. Thus, Santiago Fernández, Vicar to Eastern Tunkin, mandated that the profits of his legacy fund be given to the next Apostolic Vicar to the region "*as long as he is a Spaniard of the habit of Saint Dominic*".[126] Professor Medrano created scholarships for his descendants to attend the University of Santo Tomás, which belonged to the Dominican Order.[127] Juan Bautista de Uriarte, who had been a secretary of the Misericordia when he published his *Manifiesto*, also ordered the funding of scholarships for Santo Tomás, but exclusively for Vietnamese and Chinese students,[128] students likely formed in Dominican missions that were financed from the proceeds of legacy funds like that of Fernando Valdez Tamón.[129] Others, like Maria Ezpeleta, left money for hospitals and health houses managed by friars,[130] while Echeveste opened one of his funds to pay for

[124] Terpstra, Nicholas, Prosperi, Adriano, and Pastore, Stefania (editors), *Faith's Boundaries: Laity and Clergy in Early Modern Confraternities*, (Turnhout: Brepols, 2012).

[125] See Milhaud, Cyril, 'Interregional Flows of Capital and Information in Spain: A Case Study of the Theresian Carmelite Order', *Revista de Historia Económica* 37, nº 1 (2018): 81–110, Lavrín, 'El Capital Eclesiástico', Del Valle Pavón, Guillermina, 'Las funciones crediticias de las cofradías y los negocios de los mercaderes del Consulado de la ciudad de México, fines del siglo XVIII y principios del siglo XIX', *Revista de Indias* LXXIV, nº 261 (2014): 507–538, Irigoin and Grafe, 'Bounded', pp. 220–221.

[126] APSR, Tomo 284, fol. 2a.

[127] APSR, Tomo 226, ff. 1–3.

[128] APSR, Tomo 282, fol. 1.

[129] APSR, Tomo 229, fol. 1.

[130] APSR, Tomos 233, 235, 236, 237.

the funeral of members of the Third Order.[131] Most of the funds paid for the maintenance of priests, masses, candles, and the expenses of festivities like the day of the Virgin of the Rosary, strongly associated with the founder of the Dominican Order, Santo Domingo de Guzmán. It is thus undoubtable that opening legacy funds was a decision that also sought to benefit the community. But the "community" was broad, and funds, although barred from paying proceeds to other kingdoms outside the Hispanic Monarchy except for missionary purposes, could pay proceeds over vast distances. Thus, the fund of Domingo Antonio de Bermúdez in the Misericordia was instructed to finance the upkeep of the church of San Miguel in Duxerme, in his native region of Galicia.[132]

The relevance of Third Orders, brotherhoods, and the Misericordia was that they provided an institutional framework that expanded beyond family links and enabled capital pooling. They combined social functions and religious piety with investment and management, and in doing so they provided a way to channel the savings of the Manileños to the trade by administering and monitoring the legacy funds. They established an institutional framework to channel savings beyond the immediate family and friends' network into the trade through legacy funds, and their management of these funds provided assurance to founders of legacy funds and guaranteed the monitoring of investments and the redistribution of proceeds.[133] Thus, they were fundamental in creating an impersonal market in which individuals of very different backgrounds, like damsel Paula González, Armenian merchant Juan de Santa Cruz Cachic, Professor Medrano, and freighter and Manila town councillor Domingo Antonio de Otero Bermúdez, could pool their cash and participate in the transpacific trade, either while alive or after death, for their temporal benefit or that of their soul.

[131] APSR, Tomo 304, ff. 1–4.

[132] AMN 552 MS1662, Doc. 6, ca. 1790, f. 44a.

[133] This will be explored in detail in Chapter 5.

3.3 Instruments and Contracts

Censos

The most common instrument used to lend in the Hispanic world were *censos*.[134] *Censos* were essentially a credit instrument in which a creditor (*censualista*) offered a loan to the debtor (*censatario*) at a fixed interest rate. This loan was commonly attached to a property or a good whose usufruct was enjoyed by the debtor, and upon which he paid interests annually.[135] This instrument was common across the entire Hispanic world. *Censos* on agricultural and productive enterprises were fundamental in providing credit in both the American and peninsular economies, and the scale of the *censos* market was large. In early nineteenth-century Mexico, the bishop of Michoacán Abad y Queipo estimated that a total of 44.5 million pesos (about two-thirds of total invested capital in all of Mexico) were invested in *censos*, while the council of the city of Mexico calculated the sum to be 50 million, and Antonio José Arrangoiz elevated it to 60 million.[136] For Perú, Quiroz conservatively estimated that about 15 million pesos were invested in long-term credit contracts, most likely *censos*, in 1806 (about one-third of all the currency in circulation).[137] Spain also relied greatly on the credit provided by *censos*. The cadastre ordered by the Marquess of Ensenada in 1749 reveals a total between 158 to 191 million pesos invested in *censos* for the 22 provinces that comprised Castile, of which 73% belonged to ecclesiastical institutions.[138] This represented a sum greater than the agricultural production of the said provinces.[139]

[134] Ena Sanjuan, 'The imperceptible financial'.

[135] Von Wobeser, 'Las fundaciones', p. 785.

[136] Hamnett, Brian R., 'The Appropriation of Mexican Church Wealth by the Spanish Bourbon Government. The 'Consolidación de Vales Reales', 1805–1809', *Journal of Latin American Studies* 1, n° 2 (1969), p. 87.

[137] Quiroz, Alfonso W. 'Reassessing the Role of Credit in Late Colonial Peru: Censos, Escrituras, and Imposiciones', *The Hispanic American Historical Review* 74, n° 2 (1994), p. 199.

[138] Maté, Lorenzo, Prieto, Begoña, and Tua Pereda, Jorge, 'La Actividad financiera del monasterio de Silos en el siglo XVIII a la luz de sus Libros de Cuentas', *De Computis*, 1 (2004), pp. 104–106.

[139] Maté, Prieto, and Tua Pereda, 'La Actividad', p. 105.

There was an important difference in the scale in which *censos* were used in the Philippines compared to America and Spain. No study exists in which *censos* as a total of the existing economy has been indexed and compared to other regions of the Spanish empire, but the remaining notarial protocols from 1740 to 1800 reveals only 29 surviving *censo* contracts as opposed to 541 surviving *correspondencia* contracts. The difference in scale is also evident in the portfolio of the Misericordia. In 1806 the Misericordia managed 39 *censos* funds worth a total of 70,890 pesos.[140] In comparison, in 1816 the Misericordia managed 58 *correspondencia* funds with a total of 962,375 pesos under management.[141] The largest *correspondencia* fund in 1816, the *obra pía* of Echeveste, had 99,903 pesos under management, more than all the money placed in *censos*. Undoubtedly the use of *censos* in the Philippines was not as extensive as in America or the peninsula.

Two reasons can explain why *censos* in Manila were not as common as in the rest of the Hispanic world. The first reason is the opportunity cost for those that sought to establish funds, and it was the result of the Dutch Disease that Manila suffered as discussed in Chapter 2. Given that foodstuffs, semi-finished, and finished goods could be purchased far cheaper from Indian and Chinese merchants, it was impossible to develop a productive agricultural sector in which money could have been invested through *censos*. Legacy funds that operated on *censos* needed to impose the principals on properties, yet investment options on the local economy were scarce. Equally important was the large abundance of liquidity in Manila from the Pacific trade. Managers of *censos* found themselves in a position in which they had too much money to invest, and little properties to invest it on. As a result, in 1739 the Archbishop of Manila and the Misericordia petitioned the king as patron of the Church in the Indies, requesting that the redeemed principal of *censos* be invested on the trade through *correspondencias*.[142] They argued that diverging the money into *correspondencias* fitted better the wills of the original founders than maintaining the capital inactive, since this would have meant that the charity that the legacies were to finance for the salvation of the founders' souls

[140] AFIO 52/16, *Obras pías a censo y capellanías de la Misericordia*, 1806.

[141] AFIO 52/9, *Balance del caudal de las obras pías de la Misericordia*, 1817.

[142] AGI Filipinas 291, N. 33, *Expediente sobre dar a riesgo los principales redimidos de capellanías*, 1739.

would go unfulfilled, and that *correspondencia* funds and the trade they financed were a safe enough investment to meet the necessary conditions required for the investment of legacies.[143] In fact, four *correspondencia* funds managed by the *Junta de Temporalidades* after the expulsion of the Jesuits were *censo* funds transformed into *correspondencia* funds in 1775.[144] There were more savings searching for investment options than there were properties, urban or agricultural, to invest on, to the extent that even existing *censos* funds had to be converted into *correspondencia* funds.

The second reason why *censos* were not used as profusely in the Philippines was related to the business model of the Pacific trade and the relationship between the proceeds of the trade and the welfare paid out by the legacy funds. At a maximum rate of 5%, using *censos* to finance the trade would not have produced enough returns to increase the initial endowment of the funds and distribute welfare unless the volume of the trade expanded accordingly so that this 5% would represent a return in scale. However, Manileños capped the volume of the transpacific trade to the annual Galleon between Manila and Acapulco. As will be explained in Chapter 4, the market structure of the Pacific exchange favoured a strategy of expanding profit margins instead of scale. Given the limited volume of the exchange, *censos* simply could not capture enough of the profits from the trade to provide for the needs of the community as effectively as *correspondencias* could.

Correspondencias a riesgo de mar

Correspondencias a riesgo de mar were the local Manila iteration of the sea loan. The origin of sea loans goes back to Ancient Greece and the Roman *fœnus nauticum* recorded in the Justinian Code,[145] and they were used widely during the Italian Commercial Revolution of the twelfth century.[146] The principle behind a sea loan was that an investor would give a certain amount of money to a merchant to finance the operation

[143] AGI Filipinas 291, N. 33, ff. 6A-9B.

[144] Newberry Library, Vault Ayer MS 1349, 1797.

[145] Bernal, *La financiación*, p. 27.

[146] De Roover, Raymond, 'The Organization of Trade', in *The Cambridge Economic History of Europe from the Decline of the Roman Empire*, ed. M.M. Postan, Edwin E. Rich, and Edward Miller, vol. 3 (Cambridge: Cambridge University Press, 1963), Hoover,

of trade. The merchant would take this money, purchase merchandise, and freight it to a destination for sale. Upon return, the merchant would repay the investor the principal of money and a premium that was specified as a percentage of the principal. This would only be repaid upon the successful return of the proceeds of the sale, meaning that the investor that gave the money also assumed the risk of loss at sea.[147] If the loss was only partial, usually investor and merchant would share equally whatever could be salvaged.[148] Sea loans were common across all of Europe. In France they were known as *prêt a la grosse aventure*,[149] and in Spain they were called *préstamos a la gruesa*.[150] In the English world two variants were known. Bottomry loans were common, and they provided capital on the security of the hull and the rigging of the ship.[151] Another variation was the respondentia, less utilised in Britain but common in Portuguese maritime trade,[152] which covered the cargo instead of the hull of the ship. *Correspondencias* belonged to this category of sea loan.

Respondentias were used in many different contexts, also coexisting with joint-stock financing. At times the Court of Directors in London would give money in respondentia to agents, officials, or ship captains making the voyage to the East with the proceeds to be repaid in cash

Calvin B., 'The Sea Loan in Genoa in the Twelfth Century', *The Quarterly Journal of Economics* 40, n° 3 (May 1926): 495–529.

147 Ravina Martín, Manuel, 'Riesgos marítimos en la Carrera de Indias', *Documentación y Archivos de la colonización española* (1989), p. 108.

148 Bernal, *La financiación*, p. 48.

149 Carrière, Charles, 'Renouveau espagnol et prêt a la grosse aventure (Notes sur la place de Cadix dans la seconde moitié du XVIIIe siècle', *Revue d'histoire moderne et contemporaine*, T. 17e, n° 2 (1970), pp. 231.

150 Ravina, 'Riesgos Marítimos', p. 107.

151 Bernal, *La financiación*, p. 33.

152 Park, Sir James Allan, *A System of the Law of Marine Insurances*, vol. III, London (1809), pp. 552–569. Park clearly related the *respondentia* to Portuguese trade. Boyajian uses the term *respondência* referring to the Macao-Nagasaki trade of the seventeenth century, while dos Guimarães Sá uses the term *ganhos* or *riscos de mar* for the eighteenth century respondentias of the Misericórdia of Macao, see Boyajian, James C., *Portuguese Trade in Asia under the Habsburgs, 1580–1640* (Baltimore: The John Hopkins University Press, 1993), pp. 234–235, dos Guimarães Sá, 'Riscos da Terra', p. 48. In his treatise in 1806 written in Lisbon, José de Silva used *risco* and *grossa aventura* (parallel with the Spanish *riesgo marítimo* and *préstamo a la gruesa ventura*), de Silva, José, *Principios de direito mercantil*, Lisbon, 1806.

in some far-off port.[153] Country traders in Madras and other parts of English India contracted respondentias with Portuguese or Armenian merchants that sailed to Manila during the eighteenth century,[154] and similar contracts existed to finance maritime trade in Japan.[155] They were the primary instrument to finance Spanish trade, both in the Atlantic and the Pacific. Regardless of whether they were used by the EIC, the Misericordia of Macao, or Spanish traders in the *flotas*, respondentias were instruments based primarily on the flows of silver specie. They relied on the provision of cash to operate trading activities and the returns were always paid in cash. Similarly, according to Irigoin, they hedged against currency risk by specifying the currency in which premia and principals were to be repaid, which made them ideal instruments for long-distance trade.[156] Thus they provided a contractual association for the movement of silver specie across the globe.

The sea loan has usually been understood as a credit cum insurance instrument in which a lender gave a principal of money to a debtor, to be repaid with interest on condition that the investment returned safely to port.[157] The traditional view asserts that this insurance facet allowed sea loans to charge high interests.[158] Sea loans from Cádiz or Seville to ports

[153] IOR/E/1/30, *Miscellaneous Letters received,* 1741, ff. 58–59, 77–78, 84–85, 86–93, 147–150, 171–172, 179–180, 204–206, 241–242, 397–398, 517–518, 520–521, 526–529, 532–535, 542–543, 546–547, & 550–551.

[154] Quiason, *English*, p. 84.

[155] See Oka, Mihoko, and Gipoloux, François, 'Pooling Capital and Spreading Risk: Maritime Investment in East Asia at the Beginning of the Seventeenth Century', *Itinerario* XXXV, n° 3 (2013): 75–91.

[156] Alejandra Irigoin, '"De las contratas del dinero" instruments for trade finance in the Early Modern global economy' (presentation, World Economic History Congress, Paris, France, July 25–29, 2022).

[157] Bernal, *La financiación*, p. 28, Herrero Gil, María Dolores, '¿De la confusión a la negación? Reflexiones sobre la utilidad aseguradora del contrato de riesgo', *Espacio, Tiempo y Forma*, Serie IV Historia Moderna, t. 18–19 (2005–2006): 133–154, according to Oka and Gipoloux, it was the necessity of spreading risks amongst investors and merchants that caused the introduction of the *kaijō* in Japan, Oka & Gipoloux, 'Pooling Capital', pp. 78–79.

[158] Harris, Ron, 'General Average and All the Rest: The Law and Economics of Early Modern Maritime Risk Mitigation', in *General Average and Risk Management in Medieval and Early Modern Maritime Business*, ed. Maria Fusaro, Andrea Addobbati, and Luisa Piccinno (Singapore: Springer, 2023), p. 53, Marshall, P.J., 'Private British Trade in the

in the Americas could reach 50–75% early in the Early Modern period,[159] and the highest recorded rate is of 112%.[160] However, by the eighteenth century rates fluctuated around the 30–50% mark, even though 60% was still not uncommon.[161] In Manila, the premium on *correspondencias* for Acapulco fluctuated between 20% and 50% by year, with a mode of 30% for most of the eighteenth century.[162]

The fact that the premium was estimated as fixed rate of the principal of money given instead of a share of the profits like the *comenda* has resulted in the sea loan being conceptualised as a form of debt. In reality, the *correspondencia* was a partnership contract, and it was legally recognised as such in the Hispanic Monarchy.[163] The reason *correspondencias* were legally considered partnerships was because the premium that was charged on the principal was not calculated independently of the estimated profit margins of the trade it financed.[164] In other words, the premium represented the profits that could be realised, and not the price of money. The premium rates were not subject to the passage of time and were not annual but were circumscribed to the enterprise they financed: the voyages to Acapulco or any other ports. Thus, premia of 20% to 50% did not compound based on the time until repayment. When the outbreak of war with England in the late eighteenth century led to delays in the departures of the Galleons in their return trip from New Spain, the premia did not increase, neither did interest accumulate.[165] *Correspondencias* for Acapulco signed in 1795 at 25% were repaid in 1800

Indian Ocean Before 1800', in *India and the Indian Ocean, 1500–1800*, ed. Ashin Das Gupta and M.N. Pearson (Oxford: Oxford University Press, 1987), p. 287.

159 Bernal, *La financiación*, p. 193.

160 Ravina, 'Riesgos Marítimos', p. 132.

161 Bernal, *La financiación*, pp. 486–489.

162 Calculated from premium rates collected from ACCHS-CSIC and the account books from APSR. See Chapter 5 for details.

163 BNE Porcones 972(25), *Carta en que se vindica la equidad de las reales sentenciadas pronunciadas sobre la pertenencia del dinero salvado de la pérdida del Covadonga*, Anonymous, Manila, 1747.

164 Bernal, *La financiación*, p. 49.

165 In contrast, the premia on Spanish *riesgos* seems to have accrued over time, Carrasco González, Mª Guadalupe, 'Los instrumentos del comercio colonial en el Cádiz del siglo XVII (1650–1700)', *Banco de España-Servicio de Estudios de Historia Económica*, nº 35 (1996), pp. 93–94, and sea loans in medieval Venice also accrued interests as penalties for late repayment, González de Lara, 'The secret', p. 275.

at the same premium.[166] Furthermore, the premium had little correlation with measures of risk: while premiums in Manila fluctuated between 20 and 50% during the eighteenth century, risk of loss at sea was 4%,[167] and premia responded poorly to risk-increasing events such as declarations of war, as will be seen in Chapter 5.

The *correspondencia* was a partnership contract that financed a commercial enterprise (a specific voyage to a specific destination), that lasted for the duration of the enterprise, and whose only difference from an equity contract was that the taker of *correspondencias* promised a specified return to the giver expressed as a percentage of the money received in the *correspondencia*. In that regard, there was a promissory element in the contact that created an obligation on the part of the taker to produce the expected returns for the giver,[168] and for the giver to incur the risk of loss at sea. The determining variable that dictated the premium rates was not the opportunity cost of money over time, but the profit margins of the trading enterprises that *correspondencia* contracts financed. Trade routes with higher profits beckoned higher premium rates. Thus, while premia of 20–50% may seem high if understood as interest rates, they were actually very low when compared to estimated profit margins estimated to be between 200% and 1,400% according to the literature, evidencing the cheapness of capital in Manila (this will be analysed in more detailed in chapter 5).

Correspondencias in Manila were used to finance both the Galleon trade to America and the intra-Asian trade. By the end of the seventeenth century and during most of the eighteenth century, *correspondencias* seem to have been very streamlined and there were few differences amongst contracts.[169] Repayment was contractually established as taking place fifteen days upon the arrival of the ship, and most *correspondencias* covered the outbound and return voyages. Formulaic language remained

166 Escribano Miguel José Flores, 1795 [Legajo #26], ACCHS-CSIC.

167 Calculated from Yuste, *Emporios*, Cuadro I, & Cheong, 'The Decline', p. 153.

168 This is similar to a modern contract of *participación en cuenta* recognised in Spanish law Spain. *Código de comercio y legislación complementaria*, Boletín Oficial del Estado (BOE), 2022.

169 Two examples of Manila *correspondencias* for the years of 1766 and 1795 can be seen in Escribano Martín Dominguez de Zamudio, 1766 [Legajo #8], ACCHS-CSIC, f. 211, Escribano Miguel José Flores, 1795 [Legajo #26], ACCHS-CSIC, ff. 47a-48b.

and contracts were written from a common template, specifying repayment in gold, although the currency mentioned in each contract was Mexican silver pesos.[170] A particularity of Manila was that *correspondencias* were issued without the need for collateral, using the surety of guarantors instead. Even then, the account books of the Third Order of Saint Dominic reveal that most unperforming *correspondencias* were eventually written-off. Only in two recorded cases in the Dominican account books did insolvent takers repay with property: Simona de Villanueva had to sell her house in 1775 for a *correspondencia* of 375 pesos contracted in 1761, after being reduced 100 pesos in 1771[171]; Pedro Crisólogo Favié had his ship seized in 1792 for a *correspondencia* originally signed in 1790.[172] Defaults, nevertheless, were not inexpensive, and resulted in exclusion from the capital markets, as explained in Chapter 5.

Correspondencias were an ideal instrument for the Pacific trade. The great demand for the peso in Asia resulted in large profit margins, as has been seen previously. This tended to lower market risk as it was difficult for the purchasing power of pesos in America and Asia to converge, leaving ample room for arbitrage. The gravest threat for profit margins was the possibility of glutting Spanish American markets with Asian goods, but the limitation of the volume of trade to the one annual Galleon lowered this risk—although the causes and functioning of the one-Galleon system were more complex, as will be explained in Chapter 4. *Correspondencias* did not protect against market risk, but this business model reduced the volatility in prices, and premia could be adjusted according to profit margins, while allowing givers of *correspondencias* to share in the profits of trade.

A question arises regarding the suitability of *correspondencias* as a partnership contract with fixed returns for financing the trade as opposed to the *comenda* as an equity investment.[173] An answer can be provided by examining the nature of the trades in which they were used, especially on

[170] This is the case of all the contracts compiled. See Bibliography section ACCHS-CSIC.

[171] APSR Tomo 304, fol. 85b.

[172] APSR Tomo 282, fol. 14.

[173] On the topic, see Harris, *Going*, pp. 164–165, González de Lara, 'The Secret'. On the Spanish *comenda*, see the work of Martínez Gijón, 'La comenda' cited above, Martínez Gijón, José, 'La comenda en el derecho español. II. La comenda mercantil'. *Anuario de Historia del Derecho Español* XXXVI (1966): 379–456, Martínez Gijón, José,

how the information flowed, the markups that existed, and the level of integration of prices. *Correspondencias* may be considered a costly instrument for takers since premia were supposedly high. Yet, premia relative to profit margins were not high, as has been argued above, and as long as price differentials remained large enough to make market risk insignificant, the *correspondencia* offered advantages. The fixed premium avoided the information asymmetries that could arise between *comenda* partners once the partnership had to be liquidated.[174] Thus, from the point of view of an investor, a return denominated as a share of the profits potentially opened the door to larger gains, but it required enough information to control for asymmetries. This was difficult in the Pacific, which rested on the one-Galleon system. However, fixing the returns of *correspondencias* in terms of a rate on the principal calculated on the profit margins of the trade allowed the issuer to participate in the gains of trade while doing away with potential information asymmetries and costly monitoring mechanisms. At the same time, the taker could be assured that the limiting of volume of the trade to one annual ship and the great demand for pesos reduced market risk.

Correspondencias as insurance against risk of loss at sea also made sense given the business model of the one-Galleon, where it was impossible to diversify across ships unlike in Cádiz. With the Pacific trade relying on the crossing of one single ship, diversification across vessels was impossible. Premium insurance required large amounts of capital for cataclysmic scenarios including warfare or off-season storms that were hard to predict, while it offered low premiums in the range of 1.5–2.5% in eighteenth-century Cádiz, making the development of firms a necessity.[175] However, liquidity was not a constraint in Manila, and in fact the easy availability of cash in the city made the *correspondencia* a useful instrument. *Correspondencias* were primarily a means to raise working capital, and what they did

'La comenda y el transporte de mercancías en el derecho español de la Baja Edad Media', *Historia. Instituciones. Documentos* 1 (1974): 265–273.

[174] Börner, Lars, 'Making Medieval Markets: A Formal Institutional Analysis' (PhD diss., Humboldt-Universität zu Berlin October 2007).

[175] Baskes, Jeremy, *Staying Afloat: Risk and Uncertainty in Spain's Atlantic World Trade, 1760–1820* (Stanford: Stanford University Press, 2013), p. 214, Carrasco González, María Guadalupe, 'El Negocio de los Seguros Marítimos en Cádiz a finales del Siglo XVIII', *Hispania*, LIX, n° 1 (1999), p. 275.

was to transfer the risk of loss at sea to the investor who issued the *correspondencia* in exchange of a share in the profits. There is no evidence that *correspondencias* themselves were insured, but legacy funds were well capitalised and diversified in their investments, enough to make them resilient to sharp losses when they happened, while the premia of *correspondencias* fluctuating between 20% and 50% allowed for a fast recapitalisation.

The availability of liquidity in Manila also made *correspondencias* a suitable instrument for trade because they allowed the participation of outsiders and smaller investors. Well-capitalised legacy funds were not the only originators of *correspondencias* in Manila, and neither were all funds endowed with equal generosity. Because *correspondencias* could be signed for any quantity of money, a wide range of individuals were able to provide *correspondencias* and participate in the Pacific exchange. The collected *correspondencia* contracts from the surviving notarial protocols vary from maximums of 57,000 pesos to minimums of 100.[176] Many of the participants were in fact widows, soldiers, or sometimes natives. For example, Manuela Rosa Paasines, a Filipino headwoman from La Ermita, received 400 pesos in a *correspondencia* to Acapulco from Tomás de Endaya in 1741.[177] In 1766, two *sangleyes*, Vi Guangqua and Voyingqua received a *correspondecia* for Amoy worth 1,600 pesos from the Spanish governor of the Parián. Among their partners there was one José Tengqua, described as a confectioner.[178] Similarly, María Ana de la Cruz, a *mestiza de sangley*, invested 1,000 pesos to Acapulco in 1755,[179] and Isabel Suzitas, *mestiza* as well, invested another 2,000 pesos in 1766.[180] These were occasional participants, who appear in the record only once, which indicates that the marketplace in Manila was open enough for outsiders to complement their incomes or rents with sporadic investments in trade.

[176] Data collected from the *correspondencia* contracts in ACCHS-CSIC (see Bibliography).

[177] Escribano Baltasar Javier Sánchez de Cuenca, 1740–1741 [Legajo #2], ACCHS-CSIC, ff. 175a-176a.

[178] Escribano Martín Dominguez de Zamudio, 1766 [Legajo #8], ACCHS-CSIC, f. 210.

[179] Escribano Domingo Cortés de Arquiza, 1755 [Legajo #5], ACCHS-CSIC, ff. 83b-84b.

[180] Escribano Martín Dominguez de Zamudio, 1766 [Legajo #8], ACCHS-CSIC, ff. 86–87.

Correspondencias were therefore a partnership contract, an instrument that allowed investors to participate in the profits of the Manila trade and provided merchants with working capital in the form of silver cash and a guarantee against the risk of loss at sea. *Correspondencias* produced enough returns to the legacy funds to satisfy the welfare needs of Manila and internalise the risk of the Pacific exchange. They were ideally fitted to the characteristics of this trade. The reduction of market risk meant that takers of *correspondencias* needed not fear that profits from the trade may have been lower than the premia set in the contracts, while the availability of pesos in Manila and the lack of minimum quantities allowed outsiders to invest in the trade by originating *correspondencias*. Most importantly, *correspondencias* provided in hand the silver pesos that were the engine of commerce with Asia. The use of *correspondencias* was only discontinued when the standard of the peso coin imploded after the wars of independence in Spanish America in the first decades of the nineteenth century, highlighting the relationship between the instrument and the currency. *Correspondencias*, together with the pooling capacity of legacy funds, solved the challenge of raising enough working capital to keep the trade going.

Cash Substitutes

The capacity of lay confraternities, in the context of the need to organise the financing of long-distance trade, to adapt and become financial intermediaries is an interesting feature of Manila not shared with many other commercial harbours of the time. The lack of a market for bills of exchange in the city is equally intriguing, and it evidences the nature of the exchange in which the capital market of the city emerged and evolved. Due to the need to settle transactions in Asia with silver pesos, merchants involved in Asian trade—including both the East India companies and the Manila trade—found themselves in constant need of liquidity for trade. North-western Europe and the British Atlantic developed a sophisticated multilateral payment system based on money substitutes, such as bills of exchange.[181] In contrast to this, both the Atlantic and the Pacific trades in the Hispanic world had no recourse to such money substitutes. A simple reason for this is that money-like instruments like bills of exchange were

[181] Price, Jacob, 'Transaction costs: A note on merchant credit and the organization of private trade', in *The Political Economy of Merchant Empires* ed. James D. Tracy

not needed. The logic of the Pacific exchange was to provide Asia with a silver currency that could perform as a method of payment. Cash substitutes were therefore not important in a trade characterised by fulfilling Asian demand for silver cash in which pesos were simultaneously the currency for settlement of commercial transactions and the main good of export of Manileños. The demand for the Mexico-minted coin and its relative abundance made it ubiquitous in the city, and Manila lacked any significant money exchange businesses or banks.

Manila's *correspondencias* were not cash substitutes and did not trade separately in any secondary markets. Instead, they were the legal scaffolding that buttressed a cash transaction, apportioning risks and claims over future returns between the parties involved, but it always entailed the exchange of cash. To the extent that bills of exchange existed in the wider Manila trade, they were used to settle transactions incurred somewhere else, and thus were drawn against funds held in Manila. The protest of two bills of exchange issued by an Armenian merchant to be paid in Manila by another Armenian partner shows that merchant networks with access to Manila used this access to the liquidity of the city to back their purchases.[182] The bills of exchange were signed in 1801 by Gregorio H. Babum for a total of 70,000 pesos (approximately 1.7 tons of silver). In that year, while in Calcutta, Babum had entered two transactions worth 30,000 and 40,000 pesos with Bengal-based merchant Isaac Malchus, the payee of his bills, instructing his banker in Manila, Nazar Jacob Samir, to pay the amount to Malchus' agent in the city. However, both bills were rejected by Samir back in Manila. The reason for rejecting the bills of exchange is not stated in the notarial documents. The notarial document is called a *protesto* (protest or rejection), meaning that the only reason it was recorded was because Samir had rejected to pay the bills on behalf of Babum, and it is the only such document that has survived in the notarial protocols.

Whether drawing bills payable in Manila was exceptional, or rejecting them was rare, is impossible to know, but this case shows that at least the Armenian trading community took advantage of the abundance of cash

(Cambridge University Press, Cambridge, 1990), pp. 276–297, Sperling, J., 'The International Payments Mechanism in the Seventeenth and Eighteenth Centuries', *The Economic History Review* 14, nº 3 (1962), pp. 446–468.

[182] Escribano Vicente González de Tagle, 1800 [Legajo #19], ACCHS-CSIC, ff. 62b-65a.

in the city to back their commercial transactions in India by drawing bills against Manila. There was no liquidity constraint in Manila that bills, or other money substitutes needed to solve, neither were bills substitutes for silver specie in the Pacific exchange. However, nothing prevented intra-Asian merchants with access to Manila to draw bills on the funds they held in the city.

3.4 Manila as a Stakeholder in the Transpacific Trade

Manila was a hub that brought silver specie from Spanish America and redistributed it across Asia through its re-export trade. This trade necessitated financing, which was provided from the Asian terminal of the transpacific exchange, the city of Manila. The emergence from the seventeenth century onwards of legacy funds that invested directly in the trade through the origination of *correspondencias* proved revolutionary. It enabled the continuous pooling of resources from citizens, many of them unrelated to the trade, and allowed for the mobilisation of increasingly large quantities of capital which could absorb some of the shocks of the exchange and smooth the operation of trade. Its most unique feature was the slow adaptation of religious, urban associations into a new role as financial intermediaries who bridged the distance between the wider citizenry and trade financing. The close connection between trade and urban life meant that there existed a large overlap between the boards of these lay confraternities and the freighters in the Galleons and in the Asian trades, but this connection went beyond purely personal bonds, and into the wider religious fabric that tied urban life together.

Manila's alternative approach to financing long-distance trade was built on the city's access to Spanish American specie. The savings that opened legacy funds often came as retained earnings from the trade. Legacy funds were opened with a cash endowment, *correspondencias* transferred cash in hand to merchants for the purchase of goods, and repayment was specified uniquely in cash. But cash was precisely what Manila had aplenty, and the emergence of the *correspondencia* funds in 1668 facilitated its accumulation. Legacy funds were founded throughout the period, and their capitalisation kept increasing as the trade continued providing returns. The fact that legacy funds were opened by those unfamiliar with the trade and that *correspondencias* were sometimes given by individuals that had no relation with the commercial activities of the city indicates both the amount of liquidity available and the development of an impersonal market.

Liquidity and capital pooling were fundamental for the maintenance of long-distance trade with Asia, which demanded cash for the settlement of payments. The fundamental problems to be solved by the advent of direct trade with Asia were the need to pool unprecedentedly large amounts of capital for unprecedentedly long periods of time, as well as the need for capital lock-in.[183] In England and the Netherlands, the joint-stock corporation provided this solution.[184] In Manila, savings in cash flowed from individuals to the legacy funds and the brotherhoods and Third Orders that administered them. These institutions in turn used this cash to provide working capital to merchants to operate the trade. Manila shows that an alternative model for financing direct trade with Asia existed, and that impersonal markets were not the unique creation of the joint-stock corporate form.

An important consequence of this financial model was the change in the relationship between the city and the trade. The emergence of the *correspondencia* funds in 1668 meant that the returns of the trade that accrued to them as proceeds of the *correspondencias* were then redistributed across the city as welfare, making the legacy funds central to the urban fabric of Manila. For the citizens, this meant that the maintenance of hospitals, dowries, schools, scholarships, etc., was directly linked to the trade through the premia which the *obras pías* could charge in the *correspondencias*, which in turn relied on the profit margin of the trade. Thus, the city of Manila as a beneficiary of the welfare generated by the *obras pías* also had a vested interest in maintaining profit margins—and premium rates—high: this was a rent-seeking arrangement encompassing the entire city.

[183] Gelderblom and Jonker, 'Completing', pp. 648–649, Gelderblom, De Jong and Jonker, 'The Formative', pp. 1072–1073 argue that the causation emanated from economic logic to legal form based on the need to raise outside finance, also Carlos, 'British Corporate', p. 40.

[184] Gelderblom and Jonker, 'Completing', pp. 659–660 & p. 666, Harris, *Going*, p. 4.

CHAPTER 4

The Business Model of the One-Galleon System

Chapter 3 showed how, through the legacy funds and the capital they generated, the gains of trade were distributed throughout the networks of the city. Chapter 2 showed that the engine that motivated this trade was the Asian—and specifically Chinese—demand that existed for the Spanish American silver. This large demand led to great purchasing power differentials of the peso across both sides of the Pacific, resulting in great profits. The large returns of the Pacific trade—estimated at anywhere between 200% and 1000%—should have been impossible to maintain over 250 years in a free market. Regardless of how large entry costs may have been for newcomers, profits should have enticed individuals or companies to try their fortunes in the Pacific intermediation. Yet for the period between 1571 and the late eighteenth century, the Manileños were the only ones to maintain a sustained commercial line across the Pacific, making the claim of a "Spanish Lake" much of a reality.[1] Even then, this trade was conducted by one ship, begging the question of why other Manileños that had participated in the Pacific crossing themselves did not feel the need to freight on their own and enter the New Spanish market outside the system of the Galleon and the Acapulco fair. Finally,

[1] Spate, Oskar H.K., *The Spanish Lake*, Canberra: The Australian University E Press (1979).

J. J. Rivas Moreno, *The Capital Market of Manila and the Pacific Trade, 1668–1838*, Palgrave Studies in Economic History,
https://doi.org/10.1007/978-3-031-71810-6_4

even when more serious attempts by outsiders were tried, such as the Dutch scheme to establish a direct line between Batavia and Acapulco in the 1740s,[2] they ended in failure.

A fundamental question that arises is how Manileños managed to defeat competition and maintain their intermediation. Not only were outsiders successfully fended off, but also, Manileños maintained a limited volume of trade. The literature has commonly explained this restrictive policy as protectionism to favour Spain.[3] Yet, as revealed in Chapter 2, it was the Manileños themselves who petitioned to restrict the volume to one annual ship. Similarly, the opposition of the king of Spain would not have necessarily been enough to prevent the development of a dense network of contraband as it happened in the Atlantic.[4] The imperial authorities had no fleet to monitor the activities of the Pacific harbours, and "contraband"—known and accepted, although technically illegal—did exist on a large scale in the Pacific between New Spain and Perú, whose direct trade had been banned in 1634.[5] This shows that no matter how restrictive the law may have been on print, it could not have been the source of the limitation. Instead, Manileños must have been efficient enough in operating their commerce to the point of fending off competitors, whether foreigners or other Hispanic subjects from Manila or America.

This chapter examines the business model of the one-Galleon in the context of the trade developed through the previous chapters. It argues that the Chinese demand for specie skewed the bargaining power in favour of Mexican wholesalers. Mexicans could operate buying cartels for textiles in both the Atlantic and the Pacific because demand for pesos was global and they controlled the supply of the coin. The one-Galleon model was the best option available to Manileños given that open trade

[2] Furber, *Rival Empires*..., p. 160, & Furber, Holden, 'The India Trade in the Pacific through Two Centuries, 1600–1800', in *Private Fortunes and Company Profits in the India Trade in the 18th Century*, collected studies of Holden Furber, Aldershot: Variorum (1997), pp. 7–10.

[3] Schurz, *The Manila*, p. 178, Yuste, *Emporios*, p. 52, Bonalian, *El Pacífico*, p. 209, Bauzon, *Deficit*, p. 142, Bjork, 'The Link', p. 40.

[4] Pearce, *British Trade*, pp. 1–32, see also Pérez Herrero, Pedro, 'La rearticulación de los mercados americanos ante la presencia extranjera en el siglo XVII (1630–1720),'*Chronica Nova*, 23 (1996): 343–380.

[5] Bonalian, *El Pacífico*, pp. 80–81.

with New Spain would have resulted in them competing against each other. The single Galleon was thus a strategy to organise a mirror seller cartel to guarantee returns in the Acapulco negotiation. This answers why Manileños adhered to the limitations of the trade—in fact, sought them. Chapters 5 and 6 explore this further by analysing why it was in the interest of Mexican wholesalers.

4.1 Structure of the Market and the Acapulco Fair

After Asian merchants brought their wares to Manila and the Manileños contracted for *correspondencias* with the *obras pías* came the freighting of the Galleon, and finally, the Acapulco fair. This fair represented the point of contact between American consumption of Asian goods, and Asia's—and specifically China's—demand for silver specie. The evolution of supply and demand had implications in how the trade was conducted and how Manileños and their Mexican counterparts negotiated between themselves. Demand for Spanish American silver specie was global, and outstripped its supply, which was controlled by the great Mexico wholesale houses. This resulted in a monopsonic market in Acapulco which benefitted those that controlled the flows of specie.

As recorded by Irigoin, the Spanish American currency went through fundamental changes during the long eighteenth century. The early Spanish American coins, recognised worldwide, were called *reales* or pieces of eight, as per the subdivisions of the peso into eight *reales*, or *rials* in England. The *rial* was a currency whose standard was steady and trustable, a very adequate currency for trade.[6] The Mexico and Seville pesos, in particular, carried a premium in markets. The illegal debasement of Peruvian coins in the mid-seventeenth century, which was punished swiftly, created distrust for the Perú-minted coins as far as Asia.[7] In 1680, the quality and design of the coin were overhauled and enhanced, resulting in the new "pillar" coin, while a monetary reform in 1686 divorced the Spanish-minted pesos from its American counterparts, while by the 1730s the Spanish state increasingly took over

[6] Irigoin, 'Rise', p. 404.

[7] Lane, Kris, 'Corrupción y Dominación Colonial: El Gran Fraude de la Casa de la Moneda de Potosí en 1649'. *Boletín del Instituto de Historia Argentina y Americana "Dr Emilio Ravignani"*, 3ª serie, 43 (2015): 94–130, Boxer, 'La plata', pp. 467–469.

control of the minting and coining of silver pesos in the Americas, introducing new coining techniques, including the use of laminating mills that produced more uniform coins with rimmed edges.[8] The introduction of new minting technology, together with policies that sought to increase mining output in America,[9] resulted in expanded production of pesos. 461 million pesos were coined in the Mexico mint between 1730 and 1772, and over a billion between 1772 and 1808. Yet as Irigoin noticed, this expansion did not lead to parallel inflationary trends within Spanish America, implying that the international market could absorb the increased production of peso coins.[10]

These changes also affected the nature of Chinese demand, which was itself undergoing serious monetary changes during the Ming dynasty as examined by Von Glahn.[11] China lacked meaningful local sources of silver by the start of the sixteenth century and did not coin silver, using instead ingots called *taels*.[12] When the discovery and exploitation of large deposits of silver in Spanish America started in the 1540s and 1570s, a voluminous portion of this silver output eventually found its way to China following the global silver routes outlined previously.[13] Von Glahn and Irigoin agree that this demand stemmed from the need to find a suitable silver-denominated coin that could perform as a certified means of payment in China.[14] The peso, a trustable and abundant coin, could fulfil this demand. As Irigoin argues, the quality and reliability of the coins played an important role in orienting Chinese demand towards the peso.[15] Von Glahn states that around 1730 foreign coins had started to supplant silver ingots as a preferred means of payment, and by 1788 the peso had become a fiduciary money in Jiangnan, the most

[8] Irigoin, 'Rise', p. 392.

[9] See Chapter 2, Sect. 2.1.

[10] Irigoin, 'Rise', p. 392.

[11] Von Glahn, *Fountain*, see also Von Glahn, Richard, 'Money Use in China and Changing Patterns of Global Trade in Monetary Metals, 1500–1800', in *Global Connections and Monetary History*, 1470–1800, ed. Dennis O. Flynn, Arturo Giráldez, and Richard von Glahn (Aldershot: Ashgate Publishing, 2003): 187–205.

[12] Irigoin, 'A Trojan', p. 11.

[13] See Map 2.1.

[14] Irigoin, 'Rise', p. 396, Von Glahn, 'Foreign Silver', p. 71.

[15] Irigoin, 'A Trojan', pp. 3 & 19.

commercialised part of China.[16] This had important implications for the Pacific exchange. The first is that demand exceeded supply. Demand for pesos as silver specie was global, but its supply in the Acapulco fair was controlled by the Mexican wholesalers. The second is that this demand was also affected by the quality of the peso coins. Chinese demand slowly evolved from a demand for silver to a preferential demand for Spanish American coins, especially the Mexico-minted pesos, which added value to exporting pesos to Asia. Third, as shown by Irigoin, because pesos were trustable and known across the world, and because they eventually performed as a means of payment in China, they reduced transaction costs, especially when it came to Europeans' trade with Asia in the later eighteenth century.[17]

These developments need to be considered together with the changes that were taking place within Asian trade as mentioned in Chapter 2. The progressive depletion of silver deposits in Japan decimated the other alternative major source of silver for China and Southeast Asia.[18] This made the Pacific route much more important as a supplier of the precious metal, and Manila became China's main source of silver. Similarly, the 1680s witnessed an expansion of trade in Asia and especially with China.[19] This must have reverberated along the entire retail chain, ultimately buttressing the position of Mexican wholesalers that controlled the distribution of pesos within New Spain.

Manileños, *peninsulares*, East India companies, and anyone involved in the global silver trade with Asia needed to acquire pesos. The East India Companies resorted to all sorts of means to acquire the coin, either from their domestic market through the issuance of bonds and debt, or from the international money market through exchange transactions or sales, but they never contracted with the American source directly.[20] For Manileños and *peninsulares* however, pesos were the proceeds of sales

16 Von Glahn, 'Foreign silver', pp. 54–55.

17 Irigoin, 'Rise', p. 405.

18 Irigoin, 'Rise', p. 385, Flynn and Giráldez, 'Silk', p. 61.

19 The reasons for this expansion are outlined in Chapter 2, Section The Asian Leg.

20 Chaudhuri, *The Trading*, Ch. 8, Chaudhuri, Susil, 'The Financing of Investments in Bengal: 1650–1720', *The Indian Economic & Social History Review* 8, n° 2 (1971): 109–133, Morse, H.B., 'The Provision of Funds for the East India Company's Trade at Canton during the Eighteenth Century', *The Journal of the Royal Asiatic Society of Great Britain and Ireland*, n° 2 (1922): 227–255.

from the fairs of Acapulco and Jalapa, respectively. Chapter 2 showed how Mexican wholesalers controlled the flow of pesos within New Spain due to their financing of the silver mines and their control of the supplies of consumption goods bought from the international fairs, and more importantly, the mercury needed to process silver ore. The implication was that the Acapulco fair had a different importance for the Manileños and the Mexican wholesalers: for the former, the fair was the best place to obtain the silver pesos closest to the source, at the cheapest prices, which were the *sine qua non* of trade with Asia. For the latter, the Acapulco fair provided them with relatively cheap textiles of cotton and silk, but these goods were also imported in the annual fleets—and from 1789, the licensed ships—of the Atlantic. Mexicans controlled the market; they were unique providers of a coin of global demand. The result was a monopsonic market in the New Spanish fairs, as the total demand for pesos far outstripped its supply, controlled by a few wealthy wholesalers. This meant that Mexicans were price setters and were capable to act as a buyers' cartel in Acapulco and Jalapa.

The relative bargaining power of the parties involved in the long-distance trade with America and the market structure have never been analysed by the literature, and it goes a long way in explaining many of the formal characteristics of the organisation of trade and its evolution. This section shows how the wholesalers' cartel in Acapulco affected the organisation of the Pacific trade and led to limitations in the volume of the exchange. Firstly, the main strategy of Mexican merchants was to delay negotiations as much as possible, knowing that the Galleon had to clear the Acapulco harbour before a certain date if it wanted to avoid the typhoon season on its return trip to Manila. Secondly, Mexican merchants did petition for restrictive legislation against their Manila counterparts, banning the Manileños from entering the country,[21] which would have allowed them to contract with the mines and internal markets, the source of the demand for Asian goods, and to undercut the Mexican wholesalers. And finally, if the Mexican clique could maintain a cartel, it would be expected that Manileños would have responded in whatever way they could. This is evidenced in the way that information was treated at the fairs. Manileños sold their goods in unopened trunks and petitioned royal officials never to publish the information on the cargoes of the Galleons

[21] Yuste, *Emporios*, p. 292.

so as to deny the New Spaniards the chance to form an idea on the annual supply of goods, and therefore, on prices.[22] Tellingly, this situation (limited access to the interior of New Spain, unopened trunks, protests against the circulation of the information of the cargo) was also prevalent in the mirror transaction of the Atlantic involving the Seville and Cádiz fleets.[23] Analysing the Acapulco fair based on the structure of the market shows that Manileños did not seek to protect themselves from the fiscal impositions on the trade, but rather to mitigate the market power of Mexican wholesalers.

The Galleon would arrive on Acapulco in late January or February of the year after departing from Manila in the late summer and had to leave Acapulco by late March. This left little time for deals to be made. Notarised proceedings of Galleons' arrival to Acapulco show that the Galleon was inspected by the castellan of Acapulco and royal officials before the crew and the passengers were allowed to disembark. During the days after arrival the cargo was unloaded from the Galleons, and goods were declared and stored in the local buildings. In the meantime, messengers would be sent inland the moment the Galleon anchored to notify the merchants in New Spain, who would come down across the Badlands.[24] Simón de Anda specifically implied that Acapulco's nefarious geography and isolation, surrounded by mountains and drylands, worked in the favour of New Spanish merchants at the fair, as it discouraged the Galleon freighters from travelling inland and bypassing the Acapulco fair, a costly enterprise that required large amounts of mules and provisions.[25]

[22] AGI Filipinas 941 N.1, 1769. This document includes the litigation around the freighting and the unloading of goods of the Galleon *San Carlos* in Acapulco in 1767. As a case folder, it includes several reports and testimonies regarding the Acapulco fairs during the mid-eighteenth century.

[23] Del Valle Pavón, 'La lucha', pp. 44–46, regarding the prohibition on *peninsulares* to enter bypass the Jalapa fair and enter Mexico, Real Díaz argued that this was done to protect the profits that Mexico City wholesalers derived as redistributors of goods to the consumers in the interior, Real Díaz, José Joaquín, *Las Ferias de Jalapa* (Sevilla: Escuela de Estudios Hispanoamericanos, 1959), pp. 76–77.

[24] AGI Filipinas 941 N. 1, 1769.

[25] AGI Filipinas 941 N. 1, 1769, the politics of the location of fairs is also evident in the Atlantic side. Veracruz, the original site of the Atlantic fair, was as insalubrious as Acapulco in the Pacific. In 1725, the merchants of Cádiz convinced the king to change the location of the fair to Orizaba in the interior, which was in a favourable commercial crossroads within New Spain. The Mexico *Consulado* resented this attempt at penetrating New Spain

Compounding the prohibition of Manileños to enter the country was the fact that Mexican wholesalers usually traded in Acapulco through agents that agglutinated the supply of pesos. While the Acapulco fair was legally open to all New Spanish merchants who willed to trade, according to Yuste by the eighteenth century, around 90% of the silver introduced in Acapulco belonged to the wholesalers of Mexico City.[26] These wholesalers usually acted through a *comisionista* (commission agent) who transported the pesos to Acapulco and negotiated on behalf of their patrons.[27] The result was an even more skewed bargaining position in favour of those agents that could agglutinate the supply of pesos.

In a commissioned report written to the king in 1769, Simón de Anda recollected the Acapulco fair he witnessed while waiting for his passage to Manila in 1761. Anda specifically reported that not only the commercial interests of Cádiz were opposed to the Manila merchants, but those of Mexico were equally hostile.[28] According to Simón de Anda, the merchants from Mexico, Puebla, and Valladolid would come to Acapulco upon hearing the news of the arrival of the Galleon. Once in Acapulco, they adopted a waiting strategy, making the opening of the fair coincide with religious festivals. New Spanish buyers were aware that the Galleon had to stick to seasonal schedules and that it could not depart without the pesos that they controlled: Manileños had incurred the investment in goods and needed to repay their *correspondencias* at home. The longer they waited, the more desperate that Manileños would be become, forcing down prices.

What Anda witnessed in Acapulco and described to the king was essentially a buyers' cartel in operation. According to his report:

> The representatives of each group [New Spanish and Manileños] try to negotiate a starting price for the fair, and since the merchants from Mexico and the other cities know that Manileños must by all means sail back by the 25th of March, they make contemptuous offers under the threat of not taking the goods to Mexico [City] and forcing [the Manileños] to remain

and managed to remove the fair to the more isolated Jalapa in 1728. Carrera Stampa, Manuel, 'Las ferias novohispanas', *Historia Mexicana* 2, nº 3 (1953), pp. 323–324.

[26] Yuste, *Emporios*, p. 278.

[27] Yuste, *Emporios*, pp. 285–287.

[28] AGI Filipinas 941 N.1, 1769.

there for one, two, or more years, [thus] they [the Manileños] find themselves in the need to hand over [their merchandise] to their opponents, so that when the Mexicans and the Pueblans (which are the main traders) are united, Manileños are sacrificed, and only when one of them, to "cut through" as they say, offers an opening price is the fair average [in profits for Manileños]: in every other circumstance Manileños always lose.[29]

This waiting strategy was the same that Italian traveller Gemelli Careri described upon his arrival to the Acapulco fair in 1699, only that back then, the arrival of Peruvian merchants with alternative supplies of pesos could ease the negotiations for the Manileños.[30] Yet, as the eighteenth century progressed, active participation of Peruvians in the Acapulco fair ended. Mexican wholesalers would monopolise the buying side in the fair, and then re-export Asian goods across the Pacific coast to Perú.[31]

Not surprisingly, this strategy was also used in the Atlantic run with the fleets from Spain.[32] In both cases, *peninsulares* and Manileños were not allowed to penetrate New Spain. Apart from linking supply and demand in one place, the fair of Acapulco, like the fair of Jalapa and the *pancada* in Manila, served the important role of controlling the inflow of merchants into New Spain and preventing them from touring the country. Through the *ferias*, the local merchants that monopolised the flows of commerce could enforce their bargaining position and prevent Manileños and *peninsulares* from bypassing them and contracting directly with the mines.[33]

Manileños adapted their business strategies to the circumstances, as evidenced by the bills of instructions that consignors in Manila gave to their consignees in the 1766 Galleon, the *San Carlos Borromeo*. In that year, the king appointed Teodoro de Croix as a special judge to examine the irregularities of the Pacific trade. De Croix's investigation on the *San Carlos Borromeo*, which landed in Acapulco in January 1767, is the only known instance in which Manileños were forced to surrender their secret instructions to a royal agent. Most of the instructions were clear. Goods

[29] AGI Filipinas 941 N.1, 1769.

[30] Careri, Gemelli, *A Voyage Around the World*, 1704, in *A Collection of Voyages and Travels*, vol. IV, printed by HC in Parternoster Row (1744), p. 447.

[31] Bonalian, *El Pacífico*, p. 290.

[32] Brading, *Miners*, p. 97.

[33] Real Díaz, *Las Ferias*, pp. 60–61.

had to be sold "*in cash, and not on credit*".[34] Secret instructions clearly ordered consignors to sell in retail, rather than wholesale.[35] Some instructions were more detailed and highlight the importance that Manileños put on never revealing the quantities of goods transported in the Galleon, nor their price. An instruction signed by the Marquess of Montecastro for Joaquín González del Rivero, explicitly instructed that sales should be done with:

> [...] great harmony and caution with all individuals, without declaring quantities or money to any person, for if not, with the slightest hint the buyers will learn about the cargo of the vessel.[36]

Galleon freighters, therefore, did the best they could to restrict information. When de Croix's investigation forced the Galleon freighters to surrender their secret instructions and their bills of lading, they complained that it infringed on their privilege, and most importantly, that it imperilled the fair.

> [...] if by any chance this information is divulged, the buyers in the fair could use these bills with great detriment of our interests [...].[37]

Following Schurz's interpretation back in 1939, the privilege of Manileños to not open their trunks and for their sworn bills to be accepted at face value in the appraising of their cargo by royal officials has been understood as a sign of widespread corruption and fiscal evasion.[38] What Schurz and those that followed him failed to consider was that the Manileños may not have been looking to protect themselves from a distant king, but from the market power of the Mexican wholesalers, who controlled the distribution of the coveted pesos and could switch them

[34] AGI Filipinas 941 N.1, 1769, the document includes the secret instructions of consignors in Manila for their consignees in the Galleon.

[35] AGI Filipinas 941, N. 1, 1769.

[36] AGI Filipinas 941 N. 1, 1769.

[37] AGI Filipinas 941 N. 1, 1769.

[38] This view is probably derived from Viana's own interpretation, see AMN 533 MS1576 Doc. 2, *Informe de Viana sobre los engaños con que se hace el comercio con los galeones*, 1760, ff. 12–14.

from the Pacific to the Atlantic negotiation with ease or refuse to trade.[39] Limiting information on the cargo of the Galleon would have benefited the Manileños: Mexico's wholesalers were undoubtedly the price setters in the Acapulco fair, and their market power was uncontested, but limiting information and selling on retail would have made the wholesalers uncertain as to the actual quantity of goods that they could buy for distribution within New Spain. The position of power of wholesalers still depended on their capacity to provide the miners with mercury and consumption goods, thus the wholesalers still needed to purchase in the fairs.[40] Restricting information was a way to spread uncertainty amongst wholesalers and force them to make bids.

Unsurprisingly, any kind of meddling that could provide Mexican merchants with information was also deeply resented by the *peninsulares* in the Atlantic side of New Spain's trade. In 1628, the *Consulado* of Seville managed to obtain from the king of Spain permission to dispense with the sworn declarations of the fleets. Since 1586 the Sevillian merchants had enjoyed the same privilege as Manileños that their trunks could not be opened.[41] Guillermina del Valle Pavón has interpreted this as a strategy to maintain prices high, and fight against the position of strength of the New Spanish merchants.[42] Factoring in the global demand for the pesos, and the prohibition for Manileños to bypass the Acapulco fair, it is evident that Mexican merchants were in an unassailable commercial position, and that sellers like the Spanish and the Manileños needed to devise strategies to face this cartel.

Finally, the efforts by Manileños to maintain their position in the Acapulco fair led to one of the most interesting aspects of the negotiation, namely, how the trunks were sold. Based in some instructions from the 1766 investigation, the bulk of the cargo shipped by the Galleon freighters seems to have been sold *in* the bundles and trunks, that is, without giving Mexican wholesalers the chance to inspect what they were

[39] On the Mexican wholesalers, the best studies are those provided by Guillermina del Valle Pavón and Carmen Yuste López (in Bibliography), see also Kizca, John, *Empresarios coloniales: Familias y negocios en la ciudad de México durante los Borbones* (Mexico: Fondo de Cultura Económica, 1986).

[40] As explained in Chapter 2, Sect. 2.4.

[41] Del Valle Pavón, 'La lucha', p. 46, also see AGI Filipinas 941 N. 1.

[42] Del Valle Pavón, 'La lucha'; 41–62.

buying.[43] Manileños always wanted to sell their goods in retail, exhibiting models for display.[44] Mexicans, on the other hand, preferred to buy in bulk, thus economising in prices by buying in volume.[45] As a result, a distinction was made between items, with some being sold in retail at higher prices, and the majority being sold in bulk, without the trunks being opened. This distinction by product reflects the negotiating capacity of the parties. Only those specific goods that Manileños knew would command a premium in the Mexican market were sold in retail, but most of the cargo was sold in bulk to the wholesalers, who could wait and lower prices. Other instructions specified that the content of the trunks should only change hands once the payment had been received, and not earlier.[46] What is surprising is the lack of litigation regarding possible cheats, violations of contract, or sale of inferior quality goods.

Manileños, like their Spanish counterparts, had their correspondents and clients in New Spain, to whom they sent some articles. Yuste has explored these connections, but she has interpreted them as the true exchange, thus arguing that Manileños were agents of the Mexican wholesalers.[47] But this fails to explain why Manileños were so concerned with concealing information from their Mexican counterparts, or why Mexicans forced a waiting strategy upon Manileños in the fair. Furthermore, these orders did not represent a large stake in the overall cargo brought over from Manila. In the case of the Galleon *San Carlos* in 1766, for which the quantities are known thanks to the investigation of Teodoro de Croix, only 116 bundles (10% of the total cargo) were sent directly to New Spanish clients on commission.[48] The relationship between Manileños and Mexican merchants was closer to a relationship of trusted purveyors in the Pacific exchange than a relationship of agency in which the Mexico houses represented the senior branches. As mentioned previously, it made no sense to finance the activities of Manileño merchants, commission goods, and then refuse to negotiate in

[43] In fact, in 1767 the Galleon freighters expressly petitioned the authorities to "open" some trunks for retail in the fair, AGI Filipinas 941 N.1, 1769.

[44] AGI Filipinas 941 N. 1, 1769.

[45] AGI Filipinas 941 N. 1, 1769.

[46] AGI Filipinas 941 N. 1, 1769.

[47] Yuste, *Emporios*, pp. 295–296.

[48] AGI Filipinas 941 N. 1, 1769.

Acapulco. The fact that New Spanish wholesalers refused to open the fair straightaway and waited for the departure date of the Galleon reflects that the transaction in Acapulco was a negotiation between buyers and sellers, and not an exchange between agents and financiers. Similarly, the bulk of the financing by the eighteenth century came from the *obras pías* in Manila. These funds bore the risks of the Pacific crossing and financed the welfare of the city. This seems an expensive way to maintain an intermediary. If Manileños were agents working for the Mexican wholesalers, one must question why Mexicans did not place their agents in China itself or in India, rather than paying wholesale for the expensive maintenance of the entire city of Manila like the *obras pías* did.

Like the *peninsulares*, Manileños sought to avoid this bottleneck while preventing the expenses of being stranded in New Spain over years. Strategies involved at times placing goods under the care of specific persons in Mexico with instructions not to sell.[49] A common clause in the private instructions that Manileños merchants issued to their consignors in the Galleon referred to the eventuality of war, specifically with England. In such eventuality, merchants like Juan de Aso y Otal instructed their consignors to send them a quantity of money—in his case in 1766, 10,000 pesos "*líquidos*"—to repay the *correspondencias*, and to store the rest under the care of a trustable person—again in his case, his brother in Mexico.[50] This has been interpreted as evidence that the Acapulco fair was a show, and that the real transactions took place behind closed doors.[51] Rather, they are the exceptions that prove that the Acapulco fair served its purpose of protecting the Mexican wholesalers' territorial control. Manileños constantly sought to bypass the fair system and to penetrate New Spain.

However, the impact of these efforts to bypass the fair were limited. Firstly, Manileños needed to realise enough profit in Acapulco to repay the financing provided by the *obras pías* in Manila. Secondly, not all Manileños had contacts within New Spain, neither is it known how the goods that went to the interior were then sold, or whether they were sold to Mexico's wholesalers. For Manileños, the Acapulco fair was the way of getting the silver pesos they needed and that wholesalers controlled. The

[49] AGI Filipinas 941 N. 1, 1769.

[50] AGI Filipinas 941 N. 1, 1769.

[51] Yuste, *Emporios*, pp. 280–281.

instructions of the Galleon freighters indicate that placing goods under the care of a third party within New Spain would only happen in case of war with England. This may have been because of the possibility of losing the returns of the Acapulco fair if the Galleon was captured by the Royal Navy.

The organisation of the Acapulco fair and the structure of the transactions may look irrational if the motivation of Manileños to remain as intermediaries and the advantageous bargaining position of the Mexican wholesalers is not considered. The great demand for pesos meant that the Manileños could not walk away from the negotiation: New Spain was the source of the Mexico-minted pesos that commanded the highest regard in international markets. On the other hand, this favoured the wholesalers that controlled the distribution of the pesos, from the mines to the mint, and from the mint to the fairs. This meant that Manileños in Acapulco were at the mercy of the wholesalers, who could maintain a buyers' cartel. Manileños, who had incurred the costs of purchasing Asian goods and contracting *correspondencias*, needed to devise a strategy to maintain a price floor. The answer was the one-Galleon model.

4.2 The One-Galleon Model

Asian—and specifically Chinese—demand for pesos increased the bargaining power of Mexican wholesalers that controlled their distribution. They could choose who to trade with for textiles and consumption goods, whether those brought from the Pacific, from the Atlantic, or even domestic production, if necessary, but everybody had to negotiate with them for the pesos. Thus, Mexican wholesalers controlled the international fairs through buyers' cartels and could drive the prices of import goods down. Manileños and *peninsulares*, having incurred heavy investments at home, needed to maintain a price floor. Given the position of strength of the wholesalers, expanding the supply of Asian goods would not have necessarily resulted in a higher return of pesos, but they could have glutted Spanish American markets with goods. Their response to the wholesalers' cartel was the rationing in the volume of trade to the annual *flotas* of the Atlantic and the Galleon of the Pacific.[52] In other words,

[52] On the Atlantic, see García Fuentes, *El Comercio*, p. 164, in this, Mexican wholesalers seem at times to have coalesced with Sevillian merchants in convincing the king to increase the intervals of *flotas* to maintain prices high in New Spain, see Lamikiz, Xabier, 'Flotistas

barred from unilaterally expanding the scale of the trade, Manileños sought to maximise returns through profit margins. This choice between scale and returns, which dictated the operation of the trade and became the one-Galleon model, can be visualised through Game Theory, specifically through two game scenarios representing the choice between the broad organisation of the trade, and the uncertainty of sailing more than one vessel across the Pacific.

The first game represents the business model choice of the Manileños given the controlling position of Mexican wholesalers in Acapulco. This is a repeated transaction game between two players with ordered decision-taking in which both players have information of each other's decisions. The logic behind this is to represent the organisational choices that both Manileños and Mexicans had to take. Two contrasting organisational choices are chosen: either Free Trade interpreted as a model in which merchants and navigators have complete freedom to charter ships, freight goods, and negotiate without any kind of artificial limitation, or a cartel organisation. This refers to an organisational choice in which either the supplier or the buyer decides to band together to impose limitations of one kind or another.[53]

This model is chosen to represent certain specific things: information is considered public because the kind of information that is needed to make an organisational decision is broad enough to have been known to both players. Manileños were aware of the importance of the peso, and that their Mexican counterparts were being supplied with goods competitive to theirs' from the Atlantic. Decision-taking is ordered to represent the temporal steps that had to be taken before contracting. Mexicans could behave opportunistically because the Manileños had to incur the heavy investment of buying the goods, freighting, and sailing across the Pacific

en la Nueva España: diseminación espcial y negocios de los intermediarios del comercio transatlántico, 1670–1702', *Colonial Latin American Review* 20, n° 1 (2011), p. 9.

[53] Authors have criticised the simplification of Game theoretical approaches to binary oppositions of complex institutional settings. While this criticism is entirely valid, and there is a risk of oversimplification of nuanced institutional problems, here this game is intended to provide an aid in visualising and understanding the effects that market structure can have in the organisation of the trade. The options presented in this game (i.e. Free Trade or Cartel) are purposely left undefined as ahistorical examples with the aim of illustrating how the market structure for pesos affected the decision taking of the participants in the trade. Grafe and Gelderblom, 'The Rise', pp. 479–480.

before negotiations could even start in Acapulco, and they faced a time limit if they wanted to return to Manila due to the typhoon season.

The organisational game is displayed in Fig. 4.1. It starts with the Manileños deciding on how to conduct their transactions with Acapulco. Two choices are open to them: either allow absolute freedom to freight whatever they choose in whatever manner suited them best, or to organise themselves in a uniform group. If Manila chooses to trade freely (i.e. chooses left), Mexico can then choose to open in return or to maintain a buyers' cartel. The option in which both choose Free Trade presents the highest payoffs for both, but this payoff calculation is impossible to corroborate because at no point was the Manila-Acapulco trade completely free of any intervention of any sort, which was also the case of most other Early Modern trade routes. What is important is to notice that Mexico's option to cartelise once Manila has decided to trade freely renders it the highest returns in the game. This reflects the bargaining power of Mexican wholesalers and the monopsonic structure of the market. Manileños, if they wanted to maintain their intermediary position in the Pacific trade, *must* trade with the Mexican wholesalers in Acapulco. However, Manileños have incurred heavy expenditures before the negotiation can start, trade with goods that can be substituted, and have a limited time to negotiate. If Manileños sail on their own account to Mexico but Mexicans decide to maintain a buyers' cartel, the only competition that can take place would be between Manileños, leading to a downward competition that would make their prices fall. Because Mexicans really do not face any constraint in Acapulco, there is virtually nothing stopping them from maintaining this pressure until the point when Manileños would settle for the price that would simply cover the costs of their enterprise, leaving no profits. Both these choices never took place in real life, but they are useful to highlight the distortionary effects of the Chinese demand for pesos.

On the other hand, Manila could choose to create a sellers' cartel before sailing to Acapulco in the expectation that they would find a buyers' cartel there. If Manila decided to create a cartel before sailing to Acapulco, Mexican merchants faced two alternative choices: to open their trade or to create a buyers' cartel. Liberalising the trade at Acapulco would be more favourable to Manileños, for they could still maintain their position, but would still not be as favourable as it would have been for Mexicans if positions were reversed, and Mexicans would still make profits even if lower than if they maintained their controlling position or

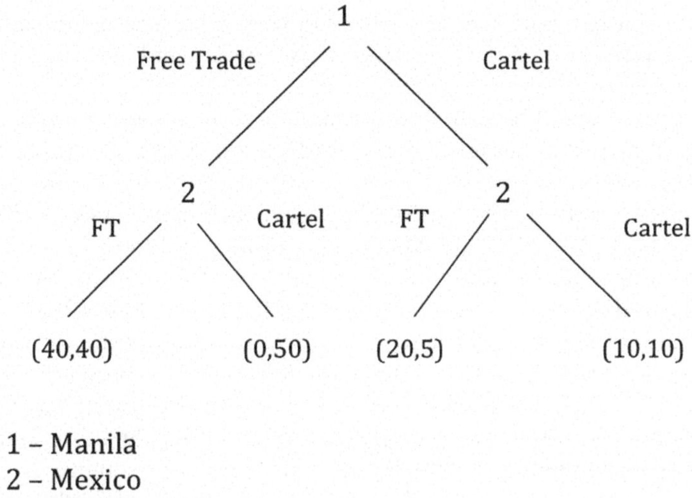

Fig. 4.1 Manila trade organisation game

the whole trade had been liberalised. This reflects again the necessity to contract with Mexican merchants in order to acquire silver pesos, the *sine qua non* of this trade. Alternatively, if Mexicans decided to establish an opposing buyers' cartel, both cartels would have had to negotiate until they reached an equilibrium. This was in fact what happened.

It is important to notice that the right-most option (the establishment of a sellers' and a buyers' cartel) represents the only possible Nash equilibrium. While the optimal choice would have been for both Manila and Mexico to open completely, the Mexicans always had a higher payoff if they decided to maintain their cartel once Manila had decided to liberalise their shipping. In such a scenario, the Manileños would predict this happening and would have simply not liberalised their trade. Furthermore, even with an overarching authority that could have forced both parties to open and liberalise their trade, Mexico would have reverted to its dominant position. In the framework of a monopsonic market characterised by the large demand for silver pesos and the potential very high profit margins, the king could have only maintained both ends of the trade completely open if he had directly intervened to break up this monopsony. This is a fundamental part of the structure of the Pacific market: this position of monopsony is ultimately not given by any strong institutional, organisational, or coercive device of Mexican merchants, but is rather a reflection of the imbalance between demand and supply when it came to pesos.

This choice would be in line with Manileños' main motivation to maintain the high profit margins of the trade upon which the proceeds of the *correspondencias* depended, rather than to achieve market integration and lower market volatility through price convergence. Given that the option of both Acapulco and Manila liberalising could not be realised, a system of opposing cartels would have achieved this aim. Manila unilaterally expanding its volume of trade would not necessarily have led to an expanding volume of silver pesos flowing in the opposite direction.[54] Limiting the trade could lead to seasonal scarcity represented in the *feria* model, rendering market risk unimportant. Asian demand for the peso laboured against price convergence but glutting Spanish American markets with competing products was a dangerous possibility. In fact it became a reality in the last decades of the Manila trade, when the opening of Mexico to free trade from the Atlantic in 1789, the creation of the RFC in 1785 with the right to supply Spanish America with Asian goods,[55] and the maintenance of the Manila-Acapulco trade, exponentially increased the supply of Asian goods.[56] The one-Galleon system would then have made sense in a context in which maintaining profits high through limiting the volume of the trade was more important than achieving market integration. In fact, in 1722 attorney Francisco de Bedoya recognised that rationing exports was in the interest of Manileños.[57] The model of the Pacific trade was one of maximising returns. Manileños had access to the source of the silver pesos, and the strategies they adopted were designed to maximise the return in pesos relative to the goods they sent in exchange given the structure of the market. This reality was different for the East India companies. Their access to liquidity was not conditioned by the market conditions in America, but by their capacity to channel

[54] Irigoin, Alejandra, 'Why was the Manila Galleon a One Ship Trade?', mimeo, 2018, pp. 19–20.

[55] As explained in Chapter 2, the RCF did not have the right to sail directly to Acapulco, but it marketed its goods in Veracruz, Guatemala, and several ports in South America, especially El Callao.

[56] Díaz-Trechuelo, *La Real Compañía*, p. 216.

[57] AGI, Filipinas 172, N.15, *Carta de Pedro de Bedoya sobre fraude en boletas*, 1722, fol. 2b.

pesos from both domestic and international markets for their financial operations or to substitute through alternative trade routes or through production of tradable goods, like the VOC did in Java after 1690, or as the private British merchants did in India during the early nineteenth century.[58] For the companies, scaling the volume and number of operations was necessary to cast a wide net. These different models are explicitly compared in Chapter 7.

This, however, does not explain the reason behind freighting only one ship. Once the need to limit the exchange had been established, expanding the numbers of ships did not necessarily alter the result of the Acapulco negotiation for the better. Nevertheless, the drawback of one unique vessel was the increased risk of losing everything in the trade season without being able to diversify the risk. In other words, market rationing could have been achieved easily with two ships as much as with just one, but using two ships, as the king ordered, would have significantly increased the chances of saving the trading season even if one of the vessels had sunk.[59] Why then use only one Galleon, even if its hold kept increasing to reach the gargantuan proportions of 2,000 tonners?

The reason is shown in Fig. 4.2, which presents a different game. Since as established in Fig. 4.1, Manileños and Mexicans established their own cartels to face the negotiations at Acapulco, sending two galleons instead of one could lead to a prisoner's dilemma for the Manileños if at some point during the Pacific crossing, both ships were separated. The Pacific crossing was the longest crossing in the world without watering stops of any kind. The Galleons also relied on the *tornaviaje*, which consisted of catching the northern Pacific current which flowed eastwards, taking ships dangerously close to the northern Pacific storm region off the coasts of Japan. There were plenty of instances of ships separating during the trip, after which chances were high that they would not reunite.[60] These

[58] On the Dutch, see Chapter 2, Sect. 2.1. On the British, perhaps the most famous case is the rise of indigo plantations in Bengal directly managed by British entrepreneurs, see Aldous, Michael, 'From Traders to Planters: The Evolving Role and Importance of Trading Companies in the nineteenth century Anglo-Indian Trade', *Business History* (online 2019):1–18.

[59] This is consistently repeated during the dispositions collected in Ávarez Abreu, *Extracto Historial*.

[60] Schurz, *The Manila*, Chapter 7 reports plenty of these occurrences. Calvo, *Espacios, climas*, also gives detailed information on the Pacific crossing for the latter half of the eighteenth century.

	Arrives	Not Arrives
Sell	1,0	0,1
Not Sell	0,1	1,0

Fig. 4.2 Two vessels accidented game

chances must have necessarily increased during the seventeenth century when a period of unstable El Niño patterns in the Pacific increased the length of the crossing by up to a third of the normal duration.[61] Given that the negotiation capabilities of the Manileños rested on maintaining a unified front in Acapulco, and that they had to clear the harbour before a specific date, two ships separating and arriving at different times would lead to potentially catastrophic consequences for the Manileños.

If two vessels lost communication during the trip, the passengers of the first vessel to arrive faced a single-transaction game with extremely high uncertainty. Without knowing whether their companion ship had sunk, or it was simply delayed, they faced two options: to start the fair and sell, or to wait. This was problematic since they were fighting against the deadline imposed by the typhoon season on the other side of the Pacific. If they waited and the other ship arrived, they would have cut down the time available for negotiation and they would have more goods to sell, driving down prices. If they waited but no ship arrived, the offer of Asian goods would have been reduced, with prices rising accordingly, but there would still be the loss of time to account for. If they decided to sell without the second ship arriving, they risked spoiling the market if the second ship managed to arrive. If they decided to sell and the ship did not arrive, they could not realise the full rise of prices that would have accompanied the increasing certainty that the other vessels would not arrive in time, but they would have more time to negotiate better prices. Each of these scenarios could lead to outcomes which may have been better than the other in practice, something that is not reflected in the notional payoffs in Fig. 4.1. The purpose of these payoffs is to reflect that there was no possible Nash Equilibrium but only a series of trade-offs. Crucially, the

[61] Parker, *Global Crisis*, pp. 15–16.

main aim is to represent that this was a one-decision process which had the potential of ruining the entire season, and it had to be taken with no information of any kind.

In this framework, it is important to mention that the structure of Manila's capital markets, the characteristics of *correspondencias*, and the inherent risk of loss at sea, meant that the true danger for the galleon freighters was not the loss of a ship, but spoiling the trade season. First, the actual risk of loss at sea was never too high in the context of the largest sailing in the world. Arteaga, Desierto, and Koyama compare 12.6% of Galleons shipwrecked in the Manila-Acapulco crossing for 3.5% of the Dutch Cape route for the period 1595–1795,[62] but they do not take into consideration the fact that the Dutch Cape route never crossed through a hurricane or typhoon region and that they had several watering stops available for repairs. Importantly, the 12.6% figure includes *arribadas*[63] rather than just shipwrecks, yet the Dutch figure only includes shipwrecks, so the two figures are not comparable. For the period 1722 to 1821,[64] only 4% of Galleons were shipwrecked.[65] This is a low rate in the context of the longest crossing of a body of water *without watering stops*. Second, the risk of loss at sea did not affect the freighters monetarily because it was internalised by the legacy funds through the *correspondencias*. This does not mean that the freighters would behave dishonestly since a shipwreck often entailed a loss of life, and even if only their consignees travelled in the Galleons, these were usually relatives, friends, or acquaintances of the citizens that remained in Manila.

Risk of loss at sea was thus not an urgent concern, but as explained in Chapter 3, the city of Manila was vested in the profits of the Pacific exchange through the legacy funds. Freighters were oftentimes also owners of legacy funds and managers of the *obras pías* that redistributed the profits of the trade in the form of welfare to the entire city. It is therefore understandable that the worst potential threat for the freighters was the possibility of spoiling the profits of the Acapulco negotiation to

[62] Arteaga et al., 'Shipwrecked', p. 1.

[63] *Arribadas* were instances in which Galleons failed to take the right winds and had to return to Manila.

[64] Thus, excluding the disastrous consequences of the changes of El Niño during the seventeenth century.

[65] Calculated from Yuste, *Emporios*, Cuadro I, and Cheong, 'The Decline', p. 153.

the point where they could not cover the costs of purchasing and shipping the goods, along with repaying their *correspondencias*—costs that they had to incur *before* participating in the Acapulco transaction. Along with the generally safe transit between Manila and Acapulco and back, it is understandable that Manileños preferred to do away altogether with the potential prisoner's dilemmas that may arise if two or more ships travelled together for one single fair, and concentrate shipping in one vessel, however big its dimensions. Hence the Manileños' offer to send one Galleon in their correspondence with the king,[66] and their challenge of the king's strict ruling that two vessels should always make the crossing to diversify the risk: the greatest problem was not that one ship would sink with the proceeds of an entire season, but that the loss of communication and resulting lack of coordination could spoil the market.

4.3 The Role of Demand in the Pacific Business Model

This chapter reveals the business logic behind the one-Galleon system based on the motivation of Manileños to remain as intermediaries, and the comparative position of strength of Mexican wholesalers resulting from their control over the supply of pesos, a coin demanded as currency for global trade which had no substitutes. Both Manileños and Mexicans were aware of this, as much as they were aware that the products shipped by Manileños could potentially be substituted by those shipped from the Atlantic by the Europeans. The result was a monopsonic market structure that required the Manileños to establish their own mirror cartel in Acapulco to maintain the profit margins that motivated the Pacific crossing and guaranteed the welfare of the legacy funds and Manila. The great demand that existed for the peso dictated the structure of the market, and therefore the operation of business.

The one-Galleon model represented a Nash Equilibrium. This model was suboptimal in the sense that it did not lower transaction costs. In essence, it maintained the profits of intermediating the Pacific exchange in pesos at the expense of limiting the scale of the exchange. Market integration was foregone, but two things need to be considered. First, as this chapter has shown, integration was not possible even if Manileños

[66] Álvarez Abreu, *Extracto*, ff: 50–56.

wanted it as long as the Mexican wholesalers grouped in their *Consulado* retained their controlling position in the flow of pesos. Second, given Manila's stake in the trade through the *obras pías*, it is doubtful that Manila wanted higher integration. The welfare that accrued to the city relied on the premia charged by the *correspondencias* given by the *obras pías*, and these premia in turn relied on the profit margins of the trade. Market integration would have entailed lowering the price differentials of consumption goods across the Pacific, and thus the profit margins of the trade, the premia of *correspondencias*, and ultimately the welfare of the city.

Thus, the Pacific trade lacked integration between its components. Asia provided consumption goods, America provided silver pesos, and Manila provided the working capital and underwrote the risk. In comparison, the joint-stock companies followed a more integrated model, in which financing and operating the trade were internalised within the same company. Joint-stock companies, which purchased goods from their own factors and agents at the source and sold in auctions to the retailers in the home markets, did not face the same kind of hold-ups as Manileños. Their problem instead was to obtain enough working capital in Asia to maintain their volume of operations.[67] In this regard, joint-stock companies faced bottlenecks, not least because in the trade with Asia, working capital needed to be in the form of silver specie, preferably pesos. The companies adopted a different strategy and a different operational model to deal with this issue, which will be reviewed in later chapters. Both models, nevertheless, failed to reduce transaction costs and usher in price convergence through trade.[68]

The high transaction costs that resulted from the lack of integration in the Pacific could be sustained by all participants as long as there was room to deflect these costs to the consumers. It is here that the most fundamental impact of the large demand for silver specie is to be found. Demand was large enough—as evidenced by the returns mentioned in Chapter 2—that it could internalise the transaction costs that resulted from the lack of vertical integration. In the context of the global specie trade, the separation of the Pacific exchange into its component parts

[67] Chaudhuri, 'The East India', pp. 24 & 29, Chaudhuri, 'The Financing', pp. 110–111.

[68] For the East India companies, see De Vries, 'The limits', p. 731, De Vries, 'Understanding', pp. 32–34.

allowed for some level of efficiency. As said at the beginning of the chapter, the Pacific trade could not remain fragmented, reaping high profit margins, without enticing new entrants into the game. It is necessary to explain how Manila managed to monopolise the operation of the Pacific trade so consistently, and in this, Manila's capital markets played a fundamental role. The capital market of the city had the tools to attract savings from individuals and to transform retained earnings from trade into working capital and reach a certain volume of economies of scale that mitigated the problems arising from the lack of integration. Manila adapted to the economic circumstances of the global peso trade and followed an alternative model of Horizontal Specialisation as defined in the introduction. How Manila managed to do this is examined in the next chapter.

CHAPTER 5

An Alternative Model of Trade Finance

Asian demand for silver specie provided ample opportunities for the Manileños to realise a profitable negotiation across the Pacific. However, as explained in Chapter 4, it also skewed the bargaining power of the Pacific Run decidedly in favour of the Mexican wholesalers that controlled the provisioning of pesos. In this context, the capital provided by the *obras pías* in Manila guaranteed the city's access to the Pacific exchange while converting it into a stakeholder of the trade, while the one-Galleon business model provided a strategic assurance that enough profits could be made in Acapulco to capitalise the legacy funds. In essence, the one-Galleon system represented Manila's best strategy to maintain the profitability of the trade given the coordination failure that followed the wholesalers' control of the supply of pesos and the lack of integration.

Economic logic suggests that the system of mirror buyers and sellers' cartels that dominated the Acapulco fair, in a trade marked by such profit margins as was the Pacific exchange, would have encouraged the emergence of interlopers, eventually provoking the collapse of the cartels. The existing trove of literature on the corporation, and its role on Early Modern trade, would also predict that chartered joint-stock companies would have the volume, the capital, and the organisational sophistication

J. J. Rivas Moreno, *The Capital Market of Manila and the Pacific Trade, 1668–1838*, Palgrave Studies in Economic History,
https://doi.org/10.1007/978-3-031-71810-6_5

to wrestle the control of the Pacific silver trade away from the Manileños.[1] Coase's theory of the firm itself suggests that vertical integration would be a rational response when high transaction costs make contracting through the market expensive.[2] Yet none of this happened.

Manila found a way to mitigate the lack of market integration and to fend off interloping attempts, whether from joint-stock companies or private merchants. The Pacific exchange as a whole seemed to have followed an alternative strategy of Horizontal Specialisation in contrast to the vertical integration of the East India Companies. Horizontal Specialisation is defined as a process in which each link of the retail chain unilaterally lowers transaction costs by specialising in one aspect of the exchange. The outcome of the specialisation of each link was a fall in overall transaction costs that kept the Manila trade competitive. In the concrete case of Manila, the city specialised as the provider of trade finance. Manila underwrote, internalised, and distributed all the risks of the Pacific exchange, providing both the Asian and American merchants at each end of the exchange a done deal. Manila became indispensable as the financier of the trade and managed to reach a certain level of economies of scale in the provision of working capital that mitigated the problems of the lack of market integration. In doing so, Manila equally solved the challenges associated with long-distance trade, namely the heightened risks of loss at sea, the difficulty of monitoring and enforcing contracts across continents, and the liquidity constraints that resulted from increased demands for capital. This chapter explores how Manila mitigated and internalised the inherent risks of exchange, and demonstrates how its capital market, in conjunction with its institutional framework and business model, mobilised enough resources to finance its trade.

5.1 Types of Risks & Mitigation Strategies

Early Modern trade suffered from three main broad categories of risk: risk of loss at sea, market risk, and agency risk. In poorly integrated markets constrained by sail technology and climate, all three risks had the capacity

[1] Steensgaard, *The Asian*, pp. 412–413, Harris, *Going*, Emmer, 'The Organisation', Carlos and Nicholas, 'Agency Problems'.

[2] Coase, 'The Nature', p. 396, Williamson's analysis is especially relevant given the potential for holdups discussed in Chapter 4, Williamson, 'The Theory'.

to ruin a trading season in one way or another. Each of these categories is reviewed, with an emphasis on how Manila mitigated them.

Risk of Loss at Sea

The risk of loss at sea was the most evident kind of risk for a trade route that crossed the largest ocean in the world. However, the risk of loss at sea was not critical, not even high. As reviewed in Chapter 4, for the period 1722–1821 the chance of a Galleon sinking stood at 4%. *Arribadas*—the failure to catch the Japanese currents and cross the Pacific—were more common, but no loss accrued from it to the *obras pías*. The accounts of the Third Order of Saint Dominic confirm that in those instances, the *correspondencias* simply remained in effect.[3] *Arribadas* can in fact be interpreted as an instance of prudent behaviour in which the Galleons' pilots and captains chose to return to port when problems arose once *en route*, as there were no watering stops where repairs could be performed in the Pacific until the coast of California. *Arribadas*, in any case, were equally uncommon during the eighteenth century.

Risk of loss at sea represented a small threat to the capital markets of Manila. Even in those instances where ships were lost, freighters suffered no losses as the *correspondencias* transferred the risk contractually to the *obras pías*. Similarly, the investments of legacy funds were diversified across the Asian and American legs (Chapter 3), which greatly decreased the chances of total loss. Furthermore, the nature of the funds, which were opened with a testament, often after death, meant that *obras pías* were immune to panic runs. The practice of spreading the risk by pooling capital for each *correspondencia* from several funds[4] meant that prospective founders of legacy funds had an interest in maintaining their funds active despite losses, since it gave them access to the capital deposited in all the funds when they requested *correspondencias*. Nevertheless, the loss of a Galleon represented a serious blow to the *obras pías*' investments when it happened, however unusual. Another important risk was the danger of capture by enemies while at sea. Anson's capture of the *Covadonga* in 1743 led to litigation between the *obras pías* and freighters

[3] APSR, this practice is evidenced in all the account books.

[4] Villacorta's audit of the Misericordia provides a breakdown of the funds used for each *correspondencia* issued by the Brotherhood in the year 1752, AGI Filipinas 303, N. 6, 1750–1752.

over returns from Acapulco that had been left in New Spain as a precautionary measure given the start of war against England.[5] The loss of a Galleon to enemies meant an irreplaceable loss for *obras pías*, reducing the overall capitalisation of the legacy funds, and therefore, the supply of capital for the next trade seasons.[6] Nevertheless, the risk of capture by enemies remained very low. Only four Manila Galleons were ever captured between 1565 and 1815.[7]

In the Atlantic, the *flotas* functioned under the *avería* system. The *avería* was a contribution to insure the fleets that travelled to the Americas. Under the *avería*, freighters would pay a rate based on the value of their freight to the *Consulado* of Seville. If the *flotas* were captured, lost, or damaged, the *Consulado* would reimburse the loss to those that had paid the *avería*.[8] In the Pacific, however, the *avería* was absent. In 1734 king Felipe V recognised that the *avería* had never been collected or enforced in the Philippines.[9] Loss at sea, when it happened, was absorbed by the legacy funds. In 1769 the king granted the collection of the *avería* on the Galleon to the *Consulado* of Manila upon its establishment.[10] *Correspondencias*, however, kept transferring the risk of loss at sea from the freighter to the legacy funds, and there is no information regarding whether the *avería* then paid the legacy funds for the loss. The cases of loss and capture were few enough to not seriously disturb the capacity of *obras pías* to generate working capital and maintain the trade afloat in the long-term.

[5] BNE Porcones 972(25), 1747, contains the opinion of a Jesuit from Manila on the case.

[6] Irigoin, 'Why was', p. 18, the impact of the *Covadonga* is also discussed in Sect. 5.2.

[7] Schurz, *The Manila*, p. 303.

[8] Orlando Díaz, Manuel, 'The Spanish Average System of Insurance and Loss Prevention', *The Journal of Insurance* 28, nº 4 (1961), pp. 85–86 & Luque Talaván, Miguel, 'La avería en el tráfico marítimo-mercantil indiano: notas para su estudio (siglos XVI–XVIII)', *Revista Complutense de Historia de América*, nº 24 (1998): 113–145, there was however a distinction between the *avería de armada*, the tax referred in this text, and the *avería gruesa* or general average, García Garralón, Marta, 'The Nautical Republic of the *Carrera de Indias*: Commerce, Navigation, *Casos Fortuitos*, and *Avería Gruesa* in the Sixteenth Century', in *General Average and Risk Management in Medieval and Early Modern Maritime Business*, ed. Maria Fusaro, Andrea Addobbati, and Luisa Piccinno (Singapore: Springer, 2023), p. 226.

[9] AGI Filipinas 268 N.1, 1752.

[10] AGI Filipinas 941 N. 1, 1769.

The situation was different for the European joint-stock companies and the independent traders that sailed across the Indian Ocean and the South China sea. In the case of the EIC, the shipbuilding interests that formed the core of the shareholders made the company hire rather than own its own ships. Thus, the EIC never insured its vessels, taking losses when they occurred.[11] Nevertheless, East India companies enjoyed the indirect benefits of scale, including forts and convoys for protection, as well as anchorages and docking waystations like the Dutch Cape colony. Private merchants unattached to the East India Companies did not have the advantage of military infrastructure and had to rely instead on private insurance.[12] Thus, private merchants could deflect the majority of their losses to insurance companies, that is, professionalised third parties that could internalise the damage once it occurred.

The one-Galleon model prevented the use of premium insurance in the Pacific crossing since it could not diversify risks across several ships. The risk of loss at sea remained low, and when losses did occur, they were transferred to the well-capitalised legacy funds through the *correspondencias*. The loss covered by *correspondencias*, however, referred only to cargo. Like the English East India company, the Manila Galleons were uninsured. Nevertheless, the loss of the vessel itself never impacted the individual freighters or the *obras pías* since the vessel legally belonged to the king. As the privilege of the city of Manila, the Galleon was built by the local treasury, which spent considerable amounts of money in the process. The labour involved in building the Galleons came from the natives, either as duties payable in labour known as *polos*,[13] or as salaried work paid by the royal officials who supervised the building of the ships and were responsible for the allocation of expenditures and the quality of the work.[14] Consequently, the cost of transport was effectively transferred to the local treasury. As a result, the Galleon did not need to be insured by any private entity or individual, but more crucially, Manileños were capable of deflecting both the costs of transportation and the risk of loss

[11] Furber, *John Company*, pp. 13 & 38, Neal, 'The Dutch', p. 222.

[12] Leonard, A.B., 'Underwriting British Trade to India and China, 1780–1835', *The Historical Journal* 55, nº 4 (2012), p. 991.

[13] Alonso Álvarez, *El costo*, pp. 169–170.

[14] AGI Filipinas 941 N. 1, 1769.

or damage to the vessel to the royal purse,[15] lowering their expenditures, which in turn meant that they had a higher margin to adjust their prices if needed.

Market Risk

The idea that price volatility can only be effectively diminished through the integration of markets implies that the lack of integration in the Pacific should have made the trade vulnerable to market risk. However, this was never considered a great problem of the line, and as seen in Chapter 3, even theologians justified turning *censos* that invested on the land to legacy funds that invested on the trade based on the security and reliability of the commerce. The paucity of data regarding prices of goods, both in Manila and in New Spain, prevent any long-term quantitative analysis of price convergence between both regions. Nevertheless, as explained in Chapter 2, profits remained large throughout the period. The great demand for silver pesos in Asia and the limited volume of the exchange meant that the purchasing power of the peso could not converge across the Pacific. The premium that the peso enjoyed in China as a means of payment also increased profits and mitigated market risk. The fact that Asian merchants (and especially Chinese) were willing to pay prices for the peso that surpassed its inherent silver content meant that exporting pesos was necessarily a good business.

Contemporaries understood that prices could not converge. As late as 1804, when the competition from the Real Compañía de Filipinas and the disruptions of the war had damaged the Galleon trade, Antonio Alonso de Terán wrote from Madrid to Mexico—likely to Gabriel Gutiérrez de Terán, president of the Mexico merchant guild—with a scheme to hoard Asian goods from the Galleon trade upon the rumour that the Philippines could be transferred to a different nation. Antonio's scheme was anchored on the principle that regardless of the outcome of the negotiations, no loss would be incurred, since the Galleon provided cheaper prices of Asian goods in New Spain than those brought by the Real Compañía de Filipinas, but also, with the understanding that "nothing can ever happen that

[15] Irigoin, 'Why was', p. 20.

would lower the price of Asian goods below what is common".[16] This mercantile correspondence highlights the extent to which market risk was mitigated in the Pacific exchange.

This similarly meant that Manileños enjoyed an absolute advantage over their competitors, since they monopolised the least-costly, most direct access route to the pesos of New Spain. The only danger that could affect prices—and therefore the profitability of the Acapulco fair—was glutting Spanish American markets with goods, thus lowering the profits that could be achieved in Acapulco. Limiting the trade to an annual Galleon and transactions to an annual fair implied limiting the amounts of goods exported to New Spain.[17] The timing of these fairs being annual also meant that American markets could not be easily glutted. Because of the situation of scarcity that existed right prior to the arrival of the Galleons, information between the regions that participated in the trade became less important since prices would have been high regardless. In fact, among the private bills and secret instructions to consignors recorded in the 1767 inspection of the galleon *San Carlos Borromeo* there is not a single mention of prices,[18] even though these documents were created for private use by the Manila merchants: the exact price of goods in Acapulco for Manileños at home—especially for the *obras pías*, whose returns from *correspondencias* were specified as a percentage of the principal—was not as important as the overall profitability of the exchange. A resilient return of 30 or 50% year on year was more important than knowing if bundles of reeled silk sold at a 190 or 210% markup one specific year.

Limiting information and transactions not only resulted in high prices, but also meant that the costs that Manileños had to incur were lower. No expensive networks of agents had to be maintained, neither were privately chartered fleets necessary. A crucial characteristic of the Manila transpacific trade was the ability that Manileños had to deflect several of these costs to either the treasury or the ultimate consumers. Penetration of New Spain was impossible precisely because Mexican wholesalers resented competition in the provision of goods to the interior of the country, especially the silver mines. The reduced costs and the assurance against prices

[16] Newberry Library, Vault Ayer MS 1823, *Correspondence between the Conde and Condesa de Casa Flórez and their financial agents, the Teráns*, 1788–1815.

[17] AGI Filipinas 229 N.1, 1724.

[18] AGI Filipinas 941 N. 1, 1769.

plummeting left Galleon freighters with room for profit margins without having to invest an increasingly higher proportion of those profits into trading infrastructure. But this was also the result of the Galleon trade's specialisation in the good that enjoyed the largest demand, the largest profit margins, and to which they had the most direct access: the silver peso.

This system not only operated in the Pacific exchange. Baskes and Lamikiz have interpreted the Spanish Atlantic system of fleets and fairs as a way of lowering market volatility by creating periodic artificial scarcity, thus reducing market risk without the need to invest in the infrastructure of informants and overseas agents.[19] However, Baskes and Lamikiz do not consider the global demand for silver and the resulting bargaining power of Mexican wholesalers. For Baskes and Lamikiz, the fairs and the restriction of supply of goods were strategies motivated to diminish market risk.[20] This book argues that fairs and the resulting mitigation of market risk were both a consequence of the market structure of the exchange. The result, in any case, was that market risk in the silver trade with America was diminished, both in the Atlantic and the Pacific.

The logic of mitigating market risk by controlling supply also guided the early sales strategies of the VOC and EIC. Joint-stock companies developed early in the seventeenth century a sales method through which their fleets could arrive at any time in the trading year without untimely depressing market prices at their destination by competing with one another and glutting the market. Chartered companies stored goods as they arrived, and only released them to the market through carefully timed auctions which smoothed prices throughout the year, essentially creating artificial scarcity, rising prices, and creating the super-profits that financed the military and commercial infrastructure of the East India

[19] Baskes, *Staying*, p. 68, & Lamikiz, Xabier, 'Patrones de Comercio y Flujo de Información Comercial entre España y América durante el siglo XVIII', *Revista de Historia Económica* XXV, n° 2 (2007), p. 239.

[20] Baskes, *Staying*, p. 98, Lamikiz, Xabier, 'Transatlantic Networks and Merchant Guild Rivalry in Colonial Trade with Peru: 1729–1780: A new interpretation', *Hispanic American Historical Review* 91, n° 2 (2011), pp. 313–314.

Companies.[21] This was the mechanism through which the monopoly obtained in foundational charters worked.

During the early history of the East India Companies, the corporations attempted to monopolise Europe's direct trade with Asia, by force if necessary. In this they not only fought against the long-established local trade, but also against other Europeans. This led to another consequence regarding market risk, which was the capacity of East India companies to manipulate the market by curtailing, or outright destroying, the trades they could not control. The Dutch had to resort to violence more often than superior trading techniques to successfully expel the Portuguese from Asian markets.[22] The Dutch came close to monopolising the supply of some spices, but their efforts were cemented in the use of violence rather than any organisational or financial advantage. A prime example was the massacre of EIC agents in Ambon in 1623.[23] During the 1650s, the Dutch stranglehold on cloves was threatened by the emergence of an alternative trade through the independent polity of Macassar. The Dutch waged a constant war against Macassar until it the flow of cloves through the country was eradicated.[24] Steensgaard shows how the VOC's control of the supply of cloves allowed for their price in Amsterdam to increase by a range of between 54% and 65% in just two years, between 1624 and 1626.[25] But controlling the flows of spices was not easy, and it required a constant investment in warfare.

Even then, the companies were never capable of bringing vast markets like India and China under their exclusive control. Interlopers, especially other European companies like the French East India company, the Ostend company, or the Danish company intermittently threatened

[21] Musgrave, Peter, 'The Economics of Uncertainty: The Structural Revolution in the Spice Trade, 1480–1640', in *Spices in the Indian Ocean World*, ed. MN Pearson, Aldershot: Variorum (1996), Neal, 'The Dutch', pp. 347–348, Steensgaard, 'The growth', pp. 121–123.

[22] Souza, *The Survival*, for the Far East and Disney, A.R., *Twilight of the Pepper Empire: Portuguese Trade in Southwest India in the Early Seventeenth Century*, Cambridge (Mass.): Harvard University Press (1978) and Subrahmanyam, Sanjay, *The Political Economy of Commerce Southern India, 1500–1650*, Cambridge: Cambridge University Press (1990) for Portuguese India.

[23] Bassett, D. K., 'The "Amboyna Massacre" of 1623', *Journal of Southeast Asian History* 1, n° 2 (1960), pp. 1–19.

[24] Souza, *The Survival*, pp. 88–89 & 108–109.

[25] Steensgaard, *The Asian*, pp. 150–151.

their direct intermediation of goods. Chaudhuri shows that the EIC eventually moved to a more market-oriented procurement strategy, focused on estimating demand in the home market and placing orders in the Asian factories.[26] The East India Companies failed to establish an effective monopoly over Asian trade, but this does not mean that they did not try. Yet, with the support of their respective governments they could suppress competition to an extent. For example, the independent merchants that formed the Ostend Company under the nominal protection of the Holy Roman Empire had to close in 1731 after the English and Dutch governments threatened reprisals.[27] The marriage of trade and violence has two important implications when it comes to studying how the East India companies mitigated market risk: first, it is impossible to clearly distinguish whether organisational or extra-economic factors were responsible for mitigating this risk, and to what extent; second, the use of violence required a heavy investment in extra-commercial expenses, which dented profit margins in the trading operations, thus increasing their vulnerability to price swings.[28]

Market risk for the EIC and the VOC within Asia were also different since they organised their intra-Asian trade in different ways. The EIC was willing to cooperate with private merchants, for which it provided help, financing, and institutional support. In exchange, these agents served as a cheap way of aligning motivation[29] and outsourcing information.[30] Networks of interlopers efficiently extended the EIC's reach while operating outside the corporate payroll,[31] an arrangement that worked as long as interlopers remained within Asian waters and did not threaten the real

[26] Chaudhuri, *The Trading*, pp. 58–60.

[27] Furber, *Rival Empires*, p. 218.

[28] Gelderblom et al., 'The Formative', pp. 1056–1057, according to Gelderblom et al. and Brandon, modern corporate features such as permanent capital and limited liability were innovations to shield the directors from investors' concerns over military extension, Brandon, 'Between…', p. 217, Harris, however, considers shareholder liability to have been a later development, Harris, Ron, 'A New Understanding of the History of Limited Liability: An Invitation for Theoretical Reframing', *Journal of Institutional Economics*, 16 (2020), pp. 646–647.

[29] Hejeebu, Santhi, 'Contract Enforcement in the English East India Company', *The Journal of Economic History* 65, n° 2 (2005), p. 517.

[30] Erikson, *Between Monopoly*, p. 108.

[31] Hejeebu, 'Contact Enforcement', p. 515.

source of profits for the joint-stock companies: the Asia-Europe direct trade. In contrast, the VOC insisted on retaining the corporate nature of this exchange. This posed a challenge for the VOC, as it meant that it had to maintain the levels of investment required in keeping the trade lines functioning, hence increasing its "vulnerability to competitive pressures" according to Neal.[32] The costs of running mercantile empires meant that the profit margins of joint-stock companies were burdened with the expenses of fortifications, navies, armies, and bureaucracies, expenditures that interlopers did not have to transfer to their selling prices. The search for goods with higher profit margins, the acquisition of increasingly diverse political commitments, and the need to constantly diversify, in short, each step in the long-term transformation from trading association to territorial empire, can be viewed as an attempt to increase revenues in the face of expanding costs in an ever-growing downward spiral. And yet the East India companies did not manage to regain their competitiveness in Asian waters. Instead, after 1795 for the VOC and 1813 and 1833 for the EIC, they lost their commercial monopolies.[33] The corporations followed the opposite model of Manila, eschewing specialisation for growth in scale, which in turn meant more vested interests, more armies, more navies, and more costs. When costs were high, profit margins were leaner, and so market risk could become a problem.

Manila's model was based on reducing costs and maximising profits by specialising in the provision of pesos, which were necessary to settle trade with Asia and thus, were demanded globally. The capacity of Manila to thrive and maintain its position in the trading world of East Asia was predicated on its advantaged access to the liquidity provided by Spanish America. As explained in Chapters 2 and 3, the commercial wealth of the city upon which the financial markets were cemented was based on their capacity to arbitrage the purchasing power of silver pesos for Asian goods. Manileños rarely sailed abroad, relying instead on the annual fleets of Chinese junks arriving from Fujian and the regular lines connecting

[32] Neal, Larry, *The Rise of Financial Capitalism: International Capital Markets in the Age of Reason* (Cambridge: Cambridge University Press, 1990), p. 139, on the profitability of the EIC intra-Asian carrier trade, Bowen, *The Business*, p. 251 & for the 1790s Cheong, Wang Eang, 'Some aspects of British Trade and Finance in Canton with special reference to the role of Anglo-Spanish Trade in the Eastern Seas, 1784–1834', (PhD diss., University of London, 1962), pp. 100–101.

[33] According to Furber, by the 1780s the EIC's India trade was already uncompetitive, Furber, *John Company*, pp. 268 & 314.

India and Java to Manila, often bringing products that could compete against each other in the markets of the city. In other words, the provision of Asian goods was outsourced and competitive. Specialisation on the provision of pesos meant that the investment of Manileños in infrastructure like vessels, harbours, agents across Asia, was unnecessary. Market risk was mitigated because the price of the peso could not converge between Spanish America and East Asia, and because Manila incurred very few costs in performing this arbitrage. If profits were high and costs were low, the capacity of market swings to diminish the profitability of the exchange was reduced. Specialisation in the provision of pesos also enhanced Manila's position making it indispensable. Market risk, therefore, was not a tangible threat to Manileños. The capital markets of Manila were instrumental in this outcome so long as they managed to provide the institutional framework that made pooling specie in large quantities possible, which in turn lowered the cost of capital and protected the profit margins of freighters sailing to Acapulco.

Agency Risk

Long distances and poor transport technology made information slow and sticky in the Early Modern period. Monitoring agents, enforcing contracts, and punishing violators were costly. Agency risk, the risk of moral hazard, adverse selection, principal-agent problems, embodied in skimming profits, embezzling funds, or outright cheating are a main concern for historians that seek to explain the emergence of long-distance trade.[34] The Manila trade presented two main different levels in which agency risk could be problematic. On the Acapulco fair level, it was difficult for the consignors to monitor that the consignees that negotiated with their merchandise behaved honestly, since they operated on a different continent, and it was these very consignees who brought back the information and the profits to Manila. On the fund level, the fact that a high number of funds were opened after the death of the donors created an unusual situation in which there was no living owner to speak of to monitor the performance of the *mesas*. Similarly, the fact that members

[34] Greif, 'The fundamental', pp. 251–284, Greif, *Institutions*, Hejeebu, 'Contract', Erikson, Emily, and Samila, Sampsa, 'Networks, Institutions, and Uncertainty: Information Exchange in Early Modern Markets', *The Journal of Economic History* 78, nº 4 (2018): 1034–1067, Carlos and Nicholas, 'Agency…'.

of the *mesas* were also the main participants—directly or indirectly—in the Galleon trade, and as such the main clients of the funds, could lead to conflicts of interest.

On the Acapulco level, as demonstrated in Chapter 4, all participants, from the consignors to the consignees and the Galleon officials acted together. They did so already in the capital markets in Manila by forming borrower coalitions, standing for one another as guarantors, often *de mancomún* (in legal association, making each individual directly liable for the actions of the other).[35] This association often went beyond legal links and into the realm of family and kinship. As an example, the consignee in charge of selling the goods freighted by José Antonio de Memije y Quirós—one of the most affluent merchants of Manila—in the 1767 Galleon *San Carlos Borromeo* was his son, Vicente Laureano de Memije.[36] Like any Early Modern merchant network, marital and trust bonds played a role, meaning that a cheating agent could expect retribution at home. Similarly, because of these connections, the profits that accrued from the Acapulco fair would eventually benefit the consignees themselves, directly or through their families and friends.

Consignees were not only members of borrower coalitions, meaning that they had enhanced access to capital from the *obras pías* by virtue of the lists of joint-guarantors they could present in their requests for *correspondencias* and the fact that managers and borrowers were all related in one way or another. They also received monetary compensation for their work as consignees. The sworn instructions of consignors attached to the bills for the 1767 galleon show that consignors were given 5% of the proceeds of the Acapulco sale.[37] Cheating was also easy to discover. Consignors usually designated three consignees to conduct the sale of their goods, with the common instruction that the general in command of the Galleon be considered as a fourth consignee.[38] The *General* of the Galleon acted as a communal defendant of the Galleon freighters. He was the elected speaker and representative of the crew and passengers of

[35] See Appendix.

[36] AGI Filipinas 941 N.1, 1769.

[37] AGI Filipinas 941 N. 1, 1769.

[38] AGI Filipinas 941 N. 1, 1769.

the vessel in front of the authorities and between themselves.[39] Attempts at cheating would have been easily spotted by the other consignees, and the network of consignors and consignees was so dense, that unless all consignees could be brought to act in coordination, it was virtually impossible to cheat on a contract without it being discovered by the consignors. Cheating on the galleon level was essentially an expensive, high-risk, zero-sum game: there was no rational motivation for it.

The informal links that connected consignors and consignees together were cemented and enhanced by the formal institutions of the trade. The prohibition of Manileños from penetrating New Spain to sell their products to the ultimate consumers forced Manileños to face a cohesive cartel of buyers in Acapulco. Given the business dynamics explained in Chapter 4, the Manileños obtained better results by sticking together than by trying to go behind each other's backs. This in turn gave more significance to the formal contracts entered by the Manileños with one another: it was not easy to go against a power of attorney in the hopes of facing no retribution when so much was at stake in Acapulco, and when the promise of returns for such an action was so uncertain.

On the fund level, the crucial characteristic of the legal infrastructure meant that while access to information on the legacy funds and *correspondencias* was difficult for anyone outside Manila, it was relatively easy for those inside. The archive of the *escribano* (notary) made this possible.[40] There is also evidence that copies of notarial documents were made for the parties to the contract, since sealed notarial writs have been found among the management books of the Third Order of Saint Dominic.[41] Since the testaments that opened legacy funds and the *correspondencias* were notarial documents, institutions managing legacy funds were able to monitor each other. As an example, the Third Orders of Saint Francis and Saint Dominic included among their management books lists of all the proceeds that accrued to them as pious destinations from the legacy funds managed by the Misericordia.[42]

[39] AGI Filipinas 941 N. 1, 1769, the role of the *general* is attested throughout the entire proceeding, and he may have performed a role akin to the "*diputados de comercio*" in the Atlantic fair of Jalapa, Real Díaz, *Las Ferias*, pp. 38–39.

[40] The documents contained in ACCHS-CSIC are the protocols that composed these archives.

[41] APSR Tomo 215, *Orden Tercera. Datos y cuentas de sus obras pías*, 1757–1806.

[42] AFIO 52/16, 1816, APSR Tomo 215, 1757–1806.

Some correspondence between the Order of Saint John (governors of the Spanish Hospital in Manila) and the Third Order of Saint Dominic regarding proceeds of funds under the management of the latter that accrued to the former have survived, showing that the Order of Saint John knew exactly how much the legacy funds of the Third Order of Saint Dominic owed them as pious destinations and providing evidence that monitoring and control were actively pursued by the different *mesas*.[43] This level of monitoring between institutions is understandable and expected given the growing influence of the *correspondencia* funds in financing the provision of public goods in Manila. The Order of Saint John, which administered the hospital of the Spanish in the city, was one of the many beneficiaries of the proceeds of the funds from different institutions. According to the order's chronicler, Maldonado de Puga, in 1742 the Order of Saint John, received 5,732 pesos annually out of proceeds of *correspondencia* funds (64% of a total annual income of 9,022 pesos in 1742). Of these, 3,746 pesos came from funds managed by the Misericordia, 1,361 from funds managed by the Order of Saint John itself, and 625 from funds managed by the Third Order of Saint Francis.[44] The importance of external financing for institutions as central to the welfare of Manila as was the Order of Saint John, as shown in Table 5.1, illustrates the communal interest in monitoring the performance of the funds, which only increased as the *correspondencia* funds grew.

Table 5.1 Income of the order of St. John, 1742

		% Total
Funds in the Misericordia	3,746	42
Funds managed by the Order of St John	1,361	15
Funds in the Tercera Orden de San Francisco	625	7
Censos/Rents on property	1,998	22
Contributions	1,292	14
Total	9,022	100

Sources Frey Juan Manuel Maldonado de Puga, *Religiosa Hospitalidad por los Hijos del Piadoso Coripheo Patriarcha y Padre de Pobres S. Juan de Dios*, Manila, 1742

[43] APSR, Tomo 215, f. 86.

[44] Maldonado de Puga, Fr. Juan Manuel, *Religiosa Hospitalidad por los Hijos del Piadoso Coripheo Patriarcha y Padre de Pobres S. Iuan de Dios*, Granada, 1742, pp. 215–253.

The composition of the *mesas* and their annual rotation made it difficult to embezzle funds or manipulate the account books. Because the members of the *mesas* usually were the wealthiest members of the *obras pías* that administered the legacy funds, they had the least incentive to steal from them since they benefitted from the capital the funds mobilised. Stealing from the *obras pías* was tantamount to stealing from their own money pot. Even if this or any other dubious practice happened, members of the *mesas* were elected every year.[45] This meant that different individuals with a vested interest on the good functioning of the funds, either as founders themselves or simply as takers of *correspondencias*, had access to the written records of the corporations. They could therefore denounce any suspicious practices they witnessed. One such case from the early eighteenth century has survived. In it, the entrant *mesa* of the Misericordia refused to repay the salient *mesa* the money that the latter had unilaterally lent to the funds due to their bad performance that year since the statutes of the Misericordia banned such loans.[46] The brotherhoods and Third Orders, through their statutes and their members, had the tools to monitor the behaviour of managers.

Finally, each fund had an appointed accountant who was a member of the congregation. Accountants had no individual decision-making power over the funds under their care, but the rotation of accountants helped monitor the integrity of the books. Accountants kept and individualised records for each fund which they often completed referencing the *Libro de Acuerdos* (the Minutes Book in which the *mesa* recorded their decisions regarding requests for *correspondencias* among other issues). These annual accounts were then signed by the individual accountant and presented to the prior of the province to be inspected.[47] Dubious recording practices by exiting accountants could be identified and reported by new accountants, as was the case of Diego Zurita, who in 1751 started managing the fund opened by Garcés. In that year, Zurita noticed that his predecessor, Domingo Rodríguez, had left no money in the treasury despite noting down 525 pesos in the previous exercise, and that instead that quantity had been given to Francisco Ustáriz in a *correspondencia* to Acapulco at

[45] See Chapter 3 Section Fund Managers: Brotherhoods, Third Orders, and the Misericordia.

[46] BNE, MSS/11014 (H.449R.-452V.), *Informe de la Mesa de la Misericordia*, undated, early eighteenth century.

[47] APSR, this is practiced in all the account books.

50% interest. Zurita brought this to the attention of the prior by making an annotation in the account book.[48]

The existence of many mechanisms for monitoring and control, and the freedom with which information circulated within Manila, does not preclude that fund managers could not choose to not follow the law, but casts doubt on the notion that they could openly cheat other agents and the authorities without the interested connivance of others. An example is provided by the 1744 investigation of the Misericordia. The capture of the *Covadonga* by Anson in 1743 led to financial problems for the House, which brought to light borrowing practices not sanctioned by Canon Law, specifically, lending the deposits left in the legacy funds to the Manila Treasury. The king instructed ecclesiastical judge Juan de la Fuente Yépez to investigate financial irregularities in the Misericordia dating back to 1738. Yépez' investigation showed that the *mesa* had been borrowing from the funds for purposes other than those specified by the donors' wills.[49]

Two details of this case are important. First, the members of the *mesa* that stood out as the main culprits in the case were the Marquises of Salinas and Montecastro, and both had opened funds in the Misericordia in the year of 1739.[50] This meant that the Marquises were—paradoxically—both perpetrators and victims of their irregular practices. Second, the king's order to enforce the wills of the donors coincided with the end of opening funds in the Misericordia. By 1784 the Misericordia managed 56 funds.[51] The king's decision to support Yépez in his inquiry was taken in 1747, which means that the news should have reached Manila by 1748 at the earliest. By that year, 47 funds already existed in the Misericordia, after which only twelve more were opened in the next four decades, one with the confiscated goods of Matías Suárez, and another one, in 1754 by Gregorio de la Fuente Yépez, a relative of the ecclesiastical judge that brought the case to the king.[52] Meanwhile the founding of legacy funds in Manila kept increasing. Of the 25 datable funds under the management of the Third Order of Saint Dominic, 18 were opened after

[48] APSR, Tomo 304.

[49] Mesquida, 'Negotiating Charity', pp. 196–198.

[50] Ibid., p. 198, AMN 552 MS1662, Doc. 6, ff. 51a-52a & 52b-53a.

[51] AMN 552 MS1662, Doc. 6. ff. 25–66.

[52] Ibid. ff. 63–64.

1748,[53] and so were 33 of the 72 identifiable funds of the Third Order of Saint Francis,[54] proving that the opening of legacy funds in Manila never ceased. That the opening of funds in the Misericordia dried up after 1748 shows that coming under royal patronage in 1733 did not bother much the prospective founders (17 funds were opened in the Misericordia between 1733 and 1748 alone), but it indicates that these individuals did not necessarily disagree with the practice of flexible lending, and certainly they did not equate it with cheating or embezzlement. In fact, no punishment followed the Misericordia other than enforcing its own statutes, and these were changed in 1754 to reflect the more financially oriented role of the Misericordia.[55]

This case shows that there was a distinction between strictly following the rules and cheating. Manileños certainly did not consider the *mesa*'s lending to the treasury as cheating, even though it was technically illegal since the wills that opened the legacy funds specified that the endowments had to be invested in *correspondencias*. It is better to understand this case in the context of other developments that were taking place in the 1730s and 1740s. The start of the decline in trade after the capture of the *Covadonga* that lasted until the late 1770s, the petitions to transform *censos* funds into *correspondencia* funds as seen in Chapter 3, indicates that there was a realignment in Manila in which *obras pías* were looking for options. For many Manileños, therefore, the practice of lending unallocated funds to the treasury instead of rigidly placing all the money in *correspondencias* may have been excusable, even rational. The alternative, in a context in which investment opportunities were becoming scarce, would have been to not invest the money, or worse, to invest it all in the trade, with the consequent potential danger of lowering the premia. Even then, Yépez' investigation and the judgement of the king demonstrate that practices that were contrary to the statutes and wills that formed the first base of regulation in legacy funds were monitored

[53] AMN 552 MS1662, Doc. 5, 1823, f. 23.

[54] AFIO 357/5, *Nueva Norma de distribución del producto de las Obras Pías de la VOT de Manila. Notas y decretos del Sr. Alcocer* - Cuaderno ms., undated. Early twentieth century. This was an account book used by the accountant of the Third Order at the time. It shows that the funds that had been established in the eighteenth century were still in operation at the start of the 20th.

[55] Mesquida, 'Negotiating Charity', pp. 199–200.

and corrected. There was an institutional framework that guaranteed the proper enforcement of contracts.

The final source of agency risk was the risk of dishonest behaviour from takers of *correspondencias*, and the risk that they may strategically default or run away with the capital of the legacy funds. This was patently anti-economical. The capital provided by the legacy funds was the best guarantee to keep accessing the Acapulco negotiation, and the welfare paid by the funds also aligned the motivation of all Manileños with the *obras pías*. Nevertheless, defaults—strategic or otherwise—kept occurring, but it was relatively uncommon for the *obras pías* to prosecute and jail defaulters. Instead, the account books of the Third Order of Saint Dominic reveal that defaulters were excluded from future *correspondencias*.[56] Again, the close connection between the managers of different brotherhoods, their broader membership, the officialdom of the Galleon, and those that freighted to Asia and America meant that someone could not realistically be excluded from receiving capital by one corporation without the others discovering it. To give an example, in 1766 Vicente Laureano de Memije obtained four *correspondencias* to freight in the Galleon *San Carlos Borromeo* for a total value of 24,000 pesos. The *correspondencias* were given by the Countess of Lizárraga (7,000 pesos),[57] the Third Order of Saint Francis of Manila (8,000 pesos),[58] the Archbishopric of Manila (5,000 pesos),[59] and the Convent of Saint Paul (5,000 pesos).[60] His joint-guarantors in all these deals were his father, José Antonio de Memije y Quirós, his brother Francisco, Alberto Jacinto de los Reyes, and Alejandro Rodríguez Varela. As seen previously, Vicente Laureano de Memije was one of the consignees nominated by his father, Jose Antonio, for the 1766 Galleon, along with Francisco José Ramírez and Demetrio Nasarre.[61] The connections between all these participants formed a dense network. At that time, the Memijes were members of

[56] APSR, this practice is also observed in all account books.

[57] Escribano Martín Dominguez Zamudio, 1766 [Legajo #8], ACCHS-CSIC, ff. 137–138.

[58] Escribano Martín Dominguez Zamudio, 1766 [Legajo #8], ACCHS-CSIC, f. 165.

[59] Escribano Martín Dominguez Zamudio, 1766 [Legajo #8], ACCHS-CSIC, ff. 165–166.

[60] Escribano Martín Dominguez Zamudio, 1766 [Legajo #8], ACCHS-CSIC, ff. 180–181.

[61] AGI Filipinas 941 N. 1, 1769.

the Misericordia, where José Antonio had been a member of the *mesa*.[62] The Countess of Lizárraga was connected to the Third Order of Saint Dominic, where she would eventually establish a legacy fund in 1783.[63] The *correspondencias* were placed on the Galleon, captained that year by Joaquín del Rivero y Quijano,[64] a relative of the Marquess of Montecastro Pedro González del Rivero y Quijano, who had legacy funds in the Misericordia, the Third Order of Saint Francis, and the Jesuits and was a member of the *mesa* of the Misericordia several years.[65] Similarly, a relative of his, José Domingo del Rivero, was the president of the *mesa* of the Third Order of Saint Francis that issued the *correspondencia* for Vicente Laureano in 1766,[66] and was the president of the *mesa* of the Misericordia in 1755,[67] while his aunt, María Rita González del Rivero, had become a member of the Third Order of Saint Dominic in 1744.[68] Had Vicente Laureano failed to repay his *correspondencias*, the Franciscan and Dominican Third Orders, the Society of Jesus, and the Misericordia would find out. In such an interconnected market, information on defaults moved quickly and resulted in exclusion from the *obras pías*. This was further the case because often the decision to exclude someone from future *correspondencias* came with insistent requests of repayments from the guarantors and by some sort of notarised documentation, including the issuing of *cartas de lasto*. There was a real threat of exclusion from the capital of the *obras pías*, which would place any Manileño at a disadvantage in participating in the Pacific exchange.

This leads to the dilemma faced by the leading citizens of Manila between their position as managers of *obras pías*, and their role as freighters in the Galleon. As both owners and managers of legacy funds,

[62] AGI Filipinas 197 N. 26, *Carta de la Mesa de la Misericordia sobre préstamo a la Ciudad de Manila*, 1743.

[63] APSR, Tomo 289, *Obra pía fundada por la Sra. Condesa de Lizárraga*.

[64] Escribano Martín Dominguez Zamudio, 1766 [Legajo #8], ACCHS-CSIC, ff. 137–181.

[65] AMN 552 MS1662, Doc. 6, ff. 51a-52a, Newberry Library Vault Ayer MS1349, & AGI Filipinas 1034 N. 4., 1805–1806.

[66] Escribano Martín Dominguez Zamudio, 1766 [Legajo #8], ACCHS-CSIC, ff. 137–138.

[67] Escribano Domingo Cortés de Arquiza, 1755 [Legajo #5], ACCHS-CSIC, ff. 96a-97a.

[68] APSR Tomo 194.

they had incentives to set the premia of *correspondencias* as high as possible to maximise the returns to the funds. Yet as freighters and takers of *correspondencias* they had a vested interest in lowering the premium, which would have resulted in higher net profits accruing to them from the Acapulco negotiation. Yet, there is evidence that these individuals in fact sided with the *obras pías* at the expense of the freighters when there was a clash. The clearest example is provided by the litigation that followed the capture of the Galleon *Covadonga* by Anson in 1743. The loss of the *Covadonga* was a serious blow to the *obras pías* that had issued *correspondencias* for that trading season, but it also resulted in a lengthy and complicated trial involving Manila, Mexico, and Madrid when the *obras pías* discovered that not all the profits of the Acapulco fair had been loaded aboard the *Covadonga*, and that a substantial part of the silver had remained in New Spain.[69] Given the fact that not all the investment underwritten by the *correspondencias* had been lost, the *obras pías* requested the repayment of principal and premium from the returns left in New Spain.

This is revealing because the *mesas* were often composed of the wealthiest freighters, which highlights that in a situation of loss in which the interest of the legacy funds was opposed to those of the freighters, these individuals decided to defend the *obras pías*. The capital that the *obras pías* provided to access the Acapulco negotiation year-on-year was more important than the profits of one trading season. That the elite of Manila decided to prioritise their role as managers of legacy funds meant that their position of power was derived not so much from their capacity as freighters but by their managerial access to the legacy funds. Not only did the *obras pías* align the motivations of the city by making it a stakeholder, but they also solved the dilemma faced by the wealthy citizens: Manila relied on its banks, the *obras pías*, and when in need, the city as a whole sought to protect them.

Aligning the motivations of the city to the well-being of the *obras pías* also meant that enforcement and monitoring were cheap. The Misericordia and other managers had their constitutions and their ways of monitoring the behaviour of managers and takers of *correspondencias*. While information between Manila and the rest of the Hispanic Monarchy may have been restricted due to distances and the prohibition

[69] BNE Porcones 972(25), 1747, ff. 7–8, Martinez de Zúñiga, Fr. Joaquín, *Historia de las Islas Philipinas*, Sampaloc (1803), pp. 544–546.

of Maníleños penetrating New Spain, information *within* Manila was easy to access. As long as the liquidity of the *obras pías* focalised the trading life of Manila, exclusion was a cheap and effective punishment. In Manila, the traditional dichotomy between formal and informal institutions breaks down. The informal institutions of partnerships, confraternities, and kin enhanced and supported the smooth functioning of the formal institutions, from *correspondencia* contracts to the statutes of the brotherhoods and the commercial legislation of the empire.

The capital markets of Manila were fundamental in providing a cheap way in which the contracts of the Transpacific trade could be upheld. This contrasts with the management of agency risk in the European joint-stock companies. Relying on private agents and outsourcing the intra-Asian trade had advantages, cheapening the overall cost of operations within Asia, and protecting the direct route to Europe, but it also led to structural problems. The downside of the EIC's strategy to cooperate with private merchants became more apparent after the conquest of Bengal. The increased military exigencies on the EIC meant that the company's trade became exponentially more expensive, allowing interlopers to undermine the company's trade.[70] The sharing of information and outsourcing of supplies that Erikson and Hejeebu point as the EIC's great comparative advantage over the VOC was equally shared with the very private interlopers that created the networks, and once the EIC's expenses rolled out of control there was nothing preventing these private individuals from filling the void.

This dynamic had gone full circle by 1765. After the EIC's conquest of Bengal, company agents reported that they were being outpriced in the procurement of textiles by private interlopers.[71] These interlopers were reportedly unbothered by questions of quality, and only cared for the return to their investments. Unencumbered by large costs, they could easily obtain a higher return than the company, and thus could offer higher prices to Bengali manufacturers.[72] Similarly, when the silver-rich Real Compañía de Filipinas sought to negotiate its first contract for the

[70] Furber, *John Company*, p. 165, Cheong, 'Some aspects', pp. 98–99.

[71] Prakash, Om, 'From Market-Determined to Coercion-Based: Textile Manufacturing in Eighteenth-Century Bengal', in *How India Clothed the World: The World of South Asian Textiles, 1500–1850*, ed. Giorgio Riello and Tirthankar Roy (Leiden: Brill, 2009), pp. 228 & 248.

[72] Prakash, 'From Market', p. 229.

procurement of Indian goods in 1790, the EIC, despite all the efforts of Cornwallis—then Governor-General—ended up being outpriced by the trading company of Lane, Lance, & Fitzhugh.[73] These independent merchants were the same intra-Asian traders that the EIC relied on for the provision of silver pesos, and that according to Hejeebu and Erikson, provided one of the advantages of the EIC over its competitors in Asian waters. The problem was that the moment trading with the EIC became uneconomical, they were also placed in a prime position to take over. They still plied the routes between India and Manila, arbitraging pesos and textiles, but without the need for any specific services from the EIC, nothing prevented them from supplanting the company in the procurement of Asian goods. Neither was the EIC the only bidder for the expertise and information of these private merchants, many of whom had been servants of the Company itself. As early as the 1720s, the French in Pondicherry were capable of attracting disaffected junior servants of the EIC to partnerships in their trading ventures in intra-Asian trade, competing with the Company's Asian procurement.[74] Outsourcing the intra-Asian trade was a good way to lessen agency risks, but this made cooperation dependent on market factors. In other words, the edifice of the EIC crumbled when the private merchants it had outsourced their intra-Asian trade to decided to *compete* rather than *complement* the company. In this outcome, profit rather than organisation played the determining role.

The joint-stock corporations, as Harris pointed out, had an excellent system to convey information from the factors on the spot to the shareholders at home, and thus enabled the pooling of capital by reducing information asymmetries.[75] But they were also vulnerable to excesses and to tension from within. Once the costs of operating the EIC skyrocketed, those that could exploit their position in the corporation took advantage of it to further their own interests, as can be seen in the Scott Case of 1798. In 1797, during the war with Britain, authorities in Manila confiscated the cargo of a Danish ship after it was discovered that it belonged to the company of David Scott & Son. David Scott had become the Chairman of the EIC's secret committee in 1797 and had

[73] Cheong, 'Changing the Rules', p. 4.

[74] Manning, 'French Country Trade', p. 287.

[75] Harris, *Going*, pp. 307–308.

been lobbying for more relaxed restrictions against private trade. Scott's involvement in the trade was found to be in violation of the EIC's privileges in India besides the fact that he was trading with the enemy, and was therefore sued by the company.[76] The case eventually ended with Scott's acquittal, and from his own position within the company, Scott kept lobbying for the end of the EIC's trading monopoly.[77] Regardless of the outcome, the case highlights that rather than reforming the EIC to make it a competitive enterprise, by the 1790s its own managers were more invested in their personal commercial enterprises to the detriment of the company. When Henry Dundas, President of the Board of Control for India since 1793, wanted to diminish the EIC's monopoly, he was able to exploit the cracks to attack the powerful London shipbuilding interests that owned the company.[78] Vertical integration did not necessarily translate into aligned motivation across the company, and the joint-stock form allowed for conflicts between owners and managers to be exploited. Manila, on the contrary, was aligned horizontally. All segments of the population were stakeholders in the trade, and this made the different actors highly complementary.

The fundamental role of the *obras pías* as providers of capital, and the wealth of information created by their financial role in the overall trade of the city, was cemented by the archive of the notary, the highly developed notarial culture in the Hispanic Monarchy, and the alignment of motivations that resulted from Manila's position as a stakeholder in the Transpacific exchange. The result was that information may have been restricted across the Pacific but circulated with ease in Manila, formal and informal institutions complemented each other, and in short, monitoring and enforcement were effective and cheap. A contrasting model is presented by the vertical integration path of the joint-stock company, where information flowed vertically from private merchants and agents on the spot to the directors at home, but where the boundaries were marked by corporate adherence. For the European East India companies, this translated into horizontal disaggregating tensions that eventually dismantled the trading power of the companies. Manila was shielded from

[76] Cheong, 'Some aspects', pp. 108–109.

[77] Cheong, 'Some aspects', pp. 110–111.

[78] Furber, *John Company*..., pp. 276–277.

this, and the capital market that emerged in the city reinforced the cohesion inherited from the Manila-Acapulco crossing not only by making capital available, but also by mitigating agency risk. Manila's position in the Pacific was never vulnerable to attacks from within, and its internal cohesion was a symptom of the political economy of the trade relative to its position in the Hispanic Monarchy, as will be analysed in Chapter 6.

5.2 Horizontal Specialisation and the Capital Market of Manila

Chapter 3 showed how Manila managed to pool pesos and transform this liquidity into working capital through the legacy funds and the *correspondencias*. The previous section has explained how the city's institutions—formal and informal—managed to internalise and mitigate the risk of loss at sea, price volatility, and the principal-agent problem. A question that remains to be answered is how Manileños maintained their intermediation in the face of the imperfect market in which they operated, where there was restricted expansion in volume and Asian demand for pesos resulted in twin cartels over the Pacific, as shown in Chapter 4. The answer is that Manila, as the financier of the trade, made itself indispensable. Manila achieved this because it specialised. Its access to the source of the pesos meant an abundance of liquidity in the city, which was then safely pooled into *obras pías* to finance the trade. Horizontal Specialisation enabled the city to mobilise and supply working capital at cheap rates, reaching a level of economies of scale and mitigating the problems derived from the lack of integration.

The profitability of the Pacific arbitrage in pesos led to an abundance of the silver coins in the city, and the social and religious functions of Third Orders and brotherhoods channelled savings from individuals into the trade, fostering impersonal cooperation. Similarly, the operation of funds through sustained periods of time also meant an expansion in their capital endowment through the retained earnings of the trade. While losses took place through the period, overall, the assets of *obras pías* kept increasing, accumulating more capital as time went on. Retained earnings from the trade and the foundation of new legacy funds and *obras pías* meant an expansion in the liquidity available to be invested as working capital. The *obras pías* fostered this abundance not only because they channelled savings to the trade, but also because they facilitated the mercantile transactions of Manileños, and thus, pesos permeated the exchanges that fed Manila with goods for export.

Manila's capacity to reach economies of scale in the mobilisation of capital was evidenced in the evolution of the premia charged by the *correspondencias*, which almost halved during the period. Premium rates were annually set by the *mesas* of the *obras pías* when they met to assess the conditions of the market. The specific information is lacking, but it is evident from the vast number of references among contemporaries that these rates were made public at a certain date.[79] Exactly how the premia was calculated is unknown. Only one document regarding the issue has survived, a letter written in 1692 by Fr. Baltasar de Santa Cruz, *prior* of the Dominican order in the Philippines, addressed to Marcos Quintero, president of the *mesa* of the Misericordia that year.[80] The letter gives a glimpse of the issues that weighed in the decision to raise of lower premium rates. The *mesa* was debating whether to lower rates to Acapulco to 40% from 50%.[81] The reason, as said in the letter, was that freighters were unwilling to take *correspondencias* from the Misericordia at 50%.[82] The *prior* however, opposed the move, arguing that a reduction in the premia would be prejudicial to the "common good" of the republic since it would reduce the income of legacy funds while their expenses—the welfare they provided—remained constant.[83] The broader social significance that *correspondencias* had taken is revealing of the communal stake that had developed through the legacy funds.

This letter reveals some important factors that were considered when assessing the seasonal premium rates. The profit of legacy funds and the provision of welfare were certainly included. Stakeholders like religious orders, priests, professionals, and all those that derived an income or rent from the funds wanted to maintain premium rates up. On the other hand,

[79] BNE, MSS.MICRO/9195, *Carta al General D. Marcos Quintero, en razón de los dineros que la Santa Mesa de Misericordia administra para dar a corresponder*. 10th April 1692, see also a 1795 contract, also offers an example of a correspondencia that references the later publishing of rates by the Misericordia and the Third Order of Saint Francis, Escribano Miguel José Flores, 1795 [Legajo #26], ACCHS-CSIC, ff. 47a–48b.

[80] BNE, MSS.MICRO/9195, ff. 585a-605a.

[81] BNE, MSS.MICRO/9195, f. 585b.

[82] BNE, MSS.MICRO/9195, f. 604.

[83] BNE, MSS.MICRO/9195, f. 585b.

members of the *mesa* were aware that freighters to Acapulco—those that ultimately realised the negotiation and brought back the pesos—were not willing to finance their operations at 50%. The price of capital, therefore, was not right. An element of crucial importance was the profit margin of the trade. As the *prior* said, the founders of legacy funds had left the money to be invested in *correspondencias* with the purpose that the funds would profit from the trade.[84] Thus, varying the premia would be licit if it followed the ups and downs of the trade.[85] However, in the instance the *prior* wrote about, the *mesa* had no authority to unilaterally modify the custom of originating *correspondencias* at 50% for Acapulco,[86] implying that no change had taken place in the profitability of the trade that would beckon a lowering of the premium. The outcome of this correspondence is not known. However, it reveals that three elements were taken into consideration when deciding the premium: the willingness of freighters to take *correspondencias*, the expenses and profits that accrued to the legacy funds, and the profit margins of the trade. The first two implied a negotiation between the needs of legacy funds and the economic imperatives of the trade. Ultimately, the premium was a compromise between the outcome of this negotiation and the profit margin of the trade it financed.

This method should have left ample room for big managers like the Misericordia, the Jesuits, or the Third Order of Saint Francis to compete among each other. Instead, for most years, their rates for Acapulco were the same. Most smaller *mesas* did not even publish their own premium rates, and from the 1770s onwards it was common to issue *correspondencias* whose returns were pegged to the three big managers—or just the Misericordia—by using the simple formula "at the premium that may come out of the Misericordia".[87] Given the great proliferation of funds and institutions that issued *correspodencias* as seen in Chapter 3, there must have been a certain level of coordination among the *mesas* when it came to deciding premium rates. This may indicate a situation in which there was a greater offer of capital than there was demand for it, meaning that competition among investors could have ended in falling premia,

[84] BNE, MSS.MICRO/9195, f. 589a.

[85] BNE, MSS.MICRO/9195, ff. 589a-589b.

[86] BNE, MSS.MICRO/9195, f. 590a.

[87] An example can be found in Escribano Miguel José Flores, 1789 [Legajo #21A], ACCHS-CSIC, ff. 119b-120a.

damaging the profits derived from the *correspondencias* and providing incentives for managers to find a floor on premia. However, this only applied to premia for Acapulco. The direct trade with America was limited to one annual Galleon, which restricted the opportunities for investment while legacy funds and liquidity kept expanding in Manila. Similarly, while there was no divergence in premia for Acapulco based on the intermediaries issuing *correspondencias*, over time the premia tended to fall, halving from 50% in 1733 to 25% in 1821.[88] *Mesas* may have tried to coordinate their seasonal premium to Acapulco, but the rates still obeyed market principles, and the abundance of capital for America led to falling premia over time. Again, there was a complicated negotiation between the supply of capital, the demand for it, and the profitability of the trade.

The Asian leg of the Manila trade had no real limitations in volume, and thus, lacked any coordination in the premia. In fact, premia charged on *correspondencias* to Asia, especially China, varied season by season depending on the originator and the principal taking the *correspondencia*, as much as by port of destination. In 1783 for example, the Misericordia lent 16,000 pesos in three *correspondencias* to Amoy on the ship *Ntra. Sra. del Rosario* at a premium of 16%, while the Third Order of Saint Francis invested 6,646 pesos at 14% on the same ship, and the legacy funds of the Archbishopric gave 4,500 pesos in two *correspondencias* to Amoy on a different ship.[89] In 1754, Andrés Blanco Bermúdez gave 1,000 pesos at 20% for Canton, while the Marquess of Montecastro issued 4,000 at 16%.[90] There were also differences depending on destination: in 1770, premiums to Amoy were at 14%, while those for Macao stood at 11%.[91] In the case of premia for Asia, differences in rates were not conditioned by limits on the volume of the trade. Different destinations provided different goods that had different profit margins in the Pacific exchange, and the Asian trade did not produce as many profits as the

[88] Data gathered from ACCHS-CSIC and APSR account books (see Bibliography).

[89] Escribano Vicente González de Tagle, 1783 [Legajo #14], ACCHS-CSIC, ff. 18a-19a, 20a-22a, 28a-29b, 31b-32a, 42a-43a.

[90] Escribano Domingo Cortés de Arquiza, 1755 [Legajo #5], ACCHS-CSIC, ff. 59ª-59b, 145a-145b.

[91] Escribano Martín Dominguez Zamudio, 1770 [Legajo #9], ACCHS-CSIC ff. 209–211, 298–302, 311–312.

Acapulco negotiation.[92] This trade served to bring textiles and staples for consumption within the Philippines and for re-export to Acapulco, where the great gains from arbitraging the purchasing power differentials of the peso could be realised. The premia thus were lower than for Acapulco.[93]

While the Pacific trade presented volume constraints, the capacity of the capital market of Manila to expand had no such limitations The abundance of liquidity and the consequent economies of scale in the mobilisation of working capital made investment cheap and mitigated to an extent the lack of market integration across the Pacific, as demonstrated by the evolution of *correspondencias'* premia in Manila. Graph 5.1 shows all the information on premia gathered from the surviving notarial protocols, as well as from the account books of the legacy funds of the Third Order of Saint Dominic. There are three things that are readily apparent. First, premia during the period between 1725 and 1821 fell by half, from 50% for Acapulco in 1725 to 25% in 1821, and from 20% for China in 1730 to 11% in 1813. Second, premia for Acapulco were generally higher than for China and other destinations like Coromandel and Java, whose observations are too few and far apart to include in the graph. Third, even if premia tended to fall during the period, in the short term they were very steady. There is as well a clear break in the trends during the 1770s. Prior to that decade, premia for Acapulco and China tended to fall in the long run, but they were generally uniform year-on-year, and there was no divergence from the premia to Acapulco published by the Misericordia. After 1779, this uniformity breaks down. Premia, both for China and Acapulco not only fall, but also diverge greatly from one season to the next. This is also the only period in which we observe premia for Acapulco varying within the same season. The end of stable

[92] There are very few observations of profit margins for Manila's intra-Asian trade. Gasch-Tomás, following data from Chuan, provides a 100% profit rate from China to Manila ca. 1600 (Gasch-Tomás, 'Transport', p. 34). However, as Ruiz-Stovel, who conducted a thorough study of the Minnan-Manila trade during the eighteenth century, has noted, it is difficult to calculate net profit margins, since the data regarding transport costs is elusive (Ruiz-Stovel, 'Chinese'). Returns of 100% by 1600 still are low compared to profit margins of 200–400% for Manila-Acapulco by the second half of the eighteenth century.

[93] The lowest recorded premium rate in *correspondencias* were 7% rates for Macao given by the *Caja de Temporalidades* in 1811, which also shows *correspondencias* at 11% to Acapulco, a unique case, AESI-A, 1052, 21, *Cartas enviadas al Padre Sebastián Sancho, Procurador General*, 1817–1818, fol. 1.

rates is better visualised by plotting the year-on-year variance, as shown in Graph 5.2. This date coincides with Spain's entrance in the American War of Independence, but it will be argued later that this hides profound changes that were taking place in the way that trade was organised across the Hispanic Monarchy.

Changes in the premia were not due to risk. *Correspondencias* transferred the risk of loss at sea to the funds, and thus, it is conceivable that fund managers would have wanted to charge higher premia during times when they perceived risk to be higher, such as at times of war. Yet, premia showed no reaction to warfare. The war of Jenkins' Ear (1739–1743) did not affect premium rates, which only rose once the war was over. Similarly, the Seven Years' War (Spain intervened from 1759 to 1763) only saw a 5% increase in premia for Acapulco, even though the English captured the city and looted the Misericordia. The end of war and the return of Manila to Spain in 1764 did not affect the premia. The Napoleonic Wars also had a limited effect. Premia rose from 30% in 1797 to 50% in 1801, but this was most likely due to financial changes introduced by the Bank

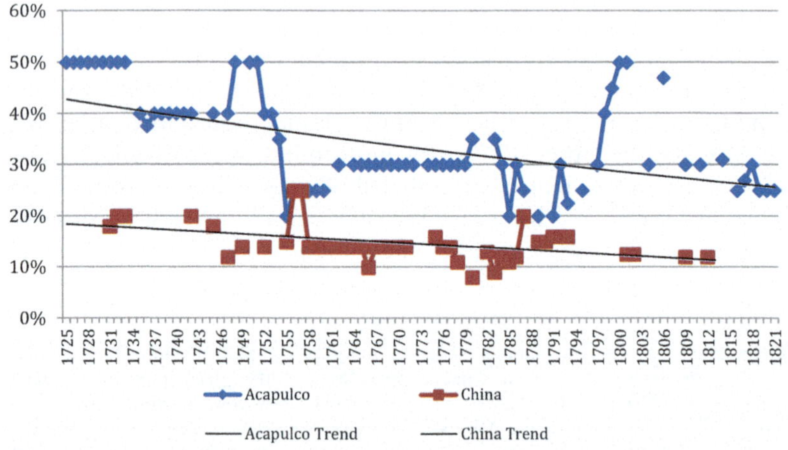

Graph 5.1 Sea loans interest rates by year and destination 1725–1821 (*Sources* Data collected from the Archivo del Centro de Ciencias Sociales y Humanas [ACCHS-CSIC], Madrid, Spain, & Archivo de la Provincia del Satísimo Rosario [APSR], Ávila, Spain)

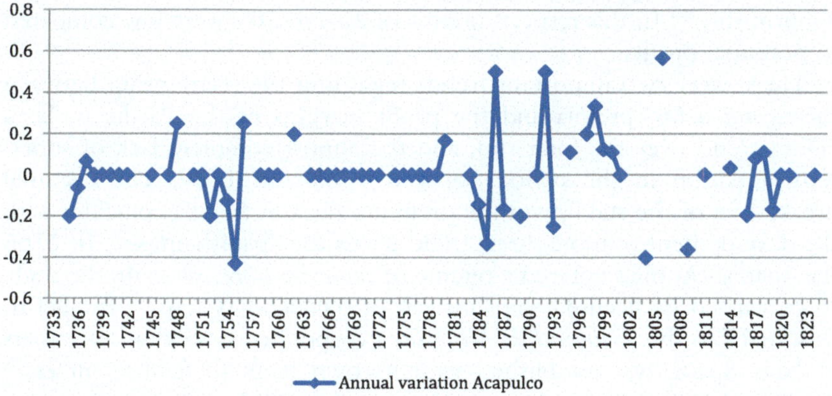

Graph 5.2 Year-on-year variation rate of premia to Acapulco 1733–1826

of England.[94] In fact, the end of the peace of Amiens and the resumption of war in 1803 led to a 20% fall of the premium to Acapulco, from 50% in 1801 to 30% in 1804, which contradicts the idea that wartime risk drove premium rates. Thus, risk does not seem to have conditioned premia in any important way. Rates fell at the resumption of war, rose with the coming of peace, or remained unfazed. Other factors determined the premium on *correspondencias*.

One factor determining the premium rates was the profit margin of the trade. As said in Chapter 2, there are no statistical records to allow for a detailed evolution of profit margins, but as argued, they were high. Chinese demand for pesos and the limitation in volume of the Pacific exchange guaranteed high price differentials across the ocean. Manileños' capacity to deflect costs and obtain subsidies further enhanced the profitability of the trade. Bonalian's estimation of 400–600% returns for the eighteenth century,[95] and this research's estimates of 120–300% for 1767,

[94] According to Irigoin, in 1797 the Bank of England suspended convertibility of its notes, provoking rising prices of silver in Europe. The effects of these changes in Asia are not well known yet but given the coincidence in time and that premia did not go beyond 30% between 1792 and 1796, when Spain was also at war, it is most likely that the upward swing between 1797 and 1800 was a response to this. Irigoin, 'Rise', p. 403.

[95] Bonialian, *El Pacífico*, p. 177.

confirm this.[96] In this respect, premia of 20% to 50% were low compared to potential profits.

There were two important trends regarding the relationship between *correspondencias'* premia and the profit margins of the Pacific trade: a falling trend over the long run, and the almost complete lack of short-term variation in the period between 1725 and 1779. The eventual breakdown of the stability of the premium rates in Manila coincides with the development of more direct trade across the Spanish empire. In 1765 the Spanish Antilles entered a regime of *comercio libre*, allowing the trade to be carried by licensed ships instead of the *flotas* system.[97] Parallel to this, in 1776 the *Tribunal de Minería*, a corporate association for miners in New Spain, was established with its own bank to finance mines.[98] As argued by Irigoin and Grafe, this may have reduced miners' dependence on financing from the wholesalers.[99] Trade in the Spanish empire became increasingly more open. *Comercio libre* was extended to mainland South America in 1778,[100] US merchants started trading between Spanish America and Asia after the Treaty of Paris of 1783,[101] and in 1785, the Real Compañía de Filipinas was chartered to conduct trade between America and Asia.[102] The delicate balance that had regulated transcontinental trade across the Hispanic Monarchy slowly came down, which affected Manila's intermediation.[103] These changes are further analysed in the next chapter. What matters here is that they fostered competition and must have undoubtedly reduced the profit margins of the Pacific exchange, even though Chinese demand for the peso and the premium the coin enjoyed abroad still warranted high profits. Importantly, the end of the balanced trading system introduced an element of volatility that explains the break in premium rates observed around the 1770s and 1780s.

[96] See Chapter 2 Sect. 2.1.

[97] Lamikiz, 'Transatlantic', p. 299.

[98] Brading, *Miners*, p. 163–165.

[99] Grafe and Irigoin, 'A stakeholder', p. 626, Irigoin and Grafe, 'Bounded', p. 211.

[100] Lamikiz, 'Transatlantic', p. 299.

[101] Irigoin, 'The End', p. 215, Irigoin, 'Rise', p. 396.

[102] Díaz-Trechuelo, *La Real*, p. 34.

[103] This is explored in more detail in Chapter 6 Sect. 6.4.

Nevertheless, profit margins do not entirely explain the evolution of premia during the period. On the one hand, the long-run fall of the premia had started much earlier than the expansion of competition, in 1735. On the other hand, swings in premium rates, although less common, did happen prior to 1780. The nature of variance in fact was different pre and post 1780. In the period that followed, it was rare for premia to remain the same year-on-year, but changes were smaller, with premia to Acapulco hovering between 20 and 30%. Before 1780, premia to Acapulco fell from 50% to 20% in four years, between 1751 and 1755.[104] Changes, when they happened, they tended to be in the space of ten percentage points, from 50% to 40% in 1735,[105] and from 40% to 50% in 1748.[106] Such drastic swings cannot be entirely explained by changes in the profit margin of a trade as stable as the Manila Galleon trade. Finally, contemporaries understood that the failure to celebrate the Acapulco fair any given year would mean higher profits the following one, and in this regard, rising premium rates from 40% to 50% after the failure to celebrate of four consecutive fairs between 1748 and 1751 would make sense. However, the premium on *correspondencias* remained stable at 30% in 1764 although the Acapulco fair had not been celebrated since 1761.[107] That is, the period before 1779 was characterised by few but violent swings in the premia, and an underlying factor that was driving premium rates down throughout the period.

This factor was the supply and demand for capital in Manila, which affected the premia as *mesas* negotiated the right rate at which freighters would be willing to take *correspondencias*. An example of this took place in the first years of the 1750s. In 1753, Governor Marquess of Ovando granted 900 *boletas* out of the 2,000-share reserved for the citizens to the officers that had participated in the expedition against Sulu as a reward for their service.[108] The city resented this reduction of their share in the galleon freight and the next year, the Misericordia was only capable of

[104] Escribano Baltasar Javier Sánchez de Cuenca, 1752 [Legajo #3] & Escribano Domingo Cortés de Arquiza, 1755 [Legajo #5], ACCHS-CSIC.

[105] APSR Tomo 304, Escribano Baltasar Javier Sánchez de Cuenca, 1741 [Legajo #2], ACCHS-CSIC.

[106] APSR Tomo 304, 228, Escribano Baltasar Javier Sánchez de Cuenca, 1752 [Legajo #3], ACCHS-CSIC.

[107] APSR, Tomo 224, 228, 304.

[108] The freighting process can be found in AGI Filipinas 268 N.1., 1752.

allocating 79,000 pesos of the 160,000 pesos it had earmarked to *correspondencias* to Acapulco,[109] even though the premium had been lowered for the first recorded time to 35%, breaking the 40% barrier. A year later, in 1755, the premium for Acapulco was 20%, a floor that had never been reached before, and that would never be pierced.[110] Nothing other than the demand for capital seems to have affected this fall of the premium. Spain was not at war, no catastrophic events affected the Pacific crossing, and there is no special indication that profits in the Acapulco fair collapsed during these years. Yet Ovando, by halving the amount of cargo that citizens could dispatch to New Spain, had correspondingly halved their demand for capital without reducing the supply offered by *obras pías*.

The profitability of the trade route that *correspondencias* financed was fundamental in determining the premium rates, but the supply and demand of working capital—the need for liquidity—were also important. In this aspect, Manila had an abundance of pooled capital that kept expanding while the trade remained limited in scale. This long-run expansion of pooled liquidity grew parallel to the declining trend of premia in the city. This was the underlying cause of the long-term fall of premia. Liquidity and capital were increasingly abundant in Manila. The cheapness of capital in Manila can be contrasted with the premia of similar instruments involved in different trades. As mentioned previously, by the second half of the eighteenth century, premium rates from the Spanish Atlantic to America also hovered between 25% and 50%, but as Bernal points out, premia could easily reach 60–75%.[111] Carriére records voyages in the 1760s between Cádiz and Perú with premiums over 60%, and in 1742, while at war with England, nominal rates to Perú could reach 130%.[112] Other Asian trades also presented higher premia, such as the diamond trade between Madras and London in the 1730s and 1740s, which ranged between 50% and 60%.[113] Of course, not knowing the profit margins of these trades makes for an incomplete comparison, but when contrasted with a median of 30% for the direct arbitrage of silver

[109] AGI Filipinas 199 N. 3, 1756, f. 78.

[110] Escribano Domingo Cortés de Arquiza, 1755 [Legajo #5], ACCHS-CSIC.

[111] Bernal, *La financiación*, p. 193.

[112] Carrière, 'Renouveau', pp. 231 & 234–235.

[113] Mentz, Søren, *The English Gentleman Merchant at work: Madras and the City of London 1660–1740* (Copenhagen: Museum Tusculanum Press, 2005), p. 132.

specie between Asia and America across the Pacific, it is possible to better contextualise the ease of financing in Manila. Barred from expanding the trade, Manila expanded its financing. This was Horizontal Specialisation in the workings.

The scale of Manila's provision of capital for its trade solved any liquidity constraints associated with long-distance trade. In fact, relative to the size of the transpacific trade, there was too much capital. The financial market of Manila represents an evolutionary case in which scarcity of capital was not the main engine of financial development, just as Irigoin and Grafe noted for the local credit markets of Spain and Spanish America.[114] Instead, it was the trade that presented restrictions due to the structure of the market for silver pesos in New Spain. This contrasts sharply with the East India companies. For the East India Companies, the joint-stock form solved the problem of acquiring enough starting capital by fostering impersonal cooperation, but it never solved the problem of acquiring timely working capital, that is, enough silver pesos to settle transactions in Asia. Instead, the East India Companies expanded in the search for working capital or, in its absence, alternatives. The different approaches reflected the diverging models of scaling and specialisation of the Companies' and Manila's trade, which is reviewed in Chapter 7.

[114] Grafe, 'An Empire', p. 23, Irigoin and Grafe, 'Bounded', p. 222.

CHAPTER 6

The Political Economy of the Manila Trade

The previous chapters have described the model of Horizontal Specialisation encompassing the large demand for pesos in Asia, and Mexican's capacity to monopolise their internal market. Facing constraints in the Acapulco fair, Manileños opted for an alternative strategy towards specialisation which resembled a process of division of labour across the Pacific exchange in which Manila focused on the provision of finance and the operation of the trade, achieving a certain level of economies of scale. On the ground, this meant that Manila's capacity to mobilise funds and pool retained earnings from the Manila-Acapulco crossing enabled the city to provide working capital in Asian waters at favourable rates, making itself indispensable. This chapter continues the work of Chapter 5 explaining why the Mexican wholesalers would, in the face of a mirror seller cartel, choose to trade with the Manileño Galleon freighters instead of anyone else given that the large and specific demand for the peso skewed the bargaining power in their favour. The chapter examines the role that the political economy of the empire played in driving Manila's alternative model of specialisation.

The argument is that the Pacific trade was an integral part of an empire-wide equilibrium that linked all territorial units of the empire together while protecting the vested interest of their local mercantile elites. The lack of integration that characterised the Manila-Acapulco exchange was

J. J. Rivas Moreno, *The Capital Market of Manila and the Pacific Trade, 1668–1838*, Palgrave Studies in Economic History,
https://doi.org/10.1007/978-3-031-71810-6_6

not unique to the Pacific, but the rule of a composite Monarchy spanning three continents.[1] The chapter explores how the institutional framework of the Spanish empire prevented the development of sustained interloper trade by conditioning each unit's control over their territory on the arbitration of the king.[2] Manila and Mexico respected their mutual privileges and had the implicit guarantee of access to the king's intermediation, thus guaranteeing Mexico's control of its internal market and vice versa. The fragmentation that defined the Hispanic Monarchy paradoxically glued the different territories (*reinos*) together through the arbitration of the king, ultimate guarantee that allowed the political system to function.[3] The chapter ends with the end of this equilibrium in the second half of the eighteenth century and the resulting collapse of the regional fairs and the advent of competition, commencing the process of market integration.

6.1 The Institutional Structure of the Hispanic Monarchy

A characteristic of the legal system of the Spanish empire was the lack of a unique legal jurisdiction that encompassed the entirety of the realm. This produced a system of jurisdictional fragmentation that manifested itself along territorial, demographic, and jurisprudential lines simultaneously. As noted by Epstein, membership to an Early Modern state usually entailed a degree of membership within a spectrum due to corporate privileges rather than an absolute measure of "citizenship".[4] Similarly, privileges and legislation differed between territorial units in a continent defined by composite monarchies in which rule and ruler were distinct, as was the case of the sixteenth-century Habsburg empire of Charles V.[5] To complicate matters further, the Canonical legal sphere, based on scholasticism and the work of the glossators, retained its legal standing in Catholic countries.

[1] Grafe and Irigoin, 'Bounded', p. 218, Yun-Casalilla, 'Las instituciones', pp. 144 & 156.

[2] Irigoin and Grafe, 'Bargaining', p. 182.

[3] Irigoin and Grafe, 'Bargaining', pp. 202–203.

[4] Epstein, *Freedom*, pp. 7 & 15–16.

[5] Esteban Estrígana, Alicia, and Floristán Imízcoz, Alfredo, 'Composición y gobierno de la Monarquía de España', in *Historia de España en la Edad Moderna*, ed. Alfredo Floristán (Barcelona: Ariel, 2004), pp. 253–254.

The Hispanic Monarchy was no exception to this rule. There was a lack of unique sovereignty in which the monarch was imagined as a guarantor of the law rather than its source.[6] Without a unique source of constitutional ordering, several institutions, amalgamated around differing schools of law, coexisted in the same space, each with its own distinct jurisdiction, often overlapping.[7] At the core of this fragmentation lied the notion that the law was distinct and separate from the ruler, that the legitimacy of a ruler was determined not by their capacity to legislate but to enforce and protect the law, and that a plurality of legal jurisdictions could exist under the aegis of one sovereign.[8] This section argues that the imperial polity was based on a delicate balance sustained by two pillars: the role of the king as arbiter of last resort coupled with the implicit guarantee that each territorial component of the Monarchy had access to the king's justice, and the resulting bargaining process between the territories—among themselves and with the king simultaneously—which maintained the equilibrium over the empire by guaranteeing that no entity had the absolute upper hand against another.[9]

The Spanish empire encompassed three main jurisdictions: Civil, Canon, and Consuetudinary. The law of the administration—or Civil Law—was the set of codified norms that composed the body of law. These were the laws that regulated the interactions of the state, with itself and with the republic, and was administered by the set of empire-wide institutions like the *Audiencia*, the *cabildos*, and the Councils. Civil Law was hierarchical in nature, with several courts of appeal and known rules regarding the monetary size that cases needed to have to qualify for an appeal. The prime example of codified legislation in the Spanish empire was the *Novilísima Recopilación de las Leyes de Indias* published in 1680, containing a compilation of all the laws pertaining to the Hispanic American territories.[10] It was also common that jurists would independently, or

[6] MacLachlan, Colin M., *Spain's Empire in the New World: The Role of Ideas in Institutional and Social Change* (Berkeley: University of California Press, 1988), p. 18.

[7] Grafe and Irigoin, 'Bargaining', p. 186, Mackay talks of a "jurisdictional cacophony", Mackay, Ruth, *The Limits of Royal Authority: Resistance and Obedience in Seventeenth-Century Castile* (Cambridge: Cambridge University Press, 1999), p. 59.

[8] Mackay, *The Limits*, p. 22.

[9] Grafe and Irigoin, 'Bargaining', p. 182.

[10] *Recopilación de las Leyes de los Reynos de las Indias*, 3 vols., Cádiz: Imprenta del Real Consejo de Indias, 1791.

at the request of a party involved in litigation or the tribunal judging the case, collect the existing *cédulas* relating to a specific case into a compilation called *cedulario*.[11] The king sat at the apex of this system and was considered as the "ultimate arbiter".[12] However, he had little legislative initiative of his own.[13] Instead, much of the king's power emanated from his capacity to issue legislation as a result of litigation, and many of the laws contained in *cedularios* were the results of sentences issued by the king.

Another fundamental body of law for the Hispanic world was Canon Law or the law of the Church. The Ecclesiastic Estate was a corporate body of universal projection yet linked to the day-to-day administration of believers' social relations. Canon Law had jurisdiction over all cases related to the clergy, and confraternities and religious orders were subject to it. It was based on a casuistic approach to cases guided by the notion of moral theology, in which precedence did not play an important role, but previous judgements of scholars on the matter were considered guiding principles.[14] Yet, the administration of law was made flexible by the Aristotelian principle of *epikeia*. As explained in Chapter 3.[15] Through *epikeia*, Canon Law had an in-built disagreement clause that made the provision of justice flexible, but also put a strong emphasis on the impact of the law, hence the importance of moral theology as a guiding principle for judging each individual case separately.

The administration of Canon Law was unitary: the hierarchy of tribunals was linked with ecclesiastical hierarchy and scholarly recognition, with the chairs of theology of universities playing a fundamental

[11] An example of an ad hoc *cedulario* is provided in AGI Filipinas 268 N.1, 1752. In this case, as the city of Manila debated the innovations introduced in the allotment of cargo space by governor Obando, the governor asked the public notary of the city to include a *cedulario* of all previous legislation regarding the allotment of *boletas* into the notarised proceedings that were sent to the Council of the Indies.

[12] Halperin Donghi, Tulio, 'Backward Looks and Forward Glimpses from a Quincentennial Vantage Point', *Journal of Latin American Studies*, vol. 24 (1992), p. 222.

[13] Irigoin and Grafe, 'Bargaining', p. 178. This is also implicit in the 1803 definition of *real cédula* provided in *Diccionario de la Lengua Castellana compuesto por la Real Academia Española, reducido a un tomo para su fácil uso*, Madrid: Imprenta de la viuda de don Joaquín Ibarra (1803), p. 187.

[14] Rodolfo Moutin, Osvaldo, '¿Qué fue el Derecho canónico indiano?', mimeo (2021), p. 15.

[15] St. Thomas Aquinas, *Summa Theologia*, pp. 2267–2268.

role. It was based on written rules (*canones*) that were universal across the entire Catholic world. In the Spanish empire, like elsewhere in the Catholic world, the canonical sphere existed separate and parallel to the civil sphere. However, due to the *patronato real* being fully granted to the Spanish monarchs by Pope Julius II, the king of Spain performed as the head and protector of the Church in the discovered territories.[16] This allowed many cases to be addressed to the king while the king's authority did not supplant that of the Pope, who was also brought in to bear his authority when it was deemed necessary. As an example, king Fernando VI had to request the issuing of a Bull from Pope Benedict XIV in 1751 to force the Jesuit order in the Philippines to accept the metropolitan visit of the Archbishop of Manila.[17]

A third jurisdiction was Consuetudinary Law, known at the time as *Derecho de Gentes*.[18] This meant the loosely defined conglomerate of traditions that minutely regulated life. There was no real understanding of what constituted tradition despite the efforts since the Middle Ages to codify it in different parts of Europe. Tradition was considered as a kind of normative legislation that emerged from the day-to-day actions of people, something reflected in its Spanish name *usos y costumbres* (lit. usages and customs), and as such was territorially fragmented. For traditions to have binding status, they had to be widely acknowledged by the population and had to have existed for a respectable time, both ambiguous concepts.[19] Consuetudinary usages were often recognised by the monarch in the form of *privilegios* or *fueros*. *Privilegios* were the recognition of a special status affecting a specific corporate group or territory, and they could be generalist. *Fueros* were a specific kind of privilege that meant exclusive jurisdiction over something.[20] When granted upon a territorial unit, a

[16] MacLachlan, *Spain's Empire*, p. 30, Egido, Teófanes, 'La Iglesia y los problemas religiosos', in *Historia de España en la Edad Moderna*, ed. Alfredo Floristán (Barcelona: Ariel, 2004), p. 340, Numhauser, Paulina, 'El Real Patronato en Indias y la Compañía de Jesús durante el período filipino (1580–1640)', *Boletín Americanista*, 67 (2013), p. 89.

[17] The Pope issued the bull after 19 *cédulas* issued by the king since 1603 had gone unheeded, AGI Filipinas 941 N.1, 1769.

[18] A contemporary manual is provided by Marín y Mendoza, Joaquín, *Historia del Derecho Natural y de Gentes*, Madrid: Universidad Carlos III (2015), 1776.

[19] Miceli, Paola, *Derecho consuetudinario y memoria. Práctica jurídica y costumbre en Castilla y León (siglos XI-XIV)*, (Madrid: Universidad Carlos III, 2012), p. 78.

[20] The first two meanings provided by the dictionary of 1803 refer to territorial and estamentary jurisdiction, *Diccionario de la Lengua Castellana…*, 1803, p. 418.

fuero meant that the said territory could keep its law without compromise to any other jurisdiction within the empire and had its own tribunals. The most famous *fueros* were those of the Basque *señoríos*, which the king of Spain swore in his dual title as king of Spain and lord of Vizcaya. Thus, the *señoríos* were an integral part of the Monarchy, yet had distinct laws of its own.[21]

Finally, the legislation of other countries could be brought to bear in litigation within the Hispanic Monarchy, emphasising the fact that the law was not originated by the king, and distinct from him. The legality of using foreign legislation in domestic cases was explained in a legal diatribe published in Manila in 1747 debating the loss of the *Covadonga*. In it, its author argued the validity of the sentence forcing the integral repayment by the freighters of the *correspondencias* contracted with the *obras pías* by quoting the legislation of Venice and the *Ordennances de Marine* of France. The author defended their validity saying:

> [...] since regarding the estatutes of Venice and the Ordinances of France they [the opposing litigants] could say that these could only have coactive force in the domains of France and Venice, and not in another country with a sovereign prince, I applied myself to search for a doctrine that could explain the force that the laws of neighbouring countries have, and their authority. [...] Among the 23 tomes of the eminent cardinal of Lucca I found the treatise [instructing] that when there is no municipal law or common law [that is applicable] there should be recourse to the law of the neighbouring princes.[22]

The result was deeply fragmented jurisdictions, lacking any single sovereign law that could bypass the swarm of corporate, territorial, and consuetudinary legislation.

This multiplicity of jurisdictions represented an equal multiplicity of avenues for those involved in the Pacific trade to defend and negotiate their interests. Economic historians have emphasised the role of the fiscal state and state building in creating the conditions for economic

[21] Lamikiz, Xabier, *Trade and Trust in the Eighteenth-century Atlantic World: Spanish Merchants and their Overseas Networks* (Woodbridge: The Boydell Press, 2010), pp. 29–30.

[22] BNE Porcones 972(25), 1747, f. 15.

growth from a quantitative perspective.[23] As a result, the literature has traditionally focused on the fragmentation between the territories of the Hispanic Monarchy,[24] and it has devoted less attention to how the legal pluralism that permeated territorial boundaries impacted trade and its financing. This was important for the capital markets of Manila because it allowed participants to navigate between jurisdictions according to their own interests. Thus, as seen in Chapter 3, the Misericordia of Manila could use the Council of Trent to resist the archbishop's audit of their legacy funds, or it could switch from archepiscopal subordination and place itself under the patronage of the king.[25] Similarly, as will be seen in the next section, Galleon freighters could use the special jurisdiction of the Galleon privilege to resist royal officials in Acapulco. This complemented the various hierarchal channels that, as argued by MacLachlan and Phelan, ensured that information could not be supressed.[26] This meant that, one way or another, Manileños, Mexicans, and everyone involved in the Pacific trade had the tools to defend their interests. Irigoin and Grafe are right in arguing that the lack of a uniform forum for negotiation in the Hispanic Monarchy akin to British Parliament makes it difficult to analyse

[23] Especially important in the case of the British world, as evidence by the work of Patrick O'Brien, O'Brien, Patrick. 'The nature and historical evolution of an exceptional fiscal state and its possible significance for the precocious commercialization and industrialization of the British economy from Cromwell to Nelson', *Economic History Review* 64, nº 2 (2011): 408–446, O'Brien, Patrick, and Hunt, Philip A., 'The Rise of a Fiscal State in England, 1485–1815'. *Historical Research* 66, issue 160 (1993): 129–176. Epstein's main focus remains territorial, but is more nuanced to accept for corporate differences. Equally interesting in this regard is the work of Julian Hoppit. Hoppit, Julian, *Britain's Political Economies: Parliament and economic life, 1660–1800* (Cambridge: Cambridge University Press, 2017), Hoppit, Julian, 'The Nation, the State, and the First Industrial Revolution', *Journal of British Studies* 50 (2011): 307–331.

[24] Elliott, John H., 'A Europe of Composite Monarchies', *Past & Present*, nº 137 (1992): 48–71, Yun-Casalilla, 'Las instituciones', Cardim, Feros, and Sabatini, 'The political', Cardim et al., 'Polycentric'.

[25] Switching canon and civil jurisdictions was not exclusive of the Misericordia, but common to all *obras pías*, see Newberry Library, Vault Ayers 1352, *Letters to Father José Victoria, Augustinian Provincial, concerning diocesan authority and episcopal visitation*, 1771, and AFIO 101/14, *Copia de un Informe del Arzobispo de Manila, Juan, elevado al Rey, acerca de las Obras Pías que administra la VOT de Manila*, 1806.

[26] MacLachlan, *Spain's*, p. 40, Phelan, John Leddy, 'Authority and Flexibility in the Spanish Imperial Bureaucracy', *Administrative Science Quarterly* 5, nº 1 (1960), pp. 53–54.

the bargaining process.[27] The advantage was that there were plenty of channels for bargaining.

Despite the multiple jurisdictions, the king, either through his role as monarch or through the privilege of the *patronato*, presided the judicial apparatus of each jurisdiction. This position of strength was derived precisely from his role as guarantor of the different legal spheres.[28] The fact that procedural law was the same for everyone in the Hispanic Monarchy also made it easier to access the king's justice. It implied equal access to the provision of the law by the king for all territorial units with no established territorial hierarchy,[29] and all shared a common procedure, opening the doors to litigation, appeals, and sentencing to all parts of the empire, that is, to bargaining.[30] This in turn meant that every unit of the empire had an incentive to remain within the monarchical system, as they had the implicit guarantees that their cases would be heard, even though the sentences issued by the king and the Council of the Indies may not fully agree with their objectives.

The main judicial organ of the Hispanic Monarchy was the *Audiencia*, a tribunal composed of several judges (*oidor*), and a prosecutor (*fiscal*) which had jurisdiction over the territory in which it had been created. The *Audiencias* functioned as an intermediate court for civil and criminal cases (and where a *Consulado* did not exist, commercial cases too).[31] *Audiencias* also guaranteed the enforcement of legislation issued by the king, assisted the governor, and checked the administration. The *Audiencia* of Manila performed specific roles in the Galleon trade when mandated by the *fuero* of the trade, the *reglamento*, until the creation of the *Consulado* of Manila in 1769.[32]

The *Audiencia* of Manila was established first in 1583, and after a brief period between 1588 and 1595, it worked uninterruptedly until the end of Spanish dominion in 1898. Nominally, the Philippines were

27 Irigoin and Grafe, 'Bargaining', pp. 204–205.

28 Grafe and Irigoin, 'A stakeholder', p. 638.

29 Cunningham, Charles H., *The Audiencia in the Spanish Colonies as Illustrated by the Audiencia of Manila* (Berkeley: University of California Press, 1919), p. 18.

30 Irigoin and Grafe, 'Bargaining', pp. 179–182, Yun-Casalilla and Comín Comín, 'Spain', p. 263.

31 Cunningham, *The Audiencia*, p. 103.

32 AGI Filipinas 941 N.1, 1769, & AGI Filipinas 268 N.1, 1752.

a captaincy-general under the jurisdiction of the Viceroy of New Spain in Mexico, and while no *Audiencia* operated in Manila, cases were appealed to the *Audiencia* of Mexico.[33] However, the moment an *Audiencia* was established in the Philippines, the archipelago and the American mainland gained equal access to the Council of the Indies and the king. Cases that expanded between territorial *Audiencias* were thus brought to the Council of the Indies, as none of them had precedence over the other. The most famous was the litigation over the nature of the Manila-Acapulco crossing between the *Consulado* of Seville (and Cádiz), and the City and Commerce of Manila, which had the exclusive right of sailing the Pacific. The case started in 1702 and lasted until 1734 and was entirely recorded by Antonio Álvarez de Abreu.[34] This litigation resulted in different modifications to the trade in 1718 and 1721 before finally settling the case in favour of Manila in 1734 with the issuance of a new, revised *reglamento*. The case, however, demonstrates that there was no stark hierarchy in the Spanish empire. The city of Manila had equal status to the trading cities of Seville and Cádiz and in fact managed to win the case. In legal terms, *Audiencias* had exclusive jurisdiction in matters regarding Civil Law on the territories under their control and had equal status among themselves.

Finally, the *Consejos* (councils) were both the ultimate representation of territorial fragmentation within the empire, as well as the courts of last appeal that rationalised the judicial process, giving it a sense of equilibrium that counteracted the centrifugal tendencies of such fragmentation. The *consejos* were the result of the composite nature of the Hispanic Monarchy, in which each territory maintained its own laws, usages, personnel, and institutions, while sharing the person of the monarch.[35] Thus, Castile had its own council (Council of Castile), while the Americas had a distinct council of their own (Council of the Indies). Councils were advisory boards for the king, but since the king was the ultimate judge in his realms, and he was bound to protect his vassals through the delivery of justice, this "advisory" role essentially took the

[33] Cunningham, *The Audiencia*, p. 39.

[34] Álvarez Abreu, *Extracto*.

[35] Elliott, 'A Europe', pp. 52–53.

form of judicial arbitration.[36] Thus, the councils essentially became the courts of last instance in their respective jurisdictions, and the only courts that could command the positive assertion of the king, therefore closing the judicial process.

Thus, the Council of the Indies was the tribunal of last instance for all matters regarding the American and Asian empire. As exemplified by the 1702–1734 litigation between Seville and Manila, cases surpassing the jurisdiction of the territorial *Audiencias* were brought to the Council. The sentences of the Council, given by the king, were also the materiel that essentially formed the corpus of Civil Law in the Spanish empire, collected in the *Recopilación de Leyes de Indias* and the different *cedularios*. This also meant, however, that the Council itself had no executive jurisdiction over the territories under its control, but rather a judicial one. As such, the Council and the king wielded great power to consolidate the institutional framework of the Hispanic Monarchy, but never had the legislative initiative.[37]

Thus, the Hispanic Monarchy had two almost contradictory facets that assured the balance of the entire system. On the one hand, it was based on a series of jurisdictions that were territorially autonomous and represented by their *audiencias*, each of which had equal standing among themselves, equal access to the king and the Council of the Indies and followed the same procedures. On the other hand, this entire structure was based on a series of levelled judicial institutions, built bottom-up with access to appeals which culminated in the figure of the king and the Council.[38] Thus, while the king had very little executive initiative of his own, he was the judge of last resort for everybody. His strength was derived from three characteristics of this legal model of state-building: he guaranteed each territorial unit's access to the law, he had supreme judicial authority, and because of the previous two factors, he had ample legislative capacity to create laws with the purpose of addressing the cases brought before him.[39]

[36] Yun-Casalilla, 'Las instituciones', p. 149, Thompson, I.A.A., 'The Rule of Law in Early Modern Castile', *European History Quarterly* 14, nº 2 (1984): 221–234.

[37] Irigoin and Grafe, 'Bargaining', p. 178.

[38] Phelan, 'Authority', pp. 50–51.

[39] Irigoin and Grafe, 'Bargaining', p. 182.

Another distinct characteristic of this system was the negotiated nature of legislation. Due to the king's paramount position in the legal framework of the Hispanic Monarchy, and the equal status among all territorial entities of the empire[40]—which all too often had conflicting interests—legislation was often bargained between the litigants and the king. This process has been termed "bargained absolutism" by Irigoin and Grafe,[41] and *pactismo* by François-Xavier Guerra.[42] This was a natural consequence of the separation between rule and ruler in which the legitimacy of the latter was built on his capacity to enforce the former. And for all practical purposes, it meant that each entity within the empire had the means to defend their interests while also had the obligation to accommodate some of their neighbours.

Finally, the multiplicity of jurisdictions and the capacity of actors to move between the boundaries of these jurisdictions made it easier for agents to defend their own interests, while simultaneously improving the access to the bargaining process. In short, there was no single sovereign law in the Hispanic Monarchy. Instead, there was a constellation of privileges and customs that enjoyed the protection of the king. The king in turn did not have the power to unilaterally alter these privileges, but as their guarantor, he could interpret and enforce the law. This implied bargaining between conflictive interests, which was facilitated by a shared procedural system. Therefore, while not all component parts of the Monarchy were equal, they all had access to bargaining under the same equal procedures. The next section will specifically apply this framework to the Pacific trade to show how Manila managed to strike a balance between privileges and duties that could protect their intermediary position in the Pacific trade.

[40] This, however, does not mean that they all wielded equal influence in the court of Madrid.

[41] Irigoin and Grafe, 'Bargaining', p. 204.

[42] Guerra, François-Xavier, 'The Spanish-American Tradition of Representation and its European Roots', *Journal of Latin American Studies* 26, n° 1 (Feb 1994), p. 3.

6.2 The Manila Trade and the Spanish Imperial Framework

As a constituent unit of the Hispanic Monarchy, Manila could utilise the institutional tools at its disposal to negotiate a settlement with the king that could protect its main objectives. Without knowledge of the *obras pías* of Manila and their role in distributing the proceeds of the trade across the city, it is impossible to discern that Manila's main motivation was to protect the intermediary role of the *obras pías* in the Pacific. Ultimately, what was at stake were the rents derived from the trade, which the city protected through bargaining in two related spheres: fiscal and jurisdictional. Firstly, through the process of bargaining, Manila managed to deflect most of the taxes on the transpacific trade and to make use of the local treasury in exchange of taking over the provision of public goods,[43] guaranteeing a minimal fiscal burden over commercial activities. Secondly, through the bargained ordering of the Hispanic Monarchy, Manila created a separate jurisdiction for the Galleon trade with its own legislative corpus, which often conflicted with others, but enjoyed the guarantee of the king. The result was a system in which Manileños could use the broader institutions of the Monarchy to enforce their intermediation, thus avoiding expensive investments and supporting the premium rates despite increasing liquidity.

Manila sought to protect the profits from the Pacific trade by reducing and deflecting costs whenever possible. This can be seen in the fiscal setup of the Pacific exchange, which was liable to four taxes. The first one was the import taxes or *almojarifazgo*, an *ad valorem* taxed levied upon the value of imports and paid by merchants entering Manila, which from the late seventeenth century had been established at a modest 6% of assessed value for non-Spanish ships, and 3% for Spanish vessels.[44] Nevertheless, as seen in Chapter 2, the great discrepancy between the recorded *almojarifazgo* collections in Manila and the documented arrival of silver pesos from the Philippines to other Asian ports suggest that the underreporting of this tax was endemic.[45] The *almojarifazgo* was also charged on the

[43] This outcome is similar to Timur Kuran's conceptualisation of the bargaining between subjects and sovereign that enabled the *waqf* system in the Middle East, Kuran, 'Why the Middle East', p. 75.

[44] Cosano Moyano, *Filipinas*, pp. 222–223.

[45] See Chapter 2, Section The Asian Leg on the Asian leg of the Manila trade.

Galleon on its departure from Manila, but this tax was a strict flat payment of scarcely 7,500 pesos,[46] a non-consequential amount in a trade whose volume is estimated to have been between 2 and 4 million pesos.[47]

The second tax was the *avería*, payable in Manila at a rate of 44 *ducados* per ton. Very little is known about this tax, and its collection does not appear to have been systematically reported or analysed by the literature. The king explicitly recognised in the 1734 *reglamento* that this tax had gone uncollected.[48] Furthermore, the king assigned this imposition in 1769 to the newly created *Consulado* of Manila to finance its operation.[49] The third tax was the *almojarifazgo* payable in Acapulco. The Acapulco *almojarifazgo* was assessed at a third of the value of the Galleon cargo according to the nominal return value of the *permiso*, which as seen in Chapter 2, was 500,000 from 1593, and changed to 600,000 in 1702, 1,000,000 in 1734, and 1,500,000 in 1776.[50] Although set at a third of this value, the *almojarifazgo* was essentially a lump payment in Acapulco. This meant that the actual tax burden was dissociated from the real value of the Galleon, which was consistently higher that the *permiso* by a large margin. Changes were introduced in the 1734 *reglamento*, which specified a rate of 17% for the allowance, while all amounts exceeding it had been taxed at 5% since 1724.[51] Finally, this rate was lowered to only 9% for the allowance, and 16% for all excess cargo in 1776.[52] To ease the burden on the Manileños further, this 5% ad valorem tax was assessed based on the price value of the goods *in* Manila instead of Acapulco until the incident of the *San Carlos Borromeo* Galleon in 1767, meaning that the import tax was assessed based on price of the goods at origin rather

46 Cosano Moyano, *Filipinas*, p. 296.

47 To place this tax in context, the 1789 dowry transferred by Antonio Tuasón, a wealthy Filipino, to his daughter rendered 5,483 pesos, 3 reales, and 3 tomines, enough to pay more than half of the Manila *almojarifazgo*, Escribano Miguel José Flores, 1789 [Legajo #21a], ACCHS-CSIC, ff 294a-295b.

48 AGI Filipinas 268 N.1, 1752, this document contains a copy of the 1734 *reglamento*.

49 AGI Filipinas 941 N. 1, 1769.

50 See Chapter 2, Section The American Leg.

51 AGI Filipinas 268 N.1, 1752.

52 Giráldez, *The Age*, p. 150.

than at destination.[53] Furthermore, tax collectors could not assess the real incidence of the *almojarifazgo* since, as seen in Chapters 2 and 4, the *almojarifazgo* was levied based on the weight of the trunks, not the value of the goods they contained.[54] To all effects, the Acapulco *almojarifazgo* was another lump payment that did not reflect the real value of the trade it was levied on.

The fourth and final tax of the Pacific exchange was the *alcábala* an ad valorem sales tax. The Manila trade was exempted from the sales tax payable in Acapulco,[55] but the Mexican wholesalers returning from the Acapulco fair had to pay a 6% tax in the entrance of Mexico City. It is difficult to assess the impact of the *alcábala* on the overall trade. The *alcábala* itself was not a uniform tax, many goods were exempted or had different rates at one time or another depending on whether the goods were brought into a region by land or by sea.[56] It is thus impossible to ascertain the actual fiscal burden that the *alcábala* imposed on the Pacific trade.

It is therefore important to notice that out of the four taxes that ingrafted the Pacific exchange including its backwards and forward linkages, only two were truly levied on the Galleon, the *almojarifazgos* on the Galleon in Manila and Acapulco. Two were also payable in Manila, and another two were payable in New Spain. Of the two taxes payable in Manila—the *almojarifazgo* on Asian vessels and the *avería*—only one was a direct imposition on the Galleon trade, and were the lowest taxes of the chain, based on nominal rates. They also amounted to the smallest quantities payable in coin, with the Manila *almojarifazgo* under-representing the real value of imports into Manila. Although Manileños only bargained for the two taxes that directly ingrafted the Galleon trade, including the entire chain of the Pacific exchange reveals the extent to which the fiscal incidence on the trade was based on notional assessments of a nominal taxable base separate from the real value of the trade. This, since the work of Schurz, has been understood as an instance of tax evasion, but

[53] In 1767 royal officials challenged the customary interpretation that the bills registered in the *contaduría* of Manila were the ones used to assess the value of the goods, instead of the bills registered upon arrival in Acapulco. AGI Filipinas 941 N.1., 1769.

[54] Viana summarised the uselessness of sworn declarations in a report to the king, AMN 533 MS1576 Doc. 2, 1760, ff. 12–14.

[55] AGI Filipinas 268 N.1, 1752.

[56] Irigoin and Grafe, 'Bargaining', p. 186.

Chapter 4 explained that the real reason behind the secrecy regarding the contents of the trunks was the role it played in the Manileños' negotiating strategy in Acapulco. Thus, fiscality was subordinated to the rationale of the exchange.

Furthermore, the largest fiscal item on the Galleon, the *almojarifazgo* payable in Acapulco, was then reimbursed to the Treasury of Manila as the *situado*, the annual transfer of cash from Mexico to the Spanish Philippines. The *situado* was an important fiscal and accounting mechanism of the Spanish empire,[57] and by extension, the Pacific trade. Its origins in the Pacific dated back to the supplies sent from New Spain to the Philippines in the context of the conquest of the archipelago,[58] but as early as 1588 it was established by Felipe II as an annual supplement to the Filipino Treasury financed from the freight and *alcabala* of the trade.[59] In 1604, Felipe III ordered instead that the *almojarifazgo* payable by the Galleon trade in Acapulco be returned to the Philippines as part of the *situado*,[60] and in 1675 or 1687, the *situado* was established as an annual payment of 250,000 pesos from New Spain to Manila.[61] The Acapulco *almojarifazgo* was not only a flat payment completely divorced of the reality of the value of the transaction it was meant to tax, but it was a legal manoeuvre to monetise a refundable imposition that went to repay the loans of the Philippines' government, thus flowing back across the city.

Another crucial contribution of the *situado* is to be found on the way it was used in Manila to the benefit of the private capital markets of the city.

[57] Grafe and Irigoin, 'A Stakeholder', p. 611, Irigoin and Grafe, 'Bargaining', p. 185, Irigoin, Alejandra, and Grafe, Regina, 'Absolutismo negociado: la trayectoria hispana en la formación del Estado y el Imperio', in *El secreto del Imperio Español: Los situados coloniales en el siglo XVIII*, eds. Carlos Marichal and Johanna von Grafenstein (México: El Colegio de México, 2012): 295–342.

[58] Alonso Álvarez, Luís, 'La ayuda mexicana en el Pacífico: Socorros y situados en Filipinas, 1565–1816', in *El Secreto del Imperio Español: los situados coloniales en el siglo XVIII*, eds. Carlos Marichal and Johanna von Grafenstein (México: El Colegio de México, 2012), pp. 256–257.

[59] Alonso Álvarez, *El costo*, p. 273.

[60] Alonso Álvarez, *El costo*, pp. 283–284.

[61] Alonso Álvarez, *El costo*, p. 287.

Nominally, the *situado* relieved the military and administrative expenditure of the islands' government.[62] However, it was often used to repay loans that the Treasury of Manila had incurred with the *obras pías*. The triangular relationship of the *obras pías* of Manila, the local treasury, and the *situado* is evidenced in the 1749 loan of the Misericordia to the Treasury. In that year, interim governor Archbishop Amechesurra requested a loan from the Misericordia to fit the annual Galleon to Acapulco to retrieve the *situado*. The Misericordia lent the Treasury of Manila 19,322 pesos from the *correspondencia* funds that it managed at no interest, and 13,000 pesos from the *censos* funds at an annual 5% rate.[63] In reality, the Misericordia had issued a 32,322 pesos loan at an annual 2% interest, with the pledge of the coming *situado*. This was problematic for two reasons: the king had continuously ordered the governors not to borrow from the Misericordia, and the capital tied in legacy funds could not be legally used to invest in anything other than what had been specified by the will of the founders, excluding thus loans to the government. Mindful of the potential legal implications, the Misericordia consulted with jurists and theologians. These jurists used canonical principles to argue that necessity overruled the ban on legacy funds.[64] Most crucially, the loan was agreed to because the governor pledged the "real palabra" (royal word) that it would be repaid from the *situado*,[65] even though such a loan was forbidden.

Regardless of the later repercussions of this loan,[66] the dynamics are worth analysing. Amechesurra, an interim governor, pledged the income earmarked by the king, in a loan from the Misericordia, which acted as a sort of communal bank, even though the governor had explicit orders not to do so. The Misericordia and the governor conducted the whole process without involving the judges of the *Audiencia* or the king's prosecutor but consulting instead with experts on Canon Law, evidencing

[62] For the nominal use of the *situado* transfers, see Alonso Álvarez, *El costo*, pp. 290–292, for the actual use of *situados* by local elites, Grafe and Irigoin, 'A Stakeholder', pp. 609–651.

[63] AGI Filipinas 198 N.9, *Carta de la Mesa de la Misericordia sobre reintegro de préstamo a las cajas reales*, 1753.

[64] AGI Filipinas 198 N. 9, 1753.

[65] AGI Filipinas 198 N. 9, 1753.

[66] Amechesurra died in 1750 before the appointed governor arrived on the islands, provoking a delay in the recognition of the loan and in its repayment.

that the multiplicity of legal jurisdictions provided the *obras pías* with avenues to advance their interests. A similar situation occurred in 1738, when the alleged scarcity of rice in the city led the municipal council to request a loan from the Misericordia of 25,000 pesos.[67] The Misericordia put forward the question to the canonical tribunal of the islands, which agreed to the loan based on three reasons: that the capital of many legacy funds was idle, demonstrating the abundance of money available for investment in the city and the lack of alternatives; that, although the situation was not urgent, the loan could be advanced by usurers if the Misericordia did not do it;[68] and, again, because the city pledged the rent of the commons as guarantee.[69]

The pattern is clear: a situation of urgency was fabricated so that, in canonical terms, it meant that it was better for the "greater good" to disobey the prohibition on lending to the treasury than to follow it. In these instances, the *obras pías*, which were under the jurisdiction of Canon Law, could bypass the *Audiencia* and appeal directly to canon tribunals. These jurists made it explicit that the *situado* was a necessary part and parcel that satisfied the condition of "certainty" necessary for the loans to be valid according to Canon Law. This was in the interest of the *obras pías* because lending money to the treasury gave them an outlet for the abundance of capital they had under their management. In a context in which the demand for working capital was limited due to the rationing of the trade but its supply was continuously growing through retained earnings and the foundation of new legacy funds, *obras pías* needed to diverge money from the trade and into any investment outlets they could find. The capital from *obras pías* lent to the treasury would reduce the available liquidity pool for *correspondencias*, potentially propping up premia.

The king of Spain perceived no real benefit from this trade, but neither did he make any serious attempt at increasing the tax rate. There was concern—especially in Seville—that too much American silver may have been deviated from the Atlantic trade by the Pacific route. As seen in Chapter 2, the constant revisions of the *reglamento* were in part a

[67] AGI Filipinas 197 N. 26, *Carta de la mesa de la Misericordia sobre préstamo a la ciudad de Manila*, 1743–1744, f. 1.

[68] Who these "usurers" may be is never specified. It is far more likely that this was an ad hoc argument used to justify the loan than a real danger.

[69] AUST, Libros, Tomo 20, *Consultas y sus Respuestas*, undated, eighteenth century, ff. 59–62 & 113–119, f. 61.

response to this conflict of interest between the Atlantic and Pacific routes, but the king's role in this litigation, and his accommodating position towards the fiscal regime of the Pacific exchange do not support the view that the main source of change in the structure of the Pacific trade was the king's aim to either tax or curtail the flow of silver east. The king's approach towards the fiscal structure of the Philippines, especially during the long eighteenth century, was a pragmatic one. The king knew that this amounted to a net profit to him, since the Philippines became for all purposes an autonomous territory, in which the fiscal resources were managed internally, and public goods were provided and distributed locally. King Felipe V himself replied to the Andalusian *Consulado* that the Pacific exchange did not amount to any sensible loss to his treasury, rather the opposite. In 1723, when lifting the 1718 ban on silk exports from Manila to Mexico requested by Seville and enshrined in the brief *reglamento* of 1720, the king noted that:

> [the rules of 1720] limit and restrict, and completely eliminate the supply of silk, in bulk and in cloth, to great damage to my Royal Treasury, for due to the rights paid by the said goods it is possible to send to these islands [the Philippines] and the Mariana islands the situado, wherein this amount would have to be paid from my Royal Treasury in Mexico, therefore causing great delay and harm in [the Royal Treasury of Mexico's] efforts to attend to all the expenditures it has.[70]

The king was therefore aware that the Philippines' autonomy was to the wider benefit of the fiscal structure of the empire, and rather than curtailing the flow of silver, the kings indirectly promoted the Pacific trade by rising the nominal *permiso* three times in the eighteenth century. Outsourcing the fiscal income did not necessarily result in a situation of bankruptcy since the provision of public goods was also outsourced. The prime example, as seen in Chapter 3, was the case of the Misericordia, which provided alms, managed hospitals, and administered the dowry fund, but in general the *obras pías* partook in this model.

The result was a situation in which the day-to-day provision of public goods was often done by the Misericordia and the *obras pías*, which often resulted in the effective privatisation of the *situado*. This setup created an equilibrium of its own that aligned the interests of the king and the *obras*

[70] AGI Filipinas 229 N.1, 1724.

pías. The king's direct expenditure was low, and the *situado* became a way of co-opting the local elites into the administration of the empire, as explained by Grafe and Irigoin.[71] This also worked to the king's advantage as Manila paid for its own defence for most of the period. For all purposes, the Philippines was an autonomous fiscal territory that provided no profits to the king of Spain and cost him no expenditure. As Irigoin and Grafe argued, this model of empire-building was focused on making the imperial polities self-sufficient and reducing the expenditure of the Monarchy while aligning the interests of the local elites with those of the king.[72] This came at the expense of tolerating the rent-seeking nature of the Pacific mercantile setup. It was a *quid pro quo* of imperial dimensions.

Manila not only obtained autonomy in fiscal matters, but through the *reglamento*, it also managed to use the bargaining process to obtain a jurisdiction of its own. As explained in Chapter 2, ever since the conquest of Manila in 1571, the city had been the centre of Spanish presence in the Philippines, and the sole commercial hub linking East and South Asia with Spanish America. The exclusivity of this intermediary position derived from the 1593 *reglamento* into a privilege of sole intermediation like that enjoyed by the city of Seville (and later Cádiz) with America, through which Manila enjoyed the exclusive right to freight across the Pacific. Due to its nature as a royal privilege, the Manila-Acapulco trade thus enjoyed an exclusive jurisdiction that was self-encompassing. Essentially, the Manila-Acapulco trade was regulated by its own laws, which were however enforced by all the echelons of administrative justice, including the *audiencia* of Manila and the Council of the Indies. This regulation, which was indissoluble from the privilege, was compiled in the trade's unique *reglamento* or ordinances.

The first *reglamento* was granted in 1593 by the king with the implicit recognition of the privilege. The *reglamento* ended the previous period of free-for-all which had seen no limits in ships sailing across the Pacific, and during which Peruvians had also attempted to establish a direct commerce with the Philippines.[73] The *reglamento* recognised Manila's exclusive privilege to sail across the ocean but included several restrictions: it limited

[71] Irigoin, Alejandra and Grafe, Regina, 'Response to Carlos Marichal and William Summerhill', *Hispanic American Historical Review* 88, nº 2 (2008), p. 239.

[72] Grafe and Irigoin, 'The Spanish Empire', p. 263.

[73] Schurz, *The Manila*, p. 194, Borah, Woodrow, *Early Colonial Trade and Navigation between Mexico and Peru* (Berkeley: University of California Press, 1954), pp. 117–118.

the trade to a *permiso* of 250,000 pesos in the outbound trip and 500,000 pesos in the inbound trip and to two galleons of 300 tons each destined exclusively to the port of Acapulco in New Spain, as seen in Chapter 2. The *reglamento*'s most extensive changes came during the trials of 1702–1734. In 1720, an addendum banned the export from Manila of Chinese silk,[74] a ban that was rescinded in 1723 when the impossibility of this change became apparent to the king.[75] Only with the king's sentence in favour of Manila in 1734 did the *reglamento* take its final form.[76] The 1734 *reglamento* was in force until the end of the privilege in 1815, with the only major change of the addendum on 1769 which created the *Consulado* and placed all commercial disputes under its jurisdiction.

These constant changes show that the process of issuing or reforming the *reglamento* was bargained. There has been a persistent interpretation in the historiography that the *reglamento* and the limitations it crystallised into law represent the king's unilateral and ineffectual attempts at curtailing the flow of silver to Asia.[77] This approach has tended to conceal the agency of Manileños in crafting the *reglamento*. The focus here is placed on how the *reglamento* created a legal guarantee that placed Manila's trade directly under the protection of the king. This not only allowed access to the king's arbitration in case of litigation, but it also meant that Manileños enjoyed another avenue for bargaining thanks to the jurisdiction created by the privilege of sole intermediation across the Pacific.

This can be seen in the litigation that led to the 1769 addendum and foundation of the *Consulado* of Manila.[78] The case was a dispute between the Galleon freighters and the port authorities in Acapulco regarding the trip of the Galleon *San Carlos Borromeo* in 1766–1767. The Galleon freighters presented a case through their representative in Mexico City, Domingo Casal Bermúdez,[79] against the royal officials in New Spain,

[74] AGI Filipinas 268 N.1, 1752.

[75] AGI Filipinas 229 N.1, 1724.

[76] AGI Filipinas 268 N.1, 1752.

[77] Bonalian, *El Pacífico*, pp. 63–64, Yuste, *Emporios*, pp. 35–36, Schurz, *The Manila*, p. 155.

[78] The complete 1769 *addendum* is reproduced in AGI Filipinas 941 N.1, 1769.

[79] A member of the Bermúdez family, which were some of the most important merchants in Manila.

arguing that they had exceeded their authority and violated the *privilegio* of the Manila-Acapulco trade in the unloading of the cargo.[80] An especially poignant issue was whether the valuation of the cargo had to be assessed based on the value of the bills of lading presented in Manila, as the freighters insisted, or upon bills presented in Acapulco, as the royal officials claimed,[81] since officials understood that the bills presented at origin grossly undervalued the cargo.[82]

Underscoring the entire process was an issue of jurisdiction, nominally, to what extent the royal officials could interfere with the Galleon privilege embodied in the *reglamento*, for the purpose of enforcing the law compiled in the *Recopilación*. This point led to a fierce debate regarding the capacity of the royal officials to inspect the privately drawn bills of instructions that consignors in Manila had given to their consignees. In this regard, Domingo Casal Bermúdez described the right of the freighters to hide their bills of lading from the officials as a royal "amnesty"[83] and argued:

> Regardless of the fact that the bills contain various confidences shared to the freighters in their footing, the common law [Derecho de gentes in the original] does not allow for their publication, even if it were in the interest of the king, as mandated by the Supreme Council of Castile as sentenced on 14th December 1745.[84]

Paradoxically, both the freighters and the officials based their case in a copy of the *reglamento* of 1734, a fact recorded in the notarial proceeding crafted on the spot, a copy of which was submitted upon request to the representative of the Manileños in Mexico.[85] In it, the freighters asserted that "we cannot be compelled without an express order of His Majesty".[86] Basically, the privilege of sole intermediation guaranteed the king's protection against perceived excesses from his own officials until

[80] AGI Filipinas 941 N.1, 1769.

[81] AGI Filipinas 941 N.1, 1769.

[82] AGI Filipinas 941 N.1, 1769.

[83] AGI Filipinas 941 N.1, 1769.

[84] AGI Filipinas 941 N.1, 1769.

[85] AGI Filipinas 941 N.1, 1769.

[86] AGI Filipinas 941 N.1, 1769.

a decision was reached. In fact, the royal officials had to recuse themselves from the case, which was derived to an independent judge brought specifically to mediate the dispute, and who ultimately agreed with the officials.[87]

Again, what was at stake in the case of the *San Carlos Borromeo* was not the fiscal burden of the Galleon trade, but the strategy of secrecy that enabled Manileños to negotiate in Acapulco. To defend this strategy, Manileños pitted the *reglamento* against the laws of the Indies. The legal pluralism of the empire described in the first section of this chapter provided multiple avenues for negotiation, as well as multiple tools for the members of the Hispanic Monarchy to defend their own interests. The king's solution to the case of the *San Carlos Borromeo* was to grant Manila a *Consulado* in 1769, an association of merchants that enjoyed exclusive jurisdiction regarding the privilege of the Galleon trade and over commercial cases.[88] The king healed the wound inflicted by his officials through further devolving authority on the merchants of Manila, shielding the trade. In this framework, legislation was not the driver of the evolution of the trade, but rather the outcome of constant bargaining through which the different parties involved advanced and defended their interests.

The privilege of sole intermediation between Manila and Acapulco had its own jurisdiction, compiled in the *reglamento*, which enjoyed the king's protection, although it was modified following judicial processes. Access to the judicial process was therefore fundamental since it could lead to changes in the way the trade was conducted. The king's guarantee meant that no single institution or lobby had enough strength on their own to modify the *reglamento* according to their own wishes, but the separate jurisdiction and the access to justice meant that there were ways in which changes could be introduced through litigation and bargaining. Neither Mexican, nor *peninsular* Spanish institutions, could change the terms of contracting without appealing through the Council of the Indies, as the Andalusians tried in 1702–1734. The legal pluralism of the Hispanic Monarchy thus worked to make Manila's position unassailable from within the empire. The *obras pías*, as seen in Chapter 3, aligned the interests of everyone in Manila towards protecting the rents

[87] AGI Filipinas 941 N.1, 1769.

[88] Cunningham, *The Audiencia*, p. 115.

of the trade. The jurisdictional fragmentation thus operated to limit the market to a set of invested groups that enjoyed local support, to the detriment of market integration. The same model was in operation in New Spain, where, as seen in Chapter 4, *Consulado* merchants controlled the transcontinental trade of the international fairs and were immune for outsiders' attacks on their control over the local market.[89] This territorial fragmentation in turn meant that solutions to challenges had to be bargained. Manila, Mexico, and Seville/Cádiz were thus entwined in a complex process of bargaining and negotiation with the king to protect their own interests, which in turn enhanced the position of the king as arbiter between all polities. This was a source of friction but also of cohesion, as will be seen in the next section.

6.3 The Equilibrium of Spanish Imperial Trade

The fiscal setup of the Hispanic Monarchy was built on a series of "conflictive pacts" between distinct territorial units that had varying interests.[90] The constitution of the Spanish empire meant that all territorial units had legal capacity to defend their own interests. It also placed the king as an institutional guarantee that kept all parties in the negotiating table. This was a system in which centrifugal tension was in-built, but that had the means to provide a negotiated outlet for such tensions.[91] It was through these bargaining and conflictive pacts that territorial units would seek to further their respective positions, but it was as much a guarantee of their continued belonging to the system as a whole. From the perspective of Manila and the transpacific trade, this institutional model provided the tools to advance its intermediary position given the skewed bargaining power that Mexican wholesalers enjoyed due to the large demand for pesos in Asia. The king's guarantee of sole intermediation through the Pacific meant that Manileños could respond to Mexico's Acapulco cartel with their own cartel embodied in the single Galleon. Manileños and Mexicans could then negotiate in the Acapulco fair to guarantee the mutual profit of the exchange, and thus of *obras pías*. This system of trade imposed a limitation in the volume of the exchange in return for a higher

[89] Irigoin and Grafe, 'Bargaining', p. 179.

[90] Yun-Casalilla and Comín Comín, 'Spain', p. 263.

[91] Irigoin and Grafe, 'Bargaining', pp. 203–204.

scope for profit, and this approach rested on balancing the interests of Manila and New Spain.

But this does not explain why Mexican wholesalers, given their skewed bargaining power, would agree to trade exclusively with Maníleños since this implied meeting some of their price demands when they had the option to choose somewhere else. Chapter 5 has explained the economic logic of this: Manila was capable of supplying capital in Asian waters more efficiently than any of their existing competitors at the time. Furthering market integration through freer trade would have meant not so much bypassing Manila's intermediary role in the Pacific, but the wholesalers' intermediation between the silver mines, the internal consumer market of New Spain, and the Mexico mint, which was the true source of the fragmentation of the market and was not in the interest of the wholesalers of the Mexico City *Consulado*. There was similarly an institutional side to this story that is explained by the jurisdictional equilibrium of the Hispanic Monarchy. The same way that Maníleños protested to the king when well-capitalised Mexicans penetrated Manila and offered financing in the city, Mexicans could bear the authority of the king to prevent Maníleños bypassing the Acapulco fair and selling Asian products directly to consumers. Maníleños and Mexicans were therefore locked in a balance that respected their ultimate sources of income: their intermediation in their respective local markets.

Manila's capacity to mitigate to an extent the problems derived from this lack of market integration through economies of scale in the mobilisation of capital enabled this balance because it offered potential interlopers the option to contract directly with Manila instead of attempting the Pacific crossing. As mentioned in previous chapters, contraband with third parties outside of the Hispanic Monarchy was missing in the Pacific exchange. The English were pioneers in opening their relationship with Manila in 1644, but they settled quickly for integrating their trade with Manila, which provided them with abundant pesos through private traders.[92] Not even when the English conquered Manila in 1762 did they seriously consider the possibility of bypassing the city and sailing straight to America.[93]

[92] Quiason, *English*, Cheong, 'Changing', and Cheong, 'Some Aspects'.

[93] Instead, the English left Alexander Dalrymple in Manila as provisional deputy governor until the return of the Spanish authorities in 1764 and to oversee the establishment of a factory in Sulu, which Dalrymple had studied since 1761,

But Manila's specialisation was not the only force labouring to produce this balance between Manila and Mexico. The Dutch attempted to bypass Manila in the Pacific in the 1740s.[94] The VOC fitted an expedition to trade directly from Batavia to Acapulco taking advantage of the onset of the War of Jenkins' Ear and the capture of the *Convadonga* by the English. The expedition was organised with the support of Jesuit priests in Manila that had contacts among the California missions and the city of Mexico, and with the advice of Andrés Blanco Bermúdez, administrator of the legacy funds of the Jesuits in Manila, and one of the wealthiest merchants in the city, whose brother was a member of Mexico's municipal government.[95] The Dutch hoped to capitalise on the temporary stoppage of the Manila-Acapulco line, however when they arrived to America it was the Mexicans themselves who refused to trade with them.[96]

This illustrates an interesting characteristic of the Pacific trade, which is that while the Mexican wholesalers had deal with the opposing cartel of the Galleon freighters in the Acapulco fair, they still refused to trade with outsiders. In reality, what Mexicans—like Manileños—were protecting was the fair system from which they derived their capacity to intermediate between international trade and internal consumption. As shown in Chapter 4, the fair system enabled the local merchants to control the flows of goods and silver within their territories. In this, all mercantile interests of the Hispanic Monarchy were united. The lack of integration in the Spanish imperial trade, as argued previously, did not mean that motivations were not aligned horizontally. Manileños and Mexicans were united in trying to defend the rents they derived from their respective fairs. For them, the greatest threat was direct trade, and the Dutch attempt of 1747 was to all effects a VOC scheme to open trade relations directly with the city of Mexico. The threat of outsiders was compounded by the fact that they were not under the jurisdiction of the king of Spain. As said in previous sections, legislation was subordinated to mercantile interests. If Mexicans, Manileños, or *peninsulares* tried to penetrate each

Manilha Consultations, vol. 10, 1764, p. 5, & IOR/E/1/47, *Letters 135–136 Alexander Dalrymple, London to the Court of Directors giving an account of his transactions at Sooloo and enclosing a Treaty he concluded with that place*, Nov. 1765, ff. 286–298, see also Quiason, *English "Country Trade"*, pp. 122–133.

94 Furber, 'The India', pp. 8–9.

95 Furber, 'The India', p. 11.

96 Furber, 'The India', pp. 12–13, Furber, *Rival Empires*, p. 160.

other's markets, they could all appeal to the king of Spain to enforce their respective privileges. Manileños petitioned the king against Mexicans settling in the islands.[97] Similarly, the *Consulado* of Mexico managed to change the location of the Atlantic fair from Orizaba to Jalapa in 1728 because Orizaba was too well connected to effectively prevent *peninsulares* from travelling into New Spain.[98] But the Dutch and the English operated outside of the institutional umbrella of the Hispanic Monarchy, and there was no guarantee that they would respect this arranged system of rent protection. It was thus easier to exclude them.

English and Dutch attempts through the Pacific were never consistent or serious enough to represent a real threat to the balance of fairs and merchant interests that characterised Spanish imperial trade. Undoubtedly, the capacity of Manila to offer silver pesos in Asia played a role in pre-empting this, since both the English and the Dutch ultimately found it easier to sell Asian goods in Manila to generate cash flows than trying to navigate the Hispanic commercial equilibrium. But the case of the Dutch attempt to open direct commercial relations with America illustrates the argument of this section: that the participants of the Spanish imperial trade preferred to protect the rents they derived from their control of their internal markets over expanding their trade options. Imperial trade, from the peninsula to the Filipino archipelago, rested on a balance between local mercantile interests in which all participants respected each other's rents to an extent. Just like the fiscal structure of the Spanish empire represented a balance between "conflictive interests", the private trade rested upon the same principle. This balance was in constant tension, but it was a balance nonetheless in which the intermediaries enjoyed the lion's share of profits and deflected the costs to the consumers.

Direct trade was a threat because it imperilled this balance. Thus, when French interlopers started sailing directly between Europe, Perú, and Asia in 1699–1720, Manileños felt threatened, since this trade diverted money from the re-export trade of Asian goods between Acapulco and Perú.[99] In the same way, Manila resented the creation of the RCF in 1785. The company's permission to acquire Asian goods at origin and

[97] Schurz, *The Manila*, pp. 363–364.

[98] See Chapter 4 Sect. 4.1.

[99] See the dedicated monography by Malamud Rikles, Carlos D., *Cádiz y Saint Malo en el comercio colonial peruano (1698–1725)*, (Jerez de la Frontera: Diputación Provincial de Cádiz, 1986), Bonalian, *El Pacífico*, pp. 246–247.

export them to America through Veracruz and El Callo was a direct threat to the system of fairs and Galleons that had existed until then because it had the potential to glut American markets with Asian goods and drive prices down. Manila, after all, was defending the share of the silver profits that accrued to it as the supplier of Asian goods from the Pacific. The expansion of trade, of which the French expeditions were just a symptom, had destabilising consequences. Globalisation did not just corrode the political scaffolding of the Hispanic Monarchy, as argued by Yun-Casalilla.[100] Since this scaffolding ultimately reflected the vested interests of the merchants trying to control the rents from trade, it similarly corroded the careful equilibrium between regions that was at the core of the imperial trade system.

It is at this point that most historians have confused the causal role of the king's regulation and have seen the limitation of the trade to the *permiso* and the single Galleon as imposed by the king.[101] According to them, scaling the trade was not possible because of institutional reasons. There are two caveats to this. Firstly, as seen in this work, the *permiso* was to all effects ineffectual. The quantities of silver that crossed the Pacific were consistently higher than what the *permiso* allowed. Even then, the king often responded favourably to demands for expansion of the trade, rising the *permiso* three times in the eighteenth century. The constant upward revisions of the *permiso* during the eighteenth century do not fit with the interpretation that the sole objective of the king was to stop the flow of silver in the Pacific. Secondly, it overlooks the cartel of wholesalers in Mexico and their bargaining strength given their control of the flows of pesos. As seen in Chapter 4, when this is taken into consideration it is possible to understand why Manileños were interested in rationing the volume of the exchange.

Not enough attention has been paid to the interest that all components of the Hispanic Monarchy—Manileños, New Spanish, and *peninsulares*—had in maintaining this equilibrium. The Seville *Consulado* may have been instrumental in bringing the first limitation of the Pacific trade in 1593, but historians ignore that this first *reglamento* also ordered that all trade with Asia through the Pacific had to be conducted through

[100] Yun-Casalilla, *Iberian*..., pp. 345–346.

[101] Bonalian, *El Pacífico*, pp. 63–64, Yuste, *Emporios*, pp. 35–36, Schurz, *The Manila*, p. 155.

Acapulco, cutting off Peru. This was an accommodation of New Spanish interests, which in this instance, as argued by Spate, went hand in hand with Seville.[102] The *reglamento* of 1593 also meant the virtual end of the "Galeones de Cebú". Azcárraga, in his treatise on the history of free trade in the Philippines, asserted that in the beginning of Spanish presence in the islands, two routes to trade with America existed: the Manila Galleons that went to Acapulco, and the Galleons of Cebú, sailing to Perú from the city of Cebú, the first Spanish settlement founded by Miguel de Legázpi in 1565.[103] The city of Cebú sent Galleons to America in competition with Manila, and in fact the latter—like Seville and Cádiz did in 1702—sued against Cebú and its American trade. A cédula from 1594 that complemented the *reglamento* of 1593 banned Cebú from transporting silk to America, which remained the exclusive privilege of Manileños.[104] Barred from the most lucrative trade, the Galleons of Cebú faded. The regulation of 1593 illustrates how the king at the centre negotiated a settlement that aimed at aligning the interests of as many players as possible. The first *reglamento* was not exclusively the imposition of an artificial limit on the Pacific trade for the benefit of *peninsulares*, it was also a guarantee for both Mexico and Manila over their control of the Pacific route. Mexico and Manila preferred trading with one another because they both enjoyed the explicit guarantees that their respective areas of control would be respected. In other words, the legislation—including the Manila *reglamento*—was the result of the balancing act in which the king had to accommodate as many conflictive interests as possible to reach an equilibrium. The emphasis on fiscality as an explanation for changes taking place across the Hispanic Monarchy from the second half of the eighteenth century—territorial as well as jurisdictional—[105]has tended to obscure the

[102] Spate, *The Spanish*, pp. 217–218.

[103] The first Galleons that brought silver and transported Asian goods to America departed from Cebú, Azcárraga, Manuel, *La Libertad de Comercio en las Islas Filipinas* (Madrid: Imprenta de José Noguera, 1872), p. 66.

[104] Azcárraga, *La Libertad*, p. 67–68.

[105] Two seminal works from such perspective are Marichal, Carlos, *La bancarrota del virreinato. Nueva España y las finanzas del Imperio español, 1780–1810* (Mexico D.F.: Fondo de Cultura Económica, 1999) and chapter on "Campomames y los preliminares de la desamortización eclesiástica" in Tomás y Valiente, Francisco, *Gobierno e instituciones en la España del Antiguo Régimen* (Madrid: Alianza Editorial, 1982).

importance of market structure, which was as much a source of rents as of contention across the imperial polity.

The political economy of trade across the Hispanic Monarchy rested in a balance between territorial units in which local merchants controlled their respective internal distribution channels. The downside to this was rationing in volume and a lack of market integration, but as long as the cost of this lack could be passed on to the ultimate consumer and interlopers could be kept away, the intermediaries that controlled this system did not suffer the consequences. The upside was trade partners that respected each other's autonomy. The institutional solution to the Fundamental Problem of Exchange rested on this union in disunion: Mexicans preferred trading with Manileños because Manileños respected Mexicans' boundaries, and if any attempt was made to break this balance, both Mexicans and Manileños could resort to their common king to restore the equilibrium between both.

6.4 The End of the Balance and the Path to a New Equilibrium

The imperial system of trade that connected Europe, America, and Asia rested on a balance between privileged merchant bodies that controlled their respective internal markets. At the core of this balance was the promise of rents to be gained from the silver trade. Each merchant group respected each other's boundaries and scaled down the volume of the exchange to guarantee profits. However, this equilibrium started to fade during the second half of the eighteenth century. After the Seven Years' War there was an expansion of trade that placed the balance under stress. In the Pacific, the looting of the legacy funds by the English and the occupation of Manila between 1762 and 1764 weakened the *obras pías* and led to changes in the organisation of the trade. The expansion of direct trade, with the chartering of the RCF in 1785 and the start of US-China trade,[106] also affected the profitability of the Manila-Acapulco commerce. Similarly, the *comercio libre* edicts that enabled licensed ships to sail directly to America from Spain, bypassing the fair system, eventually led to the glutting of Spanish American markets. It is not the purpose

[106] On the RCF, see Díaz-Trechuelo, *La Real*, on US-China trade, see Irigoin, 'The End', pp. 210–211, and Fichter, *So Great*.

of this work to examine the causes of the late eighteenth century breakdown of the imperial trading equilibrium, but only to analyse the effects and to explore what the end of this balance can tell us about the previous system it replaced. Ultimately, all of these changes, whether intentionally or not, reduced the rents derived from intermediating imperial trade.

In the Pacific, the end of the balance came in two ways. On the one hand, the English looting of the *obras pías* gave the king the chance to slowly start the reforms on the organisation of the trade and to emancipate the Manila Treasury from its dependence on the legacy funds. This in turn had the effect of denying the *obras pías* a strategy to divert their capital away from the trade, which increased the supply of capital for trade and made it difficult to maintain the rates of *correspondencia*'s premia. On the other hand, the chartering of the RCF, which had the privilege of carrying the same overall business model as the Manila Galleon (American silver for Asian goods in direct intermediation with Veracruz and El Callao, but not Acapulco) glutted American markets with Asian goods and lowered the profits of the exchange. As a result of these changes, the previously safe rents of the trade became more volatile, and Manila's *obras pías* had to engage with the new game by lowering the premia of *correspondencias* further and expanding the range of their investments. Horizontal Specialisation came under attack, so Manila had to scale up.

As mentioned in Chapter 5, the English occupation of Manila and the looting of the *obras pías* in 1762, together with Admiral Cornish's capture of the outgoing Galleon and the Spanish loyalist forces' confiscation of the incoming one, essentially bankrupted the *obras pías*. The king had to come to the aid of the *obras pías* and recapitalised them in 1764.[107] This rare event weakened the *obras pías* and strengthened the king's hand. Thus, after the king recapitalised the legacy funds of the Misericordia, the brotherhood sent a report of their accounts every five years to the Council of the Indies.[108] To an extent, the king managed to open the lock to Manila. This was followed by the appointment of Simón de Anda – the judge of the *Audiencia* who in 1762 had led the guerrilla war against the occupying British forces and who had confiscated the silver of the

[107] AGI Filipinas 595, Libro primero, 1762–1764.

[108] The reports are all kept in various folders in AGI Filipinas 595, 1764–1823.

Galleon *El Filipino* – as governor of the islands in 1770.[109] Anda started the slow process of reforming the Treasury of Manila that culminated with its emancipation from the *obras pías*.

As explained previously, the *situado* made the treasury dependent on the arrival of the Galleons and led them to rely on loans from the *obras pías*. An early attempt at rationalising the operation of the treasury was done by governor Fausto Cruzat y Góngora in the final years of the seventeenth century, but it was highly unpopular since it altered the framework of private–public contracts that enabled the city's corporations to derive profit from the treasury, and was abandoned by the next governor.[110] The appointment of Simón de Anda as governor led to an effort to improve the situation of the Manila Treasury. As reported by Cosano Moyano, the structure of the *contaduría*[111] was modified in 1776, and again in 1784, rationalising the information flows in the treasury, creating new offices where needed and establishing clear decision-making hierarchies, and providing for ways to effectively collect taxes without relying on outsourcing.[112] Parallel to these reforms, governor José de Basco y Vargas introduced a monopoly on tobacco in 1782.[113] By the late eighteenth century, the Philippines were able to achieve a fiscal surplus, and by the early nineteenth century the tobacco monopoly was the single largest source of income for the treasury.[114]

These reforms have been interpreted from a fiscal point of view as a process through which the Philippines stopped being reliant on monetary injections from New Spain and became an autonomous fiscal region that even managed to remit surpluses to the metropolis, culminating in the

[109] Escoto, Salvador, 'The Administration of Simón de Anda y Salazar, Governor General of the Philippines, 1770–1776' (PhD diss., Loyola University Chicago, 1973), p. 11.

[110] Alonso Álvarez, *El costo*, pp. 288–289, Fradera, *Filipinas*, pp. 65–67.

[111] The office in charge of the accounts of the treasury, similar to the Comptroller in Britain.

[112] Cosano Moyano, *Filipinas*, pp. 38–39 & 53.

[113] Legarda, *After*, pp. 76–77.

[114] Fradera, *Filipinas*, pp. 191–192.

supposed end of the *situado* in 1804.[115] Others, like Fradera, have questioned that fiscal emancipation from New Spain was the purpose of the reform, and argued that rationalising the tax collection and the administration of the Manila Treasury was an end in itself.[116] It is true that the amounts sent as the *situado* were drastically reduced during the 1770s and the 1780s as Anda's and Basco y Vargas' reforms consolidated the Manila Treasury. However, according to Alonso Álvarez, the *situado* did not end in 1804 despite the royal decree prematurely announcing its demise. Shipments of pesos from New Spain under the title of *situado* continued at least until 1816. Most of these shipments were small, amounting to less than 10,000 pesos, but some, especially those for the years of 1806–1807, were above 500,000 pesos.[117]

What historians have failed to realise is the connection that existed between the *situado* and the private capital market of Manila. The exact nature of the relationship needs further research, but as the previous sections have shown, to all effects the *obras pías* were diverting money from the trade, independently of whether there was a conscious strategy to do so or not, which helped maintaining the premia for *correspondencias* stable in a capital market where, as argued previously, the investment options for working capital were limited but its supply was not. This link needs to be considered because the *obras pías* were central to Manileños' motivations. Alonso Álvarez is right in noticing that the Treasury of New Spain sent a total of 1,080,078 pesos to Manila between 1806 and 1807,[118] but it is also true that, as the account books of legacy funds reveal, in 1804 the king had requested large amounts of money from the *obras pías* to finance extraordinary war expenditures.[119] Nevertheless, it can be argued that the Napoleonic Wars represented exceptional

[115] Bauzón, *Deficit*, Chapter 5, Legarda, *After*, p. 72, Alonso Álvarez, Luís, 'El impacto de las reformas borbónicas en las redes comerciales. Una visión desde el Pacífico hispano, 1762–1815', Ponencia presentada al II Congreso de la Asociación Mexicana de Hist. Económica, *Simposio Redes sociales e instituciones comerciales en México, ss. XVII-XIX* (2007): 1–29.

[116] Fradera, *Filipinas*, pp. 71–72.

[117] Alonso Álvarez, 'La ayuda', p. 284.

[118] Alonso Álvarez, 'La ayuda', p. 284.

[119] The accounting entries can be seen in the books of the Domincan legacy funds (see Bibliography, APSR section), and also in the Franciscan accounts from 1805–1806, AGI Filipinas 1034.

circumstances, and that the *situado* as a device to transfer money to the Philippines did indeed end in 1804. What matters here is that from the start of Anda's governorship in 1770, there was a new approach to make the Manila Treasury more independent, both from New Spain and from the *obras pías*.

These changes to the structure of the treasury happened simultaneously with other reforms to the *reglamento* that modified the organisation of the Manila trade. As mentioned in previous chapters, an *addendum* to the *reglamento* of 1734 created the *Consulado* of Manila in 1769, establishing the local merchants into a corporate body of its own distinct from the formula of the "City and Commerce" that had existed since the first *reglamento* of 1593, and giving the *Consulado* exclusive jurisdiction over all matters pertaining to the Galleons.[120] Among the changes introduced in it, there were three of great importance: all *boletas* would be given to the *Consulado* to allocate exclusively among its members; similarly, the *Consulado* obtained exclusive jurisdiction over all commercial cases, excluding the *audiencia* from the process, but also putting all responsibility on the corporation; finally, a provision of the *addendum* stated that the numbers of *boletas* allotted would be favoured by the investment on the local economy, in an attempt to incentivise the development of the islands, and banned *obras pías* from holding *boletas*.[121]

In essence, *obras pías* lost the half of the cargo of the Galleons that they had owned since the 1734 *reglamento*. Since it is not known what the *obras pías* did with the share that belonged to them, it is impossible to analyse the full extent of these modifications. The *addendum* of 1769 implies that the usufruct of the 2,000 *boletas* that accrued to the *obras pías*

[120] This can be seen in the shortening of the freighting proceedings of the Galleons, as less information was made reportable to the Council of the Indies. The freighting proceeding of the Galleon *San José* in 1781 (AGI Filipinas 936 N.3) was considerably less detailed than those of the *San Carlos Borromeo* in 1767 (AGI Filipinas 941 N.1), the *Santísima Trinidad* in 1753 (AGI Filipinas 268 N.1), or the *Santo Cristo de Burgos* in 1723 (AGI Filipinas 229 N.1).

[121] AGI Filipinas 941 N. 1, 1769, the development-focused purpose of the *consulados* created in the second half of the eighteenth-century contrasts with the more corporate function of the first *consulados* of Lima, Seville, and Mexico. This distinction is implicit in Gabriel Paquette's survey of the later *consulados*, see, Paquette, Gabriel, 'State-Civil Society Cooperation and Conflict in the Spanish Empire: The Intellectual and Political Activities of the Ultramarine Consulados and Economic Societies, c. 1780–1810', *Journal of Latin American Studies* 39, nº 2 (May 2007), pp. 270–271.

were sold to freighters each year, although the evidence is scant.[122] Given the overlap between managers of *obras pías* and Galleon freighters, it is unlikely that this changed at all the structure of ownership of the Galleon cargo. However, it may have changed the motivation of the wealthiest citizens of Manila, since the advantages of being a manager of legacy funds were somewhat reduced. In short, a wedge opened between the *obras pías* and the merchants, and the former lost some of their influence.

The 1769 *addendum*, however, was not a frontal attack to the vested interests of the merchants that ensured the balance of trade across the Pacific. Article 30 reiterated the ban on any Manileño to enter New Spain until the fair was finished, essentially preventing them from bypassing the Acapulco negotiation.[123] Article 42 allowed the representative of the city of Cádiz in New Spain to physically audit the Acapulco fair.[124] In this respect the reforms of the 1769 *addendum* did not break the invested position that the different trading groups held over the commercial lines that crossed the empire, something that the king lacked the power to do unilaterally. But together with the fiscal changes outlined above, this paints a picture in which the rents of the *obras pías* were put increasingly under stress because they no longer had the influence they enjoyed before.

Other events were taking place that were a much more direct threat to the rents of the Pacific exchange. The Seven Years' War had exposed the fragility of the Spanish Pacific due to its reliance on the annual crossing of the Galleons, but proponents of reforms had been arguing on the necessity of expanding the trade of the Philippines for a long time already.[125] After 1764, the king seized upon the chance to create a direct route between Spain and Manila across the Cape of Good Hope, financing commercial expeditions conducted by navy frigates. The first voyage was

[122] Ibid., also see Chapter 2 Section The Asian Leg

[123] AGI Filipinas 941 N. 1, 1769.

[124] Ibid.

[125] One of the most influential plans was presented by Manila prosecutor Leandro de Viana to the king in 1765 (AMN 233 MS0405, *Demonstración del mísero y deplorable estado de las yslas Philipinas*, 1765). The literature has tended to focus on officials' plans and projects when talking about reforms Bonalian has a section devoted to the different plans from Spain to establish a trade company in the Pacific (Bonalian, *El Pacífico*, pp. 119–141). But this has sidelined the many proposals from private citizens and from institutions like the *Consulados*, and that were part of the process (see documents AMN 533 MS1576, 1785, and Newberry Ayer MS 1423, and Paquette, 'State-Civil Society', pp. 267–268).

that of the *Buen Consejo* in 1766, which was said to have been pierced by the Manileños before its return trip and almost sank.[126] Nevertheless, thirteen direct voyages were completed, and in 1777 agents of the financial company of the *Cinco Gremios* of Madrid arrived in Manila with the purpose of opening trade with Spain.[127] The king granted commercial privileges to Cádiz private companies like that of Aguirre, del Arco, and Alburquerque, and Ustáriz, San Ginés, and Cia in order to pry open the Philippines, all to no avail.[128] It was not until 1785 that the creation of the Real Compañía de Filipinas commenced an organised attempt to end the dependency of the Philippines on the Pacific trade by expanding its trade options. As seen in Chapter 2, the RCF failed in its long-term objective of switching the economic orientation of trade in the Philippines, but competition managed to saturate the Spanish American market for Asian products.[129]

Thus, authorities tried different formulas to expand the volume of trade, but none of these projects managed to displace the Manila Galleon, evidencing the resilience of the city and its capital markets. Yet, by glutting the Spanish American markets and lowering the profit margins of the trade, the advent of trade expansion forced changes upon the model of Horizontal Specialisation. Unable to maintain the rents of the Pacific trade by controlling the expenditures and the scale of the trade, Manileños were forced to expand the investments of the *obras pías*. As seen in Chapter 5, this period witnessed the breakdown of the stable premia on *correspondencias*. Their premia may have not fallen by much during the 1780s and 1790s, but they remained below the previous mark of 30% and now varied year-on-year and started diverging between managers.[130] *Obras pías* and private individuals no longer scrupulously adhered to the premia established by the Misericordia, and some even included clauses in the contracts regarding how to negotiate the premia.[131] Similarly, the *obras pías* sought to increase their returns by expanding in

126 Díaz-Trechuelo, 'El comercio', p. 479.

127 Díaz-Trechuelo, 'El comercio', p. 480.

128 Cosano Moyano, 'Un nuevo intento', pp. 261–281, Ruíz Rivera, 'Intento gaditano'.

129 Díaz-Trechuelo, *La Real Compañía*, p. 199 & 216.

130 See Graph 5.1.

131 See for example Escribano Miguel José Flores, 1795 [Legajo #26], ACCHS-CSIC, ff. 47a-48b.

scope, financing trips to Sorsogon and Nanjing in 1789,[132] Camarines in 1792,[133] and Sulu in 1806.[134] The 1806 accounts of the VOT of Saint Francis reveal that by that date, *correspondencia* funds were investing in *riesgos de tierra* or overland trade to the interior of Luzon.[135] As the rents from the trade came under attack, *obras pías* attempted to maintain their level of returns by expanding their investments. Thus, during the last decades of the eighteenth century, the Pacific trade slowly turned from increasing profit margins to a different equilibrium that aimed at increasing the scale.

This expansion on the volume of trade affected all participants. The RCF agents interpreted the increasing volume of Asian goods exported to America by Galleon freighters as a concerted plan to expel the company by forcing prices down and sinking the profits of the exchange.[136] It is interesting that both the RCF and the Galleon merchants blamed each other. Regardless of whether Manileños were consciously attempting to expel the RCF by glutting the market or they were simply reacting to the increased competition in the Pacific, the result was similar: once the trade expanded beyond the previous equilibrium, the only course of action left was to increase the volume of the trade to make up for the loss of profit margins with returns in scale. But this was a general occurrence in Spanish imperial trade at the end of the century, not exclusively a circumstance affecting the Pacific exchange. In fact, changes in the Atlantic had started earlier and had an impact in American markets that Manileños could not ignore.

After the Seven Years' War, the structure of trade in the Atlantic was also tackled. Slowly, the previous system of Seville and Cádiz' American monopoly and the fleets was dismantled through the edicts of *comercio libre*. These edicts allowed other ports in Spain to send licensed ships to

[132] Escribano Miguel José Flores, 1789 [Legajo #21a], ACCHS-CSIC, ff. 122b-122a & 288b-289a.

[133] Escribano Miguel José Flores, 1792 [Legajo #24], ACCHS-CSIC, f. 122a.

[134] AGI Filipinas 1034 N. 4, 1805–1806, ff. 12a, on the trade of Sulu, see Warren, James. 'Sino-Sulu Trade in the Late Eighteenth and Nineteenth Centuries'. *Philippine Studies* 21, nº 1 (1977): 50–79, Warren, James, 'Slave Markets and Exchange in the Malay World: The Sulu Sultanate, 1770–1878', *Journal of Southeast Asian Studies* 8, nº 2 (1977): 162–175.

[135] AGI Filipinas 1034 N. 4, 1805–1806, f. 12a.

[136] AGI Filipinas 985, *Documentos relativos a la Compañía de Filipinas*, 1780–1786.

trade in America. In 1765, after the English occupation of Cuba, *comercio libre* was tentatively introduced for trade with the Antilles after bargaining between the royal representatives and the Cuban elites.[137] Its success witnessed its expansion to the Caribbean mainland in 1778. Mexico successfully resisted the introduction of *comercio libre* until 1789.[138] Once again, legislation was more a reflection of the circumstances than the real prime mover of change:[139] since 1739, due to the wars against England and the weakness of the fleet system with Perú, a system of licensed vessels to Perú and Río de la Plata had coexisted with the official *flotas* to New Spain.[140] Similarly, according to Baskes, while *comercio libre* was only officially extended to New Spain in 1789, the reality was that most trade with New Spain was already conducted by licensed ships after 1778.[141] Whatever the cause, after 1765 the system of convoys and fairs was coming to an end in the Atlantic, and the implications of this were important for the Pacific as well since it was an integral part of the empire-wide balance.

The literature has debated the real impact of *comercio libre* on trade across the Spanish empire. In his book *Staying Afloat*, Baskes presents a

[137] Irigoin and Grafe, 'Bargaining', pp. 199–200, also for an account of the events see Kuethe, Allan J., and Inglis, G. Douglas, 'Absolutism and Enlightened Reform: Charles III, the Establishment of the Alcabala, and Commercial Reorganization in Cuba', *Past & Present*, nº 109 (1985): 118–143.

[138] Brading, *Miners*, pp. 116–118.

[139] John Lynch offers a classical interpretation of *comercio libre* as directed by the Spanish state to guarantee control of trade flows, clearly adjudicating to the Bourbon state the initiative in the organisation of the trade. Lynch also talks of a switch in the governance of the Spanish empire from a Habsburg system of "consensus" to one of "non-negotiable demands". Irigoin and Grafe offer an opposing view in which the reforms of the late eighteenth century were bargained. This chapter does not seek to establish the causes for the *comercio libre* edicts, but it is certain that the changes taking place in the Pacific trade were caused as well by developments beyond the control of the king of Spain, and that Manileños had a say in the process. See Lynch, John, 'The Origins of Spanish American Independence', in *The Cambridge History of Latin America*, ed. Leslie Bethell, vol. 3 (Cambridge: Cambridge University Press, 1985), p. 15, Lynch, John, 'The Institutional Framework of Colonial Spanish America', *Journal of Latin American Studies*, vol. 24 (1992), p. 78, Irigoin and Grafe, 'Bargaining', p. 200.

[140] Lamikiz, "Patrones", pp. 237–238 and Lamikiz, *Trade*, p. 83.

[141] According to Lamikiz, no *flota* had sailed for New Spain since 1776, Lamikiz, 'Patrones…', p. 258, Baskes, *Staying*, p. 86.

summary of this debate.[142] It seems probable that the new regime of *comercio libre* led to an overall expansion of the volume of the trade between Spain and America across the Atlantic, although its exact rate of growth may have been smaller than previously considered. Nevertheless, according to the evidence gathered by Baskes, during the 1780s and 1790s merchants across the empire complained that American markets were glutted with goods, resulting in prices plummeting and, therefore, shrinking profit margins for traders.[143] It seems contradictory that Spanish American markets could have become glutted in such a dramatic fashion if the volume of trade before and after the advent of *comercio libre* had not changed radically. What matters here is not the exact changes in the volume of trade during the last quarter of the eighteenth century, but rather, the impact of the new way of organising trade. Prices could have plummeted and profits vanished, not necessarily—or exclusively—because there was a larger volume of goods being sent to America, but also because the new trade regime represented a more *direct* trade with a greater ability to bypass intermediaries.[144]

Relative to their importance, comparatively little is known about the intercontinental fairs that vertebrated commercial exchange in the Spanish empire,[145] but following the analysis of Chapter 4 it can be argued that these fairs were the mechanism through which local merchants enforced their privileges and controlled the market. The system of licensed vessels, through which merchants could sail independently of the convoys and trade at any time of the year irrespectively of the trading fairs, made it much more difficult for the Mexico *Consulado* to control market penetration. Baskes, placing the conditions of uncertainty and risk at the centre of his analysis, argues that the system of fleets and fairs was necessary

[142] Baskes, *Staying*, pp. 71–77, see also Cuenca-Esteban, Javier, 'Statistics of Spain's Colonial Trade, 1747–1820: New Estimates and Comparisons with Great Britain', *Revista de Historia Económica* XXVI, nº 3 (2008): 323–354 for a review on the statistical evidence.

[143] Baskes, *Staying Afloat*, pp. 78–82.

[144] Nevertheless, these two causes are not mutually exclusive, and it is probable that they were taking place simultaneously.

[145] Carrera Stampa published on the fairs of New Spain, (Carrera Stampa, 'Las ferias') and Real Díaz devoted a monograph to the fair of Jalapa (Real Díaz, *Las Ferias*). Yuste has conducted some research on the fair of Acapulco, but her conclusions differ from those presented in this book as explained in Chapter 4 (Yuste, *Emporios*, pp. 277–316).

to deal with the sluggishness of information of Early Modern trade.[146] What he fails to see is that this sluggishness of information, as shown in Chapter 4 and argued in Chapter 5, was not a cause for the fair system, but the consequence. Manileños needed to protect their return from the bargaining power that Mexicans enjoyed thanks to the large demand for silver specie. Their answer was rationing the trade through the one-Galleon model. This way, both Mexicans and Manileños enjoyed a share of rents. Lack of uncertainty was a side-effect of the protection of rents because profits were guaranteed in a trade whose volume was rationed. This "sluggishness of information" was *by design*, the result of the market structure of the imperial silver trade, and it was part and parcel of the negotiating strategies of intermediaries like Manileños that were at the expense of those that controlled the silver flows. When profits were guaranteed by the limited volume of the trade, no investments in information were needed.

Regardless of whether it was the decline of the fairs that brought about the new system of licensed ships, or if *comercio libre* was the last stroke that terminated the fairs, what is important here is that this meant a kind of trade that could bypass the control of the privileged merchants of each region of the empire, and that could thus glut the markets and lower profits. Once this happened, Manila could not simply hope to maintain its intermediary position in the trade without any change. The goods brought to America from the Atlantic were ultimately competitive with the Asian goods from Manila, and Asian goods were also being sent to Veracruz and other ports by the RCF.[147] Only the silver pesos had no substitutes in Spanish imperial trade. If prices fell in New Spain, the profits of the Manila trade were equally affected.

The importance of *comercio libre* and of the equilibrium that slowly emerged in the last quarter of the eighteenth century resides in what it can tell about the system that existed before. The fairs were the valves that ensured the rent-sharing balance of trade across the Spanish empire. Once they were bypassed, these rents were under threat, and the model that had been built on them crumbled. The end was not immediate. As shown

[146] Baskes, *Staying*, p. 98.

[147] Díaz-Trechuelo, *La Real*, pp. 216–218.

in Chapter 5,[148] there was still room for profits, and Manileños could adapt to the changing circumstances by issuing more *correspondencias* and investing in different trade routes. A new system started to emerge that accommodated these new circumstances. The end of the Pacific trade was not due to the new equilibrium that emerged at the end of the eighteenth century, but because events in Spanish America resulted in the implosion of the standard of the peso and, therefore, ended the Pacific silver trade, as shown in Chapter 3. An exogenous shock thus terminated the first direct trade between Asia and America. Whether the *obras pías* of Manila and the Galleon freighters would have ultimately succeeded in adapting to the new circumstances cannot be known.

The commercial system of the Spanish empire thus rested on a careful balance in which each merchant group had control over their internal markets, and each could rely on the rents of the trade. This system worked because silver pesos had enough demand abroad to allow those involved in the Pacific exchange to deflect the higher costs of rationing the trade to the consumers, and because the political economy of the Hispanic Monarchy made it better to agree with their neighbours than to try to step out of line. This hindered market integration across the regions of the Monarchy, but it did not mean that each of them went alone at it. Manila could not ignore how *peninsulares* overflowed the American market from the Atlantic and lowered profit margins. All regions of the Hispanic Monarchy were part of a whole. The link between political economy and trade means that market pressures need to be considered an endogenous part of the system, specifically the large demand for pesos in Asia. It was the profit margins of the peso trade that maintained the imperial structure in balance and allowed for Horizontal Specialisation as much as it was its ultimate cause as the source of bargaining power of Mexican wholesalers.

The fragmentation embodied in the prisoner's dilemmas faced at the trading fairs was first and foremost a result of economic conditions, of the large demand for pesos in Asia. Mexicans and Manileños had different bargaining positions. The political model in which each territory protected itself from penetration from one another was the result, and similarly, a way of binding each region's interest to that of their trading partners through the arbitration of the king. It was the partial

[148] As shown in the letter of Antonio Alonso de Terán from 1804, demand for silver in China still allowed for profits in exporting pesos to Asia.

demise of this system that reveals some of the most important pillars and fault lines of the careful equilibrium that linked all parts of the Monarchy together. The purpose of this chapter is to show that Horizontal Specialisation and the tools provided by the political economy of the Hispanic Monarchy aligned motivations horizontally across the actors involved. Mexico, Manila, Cádiz, and Lima ultimately respected this system and each other because their rents depended on this balance.

CHAPTER 7

Manila in Financial History

Asian demand for silver specie shaped all European trade with the continent throughout the Early Modern period and that equally defined the institutions that emerged in Manila. The city, from its earliest days, functioned to intermediate between this demand and the Spanish American supply of specie. This book shows that in doing so, Manila developed an alternative business and financial model different from the model of the European East India Companies. It was not based on scaling but on specialisation on the provision of liquidity in Asian waters, and it was not built on joint-stock companies, tradable shares, and bills of exchange, but on adapting vehicles and contracts such as legacy funds and respondentias to the context of Asia's demand for specie.

Manila's intermediation of pesos resulted in a Dutch Disease in the islands. Everything could be imported cheaply from China or India given the purchasing power of Mexico-minted silver pesos, which in turn resulted in the absence of a plantation economy in the Philippines. The fewer costs incurred and the purchasing power differentials of pesos between Asia and America granted unrivalled profits which proved an insurmountable challenge for the development of a local plantation economy. The answer of Manileños was to go further down the "rabbit hole" of liquidity, to specialise in its provision, and from 1668, to create the *correspondencia* funds that invested directly in the trade.

J. J. Rivas Moreno, *The Capital Market of Manila and the Pacific Trade, 1668–1838*, Palgrave Studies in Economic History,
https://doi.org/10.1007/978-3-031-71810-6_7

The legacy funds were an alternative solution to the problems associated with long-distance trade. Faced with long trips—with the resulting long waiting times of locked investment until the realisation of profits—and increased capital needs to outfit longer voyages, the legacy funds retained earnings in cash from the Acapulco fair and transformed it into working capital, ready to be invested as cash in hand for the operation of the trade. It was a model built on doubling down on what Manila could offer at better terms than anyone else within Asia: specie. Access to the *obras pías* meant capital upon request, rendering waiting times less problematic. Liquidity for purchases was available at any time of the year. Cash in hand allowed for a large number of occasional participants from many backgrounds alongside the established merchants. All in all, the *correspondencia* funds revolutionised the capital market of Manila. Over 260 identified individual funds across three dozen managing institutions mobilised increasingly larger volumes of capital. Manila was awash with cash in the centre of Asia's maritime trade, where cash was scarcest. It provided a fundamental part of international trade that nobody else within Asian waters was in a better position to supply. English, Armenian, Portuguese, Chinese, Malabaris, and many other came to Manila because Manila had what they all needed, and nobody could provide cheaper.

As much as the nature of the trade affected the financial model of Manila, it also affected its business model. Asian demand for the Spanish American peso meant that there were no immediate substitutes to the coin, and thus, demand from consumers rippled across the whole retail chain, skewing the bargaining power to the ultimate suppliers of pesos, the Mexican wholesalers. The wholesalers controlled the supply of goods for the mines and the flow of silver for coinage at the Mexico City mint. In this way, they controlled the movement of pesos within New Spain and could transfer them to the international fairs at Acapulco and Jalapa, from whence they obtained the goods to sell to the miners in a closed circuit. Their position of power was as much derived from their control on the internal commercial network as from the demand for pesos. Everyone came to trade with Mexico, from the Atlantic, the Pacific, and the Caribbean, so wholesalers could choose their providers. But providers could not afford to ignore Mexico. This position of strength translated into buyer cartels in the international fairs in a monopsonic market. Manileños were forced to face this cartel under the obvious threat that an expansion of the volume of exports to America needed not translate into a greater value of returns. Competition across suppliers of imports in the absence of a reciprocal expansion of the offer of pesos would translate into glutted markets in America and collapsing profit margins. The one-Galleon business model served three purposes as explained in Chapter 4: to limit the volume of exports to America and prevent market gluts there, to maintain a mirror seller cartel among Manileños, and to avoid the uncertainty of separation *en route*, which had the potential to spoil the fairs. This in turn affected the financial markets in Manila: rationing the volume of the Pacific exchange meant limiting the investment options of *obras pías* in the most profitable leg of the trade. With only a Galleon of between 1,200 and 2,000 tons crossing the Pacific, the freight was limited, and so was the demand for capital. The capacity of the *obras pías* to accumulate cash for investment in the long-term, however, was not limited, and neither was the foundation of new legacy funds, that is, the increasing supply of investable capital.

Thus, the collapse of premia in Manila from 50% to lows of 20% occurred in the 1750s, before the advent of *comercio libre* but after the great expansion of legacy funds in the 1730s and 1740s. Capital was simply cheap, because Manila was awash with cash if nothing else, and the cheapness of the premia was an indication of that abundance. The Pacific's model was one of Horizontal Specialisation across the trade, in which Manila absorbed the risks of the exchange and internalised them while offering capital at lower rates than anyone else. Everything else, the acquisition of goods and the operations of supply lines other than the voyage across the Pacific, was outsourced to the myriad agents in need to acquire silver through sales in Manila for re-export to America. This allowed Manila to capitalise on liquidity, reaching economies of scale in the provision of capital. The entire system had developed to optimise liquidity and maintain Manila's intermediary position. Through its capital markets, Manila made itself indispensable.

Manila also managed to mobilise the institutions of the Hispanic Monarchy to defend this model and enhance it. There were two fundamental ways in which the city managed this. Devolution of fiscality allowed Manileños to deflect some costs of the trade to their local treasury, as well as to bankroll the exchange through the salaries of Galleon officials. The political economy of the Monarchy allowed for a measure of subordination of fiscality to local imperatives. *Obras pías* used this to their advantage by privatising the *situado*, forcing the Manila Treasury to incur debts with them. Lowering and deflecting costs unnecessary for specialisation effectively increased markups across the Pacific and allowed for larger profit margins. On the other hand, its role within the Hispanic Monarchy helped its efforts to prevent being bypassed in exchange of respecting the Mexican's control of their local market. Manileños were the wholesalers' preferred trading partners because the political economy geared them towards mutually guaranteeing each other's trade impera tives. Importantly, the bargained nature of political institutions gave room to Manileños to steer the institutional formation process according to their economic interests. Thus, Asian demand for silver specie and the resulting market structure defined the trade and its institutions.

7.1 The Case of Manila

The capital market of Manila mitigated the challenges of long-distance trade by optimising Manila's access to silver specie and specialising in its intermediation, and by using the institutional framework to its advantage. This institutional framework was radically different from the one developed in North-western Europe to face similar challenges. Manila represented an alternative business model. But this poses a historiographical challenge: an alternative to what? The reality is that the East India companies have proved a fruitful topic for historians and economists to test their models and hypothesis, to the point that there are almost as many East India companies as there are publications on the topic.

The problem with the historiography on the East India companies is twofold. On the one hand, there is a dichotomy between theory and evidence. The literature on the East India companies is divided between authors that have applied economic models to the historical case of the joint-stock corporations in an attempt to teleologically explain their history,[1] and historians such as Holden Furber for the EIC[2] or Glamann for the VOC[3] that have researched the archives of the East India companies with a purely historical approach that sought instead to historicise the evolution of the companies in their context. And often, these two groups present contradictory views and evidence.

[1] Carlos and Nicholas, '"Giants"', Carlos and Nicholas, 'Agency', Anderson, McCormick, and Tollison, 'The Economic', Chaudhuri applied systems analysis to the EIC, Chaudhuri, *The Trading*.

[2] Furber, *John Company*, Furber, *Rival*.

[3] Glamann, *Dutch-Asiatic*.

On the other hand, there is, especially with regards to the EIC but to a lesser extent also affecting the VOC, a mismatch in chronology. Almost every publication on the joint-stock companies focuses on either the seventeenth or the eighteenth centuries, without encompassing their entire lifespan. Chaudhuri, for example, has a book spanning the formational years of the EIC from 1600 to 1640,[4] and a different one for the period between 1660 and 1760.[5] Furber attempted a complete review of the period between 1600 and 1800,[6] but his masterpiece on the EIC focused on 1770–1800.[7] Bowen focused on 1760–1820.[8] Hejeebu applied her analysis of principal-agent problems in the EIC to the period immediately prior to 1760.[9] Even Harris' *Going the Distance* only covers the seventeenth century.[10] More intriguing is the fact that the nineteenth century, arguably the zenith of the EIC's power in India, is entirely absent in the debate regarding the origin, nature, and efficiency of the joint-stock form, as if the EIC in 1600 and in 1857 was an entirely different entity.

This issue is important because this dichotomy between theory and evidence and pre- and post-1760 periodisation is not accidental, neither are they unrelated, and the failure to see the connection between the periods before and after the deciding decades of 1760 and 1770 has prevented a complete analysis of the weaknesses of the vertically integrated joint-stock business model. The result has been a "coordination failure" of sorts between authors more focused on economic analysis, and those that perform historical analysis on the documents of the companies. Economists like Carlos, Nicholas, Hejeebu, Erikson, and others have praised the capacity of vertical integration to afford more efficient transactions, thus explaining the alleged superiority of the joint-stock companies over their competitors in organising long-distance trade.[11] On the other

[4] Chaudhuri, K.N., *The English East India Company: The Study on an early joint-stock company, 1600–1640*, London: Frank Cass and Co. (1965).

[5] Chaudhuri, *The Trading*.

[6] Furber, *Rival*.

[7] Fuber, *John Company*.

[8] Bowen, *The Business*.

[9] Hejeebu, 'Contract'.

[10] Harris, *Going*.

[11] Carlos and Nicholas, '"Giants"', Carlos and Nicholas, 'Agency', Erikson, *Between*, Hejeebu, 'Contract', Anderson et al., 'The Economic'.

hand, historians, especially those of the late eighteenth century, have presented plenty of information to show that the incapacity of the East India companies to retain the loyalty of their employees and the private merchants that carried their intra-Asian trade condemned their business.[12] This contradiction is exacerbated by the even more paradoxical fact that whatever systems the EIC had in place to deal with this problem seemed to work—at least on the surface—before 1760. What happened after that decade that relentlessly pushed the EIC to its demise as a trading enterprise? Something happened between 1760 and 1770 that dramatically changed the EIC. This has gone unnoticed because the source of the change was not the organisation of the company. But this also implies that this extra-organisational "variable" may have been driving the growth of the company before 1760.

It is here that a comparison with the model of Manila can make its contribution. The argument is simple: the EIC's trade collapsed because of the very same factor that had enabled its rise, that is scale. The crux of the problem is the literature's conception that efficiency in transaction costs can *substitute* efficiency in fundamentals, that is, the more efficient use of resources (in business terms, to obtain the largest possible profits incurring the fewest possible costs).[13] The reality is that vertical integration, in the long-term, cannot substitute for business fundamentals. Although the gains in scale that accrued from vertical integration may have allowed companies to manipulate the market or transact more efficiently, the EIC could not operate against market fundamentals perennially. At some point, the cost of maintaining the size of the EIC was so large that it affected its operations.[14] It was at this point, as shown in Chapter 5, that the company suffered the slow demise of its trade. This is important because through this comparison it is possible to understand the resilience of Manila's horizontal approach. The Pacific trade,

[12] Chaudhuri, *The Trading*, pp. 208–210, Furber, *John Company*, p. 18.

[13] This is explicitly indicated by Anderson et al., 'The Economic', p. 221, and Carlos and Nicholas, 'Theory', p. 916.

[14] Gelderblom, De Jong, and Jonker ('The Formative') would argue that it was extra-commercial costs as well that shaped the form of the companies. While the original sin of combining armed violence with commercial profit was present in the companies since their foundation, a deeper study of how the growing costs of territorial protection affected trading profits still needs to be undertaken.

characterised by bargaining, both in the political level and in the commercial level, could not ignore market imperatives. *Obras pías* could not impose their premia over merchants, neither could Mexican wholesalers impose their prices over Manileño Galleon freighters. It was all negotiated because nothing was integrated, because no one had the upper hand. But this does not mean that they were not united. Ultimately, *obras pías* issued their *correspondencias* and merchants took them to buy their cargoes for America. Mexican wholesalers bought the Asian goods they needed to supply the mines while Galleon freighters returned home with their proceeds in pesos to repay their *correspondencias*. They all needed each other. The rationale for this union in disunion, the cohesive glue that kept it all together, was the trade: specifically, Asia's demand for silver specie and Spanish America's capacity to provide it. Manila specialised, and Manila specialised horizontally, through the market. Manila—and the Pacific at large—could not afford to step out of this equilibrium.

The debate regarding transaction costs is also important to properly contextualise Manila and the global silver trade. In Asia, the best way to mitigate transaction costs was not through integration—a daunting task given the size and complexity of the continent's markets—but through liquidity. Demand for silver specie, and especially as the eighteenth century progressed, silver pesos, lowered all costs associated with transactions.[15] They were universally accepted as a means of payment. Relative ease of access to silver, whether through Japan, Manila, or the deep money market of Amsterdam, not vertical integration, needs to be explored as a cause of the relative success of the EIC and the VOC. These companies succeeded in Asia even though all other joint-stock corporations, organised as a copy of the English and the Dutch, failed. If the joint-stock corporation offered enough guarantees ex-ante to potential investors, and it was their capacity to foster impersonal cooperation that enabled their success, why could the Danish or the Genoese[16] not attract a similar scale of resources? The capital raised through the joint-stock was not the determining factor for performance in Asia. As historians have noted, the

[15] Irigoin, 'Rise', p. 405, and Irigoin, '"De las contratas"', WEHC, Paris, 2022.

[16] On the Genoese Company, Subrahmanyam, Sanjay, *The Political Economy of Commerce: Southern India, 1500–1650* (Cambridge: Cambridge University Press, 1990), pp. 283–295, for an overview of the Danish companies, see Feldbaek, Ole, 'The Danish Trading Companies of the Seventeenth and Eighteenth Centuries', *The Scandinavian Economic History Review* 34, n° 3 (1986): 204–218.

problem of joint-stock companies was not raising the initial capital but maintaining a constant stream of working capital at the ready.[17] Organisational form alone cannot account for this divergence in their fortunes. Access to silver does. As explained in Chapter 2, in a commerce characterised by the persistent demand for silver, in which it was fundamental to have liquidity in Asia, the Dutch and the English succeeded in this, the Dutch with the Japanese silver, and the English, with their access to Manila. The Danish, the Swedish, the Genoese, or the Ostend companies could mimic the organisation of the VOC and the EIC, but they could not mimic their access to Japan or the Philippines. This has often escaped the attention of historians of the trading corporations because this source of liquidity was not in Europe, but in Asia, and the financial history of the East India companies has focused on the capital markets at home without considering that capital could be acquired *within* Asia.

In this regard, the business model of Manila also had its strengths. Manileños specialised in the provision of silver specie and capitalised on the abundance of liquidity that resulted from their close ties with Spanish America. This ensured the continued arrival of merchants from all over Asia and of silver from America to the city, and it made it possible for religious orders and brotherhoods to channel the savings of outsiders to the trade through their social and religious networks. *Obras pías* and legacy funds multiplied, and consequently so did the supply of capital for trade. Thus, the Pacific trade boasted profits ranging anywhere between 200 and 400%, while premia for *correspondencias* fell over the period from 50% to 20%. Nothing solved principal-agent problems more efficiently than the guarantee of profit. As seen in Chapter 5, Manila's model managed to solve agency problems by aligning interests horizontally (i.e. the *obras pías* were invested in the success of freighters, and all citizens were invested in the well-being of the legacy funds) and through the credible threat of exclusion from the cheap capital of *obras pías*. Horizontal Specialisation meant scale as well, but in a different way. The EIC scaled up to control territory and markets and to improve its terms of trade or searching for alternatives for silver specie. Manila achieved a certain degree of economies of scale in the mobilisation of working capital because it specialised narrowly on the provision of silver specie. In

[17] Harris, *Going*, p. 312, Chaudhuri, 'The East India', p. 24.

what follows, this argument is developed by contrasting Manila's model as developed in this book with the EIC.

7.2 Silver and Scale

The joint-stock corporation, as argued by Ron Harris, was a strategy to access a larger pool of liquidity through the design of a repeated transaction-based reputation mechanism which could foster impersonal cooperation.[18] Hence it is paradoxical that the emergence of a modern, permanent joint-stock resulted in no more offerings of shares and a switch to debt-financing. After the creation of the permanent stock in 1651, the EIC only issued new stocks worth £800,000 in 1786. Interestingly, stock issuances picked up after 1786. In 1789 the company issued £1 million of stock,[19] followed by another £2,900,000 in 1793.[20] Harris solves this dilemma by focusing on the period in which the EIC lacked a permanent joint-stock, raising capital in separate offerings for each voyage.[21] This way, the money raised through stock offerings for each expedition allegedly financed the procurement of goods in Asia. Thus, initial capital and working capital are considered the same. There are two problems to this. First, costs were constant. While Harris is right is arguing that the core problem facing the EIC was the acquisition of working capital instead of the maintenance of forts and factories abroad, these two were not unrelated.[22] Whether the joint-stock was organised on a per-voyage or a permanent fashion, the increase in volume and assets necessitated a constant flow of resources, hence the paradox that the EIC could increase its scale so rapidly after the establishment of a permanent stock given the absence of new issuances of shares.

At the core was the issue of obtaining a reliable supply of working capital, and specifically, as argued in Chapter 2, silver specie, which was a universally accepted means of payment common to America, Europe, and Asia. The East India companies had different ways to acquire silver specie. As Coen had already noted in 1619, intra-Asian trade could serve this

[18] Harris, *Going*, p. 4 & 312–313.

[19] Furber, *John Company*, p. 268.

[20] Furber, *John Company*, p. 265.

[21] Harris, *Going*, pp. 295–303.

[22] Harris, *Going*, pp. 312–313.

function by trying to substitute for reliable supplies of specie and boost available capital.[23] Intra-Asian trade, as practiced by the VOC, was a way of mitigating liquidity constraints by arbitraging the demand for different Asian goods within different Asian destinations. As an example, the Dutch famously bought Indian cotton goods to exchange for pepper and other spices in Indonesia.[24] However, as Furber noted, whether directly or indirectly, a certain volume of silver was still needed to operate intra-Asian trade.[25]

Another alternative was to look for local sources of silver within Asia. Asian silver was a profitable option to the East India Companies when silver in Europe was dear and to diminish transport costs. During the Early Modern period, there were two major sources of silver: Japan and Manila. The Dutch had access to Japan, but from the second half of the seventeenth century, the English had access to Manila. The English moved in first, and the Dutch were left with little room to manoeuvre once the Japanese silver mines gave out. This granted the EIC access to the pesos in Asian waters, solving many of the problems of acquiring this specific currency. Thus, the importance of Manila in solving the liquidity and capital constraint of the EIC. Access to silver in Asia, as argued previously, improved the terms of trade within the continent and went a long way in solving the capital constraints of East India Companies, giving the English and the Dutch an edge over all others.

In 1670–1680, the EIC managed to link itself to Manila's silver circuits. Silver specie allowed for expansion. The problem, however, came in 1760–1770. The looting of the *obras pías* by the English and the costs of running Bengal meant an increase in expenditures at a time when the Pacific silver flow stopped. Once the dust settled, Manila preferred to negotiate with private merchants that were unencumbered with the expenses of running a territorial empire, and these private merchants found it more profitable to bypass the EIC than to negotiate with it. Private merchants outcompeted the EIC even in the procurement of textiles in Bengal, as shown in Chapter 5. The same independent agents that according to Hejeebu and Neal gave the EIC its edge to

[23] Gaastra, Femme, 'The Dutch East India Company and its Intra-Asiatic Trade in Precious Metals', in *European Commercial Expansion in Early Modern Asia*, ed. Om Prakash (London: Routledge, 1997), p. 97, Marshall, 'Private', p. 278.

[24] Prakash, 'European', p. 91, Gaastra, 'The Dutch East India', p. 154.

[25] Furber, *Rival*, pp. 230–231.

dethrone the VOC became the cause for its demise.[26] Two related things had changed: the fundamentals of the EIC were now burdened with mounting expenses, and thus, silver flowed somewhere else.

By the eighteenth century, the East India companies were burdened by their scaling model. Expansion in goods, destinations, and factories meant an equivalent expansion in sunk costs, in salaries, navies, and facilities. As recorded by Riello, between the 1690s and the 1760s the profit margins of EIC sales of Indian products in England decreased faster than prices increased in India.[27] It could be argued that perhaps competition from private merchants or other companies were reducing prices for Indian goods in London, forcing profit margins down. However, according to Chaudhuri, London prices for Indian goods remained stable during the period or increased.[28] The implication is that the EIC's costs must have expanded from the 1690s uninterruptedly. This had been a long time in the making, but the crisis of 1760–1770 seems to have finally tipped Manila's trade towards interlopers instead of company agents, which also deprived the EIC from its flow of pesos from the city.[29] Progressively, the EIC lost its trade proficiency to private merchants.[30] According to Furber, by 1784 the large debts and expanded militarisation had rendered the EIC's India trade unprofitable.[31] In the 1780s as well, agency houses and private merchants had begun to use the EIC's homeward shipping privilege to wrestle the monopoly of direct intermediation between Europe and Asia from the company.[32] By the 1790s, virtually the only profitable trade in which the Company still operated as a merchant was the China trade, regulated by the Hong system of Canton, which served to mask

[26] Hejeebu, 'Contract', pp. 517–518, Neal, 'The Dutch', pp. 221–222.

[27] Riello, Giorgio, *Cotton: The Fabric that Made the Modern World* (Cambridge: Cambridge University Press, 2013), pp. 107–108.

[28] Chaudhuri, *The Trading*, pp. 440–448 & 499–502.

[29] The exact data is missing for the second half of the eighteenth century, however, Bowen quotes evidence comparing profit margins for the EIC across all Asian goods of 57% between 1761–1765 to just 9% between 1776 and 1779, Bowen, *The Business*, p. 240.

[30] Bowen, *The Business*, p. 251, and for the 1790s Cheong, 'Some aspects', pp. 100–101.

[31] Furber, *John Company...*, pp. 268 & 314.

[32] During the same period, the Company lost the re-export trade of coarse cotton goods to Africa to private merchants, Furber, *John Company*, pp. 282–290.

the deficits incurred in India.[33] Costs derived from scale were rendering the company uncompetitive. Access to Manila's silver helped scaling, the greater efficiency of transacting directly with pesos in Asia mitigated the costs of expansion, but when this leg of the company's trade switched, the decline was absolute. The case of the VOC is also illustrative of the importance of silver. As seen in Chapter 2, the depletion of Japanese silver mines led to increased exports of silver from Europe to Asia and the search for alternative sources of silver *within* Asia.[34] This all points to the same thing: silver was necessary to maintain trading operations within Asia, and therefore, for the direct trade with Europe.

The present characterisation of the joint-stock corporations' strategies to acquire capital and liquidity may be an oversimplification. The very conceptualisation of the massive East India companies as merely profit-focused private enterprises, is in itself ahistorical, even if such a dimension existed, it was part of a broader system.[35] Undoubtedly, other factors had important implications in the timing and evolution of the EIC and VOC. But the emphasis on intra-Asian silver flows highlights the importance of silver specie in providing working capital. This book does not seek to explain the growth and demise of the joint-stock corporation, but how the Manila trade worked. The goal here is to illustrate that since acquiring silver specie was fundamental to maintain operations in Asia, there were other ways apart from the joint-stock corporation to organise the market. Similarly, understanding the importance of cash flows for the organisation of trade and the—previously unknown—level of integration of the Indo-Pacific silver circuits opens new avenues for historical research.

This reveals Manila's business model. As shown in Chapter 2, direct access to silver pesos and the large demand for silver specie in Asia resulted in returns ranging between 200 and 400% by the eighteenth century. The situation in Manila regarding specie was the inverse: there was too much of it relative to investment options as argued in Chapter 5. In that context, there was simply no need to set up an organisational structure

[33] Furber, *John Company*, p. 302.

[34] See Chapter 2, Sect. 2.1.

[35] Perhaps the most comprehensive characterisation is presented by Philip Stern, see Stern, Philip J., *The Company-State: Corporate Sovereignty & the Early Modern Foundations of the British Empire in India* (Oxford: Oxford University Press, 2011), Stern, Philip J., *Empire Incorporated: The Corporations that Built British Colonialism* (Cambridge (Mass.): Harvard University Press, 2023).

like the joint-stock corporation. Manila had other ways to organise the market: it generated working capital through *correspondencia* contracts and through the pooled liquidity of the legacy funds; it fostered impersonal cooperation and channelled the savings of outsiders through the social networks of brotherhoods and Third Orders; it maximised profit margins by reducing costs in the absence of options to scale up the volume of the exchange. Financial intermediaries emerged as lay confraternities, providing the bridge between neighbours' savings and trade finance, solving the challenges of mobilising resources. Yet without recourse to vertical integration into the American market, and with Asian demand for specie attracting fleets of merchants annually to Manila to sell their produce, Manileños were better positioned to exploit their control over the flow of pesos and specialise as silver merchants than to attempt to integrate the trade through joint-stock corporations.

The English and the Dutch did not have such an easy access to silver. They had to acquire it through other means. Thus, the joint-stock corporation offered information and guarantees to potential investors, while the trading infrastructure in Asia allowed the companies to search for alternatives like local sources of silver, or for substitutes as was the Dutch cloth for pepper trade. Manila, on the other hand, did not form a joint-stock company because it did not need to. Ultimately, silver specie affected the profitability of the trade. Access to it had enabled the Dutch and English companies' expansion. Vertical integration allowed for scale, but it was not a substitute for fundamentals: the moment the silver flows changed, both companies found it difficult to maintain their size. This highlights what was happening in Manila. Scale in operations was not an option, or even necessary. Instead of organising transactions vertically to economise, Manila organised horizontally: it reached scale in the pooling of liquidity and the mobilisation of working capital. That is, it maximised the abundance of liquidity it enjoyed and made it its comparative strength.

7.3 Integration and "Horizontalism"

The organisation of commercial operations—whether vertically or horizontally—is related to the principal-agent problem. A paradox for the literature, as mentioned previously, is that systems that were put in place by the East India companies to solve the principal-agent problem in the seventeenth century seem to have lost their edge in the second half of the eighteenth century. The problem is that those that have sought to explain the dominance of the joint-stock company based on their capacity to act as a modern multinational have obviated the fundamentals of the companies: net profits. These are related factors, for the EIC's capacity to align motivations and solve agency risks depended as well on its capacity to provide benefits. Furthermore, the benefits that the companies had to provide to guarantee loyalty had to be greater than the opportunity cost of its agents to switch to interloping or corruption. In this sense, the changes of 1765 were important. The looting of the *obras pías*—and the consequent disruption of the Pacific silver trade—and the large expenses of running Bengal impacted the commercial operations of the EIC. Suddenly, the EIC simultaneously lost is preferential access to Manila's pesos and found itself burdened with the costs of managing a large territorial state.

Vertical integration enabled the joint-stock companies to organise several transactions internally instead than through the market. But vertical integration also allowed the companies to channel resources to try to control the markets, as seen in Chapter 5. Integration allowed scale at the expense of increasing systemic vulnerability to shifts that affected the companies' fundamentals. When silver flows in Asia changed, both the English and the Dutch were left exposed. Hence the difficulty for the literature to make sense of the Seven Years' War divide. The reality was that the main strength of the EIC became its weakness once the scale of the company started affecting its net profits. Since, as argued in Chapter 5, the solution to the principal-agent problem was solved along corporate boundaries, with the companies offering more benefits than their agents could achieve otherwise, crossing this threshold had an exponential effect, because it also affected the way transactions had been organised within the company. This is important because it highlights the comparative weaknesses and strengths of Manila's alternative approach to trade finance.

Spanish commerce in the Pacific was organised horizontally. There was no integration between Asian merchants coming to Manila, Manileños, or Mexican wholesalers as shown in Chapter 2. Neither was there integration across sectors. Miners were distinct from Mexico City's wholesalers. Legacy funds and *obras pías* that mobilised capital were also not integrated with Galleon freighters and merchants that requested financing, even if there was an overlap in membership. As explained in Chapter 4, this provided room for hold-ups. The demand for pesos and the control of silver flows by Mexico's wholesalers allowed them to pursue dilatory tactics in the Acapulco negotiation. The Galleon freighters responded by rationing the trade with the Galleon. Undoubtedly, this was a rent-seeking arrangement, and it was designed to be so. There was a lack of market integration, and therefore, transaction costs were high.[36]

These costs were ultimately absorbed by the consumers of Asian goods in New Spain and by the Asian merchants that demanded pesos, while the intermediaries were shielded. But silver made this system work. The large purchasing power differentials of pesos between each side of the Pacific sustained this trade. There was no pressure to integrate or to increase efficiency when profit margins were so large. Even then, Manila's specialisation in the provision of finance eased these problems. As argued throughout this book, Horizontal Specialisation came to mitigate the lack of integration. The vast capital market of the city, the increasing number of legacy funds and pooled liquidity waiting to be invested, led to different problems. The main issue in Manila was to find enough trade for so much capital, not enough capital for so much trade.[37]

This, however, does not mean that Manila was impervious to market forces. In fact, in this respect at least, the lack of vertical integration worked to the advantage of Manila's "horizontalism". The Pacific exchange was bargained on a commercial, financial, and political level. This meant that, unlike the vertically integrated joint-stock companies, the participants needed to accommodate to the forces of demand and supply at every instance. As seen in Chapter 5, *mesas* needed to negotiate the optimal premia for *correspondencias* so that merchants would be willing to take them while offering returns to the funds, and thus welfare to the city. Mexican wholesalers could not force the hand of Galleon freighters in the Acapulco negotiation, and equally, Galleon freighters could not walk away from the wholesalers. Because no one had the upper hand, everything had to be bargained, and this meant that the whole Pacific exchange rested in an equilibrium that ultimately benefitted everyone involved.

This was important to solve the principal-agent problem. As argued in Chapter 5, this lack of integration meant that motivations in the Pacific trade were aligned horizontally rather than vertically or hierarchically as

[36] Epstein, *Freedom*, p. 36, Grafe, *Distant*, pp. 199–201, Irigoin and Grafe, 'Bounded', pp. 218–219.

[37] Irigoin and Grafe, 'Bounded', pp. 222–223, see Chapter 5, Sect. 5.2.

it was in the companies. Almost every member of the city of Manila was involved in one capacity or another in the Pacific trade. The great contribution of the *obras pías*, as explained in Chapter 3, was not only their capacity to pool liquidity and generate working capital, but also the way they made everyone a stakeholder in the trade. Ultimately, everyone in the Pacific exchange had a vested interest in their neighbours' success. *Obras pías* wanted merchants to take *correspondencias* and have a profitable fair at Acapulco, because their profits depended on the proceeds from these *correspondencias*. Galleon freighters were invested in the wholesalers having a successful commercial season in the interior of New Spain because it would mean that they could bring more pesos to the fair, and wholesalers were invested in the Galleon freighters bringing plenty of Asian goods every year because their position within New Spain's commercial network depended on their capacity to supply the mines and the internal market with consumption goods. Thus, the Pacific avoided the centrifugal tensions that afflicted the corporate boundaries imposed by the joint-stock companies.

Similarly, as long as the Manila trade remained profitable, aligning motivations was not difficult. The *obras pías* could credibly threat defaulters with exclusion from their capital, and therefore, from the trade. One of the most important problems for the EIC was to keep attracting the trade of private merchants once it became more profitable to bypass the company than to trade with it. The difficulty of maintaining the loyalty of servants and directors compounded this problem, for, as argued previously, hierarchy depended on offering better prospects internally than through the market. The case of Scott, presented in Chapter 5, is illustrative of this situation. By the 1790s it was more rational for the directors of the EIC to undermine the company's trade than to attempt to solve its problems. Extra-commercial sources of income such as taxes in Bengal, or debts incurred under the surety of this fiscal income, shored up the finances of the EIC, but by then the company had started its transition towards a territorial empire.[38]

[38] Peers, Douglas M., *Between Mars and Mammon: Colonial Armies and the Garrison State in Early Nineteenth-Century India* (London: Tauris Academic Studies, 1995), pp. 117–120, Chaudhuri, K.N., 'India's Foreign Trade and the Cessation of the East India Company's Trading Activities, 1828–40', *The Economic History Review* 19, nº 2 (1966), pp. 345–346.

The organisation of the trade, its constant bargaining, and the horizontal alignment of motivations, served to solve the Fundamental Problem of Exchange, interpreted broadly as the challenge of offering enough guarantees and generating enough trust to maintain repeated transactions. But in this regard the role of the political economy was also important. As shown in Chapter 6, the Hispanic Monarchy rested on a balance. No territory could unilaterally change the terms of the mutual relationship that existed across the empire. Importantly, it shielded each other from internal competition and aligned the interests of all participants to maintain the balance. This was in detriment of market integration and at the expense of higher transaction costs but was compensated with high profits. Participants in the Pacific exchange took advantage of their devolved authority to deflect costs to consumers and to their local treasuries, thus maintaining profit margins.[39] The organisation of commerce for both the Manila trade and the East India companies had the objective of obtaining rents from their intermediary role. But they followed different strategies. The East India companies, with a comparatively worse access to silver, sought to increase their rents by expanding the scope of their trades, looking for alternatives and for ways of maximising profits while investing in scale. The Pacific exchange was in the best position to profit from the rents derived from arbitraging Asian demand for silver and Spanish American supply. It adopted an alternative model, one oriented to maximising profits by reducing costs and investments with the cognisance of all parties involved.

7.4 An Alternative Narrative of Global Trade

The emergence of the *correspondencia* legacy funds in 1668 represented a revolution in the financing of the Pacific trade. Long-distance trade created unprecedented requirements of capital mobilisation and lock-in and supposed unprecedented challenges in monitoring and enforcing contracts. Solving these issues allegedly led to the emergence of "modern" and impersonal capital markets, establishing a direct causal link between long-distance trade and financial development.[40] But the very

[39] See Chapter 6, Sect. 6.2.

[40] Carlos, 'British Corporate Finance', Ebert, Christopher, 'Early Modern Atlantic Trade in the Development of Maritime Insurance to 1630', *Past & Present*, n° 213 (2011), p. 89.

question of modernity, which still today remains associated with the birth of capitalism,[41] sits uneasily with the case of Manila. As much as the joint-stock chartered companies have been hailed as the harbingers of a modern world of trade, the *obras pías* of Manila managed to solve the problems associated with long-distance trade and to create an impersonal financial market. A market built on contracts that hailed back to ancient times, using vehicles and institutions rooted in canonical tradition and medieval Catholic associations. It was an alternative model that questions whether some institutional designs were inherently better than others. The model of Manila was not necessarily more efficient than the joint-stock companies. Each model adopted different strategies to solving the same challenges, although the context in which they emerged and operated, especially the comparative access to silver, were not the same. What is important is to analyse institutional processes alongside the economic and market conditions in which the former develop, based on the motivation of the agents involved.

This book has provided a new interpretation of the process of institutional formation in Manila, rooted on the broader circumstances of the trade it financed. It has incorporated new sources, a new reconstruction of the capital market of Manila, and an analysis of the market structure of the peso trade. However, the interpretations and lessons of this book are not written in stone. There are still many corners to explore, and much more information to obtain from the archives. But the case of Manila, and of the Hispanic Monarchy at large, needs to be integrated into economic history debates. The potential of Manila to qualify our notions of modernity in financial markets, of institutional performance and formation, and of the importance of monetary factors in global trade is only starting to be revealed. This book aims to highlight this potential and is an open invitation for researchers to fully unveil the dynamics at work in the city and the world beyond.

[41] Wallerstein, Immanuel, 'Capitalism as an Essential Concept to Understand Modernity', in *Capitalism: The Reemergence of a Historical Concept*, eds. Jürgen Kocka and Marcel van der Linden (London: Bloomsbury, 2016): 187–204.

Appendix

Borrower Coalition of the Vélez Escalante family in the *correspondencia* market, 1795.

Taker	*Joint-guarantor*	*Giver*	*Quantity (pesos)*	*Rate*	*Destination*
Juan de Zúñiga	Felipe Vélez Escalante Juan Pablo Infante de Sotomayor Vicente Vélez Escalante	VOT de Santo Domingo	7,000	Pegged to Misericordia	Acapulco
Felipe Vélez Escalante	Juan de Zúñiga Juan Pablo Infante de Sotomayor	VOT de Santo Domingo	8,676	Pegged to Misericordia	Acapulco
Marqués de Montecastro	Felipe Vélez Escalante Vicente Díaz Conde	Caja de Temporalidades	3,536	Pegged to Misericordia	Acapulco
Marqués de Montecastro	Felipe Vélez Escalante	VOT de Santo Domingo	14,000	25%	Acapulco

(continued)

J. J. Rivas Moreno, *The Capital Market of Manila and the Pacific Trade, 1668–1838*, Palgrave Studies in Economic History, https://doi.org/10.1007/978-3-031-71810-6

(continued)

Taker	*Joint-guarantor*	*Giver*	*Quantity (pesos)*	*Rate*	*Destination*
	Juan Pablo Infante de Sotomayor				
Manuel González del Rivero	Felipe Vélez Escalante Diego García Herreros	VOT de San Francisco de Manila	8,000	27.50%	Acapulco
Francisco Vélez Escalante	Juan de Zúñiga José Fernández	VOT de San Francisco de Manila	4,000	27.50%	Acapulco
Jacinto Celís	Felipe Vélez Escalante Juan Pablo Infante de Sotomayor	VOT de San Francisco de Manila	9,900	27.50%	Acapulco
Antonio de Zúñiga	Felipe Vélez Escalante Juan de Zúñiga	VOT de San Francisco de Manila	6,000	27.50%	Acapulco
Marqués de Montecastro	Felipe Vélez Escalante Pedro Agustín de Vivanco	Convento de San Nicolás Tholetino	9,934	27.50%	Acapulco
Domingo Infante	Felipe Vélez Escalante Juan Pablo Infante de Sotomayor	VOT de San Francisco de Manila	5,000	27.50%	Acapulco
Andrés de Ainziburu	Felipe de Ceraín Miguel Vélez Escalante	Provincia de San Nicolás de los Agustinos Descalzos	7,466	27.50%	Acapulco
Miguel Vélez Escalante	Felipe Vélez Escalante Juan Pablo Infante de Sotomayor	Andrés de Ainziburu	16,251	26%	Acapulco
Felipe Vélez Escalante	Miguel Vélez Escalante Juan Pablo Infante de Sotomayor	Pronvincia del Santísimo Rosario	3,500	26%	Acapulco

(continued)

(continued)

Taker	*Joint-guarantor*	*Giver*	*Quantity (pesos)*	*Rate*	*Destination*
		Total quantity coalition (pesos):	103.263		
		Total quantity of market (pesos):	607.194		
		Share over total:	17%		

Sources Escribano Miguel José Flores, 1795 [Legajo #26], ACCHS-CSIC

A Note of Demonyms

The text uses the terms "Manileños", "Mexicans", and *peninsulares* profusely. To clarify, this book is primarily interested in analysing the investment and business strategies and institutions of the Pacific trade within the broader framework of the political economy of the Hispanic Monarchy. Given the importance of corporate affiliation and of territorial bargaining for this political economy, the book mainly uses these terms along corporate lines, instead of racial or political lines. In essence, "Manileños" does not refer to all the inhabitants of the city of Manila, which were mostly *Sangleyes* and natives, but rather to the registered neighbours of the city, which were mostly Spanish-born or America-born individuals of Spanish descent. In a similar way, the term "Mexicans" does not refer to citizens of the later republic of Mexico, but the registered citizen of Mexico City, capital of the Viceroyalty of New Spain, and often members or agents of the Mexico *Consulado*. The only exception is the use of the term *peninsulares* to refer to the merchants coming from Spain in the Atlantic trade. The use of the term *peninsulares* is in accordance with some of the sources, but is used to avoid confusion given the change of the *Consulado* and the Atlantic trade from Seville to Cádiz in 1707. Since it is of the utmost importance for this work to explain how trade was conducted between the different regions of the empire, this distinction is employed to signify mostly the chartered traders of the Pacific and the Atlantic trades.

Glossary of Terms

Almojarifazgo: An import and export tax levied in the Spanish empire over commodities and goods introduced by sea.

Alcábala: Sales tax of Arabic origin, most often levied upon entrance on the market of destination.

Arribadas: Instances in which the Galleons failed to take the northern currents leading them eastwards to America closer to the coasts of Japan. Arribadas prevented the completion of the voyage to America, and forced the return of the Galleons to Manila.

Carta de lasto: A notarised document issued by *Obras Pías* to the joint-guarantors to a *correspondencia* when they repaid the principal and premium instead of the specified taker in the contract. Cartas de lasto served as an official receipt of repayment, which then entitled the joint-guarantors to seek compensation from the taker in a court of law if necessary.

Censo: A credit instrument amply used by institutions and individuals in the Hispanic world. Its origin dated back to the Middle Ages, and there were different types of censos with different characteristics. They often entailed the cession of the usufruct of a good or property in exchange for a sum of money upon which interests were paid.

Correspondencia: A type of *respondentia* sea loan used in Manila during the Early Modern era. As a sea loan, *correspondencias* were

J. J. Rivas Moreno, *The Capital Market of Manila and the Pacific Trade, 1668–1838*, Palgrave Studies in Economic History,
https://doi.org/10.1007/978-3-031-71810-6

contracts through which investors and merchants structured transactions destined to finance trade.

Consulado: Officially sanctioned merchant guild. *Consulados* existed in important cities of the Hispanic Monarchy and incorporated registered merchants of each locality. Members enjoyed the privileges granted to the *consulado* in exchange for membership fees. Usually attached to a commercial line over which they had prerogatives as a method to agglutinate all merchants involved in the trade. Where they existed, *consulados* often had legal jurisdiction over commercial cases.

Escribano: Public notaries in the Spanish empire and in the city of Manila.

Mesas: Governing boards of lay confraternities and third orders that administered *obras pías* according to the institutions' statutes. *Mesas* usually served for one year, and were tasked with the administration of the resources of the lay confraternities, including the legacy funds. *Mesas* agreed to the *correspondencias* issued by the *obras pías*, and decided on the premium rates to charge based on destination.

Obras Pías: During the period, Manileños often conflated the legacy funds that originated *correspondencias* and the lay confraternities managing them under the term *obras pías*, which was often also used to describe the public goods that they generated from the investments of the funds. To avoid confusion, this book uses the term *obras pías* to refer to the institutions that managed legacy funds. These institutions were often religious in nature (i.e. brotherhoods, confraternities, and third orders) but they could also include secular or lay bodies. *Obras pías* thus refer to the totality of those corporate-like bodies that managed legacy funds, and the term "lay confraternities" will be used more specifically to refer to that vast majority of them that were of religious persuasion and were therefore under the jurisdiction of canonical hierarchies.

Reglamento: Set of rules that regulated the Manila Galleon trade since its official establishment in 1593 by King Felipe II. The reglamento was the first set of codes and laws that legislated on the Pacific trade, and it was separate from the Laws of the Indies.

Sangleyes: Name given in Manila to merchants, artisans, and labourers of Chinese origin that settled in the city. The *Sangley* community was one of the largest communities in Manila and soon spread across the archipelago.

Situado: A fiscal transference of cash between imperial treasury districts in Spanish America and the Philippines.

Bibliography

Archival Sources

Note on archival sources: Some of the primary sources used in this book included the number of the folios, while others were not foliated. The footnotes have tried to reflect this fact. Whenever the document provided a folio number, they have been included in the footnotes. In those footnotes where no folio numbers are provided, this means that the original document was not foliated.

Archivo Histórico de la Provincia de Toledo de la Compañía de Jesús (AESI-A)

Legajo 1052.

Archivo del Centro de Ciencias Humanas y Sociales (ACCHS-CSIC)

Colección de Microfilmes de la Sección de Documentos Españoles del Archivo Nacional de Filipinas, Biblioteca Tomás Navarro Tomás, Madrid, Spain.
Escribano Unknown, 1674 [Legajo #1].
Escribano Baltasar Javier Sánchez de Cuenca, 1740 [Legajo #2].
Escribano Baltasar Javier Sánchez de Cuenca, 1752 [Legajo #3].
Escribano Baltasar Javier Sánchez de Cuenca, 1758 [Legajo #4].

J. J. Rivas Moreno, *The Capital Market of Manila and the Pacific Trade, 1668–1838*, Palgrave Studies in Economic History,
https://doi.org/10.1007/978-3-031-71810-6

Escribano Domingo Cortés de Arquiza, 1755 [Legajo #5].
Escribano Manuel José de Vizcarra, 1762 [Legajo #6].
Escribano Martín Dominguez de Zamudio, 1765 [Legajo #7].
Escribano Martín Dominguez de Zamudio, 1766 [Legajo #8].
Escribano Martín Dominguez de Zamudio, 1770 [Legajo #9].
Escribano Martín Dominguez de Zamudio, 1771 [Legajo #10].
Escribano Juan Antonio de Silva, 1778 [Legajo #12].
Escribano Vicente González de Tagle, 1783 [Legajo #13].
Escribano Vicente González de Tagle, 1783 II [Legajo #14].
Escribano Vicente González de Tagle, 1796 [Legajo #15].
Escribano Vicente González de Tagle, 1796 II [Legajo #15A].
Escribano Vicente González de Tagle, 1799 [Legajo #18].
Escribano Vicente González de Tagle, 1800 [Legajo #19].
Escribano Miguel José Flores, 1789 [Legajo #21A].
Escribano Miguel José Flores, 1792 [Legajo #24].
Escribano Miguel José Flores, 1795 [Legajo #26].

Archivo Franciscano Ibero-Oriental (AFIO-SFG)

357/5, 52/9, 52/16, 101/14, 357/5.

Archivo General de Indias (AGI)

Filipinas 31, 96, 98, 129, 149, 172, 197, 198, 199, 229, 268, 291, 292, 303, 595, 936, 941, 985, 1034.
Contaduría 1282.

Archivo General de la Nación (AGN)

GD Filipinas 48.

Archivo del Museo Naval (AMN)

MS 233, 533, 552, 700.

Archivo de la Provincia del Santísimo Rosario (APSR)

Tomo 17, *Obras pías del Convento de Santo Domingo de Manila*, 1600–1739.
Tomo 194, *Orden Tercera Lista de Terciarios*, 1697–1818.
Tomo 218, *Extracto de aquellas obras pías de la VOT cuya noticia puede ser interesante al Padre Prior del Convento*, 1820.

Tomo 223, *Obra pía del Señor Fernández con el título de NPS Domingo*, 1745–1847.
Tomo 224, *Obra pía del General Juan Domingo de Nebra*, 1755.
Tomo 226, *Obra pía de Luís Beltrán de Medrano*, 1780.
Tomo 228, *Obra pía fundada por el General Don Juan Infante de Sotomayor*, 1760.
Tomo 229, *Obra pía del Señor Fernando Valdéz y Tamón*, 1790–1847.
Tomo 230, *Obra primera de Nuestra Señora de Guadalupe fundada por varios interesados*, 1764.
Tomo 232, *Obra de Dña. Paula González, doncella difunta*, 1778.
Tomo 233, *Primera obra pía de Doña María Josefa de Espeleta*, 1777.
Tomo 235, *Segunda obra pía de Doña María Josefa de Espeleta*, 1777.
Tomo 236, *Tercera obra pía de Doña María Josefa de Espeleta*, 1777.
Tomo 237, *Cuarta obra pía de Doña María Josefa de Espeleta*, 1777.
Tomo 247, *Obra pía de Doña Raymunda Brionis*, 1822.
Tomo 262, *Obra pía del General Echeveste para las misiones de Tunkín*, (Cavite) 1754.
Tomo 263, *Obra pía del General Echeveste para misioneros de Tunkín y China*, (Manila) 1754 (Tomo 262 and 263 refer to two separate legacy funds founded in the same year of 1754 and for the same purpose of financing missions in Tunkin and China, but one was founded with the Third Order of Saint Dominic in Cavite and the other with the Third Order of Saint Dominic in Manila)
Tomo 263b, *Obra pía del General Echeveste para misioneros en Ity y Panigui*, 1754.
Tomo 274, *Obra pía fundada por Doña María Balansao*, 1783–1799.
Tomo 275, *Obra pía fundada por Doña María Balansao*, 1799–1847.
Tomo 276, *Obra pía del General Francisco David*, 1779.
Tomo 281, *Obra pía de Lucas de Sousa*, 1799.
Tomo 282, *Obra pía del Capitán Juan Bautista de Uriarte*, 1783–1799.
Tomo 284, *Obra pía de Santiago Fernández Obispo de Tunkín*, 1775.
Tomo 284b, *Obra pía del Capitán Juan Baustista de Uriarte*, 1799–1847.
Tomo 289, *Obra pía fundada por la Sra. Condesa de Lizárraga*, 1783.
Tomo 304a, *Obra antigua del General Francisco Echeveste*, 1735.
Tomo 304b, *Obra pía de José Garcés*, 1739.

Archive of the University of Santo Tomás (AUST)

Libros Tomo 20, Becerros 13.

Newberry Library

Ayer MS 1331, 1349, 1352, 1398, 1448, 1823.

Biblioteca Nacional de España (BNE)

MSS/8990, MSS/11014, MSS/9195.
PORCONES 972(25).

India Office Records (IOR)

IOR/HMS/606.
IOR/HMS/795.
IOR/D/150.
IOR/E/30.
IOR/E/1/47.

Online Databases

Ruiz-Stovel, Guillermo, (2021). Manila Intra-Asian Trade Database (MIAT) (1.0) . Zenodo. https://doi.org/10.5281/zenodo.4836052, accessed 25/07/2022.

Published Primary Sources

Álvarez de Abreu, Antonio, *Extracto Historial del expediente que pende en el Consejo Real, y Supremo de las Indias, a instancia de la Ciudad de Manila, sobre la forma en que se ha de hacer y continuar el Comercio, y Contratación de los Texidos de China en Nueva España*, Madrid, 1736.

Blair, Emma Helen and Robertson, Alexander, (eds.) *Philippine Islands 1493–1898*, 55 vols., Cleveland: A.H. Clark Company, 1905.

Careri, Gemelli, *A Voyage Around the World*, 1704, in *A Collection of Voyages and Travels*, vol. IV, London: Printed by HC in Parternoster Row, 1744.

Comyn, Tomás de, *Estado de las Islas Filipinas en 1810*, Madrid, 1820.

Concepción de las Isla, Fr. Juan, *Historia General de Philipinas*, 14 vols., Manila: Sampaloc, 1792.

Cushner, Nicholas P. (ed.), *Documents Illustrating the British Conquest of Manila, 1762–1763*, London: Royal Historical Society, 1971.

Díaz Arenas, Rafael, *Memoria sobre el Comercio y Navegación de las Islas Filipinas*, Cádiz: Imprenta de Domingo Ferós, 1838.

Diccionario de la Lengua Castellana compuesto por la Real Academia Española, reducido a un tomo para su fácil uso, Madrid: Imprenta de la viuda de don Joaquín Ibarra, 1803.

de Elhuyar, Fausto, *Indagaciones sobre la amonedación en Nueva España*, México: Tipografía Literaria de Filomeno Mata, 1880 (1814).

Maldonado de Puga, Fr. Juan Manuel, *Religiosa Hospitalidad por los Hijos del Piadoso Coripheo Patriarcha y Padre de Pobres S. Iuan de Dios*, Granada, 1742.

Marín y Mendoza, Joaquín, *Historia del Derecho Natural y de Gentes*, (1776) Madrid: Universidad Carlos III, 2015.

Martinez de Zúñiga, Fr. Joaquín, *Historia de las Islas Philipinas*, Sampaloc, 1803.

Ordenanzas de la Compañía de Comercio que se ha formado en esta ciudad de Manila, Manila: Imprenta del Colegio y Universidad de Santo Tomás, 1755.

Park, Sir James Allan, *A System of the Laws of Marine Insurance*, vol. II, London, 1809.

Recopilación de las Leyes de los Reynos de las Indias, 3 vols., Cádiz: Imprenta del Real Consejo de Indias, 1791.

Records of Fort St. George, *Letters to Fort St. George*, 1763–1764, vol. 44, Madras: Government Press, 1941.

Records of Fort St. George, *Letters to Fort St. George*, 1765, vol. 45, Madras: Government Press, 1941.

Records of Fort St. George, *Letters from Fort St. George*, 1762, vol. 37, Madras: Government Press, 1941.

Records of Fort St. George, *Letters from Fort St. George*, 1763, vol. 38, Madras: Government Press, 1941.

Records of Fort St. George, *Letters from Fort St. George*, 1764, vol. 39, Madras: Government Press, 1941.

Records of Fort St. George, *Manilha Consultations*, 10 vols., 1762–1764, Madras: Government Press, 1941.

Silva, José de, *Principios de direito mercantil e Leis de marinha*, 3 vols., Lisbon, 1806.

Spain. *Código de comercio y legislación complementaria*, Boletín Oficial del Estado (BOE), 2022.

St. Thomas Aquinas, *Summa Theologica*, Part 2, Treatise on the Cardinal Virtues, Q 120, translated by the Fathers of the English Dominican Province, New York: Bezinger Bros. (1947).

de Uriarte, Juan Bautista, *Manifiesto y Resumen Histórico de la fundación de la Venerable Hermandad de la Santa Misericordia*, Manila, 1728.

Torrubia, Fr. Joseph, *Disertación Histórico-Política, y en mucha parte Geográfica, de las Islas Philipinas*, Madrid, 1753.

Secondary Sources

Acemoglu, Daron, and Robinson, James. *Why Nations Fail?: The Origins of Power, Prosperity and Poverty*. London: Profile Books, 2012.

——— Johnson, Simon, and Robinson, James. 'The Rise of Europe: Atlantic Trade, Institutional Change, and Economic Growth'. *The American Economic Review* 95, n° 3 (June 2005): 546–579.

Adrianova, Svetlana, Panicos, Demetriades, & Xu, Chenggang. 'Political Economy Origins of Financial Markets in Europe and Asia'. *World Development* 39, n° 5 (2011): 686–699.

Aldous, Michael. 'From Traders to Planters: The Evolving Role and Importance of Trading Companies in the 19th century Anglo-Indian Trade'. *Business History* (online 2019): 1–18.

Alonso Álvarez, Luis. *El costo del imperio asiático: la formación colonial de las Islas Filipinas bajo dominio español, 1565–1800*. La Coruña: Universidade da Coruna, 2009.

——— 'Financing the Empire: The Nature of the Tax System in the Philippines, 1565–1804', *Philippine Studies*, 51, n° 1 (2003): 63–95.

——— 'La ayuda Mexicana en el Pacífico: Socorros y Situados en Filipinas, 1565–1816'. In *El secreto del Imperio Español: los situados coloniales en el siglo XVIII*, edited by Carlos Marichal, Johanna von Grafenstein, 251–293. Mexico: El Colegio de Mexico, 2012.

——— 'El impacto de las reformas borbónicas en las redes comerciales. Una visión desde el Pacífico hispano, 1762–1815', Ponencia presentada al II Congreso de la Asociación Mexicana de Historia Económica Simposio *Redes sociales e instituciones comerciales en México, ss. XVII–XIX*, 2007.

Alva Rodríguez, Inmaculada. *Vida Municipal en Manila (Siglos XVI–XVII)*. Córdoba: Universidad de Córdoba, 1997.

Álvarez-Dardet Espejo, Concha, López Manjón, Jesús D., and Baños Sánchez-Matamoros, Juan. 'Accounting at the Boundaries of the Sacred: The Regulation of the Spanish Brotherhoods in the Eighteenth Century'. *Accounting History* 11, n° 2 (2006): 129–150.

Anderson, Gary M., McCormick, Robert E., and Tollison, Robert D. 'The Economic Organization of the English East India Company'. *Journal of Economic Behavior and Organization* 4, n° 4 (1983): 221–238.

Andreau, Jean. *Banking and Business in the Roman World*. Cambridge: Cambridge University Press, 1999.

Arroyo Abad, Leticia, Davies, Elwyn, and van Zanden, Jan Luiten. 'Between Conquest and Independence: Real wages and demographic change in Spanish America, 1520–1830'. *Explorations in Economic History* 49 (2012): 149–166.

Arteaga, Fernando, Desierto, Desiree, and Koyama, Mark, 'Shipwrecked by Rents', MPRA Paper N° 102974, 2020.

Aslanian, Sebouh. 'Trade Diaspora vs Colonial State: Armenian Merchants, the English East India Company, and the High Court of Admiralty in London'. *Diaspora: A Journal of Transnational Studies* 13, n° 1 (2004): 37–100.

Atwell, William S. 'International Bullion Flows and the Chinese Economy circa 1530–1650'. *Past & Present* 95 (May 1982): 68–90.

——— 'Another Look at Silver Imports into China, ca. 1635–1644'. *Journal of World History* 16, n° 4 (December 2005): 467–489.

Austin, Gareth. 'Reciprocal Comparison and African History: Tackling Conceptual Eurocentrism in the Study of Africa's Economic Past'. *African Studies Review* 50, n° 3 (2007): 1–28.

——— and Sugihara, Kaoru (editors), *Labour-Intensive Industrialization in Global History*. Abingdon: Routdlege, 2013.

Azcárraga, Manuel. *La Libertad de Comercio en las Islas Filipinas*. Madrid, 1872.

Baena Zapatero, Alberto, and Lamikiz, Xabier. 'Presencia de una diáspora global: comerciantes armenios y comercio intercultural en Manila, c. 1660–1800'. *Revista de Indias* LXXIV, 262 (2014): 693–722.

Barrett, Ward. 'World bullion flows, 1450–1800'. In *The Rise of Merchant Empires: Long-Distance Trade in the Early Modern World, 1350–1750*, edited by James D. Tracy, 224–254. Cambridge: Cambridge University Press, 1990.

Baskes, Jeremy. *Staying Afloat: Risk and Uncertainty in Spanish Atlantic World Trade, 1760–1820*. Stanford: Stanford University Press, 2013.

Bauzon, Leslie E. *Deficit Government: Mexico and the Philippine Situado, 1606–1804*. Tokyo: Centre for East Asian Cultural Studies, 1981.

Bassett, D. K. 'The "Amboyna Massacre" of 1623'. *Journal of Southeast Asian History* 1, n° 2 (1960): 1–19.

Berg, Maxine. 'Asian Luxuries and the Making of the European Consumer Revolution'. In *Luxury in the Eighteenth Century: Debates, Desires and Delectable Goods*, edited by Maxine Berg and Elizabeth Eger, 228–244. London: Palgrave, 2003.

Bernal, Antonio-Miguel. *La financiación de la Carrera de Indias (1492–1824), Dinero y crédito en el comercio colonial español con América*. Sevilla: Fundación el Monte, 1992.

——— 'La "Carrera del Pacífico": Filipinas en el sistema colonial de la Carrera de Indias'. In *España y el Pacífico. Tomo I: Legazpi*, edited by Leoncio Cabrero, 485–526. Madrid: Sociedad Estatal de Conmemoraciones Culturales, 2004.

Bethencourt, Francisco. 'Political Configurations and Local Power'. In *Portuguese Oceanic Expansion, 1400–1800*, edited by F. Bethencourt & D. Ramada Curto, 197–254. Cambridge: Cambridge University Press, 2007.

Bhattacharya, Bhaswati. 'Making Money at the Blessed Place of Manila: Armenians in the Madras-Manila Trade in the Eighteenth Century'. *Journal of Global History* 3, (2008): 1–20.

Bjork, Katharine. 'The Link that Kept the Philippines Spanish: Mexican Merchants Interests and the Manila Trade, 1571–1815'. *Journal of World History* 9, n° 1 (1998): 25–50.

Blanco Núñez, José María. 'La fragata de S.M. *San Fernando* a el *Magallanes* en el servicio del Galeón de Manila-Acapulco'. In *El Galeón de Manila: la ruta española que unió tres continentes*, edited by Ministerio de Defensa, 194–205, Madrid: Ministerio de Defensa, 2016.

Blussé, Leonard. 'Batavia, 1690–1740: The Rise and Fall of a Chinese Colonial Town'. *Journal of Southeast Asian Studies* 12, n° 1 (March 1981): 159–178.

Bohorquez, Jesus. 'Linking the Atlantic and Indian Oceans: Asian textiles, Spanish silver, global capital, and the financing of the Portuguese-Brazilian slave trade (c. 1760–1808)'. *Journal of Global History* 15, n° 1 (2020): 19–38.

Bonalian, Mariano Ardash. *El Pacífico Hispanoamericano: política y comercio asiático en el Imperio Español (1680–1784)*. México: El Colegio de México, 2012.

Borah, Woodrow. *Early Colonial Trade and Navigation Between Mexico and Peru*. Berkeley: University of California Press, 1954.

Börner, Lars. 'Making Medieval Markets: A Formal Institutional Analysis.' PhD diss., Humboldt-Universität zu Berlin, October 2007.

Bowen, Huw V. *The Business of Empire. The East India Company and Imperial Britain, 1765–1833*. Cambridge: Cambridge University Press, 2009.

——— 'Bullion for Trade, War, and Debt Relief: British Movements of Silver to, Around, and from Asia, 1760–1833'. *Modern Asian Studies* 44, n° 3 (2010): 445–475.

Boxer, Charles R. *The Portuguese Seaborne Empire, 1415–1825*. London: Hutchinson & Co, 1969.

——— *Fidalgos in the Far East, 1550–1770: Fact and Fancy in the History of Macao*, The Hague: M. Nijhoff, 1948.

——— *The Great Ship from Amacon*, Macau: Instituto Cultural de Macau, 1985.

——— 'La plata es sangre: Sidelights on the Drain of Spanish-American Silver in the Far East, 1500–1700'. *Philippine Studies* 18, n° 3, (1970): 457–478.

——— 'Portuguese and Spanish Rivalry in the Far East in the Seventeenth century'. *Journal of the Royal Asiatic Society* 78, n° 3 (1946): 150–164.

Boyajian, James C. *Portuguese Trade in Asia under the Habsburgs, 1580–1640*. Baltimore: The John Hopkins University Press, 1993.

Brading, D.A. *Miners and Merchants in Bourbon Mexico 1763–1810*. Cambridge: Cambridge University Press, 1971.

Brandon, Pepijn. 'Between Company and State: The Dutch East and West India Companies as Brokers Between War and Profit'. In *The Corporation: A Critical, Multi-Disciplinary Handbook*, edited by Grietje Baars and Andre Spicer, 215–225. Cambridge: Cambridge University Press, 2017.

Broadberry, Stephen, and Gupta, Bishnupriya. 'Lancashire, India, and Shifting Competitive Advantage in Cotton Textiles, 1700–1850'. *Economic History Review* 62, n° 2 (2009): 279–305.

Cabrero, Leoncio. 'Las entidades económicas y financieras filipinas en el siglo XIX'. *Revista Complutense de Historia de América*, 17 (1991): 195–217.

Calvo, Thomas. *Espacios, climas y aventuras: El Galeón de Filipinas y la fragata de las Marianas en el Pacífico occidental (1680–1700)*. San Luís Potosí: El Colegio de San Luís, 2016.

Cañeque, Alejandro. 'The Political and Institutional History of Colonial Spanish America'. *History Compass* 11, n° 4 (2013): 280–291.

Cardim, Pedro, Feros, Antonio, and Sabatini, Gaetano. 'The Political Constitution of the Iberian Monarchies'. In *The Iberian World 1450–1820*, edited by Fernando Bouza, Pedro Cardim, and Antonio Feros, 34–61, London: Routledge, 2020.

———, Herzog, Tamar, José Javier Ruíz Ibáñez, and Sabatini, Gaetano. 'Polycentric Monarchies: How did Early Modern Spain and Portugal Achieve and Maintain a Global Hegemony?'. In *Polycentric Monarchies: How did Early Modern Spain and Portugal Achieve and Maintain a Global Hegemony?*, edited by Pedro Cardim, 3–8. Eastbourne: Sussex Academic Press, 2012.

Carlos, Ann. 'British Corporate Finance, 1500–1860'. In *Handbook of Key Global Financial Markets, Institutions, and Infrastructure*, edited by Gerard Carpio, 39–46. London: Elsevier, 2013.

——— and Neal, Larry. 'The Micro-Foundations of the Early London Capital Market: Bank of England Shareholders During and After the South Sea Bubble, 1720–25'. *The Economic History Review* 59, n° 3 (August 2006): 498–538.

——— and Nicholas, Stephen. 'Agency Problems in the Early Chartered Companies: The Case of the Hudson's Bay Company'. *Journal of Economic History* 50, n° 4 (1990): 853–875.

——— and Nicholas, Stephen. 'Theory and History: Seventeenth-Century Joint-Stock Chartered Trading Companies'. *Journal of Economic History* 56, n° 4 (1996): 916–924.

——— and Kruse, Jamie Brown. 'The Decline of the Royal African Company: Fringe Firms and the Role of the Charter'. *The Economic History Review* 49, n° 2 (1996): 291–313.

Carrasco González, María Guadalupe. 'El Negocio de los Seguros Marítimos en Cádiz a finales del siglo XVIII'. *Hispania* 59, n° 1 (1999): 269–304.

——— 'Los Instrumentos del Comercio Colonial en el Cádiz del siglo XVII, 1650–1700'. *Banco de España-Servicio de Estudios de Historia Económica*, n° 35 (1996).

Carrera Stampa, Manuel. 'Las ferias novohispanas'. *Historia Mexicana* 2, n° 3 (1953): 319–342.

Carrière, Charles. 'Renouveau espagnol et prêt a la grosse aventure (Notes sur la place de Cadix dans la seconde moitié du XVIIIe siècle)'. *Revue d'histoire moderne et contemporaine* 17e, n° 2 (1970): 221–252.

Cebreiro Ares, Francisco. 'Redes comerciales y traslado de herencias entre el Imperio Hispánico y Galicia: Andrés de Losada Sotomayor y los retornos monetarios a Compostela (1744–1790)'. *e-Spania*, 34 (October 2019): 1–26.

Chaudhuri, K.N. *The Trading World of Asia and the English East India Company.* Cambridge: Cambridge University Press, 1978.

——— 'Circuits monétaires internationaux, prix comparés et spécialisation économique, 1500–1750'. In *Études d'Histoire Monétaire*, edited by John Day, 49–67. Lille: Presses Universitaires de Lille, 1984.

——— 'Treasure and Trade Balances of the East India Company's Export Trade, 1660–1720'. *The Economic History Review* 21, n° 3, (December 1968): 480–502.

——— 'The East India Company and the Export of Treasure in the Early Seventeenth Century'. *The Economic History Review* 16, n° 1 (1963): 23–38.

——— 'India's Foreign Trade and the Cessation of the East India Company's Trading Activities, 1828–40'. *The Economic History Review* 19, n° 2 (1966): 345–363.

——— 'The Economic and Monetary Problem of European Trade with Asia in the Seventeenth and Eighteenth Centuries'. *Journal of European Economic History* 4, n° 2 (1977): 323–358.

——— *The English East India Company: The Study of an Early Joint-Stock Company, 1600–1640.* London: Frank Cass and Co., 1965.

Chaudhuri, Susil. 'The Financing of Investments in Bengal: 1650–1720'. *The Indian Economic & Social History Review* 8, n° 2 (1971): 109–133.

Chaunu, Pierre. *Les Philippines et le Pacifique des Ibériques (XVIe, XVIIe, XVIIIe siècles).* Paris: SEVPEN, 1960.

——— 'Le galion de manille: Grandeur et décadence d'une route de la soie'. *Annales, Histoire, Sciences Sociales* 6e, n° 4 (1951): 447–462.

Cheong, Wang Eang. 'Changing the Rules of the Game (The India-Manila trade, 1785–1809)'. *Journal of Southeast Asian Studies* 1, n° 2 (September 1970): 1–19.

——— 'The Decline of Manila as the Spanish Entrepôt in the Far East, 1785–1826: Its Impact on the Pattern of Southeast Asian trade'. *Journal of Southeast Asian Studies* 2, n° 2 (September 1971): 142–158.

——— 'The Beginnings of Credit Finance on the China Coast'. *Business History* 12, n° 2 (1971): 87–103.

——— 'Trade and Finance in China 1784–1834: A Reappraisal'. *Business History* 7, (1965): 34–56.

——— 'Some aspects of British Trade and Finance in Canton with special reference to the role of Anglo-Spanish Trade in the Eastern Seas, 1784–1834.' PhD diss., University of London, 1962.

Chia, Lucille. 'The Butcher, the Baker, and the Carpenter: Chinese Sojourners in the Spanish Philippines and Their Impact on Southern Fujian (Sixteenth-Eighteenth Centuries)'. *Journal of Economic and Social History of the Orient* 49, n° 4 (2006): 509–534.

Clark, Gregory. 'The Political Foundations of Modern Economic Growth: England, 1540–1800'. *The Journal of Interdisciplinary History* 26, n° 4 (Spring 1996): 563–588.

Coase, Ronald H. 'The Nature of the Firm'. *Economica* 4, n° 16 (1937): 386–405.

Coello de la Rosa, Alexandre. 'Los conflictos jurisdiccionales entre los arzobispos de Manila y los jesuitas por las doctrinas de indios (siglos XVI–XVIII)'. *Boletín Americanista* LXIII, n° 67 (2013): 105–124.

Cooper, Michael. 'The Mechanics of the Macao-Nagasaki Silk Trade'. *Monumenta Nipponica* 27, n° 4 (1972): 423–433.

Cosano Moyano, José. *Filipinas y su Real Hacienda (1750–1800).* Córdoba: Publicaciones del Monte de Piedad y Caja de Ahorros de Córdoba, 1986.

——— 'Un nuevo intento de comercio directo con las Filipinas: la compañía de Aguirre, del Arco, y Alburquerque'. *Anuario de Estudios Americanos*, n° 35 (1978): 261–281.

Cuenca-Esteban, Javier. 'Statistics of Spain's Colonial Trade, 1747–1820: New Estimates and Comparisons with Great Britain'. *Revista de Historia Económica* XXVI, n° 3 (2008): 323–354.

Cunningham, Charles H. *The Audiencia in the Spanish Colonies as Illustrated by the Audiencia of Manila*. Berkeley: University of California Press, 1919.

De Vries, Jan. *The Industrious Revolution: Consumer Behavior and the Household Economy, 1650 to the Present*. Cambridge: Cambridge University Press, 2012.

——— 'Connecting Europe and Asia: A Quantitative Analysis of the Cape-route Trade, 1497–1795'. In *Global Connections and Monetary History, 1470–1800*, edited by Dennis Flynn, Arturo Giráldez and Richard von Glahn, 35–106. Aldershot: Ashgate Publishing Limited, 2003.

——— 'Understanding Eurasian Trade in the Era of the Trading Companies'. In *Goods from the East 1600–1800: Trading Eurasia*, edited by Maxine Berg, Felicia Gottman, Hanna Hodacs, and Chris Nierstrasz, 7–39 London: Palgrave Macmillan, 2015.

——— 'The Limits of Globalization in the Early Modern World', *The Economic History Review* 63, n° 3 (2010): 710–733.

Díaz-Trechuelo Spínola, María Lourdes. *La Real Compañía de Filipinas*. Sevilla: Escuela de Estudios Hispanoamericanos, 1965.

——— 'The Economic Development of the Philippines in the Second Half of the Eighteenth Century'. *Philippine Studies* 11, n° 2 (April 1963): 195–231.
——— 'El comercio de Filipinas durante la segunda mitad del siglo XVIII'. *Revista de Indias* 63, n° 1 (1963): 463–485.
——— 'Religiosidad Popular en Filipinas: Hermandades y Cofradías (Siglos XVI–XVIII)'. *Hispania Sacra*, 53 (2001): 345–366.
Disney, A.R. *Twilight of the Pepper Empire: Portuguese Trade in Southwest India in the Early Seventeenth Century*. Cambridge: Harvard University Press, 1978.
——— 'The First Portuguese India Company, 1628–33'. *The Economic History Review* 30, n° 2 (1977): 242–258.
D'Ors, Álvaro. *Derecho Privado Romano*. Pamplona: ENUSA, 1997.
Ebert, Christopher. 'Early Modern Atlantic Trade and the Development of Maritime Insurance to 1630'. *Past & Present*, n° 213 (November 2011): 87–114.
Egido, Teófanes. 'La Iglesia y los problemas religiosos'. In *Historia de España en la Edad Moderna*, edited by Alfredo Floristán, 335–358. Barcelona: Ariel, 2004.
Elizalde, Dolores. 'El viraje de Filipinas hacia Asia en el filo de los siglos XVIII y XIX'. *Vegueta. Anuario de la Facultad de Geografía e Historia*, 20 (2020): 163–187.
Elliott, John H. 'A Europe of Composite Monarchies'. *Past & Present*, n° 137 (1992): 48–71.
Emmer, Pieter. 'The Organisation of Global Trade: The Monopoly Companies, 1600–1800'. *European Review* 22, n° 1 (2014): 106–115.
——— and Gaastra, Femme. 'Introduction'. In *The Organization of Interoceanic Trade in European Expansion, 1450–1800*, edited by Pieter Emmer & Femme Gaastra, Aldershot: Variorum, 1996.
Ena Sanjuán, Íñigo. 'The imperceptible financial (r)evolution of the censo'. *Investigaciones de Historia Económica-Economic History Research*, 17 (2021): 1–12.
Erikson, Emily. *Between Monopoly and Free Trade: The English East India Company, 1600–1757*. Princeton: Princeton University Press, 2014.
——— and Samila, Sampsa. 'Networks, Institutions, and Uncertainty: Information Exchange in Early Modern Markets'. *The Journal of Economic History* 78, n° 4 (2018): 1034–1067.
Esptein, S.R. *Freedom and Growth: The Rise of States and Markets in Europe, 1300–1750*. London: Routledge, 2000.
Esteban Estrígana, Alicia, and Floristán Imízcoz, Alfredo. 'Composición y gobierno de la Monarquía de España'. In *Historia de España en la Edad Moderna*, ed. Alfredo Floristán, 245–278. Barcelona: Ariel, 2004.
Escoto, Salvador P. 'Governor Anda and the Liquidation of Jesuit Temporalities in the Philippines, 1770–1776'. *Philippine Studies* 23, n° 3 (1975): 293–319.

——— 'Expulsion of the Chinese and Readmission to the Philippines: 1764–1779'. *Philippine Studies* 47, n° 1 (1999): 48–76.

——— 'The Administration of Simón de Anda y Salazar, Governor General of the Philippines, 1770–1776.' PhD diss., Loyola University Chicago, 1973.

Feldbaek, Ole. 'The Danish Trading Companies of the Seventeenth and Eighteenth Centuries'. *The Scandinavian Economic History Review* 34, n° 3 (1986): 204–218.

Fichter, James R. *So Great a Proffit: How the East Indies Trade Transformed Anglo-American Capitalism*. Cambridge: Harvard University Press, 2010.

Findlay, Ronald, and O'Rourke, Kevin. *Power and Plenty: Trade, War, and the World Economy in the Second Millennium*. Princeton: Princeton University Press, 2007.

Fisher, John. *The Economic Aspects of Spanish Imperialism in America, 1492–1810*. Liverpool: Liverpool University Press, 1997.

Flannery, Kristie Patricia, and Ruiz-Stovel, Guillermo, 'The Loyal Foreign Merchant Captain: Tomé Gaspar de León and the Making of Manila's intra-Asian Connections'. *Vegueta: Anuario de la Facultad de Geografía e Historia*, 20 (2020): 189–215.

Flynn, Dennis O. 'Comparing the Tokugawa Shogunate with Hapsburg Spain: Two silver-based empires in a global setting'. In *The Political Economy of Merchant Empires*, by James D. Tracy, 332–359, Cambridge University Press, Cambridge, 1990.

——— and Giráldez, Arturo. 'Spanish Profitability in the Pacific: The Philippines in the Sixteenth and Seventeenth Centuries'. In *Pacific Centuries: Pacific and Pacific Rim History Since the Sixteenth Century*, edited by Dennis Flynn, Lionel Frost, and A.J.H. Latham, 33–47. London: Routledge, 1999.

——— and Giráldez, Arturo. 'Arbitrage, China, and World Trade in the Early Modern Period'. *Journal of the Economic and Social History of the Orient* 38, n° 4 (1995): 429–448.

——— and Giráldez, Arturo. 'Silk for Silver: Manila-Macao Trade in the 17th Century'. *Philippine Studies* 44, n° 1 (1996): 52–68.

——— and Giráldez, Arturo. 'Cycles of Silver: Global Economic Unity through the Mid-Eighteenth Century'. *Journal of World History* 13, n° 2 (2002): 391–427.

——— and Giráldez, Arturo. 'Born with "a Silver Spoon": The Origin of World Trade in 1571'. *Journal of World History* 6, 2 (1995): 201–221.

——— and Giráldez, Arturo. 'Path Dependence, Time Lags, and the Birth of Globalisation: A Critique of O'Rourke and Williamson'. *European Review of Economic History* 8, n° 1 (2004): 81–108.

Fradera, Josep M. *Filipinas, la Colonia más peculiar. La Hacienda Pública en la definición de la política colonial, 1762–1868*. Madrid: Consejo Superior de Investigaciones Científicas, 1999.

Frank, André Gunder. *Re-Orient: Global Economy in the Asian Age*. Berkeley: University of California Press, 1998.

Fratianni, Michele, and Spinelli, Franco. 'Italian City-States and Financial Evolution', *European Review of Economic History* 10, n° 3 (2006): 257–278.

Furber, Holden. *Rival Empires of Trade in the Orient, 1600–1800*. Oxford: Oxford University Press, 1976.

——— *John Company at Work, A Study of European Expansion in India in the Late Eighteenth Century*. New York: Octagon Books, 1970.

——— 'The India Trade in the Pacific Through Two Centuries'. In *Private Fortunes and Company Profits in the India Trade in the 18th Century*, edited by Rosane Rocher, Aldershot: Variorum, 1997.

——— 'An Abortive Attempt at Anglo-Spanish Commercial Cooperation in the Far East in 1793'. *The Hispanic American Historical Review* 15, n° 4 (November 1935): 448–463.

Gaastra, F.S. 'The Exports of Precious Metal from Europe to Asia by the Dutch East India Company, 1602–1795'. In *Precious Metals in the Later Medieval and Early Modern Worlds*, edited by J.F. Richards, 447–475. Durham: Carolina Academic Press, 1983.

——— 'The Dutch East India Company and its Intra-Asiatic Trade in Precious Metals'. In *European Commercial Expansion in Early Modern India*, edited by Om Prakash, 97–112. London: Routledge, 1997.

García-Baquero, Antonio. *Cádiz y el Atlántico, 1717–1778*. 2 vols., Sevilla: Escuela de Estudios Hispanoamericanos, 1976.

García Fuentes, Lutgardo. *El Comercio Español con América, 1650–1700*. Sevilla: Escuela de Estudios Hispanoamericanos CSIC, 1980.

García Garralón, Marta. 'The Nautical Republic of the *Carrera de Indias*: Commerce, Navigation, *Casos Fortuitos*, and *Avería Gruesa* in the Sixteenth Century'. In *General Average and Risk Management in Medieval and Early Modern Maritime Business*, edited by Maria Fusaro, Andrea Addobbati, Luisa Piccinno, 215–256. Singapore: Springer, 2023.

Gasch-Tomás, José Luis. 'Asian Silk, Porcelain and Material Culture in the Definition of Mexican and Andalusian Elites, c. 1565–1630'. In *Global Goods and the Spanish Empire, 1492–1824: Circulation, Resistance and Diversity*, edited by Bethany Aram & Bartolomé Yun-Casalilla, 153–173. Palgrave Macmillan, 2014.

——— 'Transport costs and prices of Chinese silk in the Spanish Empire. The case of New Spain, c. 1571–1650'. *Revista de Historia Industrial*, n° 60 (2015): 15–47.

——— 'Mecanismos de funcionamiento institucional en el imperio Hispánico. El comercio de los Galeones de Manila y el Consulado de comerciantes de México en la década de 1630'. *Revista de Historia Jerónimo Zurita*, 90 (2015): 55–74.

Gelderblom, Oscar. *Cities of Commerce: The Institutional Foundations of International Trade in the Low Countries, 1250–1650*. Princeton: Princeton University Press, 2013.

——— and Jonker, Joost. 'Completing a Financial Revolution: The Finance of the Dutch East India Trade and the Rise of the Amsterdam Capital Market, 1595–1612'. *Journal of Economic History* 64, n° 3 (September 2004): 641–672.

——— and de Jong, Abe, and Jonker, Joost. 'The Formative Years of the Modern Corporation: The Dutch East India Company VOC, 1602–1623'. *The Journal of Economic History* 73, 4 (2013): 1050–1076.

Giráldez, Arturo. *The Age of Trade: The Manila Galleons and the Dawn of the Global Economy*. London: Rowman & Littlefield, 2015.

von Glahn, Richard. *Fountain of Fortune: Money and Monetary Policy in China, 1000–1700*. Berkeley: University of California Press, 1996.

——— 'Money Use in China and Changing Patterns of Global Trade in Monetary Metals, 1500–1800'. In *Global Connections and Monetary History, 1470–1800*, edited by Dennis O. Flynn, Arturo Giráldez, Richard von Glahn, 187–205. Aldershot: Ashgate Publishing Limited, 2003.

——— 'Foreign Silver Coins in the Market Culture of Nineteenth Century China'. *International Journal of Asian Studies* 4, n° 1 (2007): 51–78.

——— 'Myth and Reality of China's Seventeenth-Century Monetary Crisis'. *The Journal of Economic History* 56, n° 2 (1996): 429–454.

Glamann, Kristoff. *Dutch-Asiatic Trade, 1620–1740*. Copenhagen: Danish Science Press, 1958.

González Arce, José Damián. 'La universidad de mercaderes de Burgos y el consulado castellano en Brujas durante el siglo XV'. *En la España medieval* 33 (2010): 161–202.

González de Lara, Yadira. 'The secret of Venetian Success: A Public-Order, Reputation-Based Institution'. *European Review of Economic History* 12 (2008): 247–285.

——— and Greif, Avner, and Jha, Saumitra. 'The Administrative Foundation of Self-Enforcing Constitutions'. *American Economic Review: Papers and Proceedings* 98, n° 2 (2008): 105–109.

Grafe, Regina. *Distant Tyranny: Markets, Power, and Backwardness in Spain, 1650–1800*. Princeton: Princeton University Press, 2012.

——— 'An Empire of Debts? Spain and Its Colonial Realm'. In *A World of Public Debts*, edited by N. Barreyre and N. Delalande, 5–35. Singapore: Springer, 2020.

——— 'Empires of Charity: Imperial Legitimacy and Profitable Charity in Colonial Spanish America'. *New Global Studies* 12, n° 2 (2018): 131–155.

——— and Irigoin, Alejandra. 'A Stakeholder Empire: The Political Economy of Spanish Imperial Rule in America'. *Economic History Review* 65, n° 2 (2012): 609–651.

——— and Irigoin, Alejandra. 'The Spanish Empire and Its Legacy: Fiscal Redistribution and Political Conflict in Colonial and Post-Colonial Spanish America'. *Journal of Global History*, vol. 1 (2006): 241–267.

——— and Gelderblom, Oscar. 'The Rise and Fall of the Merchant Guilds: Rethinking the Comparative Studies of Commercial Institutions in Pre-Modern Europe'. *The Journal of Interdisciplinary History* 4, n° 10 (2010): 477–511.

Greif, Avner. *Institutions and the Path to the Modern Economy: Lessons from Medieval Trade*. New York: Cambridge University Press, 2006.

——— 'The Fundamental Problem of Exchange: A Research Agenda in Historical Institutional Analysis'. *European Review of Economic History* 4 (2000): 251–284.

——— 'Cultural Beliefs and the Organization of Society: A Historical and Theoretical Reflection on Collectivist and Individualist Societies'. *Journal of Political Economy* 102, n° 5, 1994: 912–950.

Guedes Cosme, Marco Antonio. 'Elites e Poder Local em Macau (1750–1848): Os Proveedores da Santa Casa da Misericórdia.' PhD diss., Universidade de Coimbra, 2020.

Guerra, François-Xavier. 'The Spanish-American Tradition of Representation and its European Roots'. *Journal of Latin American Studies* 26, n° 1 (February 1994): 1–35.

dos Guimarães Sá, Isabel. *Quando o rico se faz pobre: Misericórdias, caridade e poder no imperio portugués 1500–1800*. Lisbon: CNCDP, 1997.

——— 'Ganhos da terra e ganhos do mar: caridade e comércio na Misericórdia de Macau (séculos XVII–XVIII)'. *Ler História*, 44 (2003): 45–57.

Halperin Donghi, Tulio. 'Backward Looks and Forward Glimpses from a Quincentennial Vantage Point'. *Journal of Latin American Studies* 24 (1992): 219–234.

Hamnett, Brian R. 'The Appropriation of Mexican Church Wealth by the Spanish Bourbon Government. The 'Consolidación de Vales Reales', 1805–1809'. *Journal of Latin American Studies* 1, n° 2 (1969): 85–113.

Hang-Sheng, Chuan. 'Trade Between China, the Philippines and the Americas During the Sixteenth and Seventeenth Centuries'. In *Metals and Monies in an Emerging Global Economy*, edited by Dennis Flynn and Arturo Giráldez, 281–285. Aldershot: Variorum, 1997.

Harris, Ron. *Going the Distance: Eurasian Trade and the Rise of the Business Corporation, 1400–1700*. Princeton: Princeton University Press, 2020.

——— 'General Average and All the Rest: The Law and Economics of Early Modern Maritime Risk Mitigation'. In *General Average and Risk Management in Medieval and Early Modern Maritime Business*, edited by Maria Fusaro, Andrea Addobbati, Luisa Piccinno, 33–60. Singapore: Springer, 2023.

——— 'The Institutional Dynamics of Early Modern Eurasian Trade: The *commenda* and the Corporation'. *Journal of Economic Behavior & Organization*, 71 (2009): 606–622.

——— 'A New Understanding of the History of Limited Liability: An Invitation for Theoretical Reframing'. *Journal of Institutional Economics*, 16 (2020): 643–664.

Hejeebu, Santhi. 'Contract Enforcement in the English East India Company'. *The Journal of Economic History* 65, n° 2 (June 2005): 496–523.

Herrero Gil, María Dolores. '¿De la confusión a la negación? Reflexiones sobre la utilidad aseguradora del contrato de riesgo'. *Espacio, Tiempo y Forma*, Serie IV Historia Moderna (2005–2006): 133–154.

Hoover, Calvin B. 'The Sea Loan in Genoa in the Twelfth Century'. *The Quarterly Journal of Economics* 40, n° 3 (May 1926): 495–529.

Hoppit, Julian. *Britain's Political Economies: Parliament and economic life, 1660–1800*. Cambridge: Cambridge University Press, 2017.

——— 'The Nation, the State, and the First Industrial Revolution'. *Journal of British Studies* 50 (April 2011): 307–331.

Irigoin, Alejandra. 'Rise and Demise of the Global Silver Standard'. In *Handbook of the History of Money and Currency*, edited by Stefano Battilossi, Yousef Cassis & Kazuhiko Yago, 383–410. Singapore: Springer, 2020.

——— 'The New World and the Global Silver Economy, 1500–1800'. In *Global Economic History*, edited by Tirthankar Roy & Giorgio Riello, 271–286. London: Bloomsbury Academic, 2019.

——— and Grafe, Regina. 'Absolutismo negociado: la trayectoria Hispana en la formación del estado y el imperio'. In *El secreto del Imperio Español: los situados coloniales en el siglo XVIII*, edited by Carlos Marichal, Johanna von Grafenstein, 295–339. Mexico: El Colegio de Mexico, 2012.

——— and Grafe, Regina. 'Bounded Leviathan: Fiscal constraints and financial development in the Early Modern Hispanic world'. In *Questioning Credible Commitment: Perspectives on the Rise of Financial Capitalism*, edited by D'Maris Coffman, Adrian Leonard, and Larry Neal, 199–227. Cambridge: Cambridge University Press, 2013.

——— and Grafe, Regina. 'Bargaining for Absolutism: A Spanish Path to Nation-State and Empire Building'. *Hispanic American Historical Review* 88, n° 2 (2007), 204–205.

——— and Grafe, Regina. 'Response to Carlos Marichal and William Summerhill'. *Hispanic American Historical Review* 88, n° 2 (2008): 235–245.

——— 'The End of a Silver Era: The Consequences of the Breakdown of the Spanish Peso Standard in China and the United States, 1780s-1850s'. *Journal of World History* 20, nº 2 (June 2009): 207–244.

——— 'Gresham on Horseback: The Monetary Roots of Spanish American Political Fragmentation in the Nineteenth Century'. *The Economic History Review* 62, nº 3 (August 2009): 551–575.

——— 'A Trojan Horse in Daoguang China? Explaining the Flows of Silver in and Out of China', Working Paper nº 173/13, Department of Economic History, LSE, London, 2013.

——— 'Why Was the Manila Galleon Only One Ship Trade?', Mimeo, 2018.

——— '"De las contratas del dinero" Instruments for Trade Finance in the Early Modern Global Economy' (Presentation, World Economic History Congress, Paris, France, July 25–29, 2022).

Jones, S.R.H., and Ville, Simon P. 'Efficient Transactors or Rent-Seeking Monopolists? The Rationale for Early Chartered Trading Companies'. *The Journal of Economic History* 56, nº 4 (1996): 898–915.

——— 'Theory and Evidence: Understanding Chartered Trading Companies'. *The Journal of Economic History* 56, nº 4 (1996): 925–926.

Kamen, Henry, and Israel, J.I. 'The Seventeenth-Century Crisis in New Spain: Myth or Reality?' *Past & Present*, nº 97 (1982): 144–156.

Karagedikli, Gürer, and Tunçer, Ali Coşkun, 'Microcredit in the Ottoman Empire: A Review of Cash Waqfs in Transition to Modern Banking', in *Financing in Europe*, edited by M. Lorenzini, C. Lorandini, and D. Coffman, 239–268. London: Palgrave Macmillan, 2018.

Kizca, John. *Empresarios coloniales: Familias y negocios en la ciudad de México durante los Borbones*. Mexico: Fondo de Cultura Económica, 1986.

Kueh, Joshua Eng Sin. 'The Manila Chinese: Community, Trade, and Empire, c. 1570–1770.' PhD diss., Georgetown University, 2014.

Kuethe, Allan J., and Inglis, G. Douglas. "Absolutism and Enlightened Reform: Charles III, the Establishment of the Alcabala, and Commercial Reorganization in Cuba". *Past & Present*, nº 109 (1985): 118–143.

Kuran, Timur. 'The absence of the Corporation in Islamic Law: Origins and Persistence'. *The American Journal of Comparative Law* 53, nº 4 (2005): 785–834.

——— 'Why the Middle East Is Economically Underdeveloped: Historical Mechanisms of Institutional Stagnation'. *Journal of Economic Perspectives*18, nº 3 (2004): 71–90.

——— 'The Islamic Commercial Crisis: Institutional Roots of Economic Underdevelopment in the Middle East'. *The Journal of Economic History* 63, nº 2 (2003): 414–446.

Lamikiz, Xabier. *Trade and Trust in the Eighteenth-century Atlantic World: Spanish Merchants and their Overseas Networks*. Woodbridge: The Boydell Press, 2010.

——— 'Patrones de Comercio y Flujo de Información Comercial entre España y América durante el siglo XVIII'. *Revista de Historia Económica* XXV, n° 2 (2007): 233–260.

——— 'Flotistas en la Nueva España: diseminación espacial y negocios de los intermediarios del comercio transatlántico, 1670–1702'. *Colonial Latin American Review* 20, n° 1 (2011): 9–33.

——— 'Transatlantic Networks and Merchant Guild Rivalry in Colonial Trade with Peru, 1729–1780: A New Interpretation'. *Hispanic American Historical Review* 91, n° 2 (2011): 299–331.

Lane, Kris. 'Corrupción y Dominación Colonial: El Gran Fraude de la Casa de la Moneda de Potosí en 1649'. *Boletín del Instituto de Historia Argentina y Americana "Dr Emilio Ravignani"*, 3ª serie, 43 (2015): 94–130.

Lang, M.F. 'Las minas de Almadén bajo la superintendencia de Miguel de Unda y Garivay'. *Hispania*, 32 (1972): 261–276.

Lavrin, Asunción. 'El Capital Eclesiástico y las Élites Sociales en Nueva España a Fines del Siglo XVIII'. *Estudios Mexicanos* 1, n° 1 (Winter 1985): 1–28.

Legarda, Benito J. *After the Galleons: Foreign Trade, Economic Change, & Entrepreneurship in the Nineteenth-Century Philippines*. Quezon City: Ateneo de Manila University Press, 1999.

——— 'Two and a Half Centuries of the Galleon Trade'. *Philippine Studies* 3, n° 4 (December 1955): 345–372.

Leonard, A.B. 'Underwriting British Trade to India and China, 1780–1835'. *The Historical Journal* 55, n° 4 (2012): 983–1006.

Luque Talaván, Miguel. 'La avería en el tráfico marítimo-mercantil indiano: notas para su estudio (siglos XVI–XVIII)'. *Revista Complutense de Historia de América*, n° 24 (1998): 113–145.

Lynch, John. 'The Origins of Spanish American Independence'. in *The Cambridge History of Latin America*, edited by Leslie Bethell, vol. 3, 1–50 Cambridge: Cambridge University Press, 1985.

——— 'The Institutional Framework of Colonial Spanish America'. *Journal of Latin American Studies* 24 (1992): 69–81.

Mackay, Ruth. *The Limits of Royal Authority: Resistance and Obedience in Seventeenth-Century Castile*. Cambridge: Cambridge University Press, 1999.

MacLachlan, Colin M. *Spain's Empire in the New World: The Role of Ideas in Institutional and Social Change*. Berkeley: University of California Press, 1988.

Malamud Rikles, Carlos D. *Cádiz y Saint Malo en el comercio colonial peruano (1698–1725)*. Jerez de la Frontera: Diputación Provincial de Cádiz, 1986.

Manchado López, Marta Mª. '"Desamparo en que con la vida, se pierde el alma." Las controversias en torno a la obra pía del abad Sidoti para la recogida de niños chinos abandonados (Filipinas, 1705–1740)'. *Revista de Indias* 71, nº 252 (2011): 415–447.

Manning, Catherine. 'French Country Trade on Coromandel (1720–50)'. In *European Commercial Expansion in Early Modern Asia*, edited by Om Prakash, 282–292. Aldershot: Variorum, 1997.

Marichal, Carlos. *La bancarrota del virreinato. Nueva España y las finanzas del Imperio español, 1780–1810*. Mexico D.F.: Fondo de Cultura Económica, 1999.

Marshall, P.J. 'Private British Trade in the Indian Ocean Before 1800'. In *India and the Indian Ocean, 1500–1800*, edited by Ashin Das Gupta and M.N. Pearson, 276–300. Oxford: Oxford University Press, 1987.

Martínez Gijón, José. 'La comenda en el Derecho español. I. La comenda-depósito'. *Anuario de Historia del Derecho Español* XXXVI (1966): 31–140.

——— 'La comenda en el Derecho español. II. La comenda mercantil'. *Anuario de Historia del Derecho Español* XXXVI (1966): 379–456.

——— 'La comenda y el transporte de mercancías en el derecho español de la Baja Edad Media'. *Historia. Instituciones. Documentos* 1 (1974): 265–273.

Martínez Torres, José Antonio. 'Integrate the Empire: Proposals for Commercial and Defensive Cooperation in South-East Asia During the Incorporation of Portugal into the Monarchy of the Spanish Habsburgs'. In *A Global Trading Network: The Spanish Empire in the World Economy (1580–1820)*, edited by José Ignacio Martínez Ruiz, 221–237. Sevilla: Editorial Universidad de Sevilla, 2018.

de Mas y Oztet, Francisco. *Carriedo y sus obras*. Manila: Ramírez & Giraudier, 1882.

Maté, Fr. Lorenzo, Prieto, María Begoña, and Tua Pereda, Jorge. 'La Actividad Financiera del Monasterio de Silos en el siglo XVIII a la luz de sus Libros de Cuentas'. *De Computis*, nº 1 (2004): 97–141.

Mentz, Søren. *The English Gentleman Merchant at Work: Madras and the City of London, 1660–1740*. Copenhagen: Museum Tusculanum Press, 2005.

Mesquida, Juan. 'Negotiating Charity, Politics and Religion in the Colonial Philippines: The Brotherhood of the Misericordia of Manila (1594–1780s)'. In *Faith's Boundaries: Laity and Clergy in Early Modern Confraternities*, edited by Nicholas Terpstra, Adriano Prosperi, & Stefania Pastore, 187–206. Turhnhout: Brepols, 2012.

——— 'La población de Manila y las capellanías de misas para españoles: Libro de registros, 1642–1672'. *Revista de Indias* LXX, nº 249 (2010): 469–500.

——— 'Pious funds across the Pacific (1668–1823): Charitable Bequests or Credit Source?'. *The Americas* 75, nº 4 (2018): 661–697.

Miceli, Paola. *Derecho consuetudinario y memoria. Práctica jurídica y costumbre en Castilla y León (siglos XI-XIV).* Madrid: Universidad Carlos III, 2012.

Milhaud, Cyril. 'Interregional Flows of Capital and Information in Spain: A Case Study of the Theresian Carmelite Order'. *Revista de Historia Económica* 37, n° 1 (2018): 81–110.

Morse, H.B. 'The Provision of Funds for the East India Company's Trade at Canton During the Eighteenth Century'. *The Journal of the Royal Asiatic Society of Great Britain and Ireland*, n° 2 (April 1922): 227–255.

Musgrave, Peter. 'The Economics of Uncertainty: The Structural Revolution in the Spice Trade, 1480–1640'. In *Spices in the Indian Ocean World*, ed. M.N. Pearson, 337–349. Aldershot: Variorum, 1996.

Neal, Larry. *The Rise of Financial Capitalism: International Capital Markets in the Age of Reason.* Cambridge: Cambridge University Press, 1990.

——— 'The Dutch and English East India Companies Compared: Evidence from the Stock and Foreign Exchange Markets'. In *The Rise of Merchant Empires: Long-Distance Trade in the Early Modern World, 1350–1750*, edited by James D. Tracy, 195–223. Cambridge: Cambridge University Press, 1990.

North, Douglass. *Institutions, Institutional Change and Economic Performance.* Cambridge: Cambridge University Press, 1990.

——— 'Institutions, Transaction Costs, and the Rise of Merchant Empires'. In *The Political Economy of Merchant Empires*, edited by James D. Tracy, 22–40. Cambridge: Cambridge University Press, 1991.

——— 'Markets and Other Allocation Systems in History: The Challenge of Karl Polanyi'. *Journal of European Economic History* 6, n° 3 (1977): 703–716.

——— 'Ocean Freight Rates and Economic Development, 1750–1913'. *The Journal of Economic History* 18, n° 4 (December 1958): 537–555.

——— 'Institutions'. *The Journal of Economic Perspectives* 5, n° 1 (Winter 1991): 97–112.

——— and Thomas, Robert Paul. *The Rise of the Western World. A New Economic History.* New York: Cambridge University Press, 1973.

——— and Weingast, Barry R. 'Constitutions and Commitment: The Evolution of Institutional Governing Public Choice in Seventeenth-Century England'. *The Journal of Economic History* 49, n° 4 (December 1989): 803–832.

Ng, Chin-Keong. *Trade and Society: The Amoy Network on the China Coast, 1683–1735.* Singapore: Singapore University Press, 1983.

Numhauser, Paulina. 'El Real Patronato en Indias y la Compañía de Jesús durante el período filipino (1580–1640)'. *Boletín Americanista*, 67 (2013): 85–103.

O'Brien, Patrick. 'The Nature and Historical Evolution of an Exceptional Fiscal State and Its Possible Significance for the Precocious Commercialization and Industrialization of the British Economy from Cromwell to Nelson'. *Economic History Review* 64, n° 2 (2011): 408–446.

——— and Hunt, Philip A. 'The Rise of a Fiscal State in England, 1485–1815'. *Historical Research* 66, issue 160 (1993): 129–176.

Ogilvie, Sheilagh. *Institutions and European Trade: Merchant Guilds, 1000–1800.* Cambridge: Cambridge University Press, 2011.

——— 'Thinking Carefully About Inclusiveness: Evidence from European Guilds'. *Journal of Institutional Economics*, (2020): 1–16.

——— and Carus, A.W. 'Institutions and Economic Growth in Historical Perspective', in *Handbook of Economic Growth,* volume 2, edited by. Philippie Aghion, Steven N. Durlauf, 403–513. Oxford: Elsevier, 2014.

Oka, Mihoko, and Gipoloux, François. 'Pooling Capital and Spreading Risk: Maritime Investment in East Asia at the Beginning of the Seventeenth Century'. *Itinerario* XXXVIII, n° 3 (2013): 75–91.

Orlando Díaz, Manuel. 'The Spanish Average System of Insurance and Loss Prevention'. *The Journal of Insurance* 28, n° 4 (December 1961): 85–91.

O'Rourke, Kevin H., and Williamson, Jeffrey G. 'When Did Globalisation Begin?'. *European Review of Economic History* 6, n° 1 (2002): 23–50.

——— 'Once More: When Did Globalisation Begin?', *European Review of Economic History* 8, n° 1 (2004): 109–117.

Paquette, Gabriel. 'State-Civil Society Cooperation and Conflict in the Spanish Empire: The Intellectual and Political Activities of the Ultramarine Consulados and Economic Societies, c. 1780–1810'. *Journal of Latin American Studies* 39, n° 2 (2007): 263–298.

Parker, Geoffrey. *Global Crisis. War, Climate Change, and Catastrophe in the Seventeenth Century*. London: Yale University Press, 2013.

Parthesius, Robert. *Dutch Ships in Tropical Waters. The Development of the Dutch East India Company (VOC) Shipping Network in Asia*. Amsterdam: Amsterdam University Press, 2010.

Pearce, Adrian J. *British Trade with Spanish America, 1763–1808*. Liverpool: Liverpool University Press, 2007.

Pearson, M.N. 'Spain and Spanish trade in Southeast Asia'. *Journal of Asian History* 2, n° 2 (1968): 109–129.

Peers, Douglas M. *Between Mars and Mammon: Colonial Armies and the Garrison State in Early Nineteenth-Century India*. London: Tauris Academic Studies, 1995.

Pérez-García, Manuel. *Global History with Chinese Characteristics: Autocratic States along the Silk Road in the Decline of the Spanish and Qing Empires, 1680–1796*. Singapore: Palgrave, 2021.

——— 'Beyond the Silk Road: Manila Galleons, Trade Networks, Global Goods, and the Integration of Atlantic and Pacific Markets (1680–1840)'. *Atlantic Studies* 19, n° 3 (2022): 373–383.

Pérez Herrero, Pedro. 'La rearticulación de los mercados americanos ante la presencia extranjera en el siglo XVII (1630–1720)'. *Chronica Nova*, 23 (1996): 343–380.

Permanyer-Ugartemendia, Ander. 'Opium after the Manila Galleon: The Spanish Involvment in the Opium Economy in East Asia (1815–1830)'. *Investigaciones de Historia Económica - Economic History Research*, nº 10 (2014): 155–164.

Pezzolo, Luciano. 'Sovereign Debts, Political Structure, and Institutional Commitments in Italy, 1350–1700'. In *Questioning Credible Commitment: Perspectives on the Rise of Financial Capitalism*, edited by D'Maris Coffman, Adrian Leonard, and Larry Neal, 169–198. Cambridge: Cambridge University Press, 2013.

Phelan, John Leddy. *The Hispanization of the Philippines: Spanish Aims and Filipino Responses, 1565–1700*. Madison: The University of Wisconsin Press, 1959.

——— 'Authority and Flexibility in the Spanish Imperial Bureaucracy'. *Administrative Science Quarterly* 5, nº 1 (1960): 47–65.

Pomeranz, Kenneth. *The Great Divergence: China, Europe, and the Making of the Modern World Economy*. Oxford: Princeton University Press, 2000.

Prakash, Om. *European Commercial Enterprise in Pre-Colonial India*. Cambridge: Cambridge University Press, 1998.

——— 'From Market-Determined to Coercion-Based: Textile Manufacturing in Eighteenth-Century Bengal'. In *How India Clothed the World: The World of South Asian Textiles, 1500–1850*, edited by Giorgio Riello & Tirthankar Roy, 217–252. Leiden: Brill, 2009.

Price, Jacob M. 'A Note on Merchant Credit and the Organization of Private Trade'. In *The Political Economy of Merchant Empires*, edited by James D. Tracy, 276–297. Cambridge: Cambridge University Press, 1991.

Quiason, Serafin. *English "country trade" with the Philippines, 1644–1765*. Quezon City: University of the Philippines, 1966.

Quiroz, Alfonso W. 'Reassessing the Role of Credit in Late Colonial Peru: Censos, Escrituras, and Imposiciones'. *The Hispanic American Historical Review* 74, nº 2 (1994): 193–230.

Rahn Phillips, Carla. 'The growth and composition of trade in the Iberian empires, 1450–1750'. In *The Rise of Merchant Empires: Long-Distance Trade in the Early Modern World, 1350–1750*, edited by James D. Tracy, 34–101. Cambridge: Cambridge University Press, 1990.

Ravina Martín, Manuel. 'Riesgos marítimos en la Carrera de Indias'. *Documentación y Archivos de la colonización española* (1989): 103–157.

Real Díaz, José Joaquín. *Las ferias de Jalapa*. Sevilla: Escuela de Estudios Hispanoamericanos, 1959.

Reed, Robert R. 'The Colonial Origins of Manila and Batavia: Desultory Notes on Nascent Metropolitan Primacy and Urban Systems in Southeast Asia'. *Asian Studies* 5, n° 3 (1967): 543–562.

Reid, Anthony. *Southeast Asia in the Age of Commerce, 1450–1680. Vol. I. The Lands below the Winds*. New Haven: Yale University Press, 1988.

——— *A History of Southeast Asia: Critical Crossroads*. Oxford: Wiley-Blackwell, 2015.

——— 'An 'Age of Commerce' in Southeast Asian History'. *Modern Asian Studies* 24, n° 1 (February 1990): 1–30.

Riello, Giorgio. *Cotton: The Fabric that Made the Modern World*. Cambridge: Cambridge University Press, 2013.

Rodolfo Moutin, Osvaldo. '¿Qué fue el Derecho canónico indiano?', Mimeo, 2021.

Rodrigues, Lisbeth. 'Institutional investors in the Portuguese credit market (1550–1800): The case of the Misercórdias'. *Revista de Historia Económica/ Journal of Iberian and Latin American Economic History* 42, n° 1 (2024): 1–29.

De Roover, Raymond. 'The Organization of Trade'. In *The Cambridge Economic History of Europe from the Decline of the Roman Empire*, edited by M.M. Postan, Edwin E. Rich, and Edward Miller, vol. 3, 42–118. Cambridge: Cambridge University Press, 1963.

Rosenthal, Jean-Laurent, and Bin Wong, Roy. *Before and Beyond the Divergence: The Politics of Economic Change in China and Europe*. Cambridge: Harvard University Press, 2011.

Ruiz Rivera, Julián Bautista, 'Intento Gaditano de romper el monopolio comercial novohispano-filipino', in *Andalucía y América en el siglo XVIII*, Actas de las IV Jornadas de Andalucía y América, Universidad de Santa María de la Rábida, CSIC, Madrid, 1984.

Ruiz-Stovel, Guillermo. 'Chinese Shipping and Merchant Networks at the Edge of the Spanish Pacific: The Minnan-Manila Trade, 1680–1840.' PhD diss., University of California Los Angeles, 2019.

Russell-Wood, A.J.R. *Fidalgos and Philanthropists: The Santa Casa da Misericórdia of Bahia, 1550–1755*. London: Macmillan, 1968.

Schurz, William Lyttle. *The Manila Galleon*. New York: E.P. Dutton & Co. Inc, 1939.

Sokoloff, Kenneth L., and Engerman, Stanley L. 'Institutions, Factor Endowments, and Paths of Development in the New World'. *Journal of Economic Perspectives* 14, n° 3 (2000): 217–232.

Souza, George Bryan. *The Survival of Empire: Portuguese Trade and Society in China and the South China Sea, 1630–1754*. Cambridge: Cambridge University Press, 1986.

Spate, Oskar H. K. *The Spanish Lake*. Canberra: Australian National University Press, 1979.

Sperling, J. 'The International Payments Mechanism in the Seventeenth and Eighteenth Centuries'. *The Economic History Review* 14, n° 3 (1962): 446–468.

Steensgaard, Niels. *The Asian Trade Revolution of the 17th Century: The East India Companies and the Decline of the Caravan Trade*. Chicago: Chicago University Press, 1973.

——— 'The Growth and Composition of the Long-Distance Trade of England and the Dutch Republic Before 1750'. In *The Rise of Merchant Empires: Long Distance Trade in the Early Modern World, 1350–1750*, edited by James D. Tracy, 102–152. Cambridge: Cambridge University Press, 1990.

Stern, Philip J. *The Company-State: Corporate Sovereignty and the Early Modern Foundations of the British Empire in India*. Oxford: Oxford University Press, 2011.

——— *Empire Incorporated: The Corporations that Built British Colonialism*, Cambridge (MA): Harvard University Press, 2023.

Subrahmanyam, Sanjay. *The Political Economy of Commerce Southern India, 1500–1650*. Cambridge: Cambridge University Press, 1990.

——— and Thomaz, Filipe F.R. 'Evolution of Empire: The Portuguese in the Indian Ocean during the Sixteenth Century'. In *The Political Economy of Merchant Empires*, edited by James D. Tracy, 298–331. Cambridge: Cambridge University Press, 1991.

Sugaya, Nariko. 'Spanish Colonial Manila in Transition: Trade and Society at the Turn of the Nineteenth Century'. 愛媛大学法文学部論集. 人文学科編. vol.36 (2014): 19–32.

TePaske, John J. *A New World of Gold and Silver*, edited by Kendall W. Brown, Boston: Brill, 2010.

——— 'New World silver, Castile and the Philippines 1590–1800'. In *Precious Metals in the Later Medieval and Early Modern Worlds*, edited by J.F. Richards, 425–445. Durham: Carolina Academic Press, 1983.

——— and Klein, Herbert. 'The Seventeenth-Century Crisis in New Spain: Myth or Reality?'. *Past & Present*, n° 90 (1981): 116–135.

——— and Klein, Herbert. 'The Seventeenth-Century Crisis in New Spain: Myth or Reality? A Rejoinder'. *Past & Present*, n° 97 (1982): 156–161.

Thompson, I.A.A. 'The Rule of Law in Early Modern Castile'. *European History Quarterly* 14, n° 2 (1984): 221–234.

Tomás y Valiente, Francisco. *Gobierno e instituciones en la España del Antiguo Régimen*. Madrid: Alianza Editorial, 1982.

Trivellato, Francesca. *The Familiarity of Strangers: The Sephardic diaspora, Livorno, and cross-cultural trade in the Early Modern period*. London: Yale University Press, 2012.

del Valle Pavón, Guillermina. 'Las funciones crediticias de las cofradías y los negocios de los mercaderes del Consulado de la ciudad de México, fines del siglo XVIII y principios del siglo XIX'. *Revista de Indias* 74, nº 261 (2017): 507–536.

——— 'Bases del poder de los mercaderes de plata de la ciudad de México. Redes, control del consulado y de la Casa de Moneda a fines del siglo XVII'. *Anuario de Estudios Americanos* 68, nº 2 (2011): 565–598.

——— 'La lucha por el control de los precios entre los consulados de México y Andalucía'. *Revista Complutense de Historia de América* 32 (2006): 41–62.

Villamar, Cuauhtémoc. *Portuguese Merchants in the Manila Galleon System, 1565–1600*. London: Routledge, 2021.

Wallerstein, Immanuel. 'Capitalism as an Essential Concept to Understand Modernity'. In *Capitalism: The Reemergence of a Historical Concept*, edited by Jürgen Kocka and Marcel van der Linden, 187–204. London: Bloomsbury, 2016.

Warren, James. 'Sino-Sulu Trade in the Late Eighteenth and Nineteenth Centuries'. *Philippine Studies* 21, nº 1 (1977): 50–79.

——— 'Slave Markets and Exchange in the Malay World: The Sulu Sultanate, 1770–1878'. *Journal of Southeast Asian Studies* 8, nº 2 (1977): 162–175.

Williamson, Oliver E. *The Economic Institutions of Capitalism: Firms, Markets, Relational Contracting*. London: Collier Macmillan, 1987.

——— 'The Theory of the Firm as a Governance Structure: From Choice to Contract'. *The Journal of Economic Perspectives* 16, nº 3 (2002): 171–195.

von Wobeser, Gisela. *El crédito eclesiástico en la Nueva España. Siglo XVIII*. Mexico: Universidad Nacional Autónoma de México/Fondo de Cultura Económica, 1994.

——— 'Las fundaciones piadosas como fuentes de crédito en la época colonial'. *Historia Mexicana* 38, nº 4 (1989): 779–792.

Yun-Casalilla, Bartolomé. *Iberian World Empires and the Globalization of Europe 1415–1668*. Singapore: Springer, 2019.

——— 'Las instituciones y la economía política de la Monarquía Hispánica (1492–1714). Una perspectiva trans-"nacional"'. In *Economía Política desde Estambul a Potosí: Ciudades estado, imperios y mercados en el Mediterráneo y en el Atlántico ibérico, c. 1200–1800*, edited by Fernando Ramos Palencia and Bartolomé Yun-Casalilla, 139–162, Valencia: Publicacions de la Universitat de València, 2012.

——— 'The American Empire and the Spanish Economy: An Institutional and Regional Perspective'. *Revista de Historia Económica*, nº 1 (1998): 123–156.

——— 'Early Modern Iberian Empires, Global History, and the History of Early Globalization', *Journal of Global History* 17, nº 3 (2022): 539–561.

——— and Comín Comín, Francisco. 'Spain: From Composite Monarchy to Nation State, 1492–1914. An Exceptional Case?'. In *The Rise of Fiscal States:*

A Global History, 1500–1914, edited by Bartolomé Yun-Casalilla and Patrick K. O'Brien, 233–266, Cambridge: Cambridge University Press, 2012.

Yuste López, Carmen. *Emporios Transpacíficos: Comerciantes Mexicanos en Manila (1710–1815)*. Mexico: Universidad Nacional Autónoma de México, 2007.

——— 'Las correspondencias de riesgo a premio de mar en las *Ordenanzas* de la Casa de la Misericordia de Manila. Siglo XVIII'. In *Nueva España: puerta americana al Pacífico asiático, siglos XVI-XVIII*, edited by Carmen Yuste López, 223–250. México: UNAM-IIH, 2019.

——— 'Las fundaciones piadosas en correspondencias de riesgos a premio de mar en la Casa de la Santa Misericordia de Manila en el transcurso del siglo XVIII'. *Espacio, Tiempo y Forma*, Serie IV, n° 28 (2015): 99–115.

de Zwart, Pim, and van Zanden, Jan Luiten. *The Origins of Globalization: World Trade in the Making of the Global Economy, 1500–1800*. Cambridge: Cambridge University Press, 2018.

Index

J. J. Rivas Moreno, *The Capital Market of Manila and the Pacific Trade, 1668–1838*, Palgrave Studies in Economic History,
https://doi.org/10.1007/978-3-031-71810-6

The manufacturer's authorised representative in the EU is Springer Nature Customer Service Centre GmbH, Europaplatz 3, 69115 Heidelberg, Germany. If you have any concerns regarding our products, please contact ProductSafety@springernature.com

Printed and bound by CPI Group (UK) Ltd, Croydon, CR0 4YY
01/10/2026
02225913-0002